Costly Fix

Costly Fix
Power, Politics, and Nature
in the Tar Sands

Ian Urquhart

UNIVERSITY OF TORONTO PRESS

Library and Archives Canada Cataloguing in Publication

Urquhart, Ian T. (Ian Thomas), 1955–, author
    Costly fix : power, politics, and nature in the tar sands / Ian Urquhart.

Includes bibliographical references and index.

Issued in print and electronic formats.
ISBN 978-1-4875-9461-9 (softcover).—ISBN 978-1-4875-9462-6 (hardcover).—
ISBN 978-1-4875-9463-3 (EPUB).—ISBN 978-1-4875-9464-0 (PDF)

    1. Oil sands industry—Government policy—Alberta. 2. Oil sands industry—Economic aspects—
Alberta. 3. Oil sands industry—Environmental aspects—Alberta. 4. Oil sands industry—Social
aspects—Alberta. I. Title.

HD9574.C23A54 2018   338.2'7282097123   C2017-904206-8
                                                   C2017-904207-6

We welcome comments and suggestions regarding any aspect of our publications—please feel free to
contact us at news@utphighereducation.com or visit our Internet site at www.utorontopress.com.

North America
5201 Dufferin Street
North York, Ontario, Canada, M3H 5T8

2250 Military Road
Tonawanda, New York, USA, 14150

ORDERS PHONE: 1-800-565-9523
ORDERS FAX: 1-800-221-9985
ORDERS E-MAIL: utpbooks@utpress.utoronto.ca

UK, Ireland, and continental Europe
NBN International
Estover Road, Plymouth, PL6 7PY, UK
ORDERS PHONE: 44 (0) 1752 202301
ORDERS FAX: 44 (0) 1752 202333
ORDERS E-MAIL: enquiries@nbninternational.com

Every effort has been made to contact copyright holders; in the event of an error or omission,
please notify the publisher.

The University of Toronto Press acknowledges the financial support for its publishing activities of
the Government of Canada through the Canada Book Fund.

Printed in the United States of America.

Figures 2 and 3 Courtesy of Lee Consulting/Peter Lee.

Contents

Figure 1 Athabasca Oil Sands Map

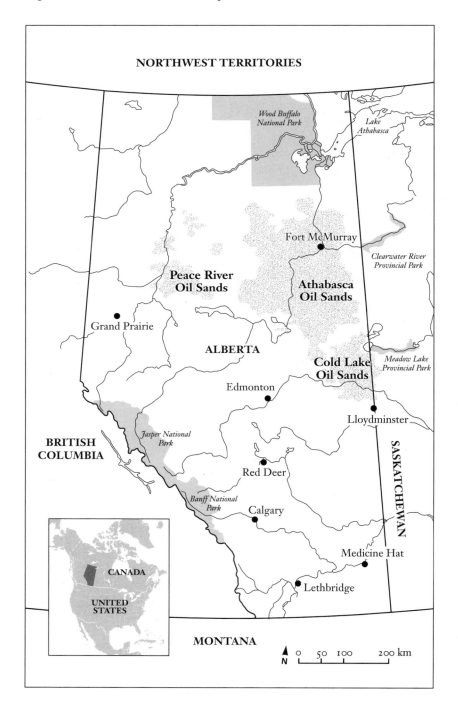

Acknowledgements

I AM VERY PLEASED TO THANK THE PEOPLE who supported in one way or another the research for and writing of this book. I am very grateful to current and former colleagues Greg Anderson, Tom Keating, Jim Lightbody, and Dave Whitson for their comments on my work. The diligence and thoughtfulness of the Press's anonymous reviewers sets a very high bar for me to meet in my future manuscript reviews I may be asked to do. Sam Gunsch and Brian Staszenki, two important figures in Alberta's environmental community, also generously gave of their time to offer their thoughts about the analysis and conclusions offered here. So too did Peter Lee, who conjured the satellite imagery in Chapter Four that offers you a stark look at the damage tar sands exploitation has inflicted on Alberta's boreal ecosystem for more than a generation now.

I also offer my thanks to the institutions that found this project worthy of support. Here I am especially grateful to the Fulbright program and the Canadian Studies Program at the University of California, Berkeley. Through the Fulbright program I was able to research and teach about the politics of the tar sands during a visit to Portland State University as a Visiting Research Chair in Canadian Studies. The John A. Sproul Research Fellowship in Canadian Studies at Berkeley offered me another wonderful research opportunity during a typically cold Edmonton winter. Publishing subventions from my university were also much appreciated.

Mat Buntin, Anna Del Col, and the staff at the University of Toronto Press have been a pleasure to work with. Michael Harrison, Mat's predecessor at the Press, deserves special thanks for his interest in this project and his patience with this author. I was also very fortunate to work with Eileen Eckert, my very talented copy editor, in the home stretch of this venture.

Thanks of a different sort are owed to my family—especially to my wife Theresa and daughters Andrea and Kali—for their untiring support of my efforts to tell this story. I thank them for that and for all they have taught me about living a good life.

Finally, those who use Google Scholar are invited to "stand on the shoulders of giants." In my career I have had the privilege to be a student and colleague of some of those giants. I am very thankful for the opportunity scholars such as Alan Cairns, Jean Laponce, and Larry Pratt gave me over the years to learn from them. I hope this book reflects their teachings well.

Tables and Charts

Tables

Charts

Acronyms

ACFN	Athabasca Chipewyan First Nation
AER	Alberta Energy Regulator
AEUB	Alberta Energy and Utilities Board
ANWR	Arctic National Wildlife Refuge
ATC	Athabasca Tribal Council
BVM	Bitumen Valuation Methodology
CAPP	Canadian Association of Petroleum Producers
CCEMC	Climate Change Emissions and Management Corporation
CEMA	Cumulative Environmental Management Association
CNOOC	China National Offshore Oil Corporation
CUSFTA	Canada–United States Free Trade Agreement
EISA	*Energy Independence and Security Act*
ERCB	Energy Resources Conservation Board (Alberta)
ESA	Environmentally Significant Areas
GHG	greenhouse gas(es)
GCOS	Great Canadian Oil Sands
IRC	Industry Relations Corporation
IRP	Integrated Resource Planning
mbd	million barrels per day
MCFN	Mikisew Cree First Nation
Mt	megatonne/million tons
NAFTA	North American Free Trade Agreement
NRCan	Natural Resources Canada
NRDC	National Resources Defence Council
NEB	National Energy Board
NEP	National Energy Program
OPEC	Organization of the Petroleum Exporting Countries
OSEC	Oil Sands Environmental Coalition
OSST	Oil Sands Severance Tax
PDVSA	Petróleos de Venezuela
SGER	Specified Gas Emitters Regulation
UNFCCC	United Nations Framework Convention on Climate Change
WCS	Western Canadian Select
WTI	West Texas Intermediate

Introduction: A Neo-Liberal Klondike

"This is the Klondike of our generation. It might end 10, 20, or 50 years from now. But right now we're riding out the gold rush."
—*Stu Wigle, Fort McMurray business owner, 2005*

"Alberta in the Klein era did not think about control."
—*Mark Lisac, 1995*

The Boom

The 1990s inaugurated what hindsight may regard as the greatest resource boom in Canadian, if not North American, history. A tsunami of petroleum industry investment in the tar sands crested over Alberta's northern boreal landscape.[1] Between 1996 and 2006 companies wrote cheques for nearly $50 billion in new projects to develop the petroleum potential locked in the bituminous sands of northeastern Alberta.[2] This exuberance grew mightily through the first decade of the twenty-first century. Tar sands developers invested roughly $201 billion in projects between 1999 and 2013.[3] At $34 billion, tar sands investments in 2014 set a new annual record.[4] These investment totals, even when measured in Canadian dollars, are staggering.

Dramatic investments reaped dramatic increases in production. By the beginning of the twenty-first century, unbeknownst to most North Americans, this boom had made Canada the largest foreign source of crude oil to the United States—not Saudi Arabia, not Venezuela, not Mexico.[5] Tar sands production in 1996 averaged nearly 432,000 barrels per day; by 2015, it had exploded to 2.381 million barrels per day.[6] Compared to many mature oil producing jurisdictions, Canadian production totals stand out because they are still increasing—this is due almost entirely to the tar sands. The calamitous post-June 2014 drop in oil prices is predicted to temper, not reverse, this growth. The Canadian Association of Petroleum Producers (CAPP) predicted oil sands production will grow to 3.08 million barrels per day by 2020 and to 3.95 million barrels per day by 2030.[7]

Profits of the corporations that went all in on the tar sands gamble also benefited handsomely during the years considered in this book. Great Canadian Oil Sands, the first company to produce commercial volumes of synthetic crude oil from bitumen for North American markets, faced long odds of surviving when it opened its Tar Island plant in 1967. Now called Suncor, this tar sands pioneer has beaten those odds and more. By 2012, Suncor had rode the post-1995 tar sands boom to become Canada's largest company by revenue in the *Financial Post's* rankings of Canada's top corporations. Suncor, now one of the largest energy companies in North America, recorded net earnings of $2.61 billion in 2013—a very great distance from the $151 million the company earned in 1995.[8]

A Modern Klondike…If Not for the Role of the State

Given the scale of the tar sands boom, allusions to past gold rushes—particularly the Klondike rush of 1897–98—have appeared in some commentaries on exploiting the tar sands. Environmentalists wrote of "oil sands fever";[9] filmmakers used "pay dirt" to help contextualize oil sands documentaries;[10] reporters described Fort McMurray as "the Dawson City of the 21st Century";[11] some locals, while joking about living in "Fort McMoney," more seriously saw themselves as modern-day Cheechakos on their own "Trail of '98" to mine the black gold locked in the Athabasca tar sands.

Personally, I found the Klondike metaphor initially appealing on a moon-less January night in 2006 driving north on Highway 63, the only major highway connection to Fort McMurray from Edmonton. In 1976, Larry Pratt used this same highway to open his classic account of the politics of exploiting Alberta's tar sands. Pratt wrote of a highway that was "a lonely strip" where you might encounter "an occasional oncoming car, hellbent out of isolation for the city."[12] When I swung north on Highway 63, the traf-fic coming at me was often hell-bent but there was nothing occasional about it. I had unknowingly selected a shift-change day for my drive. Hundreds of heavy trucks of every description, buses from work camps, pickup trucks, and cars—more than 800 vehicles in less than two hours—streamed past me on the ribbon of asphalt stretching to Fort McMurray from the junction of Highways 55 and 63. As this mechanized legion sped south, I thought of the famous photographs taken by E. A. Hegg and others of the human chain of Klondikers advancing so very slowly up "the golden stairs," the last, steepest section of the American portion of the trail to Chilkoot Pass.[13] Highway 63 is Alberta's Chilkoot Trail when workers rush north to their camps and jobs by the thousands every week.

More similarities between Dawson City during the Yukon gold rush and Fort McMurray, other than Fort McMurray likely having more escort ser-vices per capita than any other city in Alberta, could foster a belief the tar sands boom was a modern-day Klondike. Both Dawson City and Fort McMurray experienced explosive population growth and housing crises after their booms took off. Pierre Berton wrote of building lots in Dawson being sold for as much as $40,000 while outrageous rents were paid for everything from single rooms to commercial frontage. One Dawson fruit vendor paid $120 per month for a space of five feet by five feet for his fruit stand—the cost to lease a four-room apartment in New York City for two years.[14] Circumstances were little different in Fort McMurray during much of the boom. In 2005, the average selling price for a new single-family home was $462,451, 55 percent higher than the year before. By 2012, it had jumped another 83 percent to $844,433. Rental properties, if you could find them, were just as dear. Fort McMurray rents in 2012, even after declining 15 percent from their peak in 2008, remained twice as expensive as rents in Vancouver, Calgary, Edmonton, or Toronto.[15] Even after the downward spike in oil prices after the summer of 2014, the average price of two-bedroom rental accommodation in Fort McMurray in October 2016 was still 18 percent higher than rents for the same accommodation in Edmonton, 10 percent higher than in Toronto, and four dollars dearer than the Vancouver average of $1,450.[16]

Some coped with the housing crisis in much the same way as did those who came to Dawson in the spring of 1898. Newspaper stories told of people renting uninsulated, unheated garages and sheds in Fort McMurray; some called the local campgrounds home.[17] The campers stayed there year-round. The better-off lived in old, converted school buses or recreational vehicles.[18] Campground living is normal enough in this boomtown that the municipal census lists "campgrounds" alongside Abasand, Thickwood, and Fort McMurray's other conventional residential neighbourhoods.

Speculative fever and its accompanying excesses typify any gold rush worthy of the name. The tar sands rush was no different. The frantic staking and horse-trading of claims along Bonanza, Eldorado, and the other gold creeks of the Klondike found its equivalent in the Alberta government's regular auction of tar sands leases. In the early 1990s, before the boom began, provincial tar sands lease sales were tepid. Between 1991 and 1994 the provincial government leased a total of 1,176 square kilometres of land (454 square miles) to tar sands ventures for a modest $11.6 million. When George W. Bush delivered his 2006 State of the Union Address, he told the American people they were "addicted to oil" that often came from unstable dealers. Did Alberta and tar sands companies aspire to supply a more reliable fix to Americans? Tar sands lease sales between 2006 and 2008 certainly suggest so. Lease sales exploded. Nearly 44,000 square kilometres (17,000 square miles) were auctioned to companies with ambitions to turn bitumen into synthetic crude oil to satisfy America's habit. Leasing this enormous swathe of the boreal forest, twice the size of Wales or Massachusetts, generated $2.9 billion for the province.

Phenomena such as those mentioned above might encourage you to see exploiting the tar sands over the past 20 years as a reincarnation of the Klondike gold rush. This would be a mistake. The state has played a very different role in today's era of rampant resource exploitation than it did during the Klondike boom. The state took a strong regulatory and nationalist posture at the dawn of the twentieth century in order to moderate or temper the excesses of the gold rush. In our times the state instead embraced a market or business-first perspective that arguably fuelled the excesses of the tar sands boom.

What stands out from the Canadian state's actions in the late 1890s was its intent to regulate the behaviour of the tens of thousands who flooded the Yukon River valley to chase their dreams of striking it rich. Klondike histories and memoirs testify to the state's enthusiasm for regulation and order. It is found most famously in stories told by or about the North-West Mounted Police. Superintendent Sam Steele brought order and security to the streets of Dawson City. The mayhem of Skagway, Alaska, where the notorious Soapy Smith and his gang ruled for a time in the name of chaos, was nowhere to be found in the Klondike.[19]

The law-and-order focus in Klondike accounts was complemented by other steps government took to impose order on the gold rush. William Ogilvie, the government surveyor, resurveyed the claims staked on Bonanza and Eldorado creeks to settle disputes between miners on the condition that his decisions would be final.[20] The North-West Mounted Police played an active customs role on the summits of Chilkoot Pass and White Pass where they collected an impressive amount of duty on the goods accompanying the Klondikers on their way to the gold creeks. But the most dramatic illustration of the extent to which the government regulated the behaviour of those participating in the gold rush was seen on the golden stairs leading up to Chilkoot Pass during the winter of 1897–98. There, miners under heavy packs staggered and stumbled up this 35-degree slope not once, but dozens of times, ferrying supplies to caches on the summits. Their ordeals flowed from the pen of the Commissioner of the Yukon Territory; he decreed that anyone who wanted to enter the Territory that winter had to bring tents, utensils, tools, plus 1,150 pounds of food with them or they would not be allowed to enter Canada. One ton of supplies—that was the ante the Canadian state demanded from fortune-seekers to enter the Territory and play in the Klondike game.

The Canadian state was more than a strong regulator during the Klondike boom. It also was boldly nationalist. Canada asserted its sovereignty and defended its claims against American efforts to encroach on Canadian territory. This attitude appeared most clearly on the summits of Chilkoot and White Passes. Clifford Sifton, Canada's Minister of the Interior, categorically rejected the American position that the international boundary was well inland of these passes. The US colonel sent there to press the American claim backed down in the face of Canadian assertiveness. The border remained "exactly where the Mounties had placed their machine guns."[21]

Characters such as Sifton, Steele, and Ogilvie were nowhere to be seen among the politicians and officials charged with managing the tar sands boom. Recent government leaders consider Canadian nationalism to be a failing. Liberal and Conservative governments alike defined the Canadian and Albertan interest in the tar sands as nothing more than producing as much bitumen and synthetic oil as foreign—usually American—buyers would purchase, producing the petroleum as quickly as possible, and ensuring the export pipeline capacity existed to ship it abroad. Whether this attitude furthered the energy security interests of Canadians or Albertans hasn't concerned federal and provincial officials. While established and emerging industrial powers around the globe covet access to petroleum from trusted, stable suppliers, Canadian governments and corporations very rarely viewed the tar sands as an alternative supply to the foreign oil delivered to central and eastern Canadian markets, until TransCanada filed its Energy East Pipeline application in 2014.[22] Canada's status as an oil exporter obscures the fact it imports significant amounts of petroleum. Canada has behaved for decades as if no political risks are associated with the crude oil imported from countries such as Iraq, Nigeria, Russia, Saudi Arabia, and Venezuela.

That Canadian nationalism is anathema in contemporary government circles may also be seen in the treatment of foreign investment during the tar sands boom. Foreign private capital has been welcomed with open arms. American capital enjoys a privileged position here courtesy of the 1988 Canada–United States Free Trade Agreement and the 1994 North American Free Trade Agreement (NAFTA). The only foreign investments that seriously have concerned the Canadian government are efforts from some state-owned enterprises to acquire controlling interests in tar sands operations. But, as the federal government's policy makes very clear, the primary concern here is not nationalism but rather the possibility that investments by state-owned enterprises may not be commercially oriented and may be politically influenced. Furthermore, this concern didn't appear until late 2012—just over 20 years after the lobbying for the most recent phase of tar sands development began.

Orderly development was more valued by the late nineteenth-century Canadian state than it has been for state agencies concerned with exploiting the tar sands since the 1990s. Throughout the boom, federal and provincial governments have been disciples of a very puritan version of market-led development. Any tar sands development, all tar sands development, regardless of its collateral impact on the environment or society, should be seen as a blessing. On the eve of his political retirement in 2006, Alberta Premier Ralph Klein answered a question about managing tar sands growth with the phrase "it remains true that the market must prevail."[23] Amen. That response foreshadowed Klein's admission three days later that his government, ten years into the boom, didn't have a plan to try to manage growth. Premier Ed Stelmach, Klein's successor, made it clear he wasn't concerned about the pace of development when it came to exploiting the tar sands:

> The role of the government is to ensure that the services are in place as more people come to the province of Alberta and the economy grows ... We're here to deliver the services required, there is no such thing as touching the brake or anything like that.[24]

Failing to plan and refusing to touch the brake has had particularly serious consequences for the environment and for the social fabric in Fort McMurray and Aboriginal communities in Wood Buffalo. Faced with the eventual development of a vociferous international environmental opposition to the tar sands, Premier Alison Redford, Stelmach's successor, showed no signs of tempering the market-first logic of development she inherited. Her refusal to take a different tack increased her government's reliance on political tactics that may be labelled misinformation, symbolic politics, or—less politely but more honestly—propaganda. After her victory in the April 2012 provincial election, Premier Redford went on a public relations/speaking tour offensive against tar sands opponents. This foreshadowed her administration's approach to exploiting the tar sands—to seek public consent and support for the tar sands boom, in Alberta and abroad with words, not actions. Premier Redford's remarks at the Brookings Institution that "[t]ailings ponds [will] disappear from Alberta's landscape in the very near future" may have persuaded the ill-informed, but they were truly nonsensical unless the premier was talking about geological time.[25] Two months after the premier's Brookings speech, the Energy Resources Conservation Board (ERCB), the provincial petroleum regulator, revealed that tailings ponds were increasing in size in the oil sands area and that not one oil sands company met the regulator's tailings reduction directive. Tellingly, no penalties were assessed for failing to adhere to the regulation.[26] The premier likely scored a public relations coup when *USA Today* published her opinion piece supporting the Keystone XL pipeline in February 2013. There she bragged that, when it came to addressing greenhouse gas emissions, Alberta's clean technology fund had reduced greenhouse gas emissions by 32 million tons. But two days later, the most senior official in the province's environment ministry told a legislative committee the province's actual greenhouse gas reductions were far below what the premier's party had claimed. Few readers of *USA Today* would have read the corrected record.[27]

The Path Ahead

This book tries to answer several questions about the Alberta tar sands boom that started in the 1990s. Why did this flood of investment pour into the tar sands of northern Alberta? What role has government played with respect to the tar sands rush? Why? Who benefited, and who or what has paid the costs of exploiting the tar sands?

From here the book proceeds as follows. Chapter One details the analytical perspectives used here. I believe that understanding the tar sands boom requires an appreciation of interests, ideas, and institutions. The faith in markets, in the omniscience of the business community, is a key ideational plank here. The concept of market fundamentalism is vitally important to the contemporary tar sands story. So too are institutions and the extent to which they have embraced and implemented what the disciples of market fundamentalism demanded. Together with capital's perennial interest and need for profits, they combined to demand and institutionalize the reregulation of the tar sands sector.

Chapter Two presents a pre-1990s history of the tar sands' use and exploitation in Alberta. It stresses that tar sands policy-making was a bargaining process between governments and multinational petroleum companies and identifies the types of factors and circumstances actors used to pursue their objectives. By the 1980s the tar sands, as a central feature of Canadian petroleum policy, was a subject where two policy perspectives clashed. One insisted their exploitation should be market-oriented and continentalist; the other championed a nationalist and interventionist approach. Several aspects of this chapter's interpretation are novel. It highlights the extent to which industry, generally viewed as supporters of unqualified free trade, instead embraced state interventionism when it suited advancing tar sands development. It also highlights the privileged position the tar sands enjoyed in the minds of policy makers. Contrary to conventional wisdom, policy makers established an impressive suite of public policies in the 1980s that made the tar sands a profitable business indeed.

The often-ignored fact or theme—that the state helped make the tar sands profitable in the 1980s—is developed further in Chapter Three. That profitability is detailed in order to argue the extensive state support Alberta and Canada bestowed on the tar sands in the mid-1990s wasn't a lifeline to a struggling sector. Industry viewed the 1980s' taxation regime very favourably. Governments, by significantly sweetening the fiscal regime in the 1990s, enriched the already profitable. This chapter introduces and debunks another myth that corporations have used to their advantage—namely that surging world oil prices were responsible for the first wave of post-1995 tar sands investments. Oil prices were not a significant driver in this first phase of the boom. Instead, building a Canadian oil factory in northeastern Alberta began due to technological changes in tar sands production, generous fiscal policies, and a liberal renaissance in the global petroleum sector. This is the period when market fundamentalism entrenches itself as the prescription for exploiting the tar sands.

The state's warm welcome to the companies that championed this exploitation was expressed loudly in its decision to delegate policy development to industry. The industry-dominated National Task Force on Oil Sands Strategies seized this opportunity to write a generous policy prescription. Centrist and right-of-centre federal and provincial governments, facing virtually no opposition from political parties, labour, or environmentalists, happily filled it.

Measured by the flood of investment that followed this reregulation, the state's efforts to build a Canadian oil factory were a resounding success. However, this exuberance may actually threaten the long-term interests of tar sands capital and its government patrons. Financially, the state's blind devotion to market fundamentalism, its belief there couldn't be too much investment in the tar sands, exponentially increased the construction costs of tar sands projects. In a blink of an eye, the norms of project economics were profoundly disrupted. These changes, authored largely by the state when it refused to manage or regulate growth, threaten corporate profitability in a lower-price oil environment in ways that never were anticipated by the corporate leaders who drafted this development blueprint and their partners in government who so willingly implemented it. The success of the last 20 to 25 years may contain the seed of failure or serious troubles in the future.

Chapter Four is the first of three chapters examining the environmental dimension of tar sands development. Here we see what market fundamentalism in the tar sands has done to Alberta's portion of the boreal forest or taiga, a forest the Canadian ecologist Stan Rowe called the third lung of the planet. It is impossible, in my view, to see northeastern Alberta now as anything other than a landscape and ecosystem sacrificed for petroleum. Much of this sacrifice took place during the first decade of the boom considered in this chapter. Importantly, the state's environmental assessment and regulatory approval processes limited the ability to voice environmental critiques of exploiting the tar sands. But this chapter suggests this critique also was tempered, diluted, compromised by some environmentalists themselves. Recent books by Wilfried Huismann and Naomi Klein describe how some of the world's most respected environmental groups either are or have been unduly influenced by big business and government.[28] This influence, which I have pointed out previously, figures in the tar sands story.[29] The Pembina Institute, the environmental organization that emerged as an authoritative environmental commentator and critic of developing the tar sands, relied importantly on the petroleum and tar sands sector for its financial lifeblood. At times, this collaborative relationship appeared to temper the organization's environmental critique.

Chapter Five considers the place of Aboriginal peoples in the tar sands boom. It opens with an account of how First Nations, for human health and environmental reasons, have been prominent among those opposing unbridled exploitation of bitumen in northeastern Alberta. But, as in the previous chapter, Chapter Five also challenges the conventional wisdom that Aboriginal peoples are, by definition, implacable opponents of exploiting the tar sands. The reality is much different. Capital, since the early days of industrial-scale tar sands development in the 1970s, sought to involve Aboriginal peoples in the tar sands economy. First Nations leaders, whose peoples suffered from poverty and the afflictions the poor often suffer from, faced a stark choice—accommodate to industrialization or try to maintain traditional ways of life on landscapes ripped apart by the gigantic shovels and trucks of tar sands miners. Aboriginal peoples were presented with a fait accompli and, in my opinion, their leaders more often than not made the rational choice: accommodation. This choice has brought considerable wealth, in some instances obscene wealth, to First Nations and their leaders. The stereotype of materially impoverished Aboriginal peoples doesn't apply to northeastern Alberta. This aspect of the First Nations story also highlights some of the actions industry and, to a lesser extent, government will take to defend the privilege market fundamentalism has given them. Industry, as in the case of environmentalists, will try to coopt and compromise First Nations in order to temper their enthusiasm to participate in a countermovement.

Chapter Six returns to the subject of the terms of development; it revisits the politics associated with royalties and capturing economic rent. Ten years into the boom, the fiscal terms of exploiting the tar sands returned to the political agenda and became the subject of a public debate, a debate notably absent when the terms of the 1990s were set. As the spot price for West Texas Intermediate (WTI) oil tripled between early 2002 and 2006, questions arose about whether Alberta was receiving an adequate portion of the economic rent generated by higher prices. Were the owners of the resource, the public, getting their fair share? In 2006, all of the candidates to succeed Ralph Klein as Alberta's premier and Progressive Conservative Party leader campaigned on the need to review the provincial petroleum royalty systems. Ed Stelmach, the winner of that contest, made good on his promise and established a panel of experts to review provincial royalties. The panel's conclusion, that royalties should be increased significantly, stunned tar sands operators and the petroleum industry more generally. Chapter Six focuses on the development of a revised royalty policy in Alberta, the recommendations of the province's royalty review panel, and the tactics and efficacy of the industry's efforts to ensure government didn't markedly reduce the industry's share of economic rent.

Ten years into the boom, the environmental critique of development had proven woefully impotent. Its impotence, combined with new players and a domestic assessment/regulatory setting that became more and more inhospitable, prompted a twofold internationalization of the environmental opposition. First, non-Canadian environmental activists became significant, vocal opponents of exploiting the tar sands. Second, the targets of the opponents shifted importantly toward non-Canadian politicians, officials, and consumers. If Alberta and Canadian politicians refused to see the legitimacy of the environmental critique, perhaps foreign consumers and government gate-keepers of tar sands crude's access to markets, particularly American ones, would be more receptive. Beginning in about 2006, the US stage became a much more important forum for tar sands politics. Chapter Seven is our first look at this changed face of environmental politics in the tar sands. It details the new actors, venues, and strategies that became important in the conflict over exploiting this resource. It does this in large measure through a focus on the politics that came to swirl around the blight of toxic tailings reservoirs in the Athabasca tar sands area after hundreds and hundreds of waterfowl perished in Syncrude's Aurora tailings reservoir.

Chapter Eight examines climate change politics—a second example of this new, transnational character of tar sands environmental opposition. As in the previous chapter, it describes the critique and the extent to which government moved to address its substance by changing its policies. Did governments make the types of policy changes needed to give credence to what industry and government were telling foreign audiences about how serious they were about reducing the environmental footprint of development? This book suggests that the most significant environmental victory made in more than 20 years of opposition to the tar sands was President Obama's decision not to allow the Keystone XL pipeline project to proceed. This victory is a salutary reminder of the potential that institutions may offer to national or transnational opponents of the tar sands if political leaders have complementary ideological and aspirational orientations.

Most of this account focuses on the politics of the tar sands during the 44-year dynasty of Alberta's Progressive Conservative Party. That dynasty was rudely and unexpectedly dethroned in the May 2015 provincial election, when Rachel Notley's centre-left New Democratic Party turned pre-election predictions on their head and won a majority government. In opposition, the NDP consistently criticized the fiscal regime the Progressive Conservatives applied to the tar sands and chided four successive PC premiers for the environmental impact of the tar sands. Chapter Nine examines the extent to which, in its first 18 months, the new government altered the legacies they inherited from the Progressive Conservatives on royalties, tailings reservoirs, and climate change. Notley's developing record presents an excellent opportunity to consider how changing the ideological pedigree of the governing party may affect the grip of market fundamentalism on the state.

Notes

1   What should we call the bitumen-impregnated sands discussed in this study? Generally, I prefer and use the phrase "tar sands." Given the tar or pitch-like character of bitumen, I believe the term "tar sands" offers a more accurate physical description of this resource. The decision to call this resource "tar sands" or "oil sands" has been influenced strongly since the 1990s by whether the speaker favours or opposes extracting and upgrading these resources into synthetic crude oil. Governments and companies that favour exploiting the bituminous sands generally call them "oil sands." However, there have been some notable exceptions to this tendency. Today, the US Bureau of Land Management still uses the phrase "tar sands." See United States Department of the Interior, Bureau of Land Management, "Oil Shale and Tar Sands Leasing Programmatic EIS Information Center," http://ostseis.anl.gov/index.cfm. In the Alberta legislature, "tar sands development" was preferred to "oil sands development" in the official records of debates in the Alberta legislature until February 2006, the year environmental opposition to exploiting the tar sands became more public and vociferous. J. Howard Pew, the father of the first commercial tar sands operation, called them "tar sands." President George W. Bush thanked Canada for developing its "tar sands" when he met with Canadian Prime Minister Paul Martin and Mexican President Vincente Fox in March 2005. See "President Meets with President Fox and Prime Minister Martin" (United States Department of State, March 23, 2005), https://2001-2009.state.gov/p/wha/rls/rm/2005/q1/43847.htm. Most environmentalists prefer the term "tar sands." The Pembina Institute, an environmental group with important ties to the petroleum industry, is an exception to this tendency. It is more likely to refer to the "oil sands" in its publications.

2   Alberta Employment, Immigration, and Industry, *Oil Sands Industry Update* (December 2007), 27.

3   Alberta Energy, "Facts and Statistics," http://www.energy.alberta.ca/oilsands/791.asp.

4   Ben Brunnen, "Upstream Oil and Gas Industry Outlook," presentation to the Petroleum Services Association of Canada (Canadian Association of Petroleum

Producers, November 3, 2015), 31, www.capp.ca/~/media/capp/customer-portal/documents/272494.pdf.

5   US Department of Energy, Energy Information Administration, *US Imports by Country of Origin*, http://www.eia.gov/dnav/pet/pet_move_impcus_a2_nus_epoo_imo_mbblpd_a.htm. A February 2004 Ipsos-Reid poll on North American energy issues for the Woodrow Wilson Center revealed that only 15 percent of Americans knew that Canada was the largest supplier of crude oil to the United States; only 29 percent of Canadians knew this. Ipsos-Reid, *Canadians and Americans Give Their Views on North American Energy Issues*, March 1, 2004, https://www.ipsos.com/en-ca/canadians-and-americans-give-their-views-north-american-energy-issues?language_content_entity=en-ca.

6   Oil sands grew from 21.6 percent to 60.9 percent of Canadian oil production between 1996 and 2015. Canadian oil production in these respective years was 1.994 and 3.909 million barrels per day (mbd). See National Energy Board, *Estimated Production of Canadian Crude Oil and Equivalent, Annual (1998–2015)* https://www.neb-one.gc.ca/nrg/sttstc/crdlndptrlmprdct/stt/stmtdprdctn-eng.html. The 1996 figures are taken from the 1998 archived annual report.

7   CAPP, *Crude Oil: Forecast, Markets & Transportation* (June 2015), ii. The Alberta government's 2016 budget contains a similar short-term prediction; it assumes raw bitumen production will increase to 3.151 million barrels per day in the 2018–19 fiscal year. See Alberta Treasury Board and Finance, *Fiscal Plan 2016–19*, 10.

8   "FP500:2013," *Financial Post*, http://www.financialpost.com/news/fp500/2013/index.html. Suncor ranked first in terms of revenue in 2013 as well; net earnings are from Suncor Energy Inc., *Big Plans—Annual Report 1997*, 1, and Suncor Energy Inc., *Annual Report 2015*.

9   Dan Woynillowicz, Chris Severson-Baker, and Marlo Raynolds, *Oil Sands Fever: The Environmental Implications of Canada's Oil Sands Rush* (Drayton Valley, AB: The Pembina Institute, 2005).

10   Pay Dirt Pictures Inc. produced two one-hour documentaries on Alberta's oil sands in 2005. They are *Pay Dirt: Alberta's Oil Sands—Centuries in the Making* and *Pay Dirt: Alberta's Oil Sands—Making the Unconventional Conventional* (Calgary: Pay Dirt Pictures, 2005), DVD.

11   Amy Steele, "Boomtown Challenges," *See Magazine*, (December 15–December 21, 2005), 10.

12   Larry Pratt, *The Tar Sands: Syncrude and the Politics of Oil* (Edmonton: Hurtig, 1976), 13.

13   Some of these photographs may be seen in Pierre Berton, *The Klondike Quest: A Photographic Essay 1897–1899* (Toronto: McClelland and Stewart, 1983); see also Pierre Berton, *Klondike: The Last Great Gold Rush 1896–1899*, rev. ed. (Toronto: McClelland and Stewart, 1972), especially 236–47.

14   Berton, *Klondike*, 285–86.

15   Data on new home selling prices and apartment rents supplied by Canada Central Mortgage and Housing Corporation.

16   Canada Mortgage and Housing Corporation, *Rental Market Report: Canada Highlights* (2016), 5–6, https://www.cmhc-schl.gc.ca/odpub/esub/64667/64667_2016_A01.pdf?fr=1501859287406; Canada Mortgage and Housing

Corporation, *Housing Market Insight: Alberta* (2016), 11, https://www.cmhc-schl. gc.ca/odpub/esub/68779/68779_2016_M12.pdf?fr=1501858642166.

17 Deborah Tetley, "'The Richest Poor Place in the World': Garages and Sheds Provide Shelter in Black Gold City," *Calgary Herald*, October 21, 2005; Steele, "Boomtown Challenges," 10–11.

18 Steele, "Boomtown Challenges," 10.

19 Colonel Steele described the success of his efforts in language such as "everyone went about his business with as strong a sense of security as if he were in the most law-abiding part of the globe." See Colonel S. B. Steele, *Forty Years in Canada: Reminiscences of the Great North-West with Some Account of His Service in South Africa* (New York: Dodd, Mead, 1915), 299.

20 Berton, *Klondike*, 71.

21 Berton, *Klondike*, xvii; see also Jim Wallace, *Forty Mile to Bonanza: The North-West Mounted Police in the Klondike Gold Rush* (Calgary: Bunker to Bunker, 2000), 74–77.

22 Canada's National Energy Board reported that, in 2014, Canada imported 90,100 cubic metres (566,712 barrels) of crude oil per day. National Energy Board, *2015 Oil Exports and Imports Summary*, https://www.neb-one.gc.ca/nrg/ sttstc/crdlndptrlmprdct/stt/crdlsmmr/2015/smmry2015-eng.html.

23 Alberta, *Alberta Hansard*, (August 28, 2006), 1715.

24 Canadian Broadcasting Corporation, "Stelmach Prepares to Take Charge as Premier," December 4, 2006, http://www.cbc.ca/news/canada/edmonton/ story/2006/12/04/stelmach-monday.html.

25 Brookings Institution, *US-Alberta Energy Relations: A Conversation with Premier Alison Redford* (uncorrected transcript), April 9, 2013, https://www.brookings. edu/wp-content/uploads/2013/03/20130409_alberta_energy_redford_ transcript.pdf.

26 Amanda Stephenson, "ERCB Waives Tailings Penalties: Technology More Difficult than Expected," *Calgary Herald*, June 12, 2013.

27 Alison Redford, "Keystone Is Responsible Oil Sands Development," *USA Today*, February 25, 2013; Karen Kleiss, "Alberta Not Meeting Government's Own Emissions Targets," *Edmonton Journal*, February 28, 2013.

28 Wilfried Huismann, *Pandaleaks: The Dark Side of the WWF* (Bremen: Nordbook UG, 2014); Naomi Klein, *This Changes Everything: Capitalism vs. the Climate* (Toronto: Alfred A. Knopf Canada, 2014). The first time I encountered this theme was in Elaine Dewar, *Cloak of Green: The Links Between Key Environmental Groups, Government and Big Business* (Toronto: Lorimer, 1995).

29 Ian Urquhart, "Sleeping with the Enemy?—Is Safe Sex Possible?," *WildLands Advocate* 15, no. 6 (December 2007), 28–29.

1
Market Fundamentalism and the State

"From a historical point of view, for a quarter of century the prevailing religion of the West has been market fundamentalism."
–D. Joseph Stiglitz, 2009

Introduction

The role of the state in the contemporary tar sands rush begs investigation. Why were the ideas of orderly development and nationalism dead letters? This chapter outlines several signposts I use to answer that question. My approach is eclectic. It aspires to show the value a variety of approaches and schools of thought have in explaining the role the state played in exploiting the tar sands. I hope the sum of the orientation developed in this work approximates what G. Bruce Doern and Glen Toner used in their study of Canada's 1980 National Energy Program. Four components composed their energy politics framework: material/physical factors, normative factors/ideas, institutions, and interests.[1] Energy politics rested in the power relationships between interests such as governments and corporations; this politics was influenced by material factors such as world petroleum markets, institutions such as federalism, and ideas such as the sanctity of profits and a fair return on investments. Interests, ideas, and institutions figure importantly in the tar sands story.

Capital's Privilege in Market Societies

Political economy, the interdependence of economic and political power, guides the assessment of interests or actors. In both liberal and more radical versions of this approach, capital is privileged when it comes to understanding how liberal democracies attend to matters involving the affairs of business. In Charles Lindblom's neopluralist account, this privileged position is first a product of capital's structural position in liberal, market-oriented societies.[2] Market societies essentially entrust business with the vital task of generating and organizing economic production. The market system through which corporations carry out this task is one that largely operates through inducements. Business must be induced, not commanded, by the state to perform its vital economic role. This generally places corporations in

14

a privileged position relative to government and to other actors demanding state action, such as unions and environmentalists.

Business is predisposed to respond to threatening or disagreeable economic policies in ways that increase unemployment and/or restrict investment. This tendency, what Lindblom calls the "automatic punishing recoil," represses policy and institutional change not to the liking of the business community. If government treads this path, it risks losing the political support governments must fight hard for during tough economic times. "When a decline in prosperity and employment is brought about by decisions of corporate and other business executives," he writes, "it is not they but government officials who consequently are retired from their offices."[3] This relationship and these consequences lead Lindblom to characterize the market as an institution that imprisons fiscal and economic policy-making. It "imprisons our attempts to improve our institutions" and "greatly cripples our attempts to improve the social world" because even to start a debate about economic change or reform may prompt a harmful corporate reaction.[4] Lindblom does not believe change is impossible. Stricter environmental regulations, for example, may be imposed on corporations, but these impositions might need to be paired with new state benefits or supports for business. The state may have to pay ransom for such reforms.[5]

"The Market as Prison" also highlighted the importance of ideas, of the "habit of mind" we rely on when we think about the issues and challenges facing us. The market system imprisons our thinking about politics and economics. It is seldom regarded as a variable; it's a constant. "We have come to think not of human need and aspiration," Lindblom wrote, "but of the market system as the fixed element in the light of which we think about policy."[6] His account of the reaction to his first book, *Unions and Capitalism*, illustrates the market's power as an intellectual concept. The book argued that the tension between collective bargaining and the market system was likely to lead to serious economic challenges in the future. Lindblom offered no prescription to address this possibility. His reviewers did. Almost all of them believed Lindblom must be making a case against unions and collective bargaining. Such was the ideological appeal of the market that those reviewers didn't even raise the possibility of instead reforming the market system.

Lindblom's argument is concise and powerful—the latter not least because it came from such a well-respected liberal political scientist.[7] Even so it invites questions. Students of comparative government and politics may wonder what needs to be added to help explain the fact that, historically, liberal democratic governments have differed in their enthusiasm for the market.[8] While Lindblom doesn't assert that the market is escape-proof and alludes to the possibility of prison breaks, he doesn't provide clues about what's needed to engineer an escape. Is widespread popular electoral support needed to escape from the market prison? To what extent do the ideological pedigrees of governing parties or the administrative capacities of governments matter? Can business be tamed if the state possesses scarce, highly valued natural resources such as the tar sands that cannot be checked as baggage during capital flight?

Lindblom's recognition of capital's structural power and account of the corporate/government relationship may strike readers as similar to the positions of some neo-Marxist or radical scholars. His account of the privileged position of business, for example, resembles Fred Block's assessment offered contemporaneously with Lindblom's. What Lindblom calls the automatic punishing recoil appears as "business confidence" in Block's work. Major reforms introduced by left-of-centre governments may shatter this business confidence. This shattering will drag down economic performance, increase unemployment, and push government public support over a cliff. Reformist regimes are likely then to fall—either through the ballot box or, in the extreme, through the barrels of the military's guns. Replacing regimes that have the nerve to challenge business is the first step on the path to restoring business confidence.[9]

What is successful reform to the market system in Lindblom's account is rationalization in Block's. When Block wrote in the late 1970s, rationalization constituted state policies designed to encourage workers to accept their place in capitalism and accommodate themselves to the general interests of capital. Here Block's account is more satisfying than Lindblom's when it comes to suggesting the dynamics behind rationalization or reforms. Writing before the retrenchment of the welfare state began in earnest, Block linked extending the rationality of capitalism, the tempering of capitalism's excesses, to expanding the state's role in the economy and society. Class conflict and the self-interest of state managers whose power increased through bureaucratic expansion produced this growth in government; they contributed to capitalism's dynamism and its rationality. As Block pointed out, the expanded state produced by worker opposition and bureaucratic self-interest didn't try to put the brakes on capitalism; its mission instead, one that unchecked business confidence couldn't contemplate, was to pursue reforms promoting continued economic growth and capital's general interests. While class struggle had the potential to reorient societies radically, it also was key to the continuing, evolving rationality of capitalism. It was essential to the reform, not the elimination, of market systems.

These understandings of interests and power lived in John Richards and Larry Pratt's seminal study of pre-1980 natural resource exploitation in the provinces of Alberta and Saskatchewan. *Prairie Capitalism: Power and Influence in the New West* challenged two conventional wisdoms of the anglophone left in Canada. The first was that provincial governments could be nothing more than "the captive dependencies or instruments of international capital," and the second was that progressive political change demanded the centralization of power in Ottawa.[10] Their account of petroleum and potash development in the 1970s detailed the emergence of entrepreneurial provincial states that challenged the power of international capital. Buoyant commodity markets, surging corporate profits, increasingly professional public services in Alberta and Saskatchewan, and ambitions to diversify agricultural economies prompted the new provincial government assertiveness. While Saskatchewan's entrepreneurialism was primarily bureaucratic, Alberta's was propelled by both the bureaucracy and a hungry new middle class. The ability of both provinces to engineer prison breaks and renegotiate more favourable terms with business rested importantly in the professionalization of their bureaucracies and the ideological commitment to state-led diversification. They claimed:

> What begins as a relatively simple and highly unequal, often exploitative relationship evolves into a much more complex pattern of relations as the provincial government moves up a learning curve of skills and negotiating expertise and the foreign company faces the steady erosion of its monopoly power.[11]

Economic Liberalism's Resurrection: Market Fundamentalism

This change in the terms of business-government relationships during the 1970s was neither predetermined nor irreversible. But Richards and Pratt felt the interventionist tide was likely to continue to rise. It didn't. As *Prairie Capitalism* went to press, a profound ideological shift was about to rise over the political horizon in Anglo-American democracies. The elections of Margaret Thatcher in 1979 and Ronald Reagan in 1980 started to shred the interventionist ethic in earnest. Acolytes of Thatcherism and Reaganomics repudiated the Keynesian postwar bargain and preached the need to unshackle corporations and individual enterprise from the chains of government regulation and taxation. Thatcher and Reagan deserve much of the credit for resurrecting economic liberalism as a primary governing principle for the concluding decades of the twentieth century. Although it is often called "free market ideology" as well as neoliberalism or neoconservativism, this book follows George Soros, Fred Block, Margaret Somers, Joseph Stiglitz, and others generally to refer to this reincarnated version of economic liberalism as "market fundamentalism." The religious allusion arises in part because this conviction is "not based on economic science or historical evidence."[12] It also rests in the "quasi-religious certainty" expressed by the belief's faithful followers in government, industry, and academia.[13] The gospel of Thatcherism and Reaganomics aspired to create societies of "profit-maximizing firms without government regulation."[14] The dangers such societies would pose to social interests and nature were dismissed.

The authors above are among those who bring Karl Polanyi's conceptual framework to the task of interpreting the resurgence of market fundamentalism in contemporary political economies. In *The Great Transformation*, Polanyi argued the clash between economic liberalism and social protection was one key to understanding the history of the nineteenth century; a second key was the conflict between classes. Together these dynamics ultimately destroyed a century of peace and ushered in the upheavals and tragedies that began with World War I and continued until the end of World War II. With respect to economic liberalism, Polanyi contended that the normative ambition of free market ideas—to establish self-regulating markets free from politics—was utopian.[15] By utopian Polanyi did not mean "a good society but an impossible society."[16] This utopia, whether imagined by Polanyi's contemporary Ludwig von Mises or the nineteenth-century economic liberal Herbert Spencer, ignored history. To pursue the ideal of a self-regulating market was to blind oneself to the reality that markets never have been autonomous, that they always have been embedded in societies, that they always have needed to be organized and regulated by politics. A utopian ideal, contradicted by political economic history, the continuing authority of economic liberalism in political debates sometimes rested on successfully, if mistakenly, blaming state intervention for the market's failure to deliver. Laissez-faire could be reached for the good of all if only the state intervened less in social and economic life, if only the ideal of the self-regulating market had dominion over man and nature.[17]

In Polanyi's account, the movement to expand the market's role in society was met by a countermovement to protect society from the problems and damage created by that expansion. Much nineteenth-century legislation in England targeted the social problems associated either with industrialization or with "the market method of dealing with them."[18] This "double movement," where economic liberalism sparked a move for social protection, animated societies in England and Europe throughout the 1800s up until the outbreak of World War I. The landed aristocracy, peasantry, and the nascent working class were key defenders of the broad range of human, social, and natural interests affected by the expanding market mechanism.

As ideologically paradoxical as it appears, some economic liberals were also part of this countermovement. They saw that "the organization of capitalistic production itself had to be sheltered from the devastating effects of a self-regulating market."[19] They advocated restrictions on the ideal of laissez-faire such as trade union and anti-trust laws.[20] Practically speaking, they realized that a self-regulating market in all manner of economic affairs could damage the vital interests of leading industries. Consequently, industry's passion for free market ideology could be very selective. Manchester cotton manufacturers, for example, simultaneously demanded freedom from production regulations and beneficial protectionist measures. Protective tariffs, export bounties, and indirect wage subsidies joined regulatory freedom as vital to the development of England's cotton industry, an industry that was the country's leading "free trade" industry in the nineteenth century.[21]

In contemporary times, scholars have applied Polanyi's perspectives to a wide range of issues. Fisheries, President Clinton's changes to social welfare, the 2008 financial crisis and its aftermath, and globalization are among the subjects studied and explored with the help of Polanyi's insights.[22] Block and Somers use the concept of reregulation to describe the reality of contemporary market fundamentalism. The term captures very well the fact that, despite the rhetorical commitment of politicians to deregulation, market fundamentalism delivers the reregulation of markets, not their liberation. In the United States, a suite of regulations and taxes that had supported workers, consumers, and the poor were swept away and replaced with new regulations that promoted corporate interests and the wealthy.[23] Reregulation demonstrates well the contemporary relevance of Polanyi's observations about industry's selective enthusiasm for free market ideology; reregulation enabled corporations to avoid obligations to society "while they continued to rely on governmental action to help them secure a continuing flow of profits."[24] Calls for deregulation and smaller government, in other words, didn't stop corporations from seeking and welcoming government intervention if it promoted their interests. To this point Block recounts an anecdote from Joseph Stiglitz about the economist's time as the chair of President Clinton's Council of Economic Advisers. The CEOs of major American corporations approached Stiglitz professing their faith in free markets only to then argue that their business was special and required government support. Alcoa's CEO, for example, didn't let his enthusiasm for free markets stop him from asking the Clinton administration to help him organize a global aluminum cartel.[25] Furthermore, in the United States a hidden developmental state has played a vital role since the early 1980s in promoting new technologies that have boosted sectors of corporate America. It remains out of public view largely because of the partisan politics revolving around market fundamentalism's dominance. Because of that ideology's success, "there is simply no conceptual space for the idea that government plays a critical role in maintaining and expanding the private sector's dynamism."[26] Out of public sight perhaps, government intervention and assistance was not out of the corporate mind.

In this book I hope to demonstrate that reregulation featured importantly in the politics of the tar sands since the 1980s. On the one hand, an assortment of measures confirms expectations that embracing economic liberalism would generate deregulation, smaller government, and free trade. Nationally, Prime Minister Brian Mulroney's Progressive Conservative government cancelled the interventionist start Pierre Trudeau, his Liberal predecessor, had made with the National Energy Program (NEP) in 1980. The federal Liberal governments of Jean Chrétien and Paul Martin, through tax policy and a timid response to the challenge of climate change, echoed the approach of the Mulroney Progressive Conservatives. They too eliminated market-constraining measures in the tar sands. After securing a majority government in the 2011 national election, Stephen Harper's Conservatives introduced a host of measures that further strengthened this policy orientation. Shortening National Energy Board (NEB) hearings, limiting the ability of the public to participate in NEB hearings, giving the federal cabinet the final word on all NEB recommendations, exempting in situ oil sands projects from the federal environmental assessment process,[27] allowing provincial environmental assessments to replace federal ones, and narrowing the protection offered to aquatic life by the *Fisheries Act* reaffirmed the pro-market commitment to the petroleum sector that the Canadian government has shown since the mid-1980s.[28]

Provincially, Premier Peter Lougheed's Alberta found a willing partner in Mulroney's administration to pursue a free trade agreement with the United States that ensured the NEP's interventionism could only be revived with great difficulty. In the early 1990s, Alberta's treasurer insisted the days of his government taking ownership positions in the economy were over; Alberta was "simply out of the business of business."[29] To that end, in 1993 Alberta first sold its stake in Alberta Energy Company, a public-private enterprise the provincial government had created; by 1995 the province had liquidated its position in Syncrude, then the world's largest tar sands producer.[30] As we will see in Chapter Three, Premier Ralph Klein's Alberta government took an axe to energy regulations and public servants alike in the 1990s. A pro-market ideological playbook was central to the public face of the so-called Klein Revolution.[31]

But, coincidentally with these measures, these same governments intervened to promote the tar sands. We will see later how petroleum companies sought and welcomed the tax and royalty breaks Ottawa and Alberta offered them when they were blindsided by the collapse of world oil prices in 1986. The Canada–United States and the North American Free Trade Agreements are generally regarded as hallmarks of government commitment to "free markets." The energy chapters of these agreements generally shun regulatory or tax measures constraining the activities of petroleum companies. But that anti-state tone disappears in Article 608.1 where the signatories "agree to allow existing or future incentives for oil and gas exploration, development and related activities in order to maintain the reserve base for these energy resources." Incentives to assist petroleum companies maintain and expand their profit-making ventures still were welcome in this testament to market fundamentalism; taxes and unhelpful regulations weren't. Another profound illustration of this second face of market fundamentalism in the tar sands is the so-called generic royalty regime introduced by Alberta in the mid-1990s. This example of reregulation in the tar sands shifted financial risk onto governments and taxpayers and away from corporations. It offered very generous rent collection terms in the early years of projects in the hope that more revenue might be collected in the future. Government hype about its royalty changes notwithstanding, this regime wasn't "generic" at all. Established players in the sector had the option to retain the royalty regimes they already had. Reregulation for them was voluntary, a corporate choice determined by whether the government's changes would enable them to garner even more profits than they reaped under the established rules.

Examining Alberta's generic royalty regime also speaks to the dangers market fundamentalism may pose to the very corporations and wealthy interests who demand that the state reregulate in their favour. For corporations, the ideological power of market fundamentalism, when linked to the short-term profits they may reap from the lack of governance, may render these interests "incapable of constructing even the order that they need for their own long-term accumulation of capital."[32] Stiglitz asserts this incapacity contributed to the financial crisis in 2008. The lack of regulation and the subscription to market fundamentalism in both the Federal Reserve and the Bush administration helped to create, not manage, risk in the financial sector.[33] This study argues that the state's failure to temper the tar sands rush is another example of where the absence of regulation created, not managed, risk. As we see in Chapter Three, the Alberta government's decisions in the 1990s to generously promote any and all tar sands ventures helped dramatically inflate the oil price corporations claimed to need for new projects to break even. Depending on the future of oil prices, the corporate behaviour that this policy regime tolerated, if not encouraged, may be responsible for future threats to development and/or more demands for fiscal concessions from government.

Similarly, the project cost-inflating consequences of those Alberta decisions helped to scuttle the province's own ambitions to increase the amount of bitumen upgrading that would take place in Alberta. With respect to nature, Chapters Four, Seven, and Eight examine what the Canadian state's tolerance of the environmental consequences of tar sands exploitation produced: intensifying environmental controversy and a growing national and international opposition.

The notion a rejuvenated regulatory state might have benefited, and may still benefit, the long-term prospects of tar sands capital is not as ludicrous as market fundamentalists will believe. As the Harvard Business School's Michael Porter argued, it is a "false dichotomy" to suppose that environmental regulations are necessarily the bane of competitiveness.[34] In fact, if environmental regulations stimulate innovation and upgrading, they actually may boost competitiveness.[35] The possibility that some types of environmental regulations may promote corporate dynamism is strengthened further if you accept Porter and van der Linde's point that "the world does not fit the Panglossian belief that firms always make optimal choices."[36] One might have thought this point wouldn't be difficult to accept in the wake of the spectacular corporate scandals and blunders provided by Enron, WorldCom, and Lehman Brothers, or illustrated by the Libor scandal, the subprime mortgage crisis, and the Deepwater Horizon explosion and blowout. The record so far suggests otherwise.

Reregulation draws our attention toward how ideas are institutionalized in rules and organizations. I hope to demonstrate the instrumental role a range of institutions play in ensuring the vitality of market fundamentalism in the politics of the tar sands. Rules affecting political behaviour have exerted important, independent impacts on policy in the tar sands. Institutions such as government departments, legislatures, regulatory agencies, joint industry-government task forces, and courts are more than just "arenas for contending social forces . . . they are also collections of standard operating procedures and structures that define and defend interests. They are political actors in their own right."[37] Constitutions and the courts that interpret them, decision-making rules, and rules for establishing the standing to participate in regulatory and/or environmental assessment hearings join international treaties such as the free trade agreements in affecting and shaping political conduct and outcomes. For example, provisions of the Canadian constitution such as provincial ownership of natural resources aid in understanding Alberta's prominence in the politics of petroleum. Judicial decisions regarding the constitutional duty of governments to consult and accommodate First Nations when development affects Aboriginal rights may affect the policy influence of and impact on Aboriginal peoples. The need for pipelines crossing the Canadian-American border to receive a presidential permit helps to explain why the Keystone XL pipeline project became the poster child for climate change and anti-tar sands campaigns in American politics. The rules of Alberta's energy regulatory process, by severely limiting public participation in that process, became an important contributor both to the tar sands boom and also to the growth of a transnational environmental opposition to the tar sands. Taken together, these institutions, with the notable exception of President Obama's rejection of the Keystone XL pipeline, have cemented the dominance of petroleum interests and the diminishment of nature for more than a generation now. You might say these institutions ensured the fix was in.

In *The Great Transformation*, the impossible pursuit of the self-regulating market was met in the last half of the nineteenth century by "a protective countermovement tending toward its restriction."[38] The traditional landed classes—squires and peasants—joined the fledgling working class in this countermovement against industrialists, entrepreneurs, and capitalists. Like Janus, the instigators of this countermove looked both to the past (feudalism) and to the future (socialism):

> But while the landed classes would naturally seek the solution for all the evils in the maintenance of the past, the workers were, up to a point, in a position to transcend the limits of a market society and to borrow solutions from the future.[39]

In their time, the landed and working classes, animated by "a purely pragmatic spirit,"[40] secured a raft of legislation to protect society from the extremes of the market.

With respect to the tar sands case, did a countermovement emerge to challenge this expression of market fundamentalism? If so, who led this countermove and what factors shaped the countermovement's goals and strategies? While Polanyi's double movement is said to be typical of "the normal politics of market societies," there isn't a guarantee that strong national or transnational countermovements will appear to challenge the policies of market fundamentalism.[41] In studying the countermovement to the tar sands rush, we take our cues from Block and Evans and focus primarily on the ideological and organizational circumstances countermovements must either face or take advantage of. Ideology, elite unity, and the growth of the religious right in American politics help Block account for the relative weakness of the countermovement to market liberalism in the United States.[42] Evans acknowledges that national countermovements may not persuade national governments to act against neoliberalism. But he is optimistic that if social movements organize globally they may be able to secure goals such as better stewardship of environmental collective goods. Slowing the pace of climate change and increasing the capacities of many to adapt to this phenomenon would be such accomplishments. Evans believes that, to be successful, global movements for social protection would have to be transnational and bridge the North-South divide; they would have to focus on more than just single issues; they would have to campaign at local, national, and global levels; and their objective must be one that inspires many to act, one that "captures the collective imagination."[43]

Workers and state managers, the last generation's keys to promoting capitalism's rationality and dynamism, have suffered badly in most OECD countries since the early 1980s. For example, between 1995 and 2005 the percentage of the labour force employed in the public sector fell in 9 of the 11 countries for which the OECD could obtain data.[44] As we'll see in Chapter Three, Premier Klein's version of market fundamentalism imposed significant cuts on the departments with regulatory responsibilities in the tar sands. Since the Alberta Progressive Conservatives suffered a humiliating defeat in the 2015 provincial election, there have been few indications from Edmonton that the New Democratic Party (NDP) government believes it needs to increase its organizational capacity to regulate the tar sands. Numerically, organized labour has suffered too, more than state managers globally. Labour union members accounted for 17.5 percent of employees across the OECD area in 2011, virtually half the 34 percent level they claimed in the mid-1970s.[45] Trade union density in Alberta is the lowest in Canada, where 22.6 percent of the province's workers in 2010 belonged to a trade union (the national trade union density was 29.5 percent).[46] The declines in the organizational strength of these actors assists somewhat in concluding that they play a minor role in the countermovement against the tar sands.

More importantly, Alberta trade unions initially were important allies of petroleum companies in promoting tar sands exploitation. Their support for a national oil sands development strategy was part of the national lobbying effort on the issue in the 1990s. The objections that have since come from the trade union sector to developing the tar sands have focused mainly on those dimensions of development—importing foreign workers and processing bitumen in the United States as opposed to Alberta—that affect trade union jobs. Trade unions, due to the material benefits they potentially gain from accelerated tar sands development, are not likely to figure prominently in a countermovement concerned about nature.

Aboriginal peoples and environmentalists, constituencies that didn't figure in the 1970s' analyses of Lindblom and Block, are where we find much of the contemporary opposition to exploiting the tar sands at break-neck speed. If an effective countermovement to tar sands exploitation is to arise, it's likely to have its roots in the interests and leadership of these constituencies. To some extent, today's Aboriginal peoples and environmentalists approximate the visions Polanyi attributed to the landed and working classes. Aboriginal peoples, like the landed classes, may be seen to look to the past due to their interest in protecting traditional customs and practices. That ambition seems quite similar to what Polanyi called the ambition to protect "the culture of the countryside."[47] An Aboriginal land ethic bears important similarities to Polanyi's description of how man thought of the land in much more than simply economic terms. About the vital functions of land, Polanyi wrote:

> It invests man's life with stability; it is the site of his habitation; it is a condition of his physical safety; it is the landscape and the seasons. We might as well imagine his being born without hands and feet as carrying on his life without land.[48]

Environmentalists don't necessarily imagine the socialist future that nineteenth-century working classes sought. But they universally aspire to a less carbon-intensive future, one where our reliance on fossil fuels is reduced dramatically and where both Alberta and Canada make a meaningful contribution to global efforts to reduce greenhouse gas (GHG) emissions. Their additional concerns about the landscape and aquatic impacts of the tar sands industry overlap with those of Aboriginal peoples.

Four of the following chapters consider the role environmentalists and First Nations have played in the contemporary tar sands story. There we see the birth of a countermovement to protect natural features that were threatened by the tar sands rush. But, given the rapidity and gigantism of the tar sands boom, one might have expected the countermovement to be stronger, more prevalent, and more effective than those chapters will suggest. That examination will provide some suggestions for why, in the case of the Alberta tar sands, a stronger countermovement didn't emerge. Some of those suggestions will underline how the proponents of market fundamentalism structured policy-making to deny participation to and silence those who would defend nature. The regulatory process, for example, exemplified non-decision-making, decision-making that "results in suppression or thwarting of a latent or manifest challenge to the values or interests of the decision-maker."[49] This strategy was especially effective in preventing a wider range of environmental interests from participating in the state's regulatory and environmental assessment processes. Those processes for tar sands approvals have a definite David and Goliath character. The expertise and resources that industry and government bring to those processes dwarf what First Nations and environmental groups are able to muster. Such disadvantages were compounded during the first decade of the boom by the rapid-fire appearance and approval of projects. In these situations of gross disparities in resources, we will see how industry insinuated its interests into the perspective First Nations took to proposed projects. Industry would help to fund much-needed administrative capacity but only if First Nations were willing to accommodate themselves to industry's plans.

Such efforts from government and industry to tame the countermovement should be expected. What may be more striking or surprising is what these chapters will suggest about how the ties of environmentalists and First Nations to the market society affect the strength of their criticisms and the countermovement they lead. Polanyi's observation that workers could only transcend nineteenth-century market society "up to a point" suggests how the position of interests in market societies will affect the scope of their opposition. In the tar sands, some of the most significant environmental and First Nations' voices have important, profitable relationships with the tar sands companies. Those relationships have tempered their criticisms and the strength of the countermovement.

Conclusion

For more than a generation now, exploiting Alberta's bitumen resource has fuelled provincial and national material prosperity in Canada and has strengthened Alberta's position as the pre-eminent foreign supplier of crude oil to American markets. "Frenetic" best describes the pace this exploitation generally has taken since the mid-1990s. It also has been single-minded in the sense that the consequences of frenetic development for nature, such as Alberta's boreal forest or the global climate, have never figured prominently in policy-making. This work invites you to look in several directions to understand what has transpired in northeastern Alberta. Explaining the tar sands boom requires us to weave a tapestry where interests, market fundamentalism, and institutions figure prominently.

Notes

1   G. Bruce Doern and Glen Toner, *The Politics of Energy: The Development and Implementation of the NEP* (Toronto: Methuen, 1985), 11–20.
2   Charles Lindblom, "The Market as Prison," *Journal of Politics* 44, no. 2 (May 1982). Lindblom certainly wasn't the only or the first liberal American political

scientist to come to this conclusion. For an earlier account of the privileged position of business, see Grant McConnell, *Private Power and American Democracy* (New York: Alfred A. Knopf, 1966).

3   Lindblom, "The Market as Prison," 329.

4   Lindblom, "The Market as Prison."

5   Lindblom, "The Market as Prison," 326, 329.

6   Lindblom, "The Market as Prison," 333.

7   For much more negative appraisals of Lindblom's position, see Robert Solo, Daniel R. Fusfeld, and James M. Buchanan, "Three Reviews of Charles E. Lindblom's *Politics and Markets: The World's Political Economic Systems,*" *Journal of Economic Issues* 13, no. 1 (March 1979), 207–17.

8   See, for examples, Peter Hall and David Soskice, eds., *Varieties of Capitalism: The Institutional Foundations of Comparative Advantage* (Oxford: Oxford University Press, 2001); Gosta Esping-Andersen, *The Three Worlds of Welfare Capitalism* (Princeton, NJ: Princeton University Press, 1990); Peter J. Katzenstein, *Small States in World Markets: Industrial Policy in Europe* (Ithaca, NY: Cornell University Press, 1985).

9   Fred Block, "The Ruling Class Does Not Rule: Notes on the Marxist Theory of the State," *Socialist Revolution* 33 (May–June 1977), 18–19.

10   John Richards and Larry Pratt, *Prairie Capitalism: Power and Influence in the New West* (Toronto: McClelland and Stewart, 1979), 6–8.

11   Richards and Pratt, *Prairie Capitalism*, 9. Pratt and Richards explicitly drew on Raymond Vernon's concept of the "obsolescing bargain" in their work. See Raymond Vernon, *Sovereignty at Bay: The Multinational Spread of U.S. Enterprises* (London: Longman, 1971).

12   D. Joseph Stiglitz, "Moving Beyond Market Fundamentalism to a More Balanced Economy," *Annals of Public and Cooperative Economics* 80, no. 3 (2009), 346.

13   Fred Block and Margaret R. Somers, *The Power of Market Fundamentalism: Karl Polanyi's Critique* (Cambridge, MA: Harvard University Press, 2014), 3.

14   Block and Somers, *Power of Market Fundamentalism*.

15   Karl Polanyi, *The Great Transformation: The Political and Economic Origins of Our Time* (Boston: Beacon Press, 2001).

16   Fred Block, "Karl Polanyi and the Writing of *The Great Transformation,*" *Theory and Society* 32, no. 3 (June 2003), 282.

17   Block, "Polanyi and the Writing," 149–50.

18   Block, "Polanyi and the Writing," 152–53.

19   Polanyi, *Great Transformation*, 138.

20   Polanyi, *Great Transformation*, 154–57.

21   Polanyi, *Great Transformation*, 141–45. Polanyi also saw the similarities between religious devotion and faith in the ideal of a self-regulating market. Chapter 12 of *The Great Transformation* was tellingly titled "Birth of the Liberal Creed." Terms and phrases therein such as faith, fanaticism, dogma, militant creed, crusading passion, and "turned almost into a religion" suggest how similarly Polanyi regarded these two types of faith.

22   Becky Mansfield, "Rules of Privatization: Contradictions in Neoliberal Regulation of North Pacific Fisheries," *Annals of the Association of American Geographers* 94, no. 3 (2004); Block and Somers, *Power of Market Fundamentalism*; Stiglitz, "Moving Beyond Market Fundamentalism"; Peter Evans, "Is an Alternative Globalization Possible?," *Politics and Society* 36, no. 2 (June 2008).

23   Block and Somers, *Power of Market Fundamentalism*, 19–20.

24   Fred Block, "A New Era of Regulation?," *States, Power, and Societies* 15, no. 1 (Fall 2009), 3.

25   Fred Block, "Understanding the Diverging Trajectories of the United States and Western Europe: A Neo-Polanyian Analysis," *Politics and Society* 35, no. 1 (March 2007), 12.

26   Fred Block, "Swimming Against the Current: The Rise of a Hidden Developmental State in the United States," *Politics and Society* 36, no. 2 (2008), 183.

27   In situ ("in its original place") oil sands projects are not mines. Instead bitumen is extracted from below ground by injecting steam or another substance to liquefy the bitumen, enabling it to flow into extraction pipes and wells.

28   For an analysis of many of the consequences of the 2012 federal budget for federal environmental stewardship in Canada, see Theresa McClenaghan, "Bill C-38: Federal Budget Bill 2012 Implications for Federal Environmental Law" (Canadian Environmental Law Association, June 2012), http://s.cela.ca/files/Bill-C-38-Federal-Budget-Bill-Review-and-Implications.pdf.

29   "Alberta Rejects a Bailout for West Edmonton Mall," *Toronto Star*, March 18, 1994, B7.

30   The provincial government held a 36 percent share of Alberta Energy Company. It held a 16.74 percent share of the Syncrude partnership and sold a 5 percent Syncrude position to Murphy Oil in 1993 and an 11.74 percent position in Syncrude to Torch Energy Advisors in 1995.

31   Mark Lisac, *The Klein Revolution* (Edmonton: NeWest Press, 1995); Mark Lisac, *Alberta Politics Uncovered: Taking Back Our Province* (Edmonton: NeWest Press, 2004).

32   Evans, "Alternative Globalization," 280.

33   Stiglitz, "Moving Beyond Market Fundamentalism," 352.

34   Michael E. Porter, "America's Green Strategy," *Scientific American* 264, no. 4 (1991), 168.

35   Porter, "America's Green Strategy." A more elaborate expression of this argument is found in Michael E. Porter and Claas van der Linde, "Toward a New Conception of the Environment-Competitiveness Relationship," *Journal of Economic Perspectives* 9, no. 4 (1995).

36   Porter and van der Linde, "Toward a New Conception," 99.

37   James G. March and Johan P. Olsen, "The New Institutionalism: Organizational Factors in Political Life," *American Political Science Review* 78, no. 3 (1984), 738.

38   Polanyi, *Great Transformation*, 151.

39   Polanyi, *Great Transformation*, 162.

40   Polanyi, *Great Transformation*, 147.

41   Block, "Polanyi's Double Movement"; Evans, "Alternative Globalization."

42   Block, "Polanyi's Double Movement."

43   Evans, "Alternative Globalization," 287.

44   Organisation for Economic Cooperation and Development, *Government at a Glance 2009* (Paris: OECD, 2009), 66–69.

45   OECD, *OECD Database on Trade Unions*. Canadian trade union membership actually grew in percentage terms from 34.3 percent in 1975 to it peak of 37.8 percent in the years 1992 and 1993. In 2011, it had fallen to 28.8 percent. In 1960, US trade unions represented 30.9 percent of American workers.

In 1975, this percentage fell to 25.3 percent. In 2011, it had plunged to 11.3 percent.

46   Statistics Canada and Sharanjit Uppal, "Unionization 2011," http://www. statcan.gc.ca/pub/75-001-x/2011004/article/11579-eng.htm.

47   Polanyi, *Great Transformation*, 138.

48   Polanyi, *Great Transformation*, 187.

49   Peter Bachrach and Morton S. Baratz, *Power and Poverty: Theory and Practice* (New York: Oxford University Press, 1970), 44, quoted in Steven Lukes, *Power: A Radical View*, 2nd ed. (Padstow, UK: Palgrave Macmillan, 2005), 22.

2
State, Capital, and the Foundations of Exploiting the Tar Sands

"In this, as in countless other cases in both Canada and [the] United States, when the market economy failed to satisfy the immediate necessities of the business community, it appealed without the slightest qualm to the state for public provision of the service."
—H. V. Nelles, The Politics of Development, 1974

Introduction

After presenting some background information about Alberta's bitumen resources, this chapter focuses primarily on how the tar sands were developed during the period stretching from the end of World War II until the institutionalization of the Canada–United States Free Trade Agreement (CUSFTA) in 1989. It critically considers the efforts of Paul Chastko and Larry Pratt to explain the path of development in the first 30 years after World War II.[1] Their works offer fundamentally different views of the relationship between government and tar sands interests. Chastko's account is one that grants considerable autonomy to the Alberta government in the 1960s from the interests and demands of tar sands capital. Ernest Manning's Social Credit government receives considerable credit for bringing Alberta's tar sands to market in an orderly fashion that didn't coincide with the ambitions of multinational enterprises. Pratt grants much more importance to the interests and influence of those multinational firms. Pratt's book, and his subsequent work with John Richards, highlights that the relationship between government and industry is fundamentally a bargaining one, a relationship where power is exercised according to the parties' relative possession and utilization of various political resources.[2] Generally Pratt's outlook is preferred here. Its strength rests first in its recognition that the state/capital relationship is a bargaining one that revolves around factors such as institutional expertise and capacity. It highlights how real and potential developments in the international petroleum economy, such as the rise of the Organization of the Petroleum Exporting Countries (OPEC), the energy crisis of the early 1970s, and the petroleum potential in US oil shales resources, affected the interests and bargaining power of governments and multinationals with respect to the tar sands. The industry principals behind Syncrude, the second major tar sands mining project to proceed in Alberta, ably exploited the price shock and supply concerns arising out of the energy crisis of the 1970s to win government concessions for and financial participation in that joint venture.

A string of events beginning in 1980 signalled some of the logic tar sands exploitation would start to follow in the mid-1990s. Ottawa's National Energy Program (NEP) introduced in October 1980 was one such event. The tar sands sector was tied to the Liberal government's newly professed interest in petroleum self-sufficiency. Consequently, tar sands producers received policy favours from Ottawa. They were spared the federal policies that drew the ire of Alberta and foreign-controlled petroleum companies alike. The production of Syncrude and Suncor, for example, was exempted from the price ceilings the NEP set for Canadian conventional oil production. That Syncrude was first shown this favouritism—favouritism Suncor had to fight for publicly—also suggests that Ottawa wasn't about to threaten the 15 percent ownership position it held in Syncrude through Petro-Canada, the Crown Corporation Ottawa created in 1975. The state's financial and petroleum security interests in the tar sands were at odds with the norms of market fundamentalism. Those interests gave a temporary statist hue to the character of the interventionism seen in this period, one that would fade starting in the last half of the 1980s. Tar sands producers also tried to exploit Ottawa's new-found concern about petroleum self-sufficiency. In the mid- to late 1980s they demanded more state assistance to strengthen their position in Canada's petroleum economy.

Other key events in the 1980s took place internationally and significantly shifted the normative benchmark for good government. Ronald Reagan's presidential election victory in 1980 ushered in "supply-side" economics or Reaganomics. Economic growth hinged on reducing taxes and deregulating business. In Great Britain, newly elected Prime Minister Margaret Thatcher followed a similar, unwavering commitment to free markets from government rules and regulations. Through the magic of Reagan and Thatcher the spell of market fundamentalism, a doctrine many thought had died with the Great Depression, became popular once again. In Canada, the landslide victory of Brian Mulroney's Progressive Conservatives in the 1984 federal election was soon followed by free trade negotiations with the United States. The subsequent Canada–US free trade agreement testified to a renewed devotion to free market ideology in North American economic life.

Block and Somers argue that a contradiction described by Karl Polanyi in *The Great Transformation*, one where business professes its faith in free markets while simultaneously seeking government assistance, also defines contemporary business-state relations, especially in the United States.[3] In this chapter we see how well this characterization applies to the relationships formed in the 1980s between the state and the tar sands interests. Demands for government assistance and free trade in energy were essential elements of the tar sands industry's vision for future development. In the energy provisions of the CUSFTA we see how these two contradictory ideological themes were accommodated.

Alberta's Bitumen

The bituminous sands are a nonconventional source of oil. Essentially, this means that, at first glance, neither you nor I would recognize them as "oil." Crumbly asphalt, likely to become gooey on a hot summer's day, mixed liberally with beach sand would be a better physical description of what these grey or black sands look like. Most of the sands, roughly two-thirds to three-quarters of a representative sample from Alberta's Athabasca tar sands, are just that—quartz sand; water makes up another 3 to 5 percent of these deposits; bitumen, the hydrocarbon now being processed into synthetic crude oil in record amounts, constitutes a further 10 to 12 percent of the sands.[4] The phrase "tar sands," now shunned by most governments, petroleum companies, and other boosters of exploiting this resource, is truer to their physical character than the salesperson's preferred phrase—"oil sands." The phrase owes its accuracy to bitumen's tar- or pitch-like character. Bitumen, due to its high specific gravity and high viscosity, flows or pours extremely slowly if at all. Its potential commercial value as oil arises from the way the water in the tar sands surrounds the individual grains of sand. That the embrace between bitumen and water is weaker than that between water and sand makes it easier to separate bitumen from the sand, clay, and heavy metals.

As this suggests, extensive upgrading or processing is required in order to transform bitumen into synthetic crude oil.[5] A barrel of bitumen, with less hydrogen, more carbon, and more sulphur than a barrel of conventional crude oil, needs to have hydrogen added or carbon removed in order to be a suitable feedstock for most refineries. Some type of petroleum condensate must be added to the bitumen in order to dilute it sufficiently to transport it through pipelines to upgraders and/or refineries—some of them hundreds or thousands of miles from the source of the bitumen.[6] To date, natural gas condensates have been the preferred diluent. But whether or not these condensates will be plentiful in the future from local supplies is questionable given the sharp decline in Alberta's conventional natural gas reserves. The combination of the crucial need for diluents and the decline in Alberta's gas reserves has produced a seemingly bizarre scenario in Alberta's hydrocarbon-rich northeast. Canada's National Energy Board approved Enbridge Inc.'s Southern Lights project, a project to construct a 180,000-barrels-per-day pipeline for delivering light liquid hydrocarbons produced in Chicago—one destination for tar sands production—back to Edmonton in order to provide the precious diluent that tar sands operators require to move their product by pipeline.

Tar sands deposits lie beneath much of northern Alberta. Found under approximately 60,000 square kilometres (23,000 square miles) of the province, they would encompass nearly half of England; they occur in virtually as much territory as the combined area of the states of Maryland and Massachusetts. The rocks destined to become the tar sands were formed sometime in the late-Paleozoic or mid-Mesozoic eras—anywhere from 354 to 142 million years ago. The Athabasca deposits originated as light oil in the Western Canadian Sedimentary Basin—hundreds of kilometres from where they rest today. Geological pressures pushed these oil-bearing formations to the Fort McMurray region. Microbes decomposed the lighter hydrocarbons in this oil, transforming it into bitumen. This biodegradation process changed the quality of the oil and reduced its original volume by two or three times.[7] Nonetheless, Alberta still contains a staggering amount of bitumen—approximately 1.7 trillion barrels.[8] No other jurisdiction comes close to Alberta when it comes to the amount of in-place bitumen resources. Russia's bitumen reserves amount to 12 percent of Canada's; Venezuela's amounts to 3 percent; Nigeria's amounts to just under 3 percent; the United States' bitumen reserves—most of which are found in eastern Utah—amount to less than 2 percent of what is found in Alberta.

When measured in terms of recoverable bitumen reserves—those reserves expected to be recoverable given anticipated economic and technological conditions—this "bitumen advantage" propelled Canada into one of the globe's top-ranking sources of petroleum. With 169.7 billion barrels of proved oil reserves at the end of 2012 (of these reserves 168 billion barrels are bitumen), Canada now has the third largest petroleum reserves in the world. Only Saudi Arabia (265.9 billion barrels) and Venezuela (297.6 billion barrels) have larger proved reserves than Canada.[9] Today, tar sands are exploited either by mining or by in situ operations. Deposits found within 75 metres of the surface are generally exploited through mammoth open pit mining operations. Alberta estimates that nearly 20 percent of its established bitumen reserves will be exploited through surface mining operations; the remaining 80 percent will be extracted through in situ recovery.[10] Current in situ processes generally inject steam through a well bore into the bitumen reservoir in order to lower the bitumen's viscosity and coax it to flow to a second well bore through which it is pumped to the surface.

Early History

Bitumen has been used since ancient times. The Greek historian Dio-
dor described it as one of Babylon's "incredible miracles."[11] Babylonians,
Carthaginians, and Palestinians used bitumen as a mortar; it also was valued
for its medicinal qualities; supposedly Noah's Ark and Moses' basket were
caulked with bitumen in order to waterproof them.[12] Bitumen thus contributed to the "miracle" of the Phoenicians' skill at sea and the extensive
trade network they developed. The Carthaginian use of bitumen to tar the
clay walls of their dwellings tragically enabled the Romans to burn Carthage
to the ground in 146 BCE.[13] In a similar notorious vein, Middle Eastern
bitumen seepages helped to introduce flaming missiles into the warfare of
biblical times.

The Aboriginal peoples who lived for millennia along the Athabasca
and Clearwater rivers caulked their canoes with bitumen in order to help
them travel throughout these river basins. To read the opening to a government report on an 1889 expedition to the Athabasca District you would
think only white eyes could appreciate the tar sands' value to livelihoods.
The report inferred that the region's history only began when Peter Pond
reached the Athabasca in 1778 as part of his efforts to expand the fur trade.[14]
R. G. McConnell's observations made during a Geological Survey of Canada expedition spoke optimistically about the economic value of the area's
bitumen resources. While McConnell felt the commercial value of the tar
sands was uncertain, he believed their abundance, when combined with the
high percentages of bitumen found in the sands, meant they probably would
be used profitably sometime in the future.[15] Not anticipating that bitumen
itself could be converted into oil, he held out the hope that some of the oil
that biodegradation had transformed into bitumen still might be found in
the region. Disappointingly, test drilling conducted by the federal government in the 1890s did not find this more technologically friendly, more
desirable prize.

In the early white history of the tar sands, many of the men who came
to exploit this resource were as nonconventional as the oil they sought.
Most came and left northern Alberta with little more than a trunk full of
dreams. Alfred von Hammerstein, a German count, typified these pioneers.
Rumours of oil in the Athabasca region led him to abandon plans to join
the Klondike gold rush. Instead, the count leased more than 10,000 acres of
tar sands properties from the federal government. Lacking technical skills,
von Hammerstein's prospects of striking it rich north of Fort McMurray were as dim as his chances of finding gold in the Yukon. Nothing of
consequence—other than his musical contributions to the University Radio

Orchestra—came from his time in Alberta.[16] Dreams became nightmares for other tar sands pioneers. R.C. Fitzsimmons, the founder of International Bitumen, blamed the government of Alberta for the failure of his company. The government persecuted him, never gave his company "a square deal," and chose instead to support the leading oil companies. Fitzsimmons astutely saw these companies as having no interest in immediately developing these resources; they instead planned to keep the tar sands in reserve until conventional oil supplies became scarcer. In Fitzsimmons's eyes even Dr. Karl Clark, generally credited with conducting the most rigorous research into using hot water to separate bitumen from the sands, was guilty of doing more to frustrate, rather than facilitate, tar sands production.[17]

As Fitzsimmons's bitterness infers, intense interpersonal rivalries marked this era. No rivalry appears more heated than that between the Alberta Research Council's Clark and Sidney Ells of the federal government's Mines Branch. The seed for their animosity may have been planted in June 1917 when Clark, then a new Mines Branch employee, was assigned an uncomfortable job—to review a report on the tar sands' commercial properties prepared by Ells, his more senior colleague. Clark's evaluation of Ells's report, authored with another member of the department, was unflattering. Although Clark's biographer—and daughter—does not quote from Clark's "highly critical appraisal," she notes it did not challenge the opinion that Ells's research was "muddled," an opinion offered by the University of Alberta's President H. M. Tory.[18] Clark's personal letters are sprinkled liberally with skeptical comments about Ells and his work.[19]

The prickly nature of the Clark-Ells relationship resonated well with the tenor of federal-provincial relations of the time when it came to exploiting the tar sands. Who would control the tar sands? Who would determine how soon their potential would be developed? Ottawa irritated Alberta. This attitude arose almost immediately after the two governments signed a promising intergovernmental research agreement. Ells began to pursue research questions about bitumen separation that the research agreement had assigned to Clark and the provincial research council.[20] The terms outlined in the *Natural Resources Transfer Act of 1930* intensified Alberta's irritation. The federal government did not turn over the ownership of all natural resources to the province. Instead, Ottawa retained control over 2,000 acres north of Fort McMurray, acreage including the tar sands deposit Ells had been working in. It then leased the development rights to this property to Abasand Oils Ltd.

Not long after the first shots were fired in World War II, the federal government concluded that Canada's dependence on oil imports from the United States could gravely threaten Canada's contribution to the war effort. In this crisis atmosphere the federal government was desperate to secure additional oil supplies. It hoped the Abasand plant, which had processed just 52 tons of tar sands per day in 1941, could be modified to handle nearly 200 times that amount—10,000 tons per day. For C. D. Howe, the Minister of Munitions and Supply, wartime necessities transformed the tar sands into "a source of immediate oil production."[21] But Abasand flopped, first under private management and then under direct federal control. Alberta's frustrations escalated with each failure. Effectively, Ottawa used the war to bar any venture other than Abasand from trying to exploit the tar sands. Ottawa treated Alberta as little better than a bumpkin during these years. The federal government dismissed out of hand Alberta's growing expertise in bitumen extraction, expertise accumulated during more than two decades of work by Clark and the provincial research council. Instead Ottawa turned to foreign "experts" who knew nothing about the tar sands. With nothing of consequence taking place under this de facto federal monopoly, Alberta, then intent on the idea that the tar sands should be developed, wanted out of the 1942 agreement. Alberta wanted to reclaim the authority to offer development leases in the tar sands, and Ottawa agreed. But Ottawa placed a poison pill in the break-up settlement: It threatened to cut off federal research funding if new lessees used the Abasand process prior to any federal release of their findings. This threat made it very unlikely any nonfederal venture would go ahead.[22]

From the end of World War I until the end of the 1940s, Alberta generally supported tar sands research and development enthusiastically. When, at the end of World War II, the federal government's attitude became one of "benign neglect," Alberta moved into the void and financed the construction and operation of a bitumen mining operation at Bitumount.[23] Under Clark's guidance the plant overcame the technical obstacles to bitumen production. But, as Clark laboured to demonstrate the technical feasibility of tar sands development, an event occurred hundreds of miles to the south that soon cooled the province's enthusiasm. Vern Hunter, nicknamed "Dry Hole" because of his dismal drilling record with Imperial Oil, struck a gusher at Leduc #1. The discovery marked the birth of Alberta's first conventional oil boom; oil production soared, skyrocketing from 6.4 million barrels in 1947 to 137 million barrels a decade later.[24] Such explosive growth signalled Alberta's transformation into a petro-economy. It brought with it an entirely new set of challenges—most notably to secure markets for Alberta conventional crude and to placate the budding number of companies and other interests who depended on the health of conventional oil production. Developing the tar sands was no longer a pressing provincial concern. The province closed the doors on Bitumount in 1949.

The Social Credit Years: The Birth of Great Canadian Oil Sands (Suncor)

Paul Chastko, in his history of oil sands development, is lavish in his praise of the Ernest Manning administration for what it did after Bitumount shut down. The Social Credit government "coolly assessed" the predicament created by the Leduc discovery and "shrewdly plotted manoeuvres"—leasing conditions and bitumen sales requirements for the tar sands companies—"that braked business enthusiasm" and kept the tar sands out of production.[25] Manning privileged conventional oil producers and protected them to a degree as they scrambled to secure North American markets for their petroleum.

Larry Pratt is more critical.[26] He grants the Manning government far less independence from the influence of major energy corporations. He, too, sees that Alberta's policy makers were pressured to ensure the stability and profitability of the conventional oil industry. But multinationals in the 1950s controlled more than 80 percent of Canadian oil production, and most of that production came from Alberta. Supporting the conventional producers, then, shouldn't be seen as a sign of provincial independence from the heavyweights in Alberta's petroleum industry.[27] Furthermore, he views Premier Manning as essentially happy to accommodate the multinationals when it came to the feasibility and timing of tar sands production. For Pratt, commercial tar sands production failed to proceed in the 1950s less because of the province's shrewd plotting than because foreign multinationals did not believe, as Fitzsimmons had claimed, the immediate development of the tar sands was in their interest. Regarding Alberta's tar sands resources as insurance to be developed some time in the future was very much part of the global investment and production logic of the multinationals.

Chastko's impressive amount of detail notwithstanding, Pratt's perspective on government/multinational power relationships is more persuasive when it comes to understanding the Manning administration's land tenure policies and the course of tar sands development in the 1960s and 1970s. To suggest, as Pratt does, that multinationals were in a superior bargaining position in these decades doesn't mean we should expect to see every multinational development proposal receive the government's stamp of approval. The competition between Sun Oil, Shell, and a Cities Service-led consortium (this consortium was the precursor to the Syncrude partnership) in the early 1960s is a case in point. Sun Oil succeeded while the other two proposals were rejected. The task, then, is to account for the success of one multinational actor over others. To understand why Sun Oil's Great Canadian Oil

Sands (GCOS) and not Shell or Cities Service was approved, it is important to consider the close personal relationship between Premier Manning and J. Howard Pew, the chairman of Sun Oil. Their friendship was an important political resource that Sun Oil used to its advantage in the early 1960s.

Some of the strongest support for Pratt's view is found in Alberta's land tenure policies for the tar sands. The first edition of this system was unveiled in the fall of 1951 when Alberta invited the petroleum industry to Edmonton to hear about the tar sands' possibilities. Interspersed with government oaths sworn to continental (not Canadian) oil security and to preserving the Christian way of life against communism, Alberta promised very generous terms for any company willing to stake a claim in the tar sands. This generosity meant these corporate claims came with very little financial risk or exposure. Effectively, multinationals were able to bank land rights to the tar sands "until their worldwide interests tipped the scales in favour of development."[28] For the multinationals the tar sands represented "oil insurance." Multinationals adapted a decades-old global strategy when they obtained land positions in Alberta's tar sands region. Globally, the integrated majors sought to control supplies, output, and land concessions in order to maximize profit and limit their competition. They implemented this same logic in Alberta generally and in the Athabasca tar sands region in particular. Generally, as the first president of the Independent Canadian Petroleum Producers Association claimed in 1959, multinationals "can afford to sit on their Canadian holdings as a reserve for the future."[29] With respect to the tar sands, multinationals had no intention of developing the concessions they obtained in the short term. Instead, they planned to hold them in reserve and develop them at a time and in a manner that would maintain their stature and power in world oil markets. As an Alberta Energy department official suggested in a review of the post-1950 history of tar sands leasing, this corporate strategy characterized the tar sands leasing pattern in Alberta:

> By and large the bituminous sands and oil sands (now all known as oil sands) agreements were acquired by major trans-national petroleum companies anxious to add to their world wide resources holdings which, though not immediately economic to produce, they anticipated would be so in due course.[30]

None of the major multinational oil companies, individually or through Canadian subsidiaries, champed at the bit to mine the tar sands. The representatives from American and British multinationals who attended Alberta's 1951 oil sands conference did not leave with a burning desire to become pioneer tar sands miners. Imperial Oil was reaping the rewards of its strikes at Leduc. Under the watchful eyes of its parent, Standard Oil of New Jersey (ExxonMobil today), it concluded it did not have any serious designs for the tar sands.[31] But, even without serious designs, the company proceeded immediately to lease lands, lands that over the next 10 to 50 years would be the focus of exploitation through, first, the Syncrude project in 1969 and then the Kearl project in 2007.

Sun Oil is the exception to this pattern. Sun's chairman J. Howard Pew, who with hindsight may be regarded as a visionary, held views in the 1940s about the tar sands that then may have made him appear to be a crackpot among petroleum executives. Pew believed that conventional oil production would peak, a peak he saw occurring sooner rather than later. For this reason, as well as because he was reluctant to plunge his company into the volatile Middle East, Pew concentrated his attention on petroleum plays in the Western hemisphere.[32] The tar sands figured prominently here. In 1949 Pew told the manager of Sun's Canadian operations that his only important mission was to guarantee that "Sun Oil Company always has a 'significant position' in the Athabasca Tar Sands area!"[33]

The "solid friendship" between Pew and Manning helped Pew realize his ambition to produce oil from the tar sands.[34] Sun Oil would be the first company to exploit the tar sands commercially. The Great Canadian Oil Sands plant was the exception to what had been a de facto rule of the province's Petroleum and Natural Gas Conservation Board—that tar sands production must not displace conventional oil production. The Conservation Board developed this criterion out of its concern that North American markets could not be found for all of the conventional oil Alberta could produce. By 1959, more than 50 percent of Alberta's potential production was shut-in, a 20 percent increase in less than five years.[35] This percentage of shut-in production discouraged the investment needed to ensure the Alberta's industry continued growth. In the last half of the 1950s, Alberta's oil production fell by 9.3 percent. With the conventional oil industry stagnating, there was no business or economic case to be made for tapping the tar sands.[36]

The challenges to conventional oil producers in the 1950s had roots in changes taking place in global and North American petroleum markets. Oil consumption grew dramatically, beyond most expectations, but this consumption actually was dwarfed by "gargantuan" increases in production.[37] In the early 1950s huge reservoirs of oil—the elephants—were discovered year after year in the Middle East. A changing of the guard came with these discoveries; the Middle East was on the fast track to replacing the United States as the world's largest petroleum-producing region. From the late 1940s until the early 1970s, the American share of world production fell from

64 percent to 22 percent, a relative decline explained by the exponential growth of Middle Eastern production over these years.[38]

Cheap Middle Eastern and Venezuelan oil, not more expensive Texas or even more expensive Alberta crude, flooded North American markets. The end of the Korean War, the return of Iranian oil to world markets after the Anglo-American–orchestrated overthrow of Iran's Mossadegh government, and the recession of 1958—each event sent these flood levels higher. "More oil was in search of markets," wrote Yergin, "than there were markets for oil."[39] Independent American oil producers, through powerful Congressional champions such as Senator Lyndon Johnson and House Speaker Sam Rayburn, put unrelenting pressure on the Eisenhower administration to shelter them from this foreign flood. Ultimately, this political pressure trumped Eisenhower's free trade inclinations. First through voluntary import controls and then through mandatory quotas, the Eisenhower administration bowed to the political clout of the oilmen from Texas and Oklahoma.[40]

Both circumstances—the flood of cheap, non-North American oil and the efforts of the American independents to preserve some of their US market share—made it difficult for Alberta conventional oil production to penetrate American or eastern Canadian markets. Neither the multinational importers of cheap foreign oil nor American independents had any interest in seeing Alberta increase its share of the American market. And, in Canada, consumers in vote-rich Quebec benefited from cheaper foreign imports. Consequently, there was no political support there for proposals that Montreal refineries should refine Alberta's more expensive oil rather than the cheaper, plentiful feedstocks available from outside of North America.[41]

In this global oil glut, the prospects for any tar sands development appeared dim; Alberta's regulatory body, the Petroleum and Natural Gas Conservation Board (the Conservation Board), resisted overtures to bring this expensive source of petroleum to market, a rational stance arguably in the province's best economic interests. Yet, in 1962, just two years after rejecting the first GCOS proposal for a tar sands plant, the Conservation Board relented and approved the venture's proposal to bring 31,500 barrels of oil per day onstream from a synthetic crude oil plant to be built on the appropriately named Tar Island lease.

Chastko sees a convincing rationality behind this course of events. The nearly two-year delay between rejection and approval let the government compose "a strategy for orderly development" of the tar sands. It gave conventional producers time "to solidify their markets and develop strategies to cope with the competition provided by the oil sands."[42] This conclusion seems generous. At least half of Alberta's production was shut-in at this time, a situation aggravated by the dynamics of global and North American markets that weren't entirely resolved by Ottawa's introduction of the National Oil Policy in 1961. A struggling conventional sector was in no economic position to welcome one barrel, let alone more than 30,000 barrels, of new production from the tar sands.

The Pew-Manning friendship may offer a better explanation for Alberta's flip-flop. In October 1962 the government approved the GCOS project, despite the oil glut consumers were enjoying and the shut-in capacity producers, especially Canadian independents, suffered through. Less than two months after this approval, the Manning administration announced a new policy with respect to tar sands production. Tar sands production would be restricted, not prohibited; it would be limited to no more than 5 percent of the demand for Alberta's oil. This percentage fit strikingly well with proposed production from the GCOS operation. This revised government policy, coming on the heels of GCOS receiving regulatory approval, suggests a link between the two decisions, a link further legitimizing the Great Canadian Oil Sands project. To see this approval as a function of the Pew-Manning relationship we should recognize that in 1962, unlike in 1960, two other tar sands project applications were before the Conservation Board. These proposals, submitted by Shell and the Cities Service consortium, stressed the importance of economies of scale to project profitability; they imagined much larger projects than GCOS, projects producing approximately 100,000 barrels per day. Their larger size arguably placed these projects on a stronger economic footing than the GCOS project. However, their proponents, whatever the economic merit of their proposals, did not enjoy a vital political resource—Pew's personal relationship with the premier. The Conservation Board rejected these other applications.

While the Pew-Manning friendship boosted the prospects for Great Canadian Oil Sands, the financial terms negotiated for this project underlined that even good friendships have their limits. With respect to royalties, the province required GCOS to pay an 8 percent royalty on the first 900,000 barrels of crude production, a 20 percent royalty on all production above that level, and a 16.66 per cent levy on all products refined from the bitumen. In addition, in a striking departure from the norms of the business/government relationship, the province wanted some of its royalties in advance—royalties on the first 8 million barrels of production were due to land on the provincial treasurer's desk before those barrels were produced.[43] Alberta also placed other financial demands on GCOS. The company was required to pay obligations to the federal government outstanding from the Abasands venture, a $500,000 annual municipal tax, and a special 11 percent sales tax on materials imported into Alberta to construct the plant. Alberta also insisted GCOS establish a hiring preference for Albertans, reserve a small percentage of shares for Albertans to purchase, and appoint a provincial oil executive to the company's board.[44] Such conditions were strikingly absent from the agreements provincial administrations would negotiate with tar sands companies in the 1970s, 1980s, and 1990s.

When GCOS ran into serious problems after start-up—the company lost nearly $9 million in its first three months of operation—it sought royalty relief and other financial concessions from the province. Under Harry Strom, Alberta's last Social Credit premier, and Peter Lougheed, the first premier in what became a Progressive Conservative dynasty that lasted 44 years, the government gave GCOS some, but certainly not all, of the concessions the company claimed to need in order to put itself on a sound financial footing. GCOS demanded an 8 percent reduction in royalties; A.R. Patrick, Strom's energy minister, reluctantly granted a temporary, 20-month reduction of that amount. The company also demanded an increase in the price of its synthetic crude oil; Alberta flatly rejected that request. The pressure from GCOS did not stop. Pew personally lent his weight to a demand that Alberta give GCOS a five-year royalty holiday and a deductible upgrading allowance that could be used to reduce the company's synthetic crude royalty payments. Pew and senior Sun Oil officials travelled to Edmonton to insist the combination of surprisingly high operating costs and low synthetic crude prices meant their royalty arrangements with the province "were not realistic."[45] Strom gave GCOS some of what it wanted— a 50 percent remission of royalties for three years. Lougheed, who became premier after the 1971 election and someone Patrick apparently suggested to Sun officials was the spokesman for the conventional industry, also refused to make the long-term commitment to royalty reductions sought by GCOS.[46] But accommodations in the short term were fine, and Lougheed restored the GCOS remission in 1974, a decision Taylor believes may be explained by the premier's promotion of the Syncrude project. Lougheed's enthusiasm for Syncrude may have been more politically vulnerable if GCOS continued to flounder in a sea of red ink.[47]

The Great Canadian Oil Sands story contains several themes to consider as we move forward in the history of tar sands exploitation. First, it underlines the bargaining nature of the relationship between governments and the various sectors of the petroleum industry. The relative success of sectors, companies, and governments depends fundamentally on the political resources at the parties' disposal and how those resources are employed. Social Credit politicians and regulators used their concern with protecting the conventional oil industry to deflect much of the pressure they faced from multinationals intent on initiating tar sands operations in the early 1960s. But Great Canadian Oil Sands was an exception here, one that cannot

be understood without recognizing the important political resource spring-
ing from the Pew-Manning friendship. Second, the state of global oil markets, but especially the balance of foreign and domestic production in the
American market with its perennial implications for Canadian access, also
may affect the bargaining power of governments and corporations. At times
when cheap, secure non-North American production is readily available to
Americans, the task of securing a larger American market share for Canadian
oil of any type—but especially the more expensive nonconventional production served from the tar sands—will be difficult. Alternatively, when price
spreads between non-North American and Canadian production shrink and
when American ability to supply its consumers with domestic production
falls, the bargaining power of tar sands promoters should improve. Finally, the
Canadian petroleum industry is not monolithic. Common ground between
sectors in the industry will be established and will disintegrate depending on
market conditions and commodity type. The 1950s and 1960s, for example,
were decades when the interests and policy demands of Canadian independents sometimes conflicted sharply with those of the multinationals. The
independents, lacking the multinationals' refining and marketing networks,
favoured state interventions that would maintain or increase their access
to markets. Prorationing, the creation of the National Energy Board, and
Diefenbaker's National Oil Policy were such interventions.[48] When access
to markets is tight, conflict, as we have seen, also may erupt between the
conventional and nonconventional petroleum sectors.

Syncrude

In 1962, four American-controlled oil companies—Imperial Oil, Atlantic
Richfield Company (ARCO), Cities Service Athabasca Ltd., and Royalite
Oil Company—submitted an application to the Conservation Board to
build a 100,000 barrels-per-day tar sands plant. The proposal's ambitious production level raised a substantial hurdle since it ran afoul of the limit set by
the province's tar sands development policy. Rather than reject their application outright, the Conservation Board invited the proponents to resubmit
their application before the end of 1968.

Two years after the Conservation Board rejected their proposal, these
companies formed the Syncrude consortium.[49] Before reapplying to the
Board in 1968, the Syncrude partners lobbied government privately and
tried to swing public opinion in favour of their venture. To this end the
companies played the "oil shales card." Both in public forums and in private meetings with government, Syncrude's backers warned that, if Alberta
did not approve new tar sands projects, the province risked seeing any

potential tar sands development displaced by the exploitation of oil shales in Colorado.[50] In this argument, the shales threatened all sources of Canadian oil looking to enter the American market. According to Syncrude, this threat—and the need to blunt it—was made more credible by the probability that future American production could not meet US demand. In this scenario, only the tar sands or the Colorado oil shales could satisfy America's growing thirst for oil. In a private meeting called in May 1966 by Premier Manning, a gathering whose attendees were drawn overwhelmingly from companies that wanted to mine the tar sands, Syncrude argued that billions of barrels of new production were needed and that "[t]he source of supply which can be developed most rapidly and economically will certainly enjoy the most favourable supply position."[51] Provincial policy, with its limits on tar sands production, seriously impeded the development of ventures capable of generating the volume of synthetic crude oil needed for commercial success. Only the Independent Petroleum Association—the voice of the Canadian conventional oil independents—and Dome Petroleum urged the government to maintain the status quo with respect to tar sands development.[52]

This lobbying persuaded Alberta. In February 1968, the government announced several clarifications and amendments to the Oil Sands Development Policy that boosted and legitimized additional tar sands production. At a time when very significant percentages of Alberta's production were shut-in and the lifespan of the province's conventional oil reserves was increasing, the government legitimized its policy changes by arguing they would "encourage further growth in the total crude oil market and thereby permit further oil sands development."[53] It is hard to see the amended policy as anything other than a major concession to Syncrude and others who had ambitions to produce oil from the tar sands. While the policy claimed it would encourage growth in the markets serviced by Alberta oil, it was silent about how additional tar sands production would accomplish this or why measures to reduce the amount of shut-in oil would not realize just as much market growth. Another feature of the amended policy that appears as a concession to the principals behind Syncrude was the declaration that the 5 percent limit introduced in 1962 was "no longer useful and will be discarded."[54] The government didn't explain or justify why a specific percentage limit was no longer appropriate. This was a surprising omission given the province's previous declaration that the life of conventional reserves was vital to consider when evaluating any tar sands proposal. That dropping the 5 percent limit looked tailor-made for the Syncrude project may be seen in the government's decision to increase the total permissible volume of tar sands production to 150,000 barrels per day. This ceiling would just accommodate

GCOS's production plus the 100,000 barrels per day proposed in the initial 1962 application by Syncrude's principals.

Syncrude's warnings had won over the politicians; the regulators, however, were more difficult to please. The government's policy changes might have been seen as ones that should have paved the way for the Conservation Board to approve the Syncrude application—perhaps especially since, in its reincarnation, the project was downsized to 80,000 barrels per day. This was a politically, not economically, motivated change. Again the Board was skeptical. In light of the Prudhoe Bay discoveries in Alaska, the Board doubted the American market access presumed by the Syncrude application would be available for Alberta tar sands production. Based on its concern over the availability of markets, the Board did not approve the application. But the Board said approval would be forthcoming if Syncrude's principals could make a convincing case that Prudhoe Bay oil and American policy on Canadian oil imports wouldn't undermine their US market access assumptions. To this end, the Board invited Syncrude to satisfy these concerns at a third public hearing to be held in 1969. For Syncrude, the third time before the Board was lucky; two of the three Board members who heard the application felt the American supply situation in the latter half of the 1970s would open the door to greater Canadian oil imports.[55] In a two to one decision the Conservation Board finally approved the Syncrude application in September 1969. Alberta's second commercial tar sands project was born.

For Chastko, Syncrude's approval is the capstone to a lengthy period over which the provincial government "devised and implemented" its oil sands strategy. Largely absent from his interpretation of the historical record is the theme that the multinationals, rather than the provincial government, did most of the devising. By contrast, the multinationals' strategy is centre stage in Pratt's examination of the machinations surrounding the Syncrude project. In *The Tar Sands*, Pratt delivered a sharp critique of provincial and federal energy policy in a strong nationalist voice, a voice that today is little more than a whisper in Canadian energy policy debates.[56] Analytically, Pratt's strength rests in his emphasis on how the interests and power of the multinational oil industry shaped the nature of the bargain struck between the industry and the Alberta and federal governments. While Pratt's perspective may stumble in explaining the timing of Syncrude's ultimate approval—notably the early failures of the principals behind Syncrude—with the addition of the Pew-Manning relationship, it persuasively details the constituents of power and influence in energy policy-making.

In Pratt's account, neither Canada's federal nor provincial politicians were able to formulate a Canadian objective for tar sands development other than satisfying American energy demands, if and when the Americans came calling. In some measure this was due to the above-mentioned fear that a revolutionary change in energy technologies would pass the tar sands by. This would be especially concerning to the provincial government. It was riskier, in other words, to sit on or bank the tar sands than to encourage their exploitation. This was so even if encouragement meant that government would bear a significant proportion of the financial risks and costs associated with the construction and operation of tar sands ventures. Consequently, both the provincial and federal governments did not bargain particularly well with Syncrude over the terms of development after the Conservation Board approved the project. Syncrude drew on assets such as its creators' enormous financial clout, their possession of reserves and development opportunities in other parts of the world, and their control over key information and technology to set the rules of the game. Government attitudes and positions—the fear the tar sands could lose their value, the lustre of thousands of construction jobs, the federal government's growing belief that tar sands production would soon be needed to address a deteriorating domestic oil supply situation, and the categorical rejection of developing the tar sands through a state-owned enterprise—also contributed to the highly unequal nature of the bargaining process. After the first round of negotiations, Syncrude's principals walked away from the table with "a guaranteed rate of return on investment, royalty-free holidays, commitments to provide strike-free labour, promised provincial support in Syncrude's negotiations with Ottawa, expensive publicly financed 'roads to resources' infrastructure, and more."[57] Later, when Atlantic Richfield abruptly pulled out of the Syncrude project in late 1974, the federal, Alberta, and Ontario governments bailed the project out by stepping into ARCO's shoes, injecting $1 billion into the project ($4.9 billion in 2016 dollars) and creating a very favourable tax regime for the project.[58] These outcomes led Pratt to conclude, perhaps a tad melodramatically, "the politics of Syncrude are the politics of imperialism."[59]

Pratt's account is also essential for the more general linkage it makes between the international political economy of oil at this time and the pace of tar sands exploitation in Alberta. Here the impact of the OPEC cartel stands out. The balance of power in international petroleum markets shifted profoundly in the early 1970s when OPEC members began to assert their market power and to negotiate the purchase of the multinationals' assets in their countries. The cartel's assertiveness effectively redistributed power in international petroleum markets, suddenly making the integrated majors and major oil-importing countries such as the United States more vulnerable than they had ever been before about their access to oil—that most precious and essential foundation for the post–World War II standards of living in the West. Developing the tar sands, from a continentalist perspective, arguably became more urgent in this new climate. Tar sands exploitation joined developments such as those in the North Sea and in Prudhoe Bay as a lever the multinationals could use to improve their supply positions and reclaim some of the bargaining power they had lost to OPEC in the global oil market.

OPEC's willingness to use its growing power also inflamed anxiety in the United States about its petroleum security. Striking a continental energy deal with Canada, a deal that would increase American access to Canadian petroleum and would ensure that Canada would be a reliable transportation corridor for Alaskan natural gas, grew in popularity in Washington as the United States tried to strengthen its position relative to three rivals: OPEC, Japan, and Western Europe.[60] Tar sands production, from a security aspect, had some appeal to the United States as part of a continentalist energy strategy in the early 1970s. The ultimate strength of the tar sands' appeal and therefore the place of the tar sands in this continentalist strategy, however, was contingent on the success the United States would have in dealing with its rivals.[61] If, for example, the United States could strengthen its position among the Middle Eastern oil producers while the multinationals and other non-OPEC producers developed new supplies of conventional oil in the non-OPEC world, the pressure to develop aggressively even higher-cost alternatives such as the Colorado oil shales or Alberta's tar sands would lessen. This is exactly what happened in the 1970s. The combination of a strengthened American relationship with the Middle East sheikdoms and significant new additions to world production levels from regions such as the North Sea and Alaska made tar sands development on today's grand scale less urgent then.

Confused Seas on the Voyage to Free Trade

Confused seas describe a situation most mariners hope to avoid. Major, rapidly shifting winds confuse sea conditions—waves come from several directions simultaneously, making them irregular, unpredictable, and a danger to navigation. The nautical phrase describes well the course Canadian petroleum policy took in the 1980s. The decade began on a dramatic interventionist and nationalist note. The federal Liberals' National Energy Program (NEP) promised Canadians energy security through self-sufficiency in oil, a less significant foreign multinational presence in a more "Canadianized" industry, and a made-in-Canada petroleum pricing regime that would not slavishly follow world oil prices. This regime would share oil and gas revenues more equitably between Canadians and between the federal and provincial governments. Its intent to shift exploration and development activity onto lands controlled by Ottawa, to peg Canadian oil prices generally below world prices, and to increase the federal share of petroleum revenues infuriated Alberta. It also initially angered the multinationals and generated threats of retaliation from the US Congress and elements within the Reagan administration.[62]

The landslide victory of Brian Mulroney's Progressive Conservatives over the Liberals in Canada's 1984 federal election promised a dramatic reversal in Canadian oil and gas policy. Pratt summarized that approach as "supply-side economics with a strong emphasis on increased exports to the United States."[63] For the petroleum sector in Canada, the Mulroney government very much followed the script of Reaganomics—the NEP's suite of regulations, taxes, export controls, and Canadianization incentives were or would be eliminated through the 1985 Western Accord Mulroney signed with the Western petroleum-producing provinces.[64] Progressive Conservative energy policy preached market fundamentalism. With it, Mulroney reoriented Canada back toward the traditional continentalist, market-oriented direction petroleum development had followed before the NEP interlude.

The decade ended with the Canada–United States Free Trade Agreement. By institutionalizing the deregulatory thrust of the Western Accord in a wide-ranging treaty, the Mulroney government made it very difficult, if not impossible, for future Canadian governments to reincarnate the NEP's style of interventionism. The CUSFTA, in both its ideological and policy dimensions, became a key feature of the institutional foundation crucial to the explosive trajectory tar sands production would soon take. The free market and deregulatory measures of CUSFTA stand out most prominently. But it also anticipated the type of government intervention tar sands interests sought while governments were negotiating CUSFTA. Government "incentives" to maintain reserves and sustain or increase petroleum production that did not discriminate between Canadian and American capital were welcome in this free trade regime. The version of market fundamentalism unfolding in the tar sands was one where the Canadian petroleum sector swore allegiance to free markets while quietly endorsing government interventions in markets that would support their interests.

For anyone even superficially familiar with Canadian political history, the National Energy Program likely stands as Canada's most controversial and contentious energy policy. The NEP intended to increase federal power on two fronts, first, vis-à-vis the petroleum industry and, second, vis-à-vis petroleum-producing provinces such as Alberta. It sought these goals while also attempting to attain petroleum self-sufficiency and to increase the ownership and influence of Canadian capital in the petroleum sector. The federal program proposed to eliminate all oil imports by 1990, to increase Canadian ownership and control of the oil and gas sector to 50 percent by 1990, to create a made-in-Canada oil price regime, to shift petroleum exploration and development away from the provinces to "Canada lands" controlled by Ottawa, and to increase the federal share of the petroleum revenue pie.[65] Alberta, like foreign-controlled companies operating in Canada, scorned the program; Alberta Premier Peter Lougheed went on television to tell Albertans the federal government was trying to expropriate the province's petroleum resources.

According to the text of *The National Energy Program*, the tar sands sector escaped the damaging policies meted out to conventional oil producers. Depletion allowances would be stripped from companies exploring for and producing conventional oil in the provinces; these allowances would be retained for Alberta's tar sands operations.[66] Upgraders, the processing mammoths that convert heavy oil into light oil, would be designated as resource companies, not as manufacturers or processors. This designation delivered federal income tax benefits. Upgraders would be allowed to claim federal resource and depletion allowances; if they were more than 50 percent Canadian-owned and controlled they also would be eligible for payments from the Petroleum Incentives Program.[67] The "made-in-Canada" per barrel price of $38.00 set by the federal government for new tar sands production in January 1981 was more than double the $17.75 price the government set for conventional oil. New tar sands production essentially would receive what was then the world price for oil; conventional production would not.[68] With respect to prices, the NEP largely continued what had become the prevailing federal policy approach to the tar sands. Syncrude essentially had received the world price for its production since its start-up, an essential concession granted by Ottawa as part of the package of measures that rescued the Syncrude joint venture after ARCO withdrew from the partnership.[69] Given the run-up of world oil prices the federal government argued that, for Syncrude, the NEP's tar sands reference price would "provide a substantially higher return on this project than was contemplated when the initial investment was made."[70]

The NEP did not treat Suncor this well. Unlike Syncrude, Suncor had only been receiving the international price for its production since April 1979. This arrangement had been a condition of the company's agreement with the federal government to increase production. In the original NEP, Suncor would receive the tar sands reference price for its new production only; in January 1981 Suncor's production would fetch $17.75 per barrel—the price set for conventional oil. Ottawa argued that honouring the

1979 international price agreement with Suncor into the future would give the company "unwarranted windfall gains."[71] Ottawa justified the NEP's differential treatment between these two tar sands producers according to the dramatically different initial construction costs of the two projects—$185 million for the original GCOS plant versus approximately $2.4 billion for the Syncrude plant.[72]

Suncor was outraged at this discriminatory treatment. Its president questioned the federal logic and argued that, original construction costs aside, the Suncor investment was nearly as pricey as Syncrude's when the company's perennial losses during its first 12 years of operations were also taken into consideration. Ross Hennigar stated that the NEP's new tar sands reference price would deliver a modest return of 12 percent on the Suncor investment, roughly twice what the company could hope for if its synthetic crude received only Ottawa's conventional oil price.[73] Chastko, who writes as if Suncor could never receive the tar sands reference price for any of its production, clearly is sympathetic to the Suncor position; the federal government had delivered "a staggering blow" to the tar sands.[74]

Staggering or not, the impact of this blow was short-lived. In September 1981, the federal and Alberta governments concluded negotiations modifying the original terms of the NEP. According to this agreement the tar sands reference price was increased and Suncor would receive this new price for all of its production. The company expected the new arrangement to add six or seven dollars a barrel or as much as $120 million to its cash flow in 1982. Suncor's Hennigar was optimistic about the impact of this agreement; the new terms would "move the plant from a marginal operation to one with a strong future."[75] The following July, Suncor announced it was going ahead and investing an additional $335 million to increase the size of its reserves by 90 million barrels, an investment it had said was uneconomical if it did not receive the tar sands reference price for all of its production.[76]

The treatment of Syncrude, Suncor, and the tar sands sector generally during the brief life of the NEP invites a more nuanced interpretation of that program's impact on the petroleum industry than has been portrayed customarily. Unquestionably, there is merit in the view the NEP was discriminatory and devastating. Certain features of the NEP, particularly its Canadianization thrust and its system of exploration/development incentives, discriminated against foreign capital and against conventional oil and gas activities in the provinces.[77] It devastated conventional oil and gas activities and related industries in Alberta. According to Mansell and Percy, when the NEP was introduced Alberta's economy relied on investment as its key engine of growth. Any event that threatened investment expenditures was bound to have a tremendous negative impact on Alberta.

The NEP was just such an event for anyone connected to the conventional oil and gas sector.[78]

But did the NEP present a similar threat to the tar sands sector? Hardly. True, hoped-for projects such as Alsands and Cold Lake were cancelled or postponed after the NEP was announced. But it is questionable at the very least to point to the NEP as the villain here when other prime suspects such as escalating project costs, staggeringly high interest rates, an attendant recession and, most importantly, declining world oil prices beg to be interrogated. When the Alsands project finally was laid to rest in May 1982 the global recession had already knocked down the average cost of imported crude oil to the United States by 16 percent from its February 1982 high.[79] "By early 1982," wrote Doern and Toner with respect to Alsands and Cold Lake, "the two major nonconventional mega-projects were doomed by the softening prices."[80] International events, not the machinations of federal politicians, more likely deserve the bulk of the blame for the failures of those nonconventional ventures.[81]

The more favourable treatment of the tar sands seen in the birth and evolution of the NEP reflected the vital contribution the federal government saw tar sands production making to the state's oil self-sufficiency goal. Like the frontier regions in the Arctic and the Atlantic offshore, the tar sands promised the additional supplies needed to secure oil self-sufficiency in light of falling Canadian conventional oil production (conventional oil production in Canada peaked in the early 1970s as it did in the continental United States).[82] It also should be noted that, since the federal government was part of the Syncrude consortium (the government's 15 percent share was held by the state-owned firm Petro-Canada), Ottawa had important political and material interests for propping up the profitability of Syncrude. Alberta was unlikely to object to this more favourable treatment of Syncrude, since it held a 10 percent ownership position in the consortium and Premier Lougheed had invested considerable political capital into the project. The initial differences in the treatment of Syncrude and Suncor also may be seen through this lens.

While the principals in the tar sands did not always secure their preferred prices and fiscal terms during the NEP years, they certainly tried to capitalize on the NEP's linkage of tar sands production to oil self-sufficiency. In this respect the sector's principals and boosters were fair-weather disciples of market principles. When market conditions were tough or likely to be unpredictable, they ran to the state for help and concessions. They sought the type of government intervention they so stridently opposed in 1980. When world prices crashed in 1986, industry stopped chanting their "we must receive world prices" mantra from 1980. Leaders of the oil-producing provinces, strident opponents of the NEP's state-administered price regime, warmed to the idea of a government-fixed minimum price for oil as the bottom fell out of the global oil market in 1986.[83] Alberta's Premier Getty reportedly even approached Sheik Yamani, Saudi Arabia's oil minister, about the possibility of ordering a reduction in Alberta's oil production as part of a bid to raise prices.[84] The federal Progressive Conservatives, who had buried the NEP after they came to power in 1984, refused to entertain a return to state-administered oil pricing. But, with industry's encouragement, they used other fiscal tools to temper the market's effects on tar sands production; Syncrude and Suncor were exempted from paying the federal government's petroleum revenue tax in 1986.[85]

The industry's taste for government assistance lent an ironic flavour to the politics of the tar sands in the latter half of the 1980s that fits well with the policy implications attributed to market fundamentalism. On the one hand, the energy industry used the Canada–United States free trade negotiations to extend and formalize the de facto free trade in energy created by Prime Minister Mulroney's Progressive Conservative government after 1984. Through the Western Accord, a federal-provincial agreement signed in 1985 with Alberta, British Columbia, and Saskatchewan, Ottawa completely deregulated oil pricing. The accord, as Larry Pratt noted, "clearly anticipated a wide-open continental market."[86] With respect to incentives for industry, all companies—irrespective of their nationality—would be treated equally. The national government also dropped the NEP's subsidies to Canadian-owned companies for their activities on Canada Lands.[87] Free trade sought to ensure that the NEP could never be reincarnated. As well, the industry sought to prevent the United States, through quotas or other measures, from ever again threatening Canadian petroleum access to American markets. In its pursuit of free trade in energy the industry took an "extremely low" profile during the negotiations; the producing provinces represented them well and, in order to avoid arousing Canadian nationalists, industry did not participate in any of the pro-free trade campaigns.[88]

On the one hand, tar sands promoters and the Alberta government staunchly advocated the continentalist, pro-market policy direction that would be entrenched in the 1989 free trade agreement. But they also did not hesitate to champion state subsidies for the tar sands in the name of Canadian energy security. In the early 1980s the Alberta Chamber of Resources, an association of mineral resource companies, made the tar sands the Chamber's number one development priority. To that end the Chamber established an industry task force in 1984 to promote the tar sands by pinpointing and publicizing the social and economic benefits of development. In this respect the Chamber performed like a research arm of the provincial government—the energy department actually enlisted the Task Force to write a report on synthetic crude oil production costs. The study was crucial to the Chamber's rebuttal to the National Energy Board's pessimistic assessment of the feasibility of tar sands projects going ahead in the short to medium term. The NEB's 1985–2005 energy supply and demand forecast concluded there was no hope of developing additional tar sands production over that 20-year period. "No production from new mining plants," the NEB wrote, "is included in our projections."[89] This dismal assessment of the tar sands' possibilities came in a report where the NEB was predicting that anywhere between 40 and 64 percent of Canada's light crude oil requirements in 2005 could be supplied by imports.[90] The Chamber's work disputed the NEB's supply cost assumptions for tar sands production and suggested that new production could be delivered for less than C$30 per barrel (US$22.50 in 1987 dollars). Citing the success of Suncor and Syncrude in reducing their operating costs to "well below" $18 per barrel, the Chamber insisted the tar sands could be competitive with other options.[91]

Several aspects of the Task Force's research and recommendations should be highlighted. Responding to the dramatic cost escalation that had helped doom the Alsands project, the Task Force recommended future development depart from the integrated mining/upgrading model implemented at Suncor and Syncrude. It advocated instead a development model where any number of small- to medium-sized bitumen mines would feed an independent, synthetic crude oil upgrader. According to the Task Force, the regional upgrader approach would offer many benefits. They included reduced capital requirements—important in an environment where banks were putting "stringent lending conditions" on large energy projects; greater utilization of the bitumen resource—smaller leases that could not produce the volume of bitumen needed to realize needed economies of scale could help feed the upgrader; greater opportunities for smaller Alberta and Canadian capital to participate in the sector; and significant national employment gains.[92]

Security of supply considerations also figured prominently in the Chamber's advocacy of tar sands development. Given the significant production-consumption gap the NEB anticipated would emerge by as early as 1995, the Chamber argued "there are many who believe that a secure energy supply and a healthy oil industry are important enough to warrant renewed efforts to examine development alternatives for our known energy resources."[93] The tar sands figured crucially here. A regional upgrader "would enhance Canada's security of supply and improve balance of payment."[94] Linking tar sands development to Canadian oil security buttressed the Chamber's view that state support or incentives would be justified. Since a regional upgrader may not have been profitable in 1987, the initiative "may have to be supported and/or a business environment conducive to growth may have to be created by the governments if it is to be implemented."[95] Such support could take many forms. The Task Force's committee on representative costs suggested to the Task Force's chair and through him to the Alberta government that a 30-year, 50 percent interest-free loan would be appropriate. Less than three months before Canada and the United States concluded the first free trade agreement, members of the Chamber made the trek to Ottawa to request state support for the tar sands. Its managing director argued that, "for the good of the country," the federal government would be wise to ante up approximately $1 billion of assistance for the tar sands.[96] The Chamber clearly understood, like generations of Canadian capital before them, that state intervention certainly didn't need to be anti-business.

When it came to the fiscal terms of tar sands agreements, the Chamber argued they were bedevilled by too much uncertainty and a lack of clarity. The terms were not known in advance and they were negotiated separately for each project. This hindered the planning ability of firms. But, in testimony before a parliamentary committee, the Chamber suggested that Alberta had "made significant progress" toward establishing a generic regime; the rules that applied to Imperial Oil's Cold Lake heavy oil project had just been applied to a $150 million expansion of Suncor's mining operations. The Cold Lake regime was, in the words of the ACR's managing director, "a good example of what we would like to see."[97] Under that formula, new projects would pay an escalating gross production royalty until payout.[98] The gross royalty was set at 1 percent of gross revenue at the time of plant start-up; this royalty was increased by one percentage point every 18 months until it reached a maximum of 5 percent after six years of operations. Once payout was reached, the annual royalty collected was either 30 percent of net revenues (profit) or 5 percent of gross revenues, whichever amount was greater. By 1987 the Cold Lake system applied to most tar sands ventures. It typically applied to all in situ operations and its 5/30 gross/net revenue royalty formula applied to Suncor's mining operation. It did not apply, however, to Syncrude. Syncrude did not pay any minimum royalty on its gross production; it paid instead 50 percent of its net profits to Alberta as a royalty.

In addition to making these business-friendly changes to the royalty regime, Alberta joined the Chamber in forging links between Canadian energy security, the tar sands, and state aid. It did so in the aptly titled *Energy Security for Canada: The Oil Supply Option*. A key foundation of the Alberta position paper—that "committed and aggressive" state action was required to reduce Canada's growing dependence on foreign crude and increase domestic oil supply security—had been laid by an interprovincial task force struck to discover a path to oil self-sufficiency. Alberta, Saskatchewan, and

Quebec reported that deregulated market prices would not guarantee the additional supplies oil self-sufficiency demanded. One of their key observations, clearly aimed at the tar sands, read in part:

> While deregulation provides a positive environment for long-term planning— it cannot be relied upon to result in private decisions that are in the best interests of Canada when looking at major projects with seven year construction periods and 25 year operating lives. Many risks remain for private investors and if these risks diverge from government perceptions, governments can and should attempt to reduce those risks.[99]

State intervention plus deregulation were seen as essential to ensuring the tar sands would contribute to increasing Canadian petroleum production. But this imperative would be exercised in a clearly industry-friendly way: "A range of fiscal and financial vehicles is available which would reduce private sector risks in order to allow projects to proceed."[100] This report and Alberta's subsequent oil supply position paper were favourably disposed to government assistance. Alberta applauded an Informetrica study on the national economic benefits associated with oil supply investments that weren't justified by then-current world oil prices. Alberta, a passionate advocate of free trade in energy, endorsed Informetrica's conclusion that

> Canada is better off as a result of these investments *even if* some public sector support is needed to cover the full supply costs for the projects at very low oil prices. The initial investments, the continuing economic activity associated with producing crude oil and the resulting reduction in imports of crude and products together generate a powerful stimulus to the Canadian economy.[101]

The message here was clear—deregulation alone could not deliver national oil security. Governments needed to reduce the risks, constraints, and difficulties associated with large capital-intensive projects such as the tar sands. Alberta, for its part, wanted to discuss aggressively developing the tar sands, as long as any such scheme respected Canada's obligations under a free trade agreement with the United States.[102]

These two principles—deregulation and state support for the petroleum sector—animate the energy-related provisions of the 1989 CUSFTA and its successor, the North American Free Trade Agreement (NAFTA). Chapters 9 (Energy) and 16 (Investment) of the CUSFTA embrace and extend the General Agreement on Tariffs and Trade's "national treatment" principle; Canada gave away the lion's share of its ability to tax and regulate American energy companies and products destined for American markets differently than Canadian ones. The investment provisions of Chapter 16 ensured the preferential Canadian corporate treatment of the Liberals' NEP could not be established again vis-à-vis American firms. Article 1602 obliged Canada to treat American firms as if they were Canadian ones. The energy chapter extended this principle of nondiscrimination to the energy trade. Effectively, free trade erased the Canada–United States border when it came to taxing and managing energy production. Export taxes, levied by the Liberals in the 1970s on petroleum headed to the United States, were prohibited. Any tax on energy products destined for American markets could be no higher than whatever tax was applied to Canadian consumers.

Canadian governments also relinquished the supply management powers they previously had enjoyed. If a domestic petroleum supply crisis emerged, Canada could not address it by reducing or eliminating exports to American consumers in order to meet Canadian demand. Any supply disruption would have to be distributed equitably between the two countries. This proportional access provision (Article 904) ensured that, if Canada cut total production, the United States market would be guaranteed the same percentage of Canadian production it enjoyed in the most recent three-year period before the cutback. In other words, if Canada exported 76 percent of its crude oil production to the United States over the most recent three-year period, then, if Canada reduced its petroleum production, the United States would be entitled to 76 percent of this smaller amount.[103] Canadian governments shackled themselves through the energy provisions of free trade.[104]

The "Canada-first" tenor of the NEP obviously was sacrificed on the altar of free trade. But, although many accounts of free trade in energy ignore it, the energy provisions of both free trade agreements do not embrace free market principles unequivocally. Incentives or subsidies to petroleum companies to exploit petroleum were welcomed in the North American version of "free trade." Article 906 authorized the use of "existing or future incentives for oil and gas exploration, development and related activities in order to maintain the reserve base for these energy resources."[105] A truncated version of interventionism—one where aid to produce more petroleum was legitimate while restrictions on production by North American companies was illegitimate—also was institutionalized in the free trade agreements.

Conclusion

By the end of the 1980s, Canadian governments had woven a strong web of predispositions, policies, and institutions to support the development of Alberta's tar sands. This web was crucial to creating, as we will see at the outset of the next chapter, a healthy, profitable tar sands sector entering the 1990s. The period between the end of World War II and the conclusion of the CUSFTA cannot be viewed as one where government enjoyed much autonomy from the multinationals that populated the tar sands sector. Both the Great Canadian Oil Sands and Syncrude stories illustrate the privileged position that multinational corporations enjoyed when it came to shaping the development of Alberta's petroleum resources.

The NEP is significant here for several reasons. Its measures illustrate clearly that, by the early 1980s, Syncrude and Suncor enjoyed favourite son status in Ottawa and Edmonton. The label "too big to fail" seems especially applicable to Syncrude. Had the state not acted in the 1980s through the NEP to enhance Syncrude's prospects for surviving and prospering, the substantial investments of the Canadian, Alberta, and Ontario governments plus thousands of jobs would have been jeopardized. The NEP's call for Canadian petroleum self-sufficiency is also notable. While this objective lasted only briefly, the tar sands industry seized on the state's interest in self-sufficiency to justify demands for government assistance, at the very time that Canadian governments and the petroleum industry sought free trade in energy. The tar sands industry behaved just as the Manchester cotton manufacturers did in Polanyi's account—their interests led them to promote free trade and state subsidies simultaneously. By decade's end the CUSFTA institutionalized these ideologically inconsistent positions. While ideologically inconsistent, this mélange foreshadowed very well what industry would look for in government reregulation in the 1990s. An important target for that reregulation would be the very royalty arrangements the Alberta Chamber of Resources thought so highly of in 1987.

Notes

1   Paul Chastko, *Developing Alberta's Oil Sands: From Karl Clark to Kyoto* (Calgary: University of Calgary Press, 2004); Pratt, *Tar Sands*.
2   Richards and Pratt, *Prairie Capitalism*.
3   Block and Somers, *Power of Market Fundamentalism*.
4   Inorganic material, other than the sand itself, makes up the remainder of the deposits. For an introduction to the geological and chemical characteristics of the tar sands see National Energy Board, *Canada's Oil Sands: A Supply and Market Outlook to 2015* (Ottawa: National Energy Board, 2000), 4–11.
5   The amount of upgraded or synthetic crude oil produced per barrel of bitumen varies according to the upgrading technologies used and other factors. The World Energy Council reported in 2007 that Suncor produced 0.81 barrels of oil per barrel of bitumen. The respective yields for Syncrude and Albian Sands were 0.85 and 0.9 barrels of oil per barrel of bitumen. See World Energy Council, *Survey of Energy Resources 2007* (London: World Energy Council, 2007), 125.

6   The CAPP reported in 2007 that 65 to 70 per cent of the bitumen extracted in Alberta was upgraded to synthetic crude oil. Canadian Association of Petroleum Producers, *Oil Sands: Benefits to Alberta and Canada, Today and Tomorrow, Through a Fair, Stable and Competitive Fiscal Regime* (Calgary: Canadian Association of Petroleum Producers, May 2007), 38. The percentage of bitumen upgraded in Alberta has fallen steadily and rapidly since then. In May 2014, Alberta's primary energy regulatory agency, the Alberta Energy Regulator, reported that 52 percent of bitumen was upgraded in Alberta in 2013 and that this percentage was expected to fall to 36 percent by 2023. Alberta Energy Regulator, ST98–2014: *Alberta's Energy Reserves 2013 and Supply/Demand Outlook 2014–2023* (Calgary: Alberta Energy Regulator, 2014), 11.

7   National Energy Board, *Canada's Oil Sands*, 6.

8   World Energy Council, *Survey of Energy Resources 2007*, 120.

9   BP, *BP Statistical Review of World Energy June 2014*, http://www.bp.com/content/dam/bp-country/de_de/PDFs/brochures/BP-statistical-review-of-world-energy-2014-full-report.pdf, 6. The bitumen barrel estimate for Canada only includes bitumen resources in Alberta. Alberta Energy Regulator, *ST98-2013: Alberta's Energy Reserves 2012 and Supply/Demand Outlook 2013–2022* (Calgary: Alberta Energy Regulator, May 2013), 3.

10   The CAPP defines in situ as "[i]n its original place; in position; in situ recovery refers to various methods used to recover deeply buried bitumen deposits, including steam injection, solvent injection and firefloods." See Canadian Association of Petroleum Producers, "Glossary," http://www.capp.ca/publications-and-statistics/glossary#I.

11   Daniel Yergin, *The Prize: The Epic Quest for Oil, Money, and Power* (New York: Free Press, 1991), 24.

12   Yergin, *The Prize*.

13   Fernand Braudel, *Memory and the Mediterranean* (New York: Vintage Books, 2001), 188.

14   R. G. McConnell, *Report on a Portion of the District of Athabasca Comprising the Country Between Peace River and Athabasca River North of Lesser Slave Lake* (Ottawa: Queen's Printer, 1893), 5.

15   McConnell, *Report on a Portion*, 65. Interestingly, this report indicates that the respective proportions of bitumen, water, and sands in the tar sands were estimated accurately as early as the 1880s.

16   Mary Clark Sheppard, *Oil Sands Scientist: The Letters of Karl A. Clark 1920–1949* (Edmonton: University of Alberta Press, 1989), 61–62; Chastko, *Developing Alberta's Oil Sands*, 4–5.

17   R. C. Fitzsimmons, *The Truth about Alberta Tar Sands: Why Were They Kept Out of Production?* (Edmonton: 1953), 1, 11, 17, 25–26.

18   Sheppard, *Oil Sands Scientist*, 10, 16.

19   Sheppard, *Oil Sands Scientist*, 161, 170–74, 219–20, 236, 244, 275, 284–85, 289–90.

20   Chastko, *Developing Alberta's Oil Sands*, 18–19; Sheppard, *Oil Sands Scientist*, 170–74.

21   Chastko, *Developing Alberta's Oil Sands*, 33.

22   Chastko, *Developing Alberta's Oil Sands*, 35–49.

23   Chastko, *Developing Alberta's Oil Sands*, 58.

24 Canadian Association of Petroleum Producers, *Statistical Handbook*, http://www.capp.ca/publications-and-statistics/statistics/statistical-handbook.

25 Chastko, *Developing Alberta's Oil Sands*, 79.

26 Pratt, *Tar Sands*. The accuracy of Fitzsimmons's view is central to Larry Pratt's understanding of the behaviour of transnational petroleum companies.

27 The 80 percent figure is taken from Pierre R. Alvarez, "Business Interest Associations and the Canadian State: A Case Study of the Independent Petroleum Association of Canada" (master of arts thesis, Department of Political Studies, Queen's University, September 1986), 39. In 2009, after nine years as president of the CAPP—Canada's primary petroleum producer association—Alvarez became vice-president, corporate relations for Nexen. In 2015, he joined Global Public Affairs as its vice-chair.

28 Pratt, *Tar Sands*, 43.

29 Alvarez, "Business Interest Associations," 43.

30 Michael J. Day, "A New Tenure Option for Alberta Oil Sands," in *Heavy Crude and Tar Sands: Hydrocarbons for the 21st Century, Fifth International Conference on Heavy Crude and Tar Sands,* Volume 4, ed. Richard F. Meyer (Caracas: Petroleos de Venezuela, S.A., 1991), 429.

31 Chastko, *Developing Alberta's Oil Sands*, 87.

32 Graham D. Taylor, "Sun Oil Company and Great Canadian Oil Sands Ltd.: The Financing and Management of a 'Pioneer' Enterprise, 1962–1974," *Journal of Canadian Studies*, 20, no. 3 (1985), 107.

33 Quoted from an unpublished manuscript written by George Dunlap, Sun Oil's Canadian manager, and cited in Chastko, *Developing Alberta's Oil Sands*, 105.

34 The close relationship between Pew and Manning is sketched in Chastko, *Developing Alberta's Oil Sands*, 112.

35 Chastko, *Developing Alberta's Oil Sands*, 92.

36 Ian Urquhart, "Borders, Boundaries, and the Politics of Petroleum Pipelines," *Journal of Borderland Studies* (forthcoming).

37 Yergin, *The Prize*, 499.

38 Yergin, *The Prize*, 500.

39 Yergin, *The Prize*, 514.

40 Yergin, *The Prize*, 535–38.

41 David H. Breen, *Alberta's Petroleum Industry and the Conservation Board* (Edmonton: University of Alberta Press, 1993).

42 Chastko, *Developing Alberta's Oil Sands*, 109.

43 Due to serious start-up problems, the plant would not produce those 8 million barrels of petroleum until well into its second year of production.

44 Taylor, "Sun Oil Company," 108–11. Alberta did not then—and still does not—have a generally applicable sales tax.

45 Taylor, "Sun Oil Company," 116.

46 Taylor offers this characterization of Lougheed by Patrick after consulting the papers of Robert Dunlop, Sun Oil's president at that time. See Taylor, "Sun Oil Company," 116.

47 Taylor, "Sun Oil Company," 116–17. Great Canadian Oil Sands turned its first profit in 1974. See Chastko, *Developing Alberta's Oil Sands*, 136.

48 Alvarez, "Business Interest Associations," especially Chapter 3.

49   Initially Imperial Oil, ARCO, and Cities Service Athabasca each held 30 percent
     ownership shares in Syncrude. Royalite Oil held the remaining 10 percent.
50   The Center for Biological Diversity makes the following distinction between
     tar sands and oil shales: "Oil shale is a form of sedimentary rock that contains
     kerogen, which is released as a petroleum-like liquid when the rock is heated.
     Tar sands are a combination of clay, sand, water and bitumen, which is a heavy
     hydrocarbon." Center for Biological Diversity, "Oil Shale and Tar Sands,"
     http://www.biologicaldiversity.org/programs/public_lands/energy/dirty_
     energy_development/oil_shale_and_tar_sands/.
51   Chastko, *Developing Alberta's Oil Sands*, 122.
52   Chastko, *Developing Alberta's Oil Sands*.
53   Alberta Oil and Gas Conservation Board, *Report on an Application of Atlantic
     Richfield Company, Cities Service Athabasca, Inc., Imperial Oil Limited and Royalite
     Oil Company, Limited under Part VI A of the Oil and Gas Conservation Act
     (OGCB Report 68-C)* (Calgary: Alberta Oil and Gas Conservation Board,
     December 1968), A-8, A-9.
54   Alberta Oil and Gas Conservation Board, *Report on an Application*, A-11.
55   Chastko, *Developing Alberta's Oil Sands*, 130.
56   In recent years the Parkland Institute and the Council of Canadians are among
     the few organizations articulating a nationalist, "Canada-first," position on
     energy policy.
57   Pratt, *Tar Sands*, 127.
58   Atlantic Richfield's 30 percent position was assumed by the federal government
     (15 percent), the Government of Alberta (10 percent) and the Government of
     Ontario (5 percent). For a history of Syncrude's ownership, see "Reshaping a
     Giant: Syncrude Ownership 1965–2015," *Daily Oil Bulletin*, October 4, 2015,
     http://www.dailyoilbulletin.com/supplement/daily-infographic/2015/10/5/
     reshaping-giant-syncrude-ownership-1965-2015/#sthash.LGp7oZv8.dpbs.
59   Pratt, *Tar Sands*, 178.
60   For an account that describes the American interest in transporting Alaska
     natural gas across Canada, see François Bregha, *Bob Blair's Pipeline: The Business
     and Politics of Northern Energy Development Projects* (Toronto: James Lorimer and
     Company, 1979).
61   Pratt, *Tar Sands*, 56.
62   Larry Pratt, "Energy: The Roots of National Policy," *Studies in Political Economy*
     7, no. 1 (1982), 50.
63   Larry Pratt, "Energy, Regionalism and Canadian Nationalism," *Newfoundland
     Studies*, 1, no. 2 (1985), 193.
64   Pratt, "Energy, Regionalism and Canadian Nationalism," 193–95.
65   Doern and Toner, *Politics of Energy*, 3–5; David C. Hawkes and Bruce G. Pollard,
     "The Evolution of Canada's New Energy Policy," in *Canada: The State of the
     Federation 1986*, ed. Peter M. Leslie (Kingston, ON: Institute of Intergovernmental
     Relations, 1987), 153–54.
66   Energy Mines and Resources Canada, *The National Energy Program, 1980*
     (Ottawa: Supply and Services Canada, 1980), 39.
67   Energy Mines and Resources Canada, *National Energy Program,* 40–41.
68   Energy Mines and Resources Canada, *National Energy Program,* 26. According
     to the Bank of Canada's inflation calculator (based on monthly consumer

price index data), the inflation-adjusted price for that $38 barrel of oil would have been $100.11 in 2017. http://www.bankofcanada.ca/rates/related/inflation-calculator/.

69   Pratt, *Tar Sands*, 161–178.

70   Energy Mines and Resources Canada, *National Energy Program*, 29.

71   Energy Mines and Resources Canada, *National Energy Program*, 29.

72   Ronald Anderson, "Lalonde's Plans Felt Major Policy Blunder," *Globe and Mail*, November 20, 1980, B2.

73   Anderson, "Lalonde's Plans."

74   Chastko, *Developing Alberta's Oil Sands*, 185.

75   *New York Times*, "Canada Oil Accord Is Praised," September 3, 1981; *Dow Jones News Service*, "Sun Says Canadian Oil Pact Will Increase 1982 Earnings," September 2, 1981.

76   *Dow Jones News Service*, "Suncor Plans $355 Million Oil Sands Plant Expansion," July 27, 1982.

77   The NEP consciously attempted to shift the focus of the oil and gas exploration activities to the Arctic and offshore. These locations were "Canada Lands"—lands where, unlike in the provinces, Ottawa owned the natural resources.

78   Robert L. Mansell and Michael B. Percy, *Strength in Adversity: A Study of the Alberta Economy* (Edmonton: University of Alberta Press, 1990), 30–43. Mansell and Percy also identify high interest rates and large net federal fiscal withdrawals as key causes of the steep economic downturn Alberta experienced between 1981 and 1984.

79   US Department of Energy, Energy Information Administration, "U.S. Crude Oil Imported Acquisition Cost by Refiners," http://www.eia.gov/dnav/pet/hist/LeafHandler.ashx?n=PET&s=R1300____3&f=M. The refiner acquisition cost of imported crude oil in February 1981 in nominal dollars was $39.00 per barrel. In April 1982, it had fallen to $32.82. This price continued to drift lower for the next 45 months. Then in February 1986 it began the plunge that took it from $24.93 in January 1986 to $10.91 in July 1986.

80   Doern and Toner, *Politics of Energy*, 274. Further to this point, in early 1982 an oil analyst at a Toronto investment firm said the following about the Alsands project: "The problem is these things are so incredibly costly. And nowadays, given the declining world price of oil and the high costs of operations, the potential return is not all that attractive anymore." Andrew H. Malcolm, "Canadian Tar Sands: Hope and Challenge," *New York Times*, February 15, 1982.

81   In January 1981 Syncrude cited the NEP as the reason it was suspending plans to proceed with a $2 billion expansion. According to Syncrude, the reference price of $38 per barrel, indexing that price to the consumer price index, and other budget items associated with the NEP such as the new tax on revenue made the expansion uneconomic. See Timothy Pritchard, "Syncrude Plant Expansion Halted; Energy Policy Cited," *Globe and Mail*, January 14, 1981, B1. Subsequent events might call this explanation into doubt. In July 1987, after the Mulroney government had terminated the NEP, Syncrude claimed it needed a higher oil price—somewhere in the $25 to $35 range in order to proceed with a $4 billion expansion. In inflation-adjusted terms a $35 barrel of oil in 1987 would have sold for just $25.29 in 1981, 33 percent less than the NEP's oil

sands reference price. On Syncrude's 1987 position, see Canadian Press, "Major Syncrude Project Depends on Rising Oil Price," *Globe and Mail*, July 29, 1987, B6.

82   Prior to the oil sands boom Canadian crude oil production peaked in 1973. See Canadian Association of Petroleum Producers, *Statistical Handbook for Canada's Upstream Petroleum Industry* (September 2015), Table 3.1b: "Canadian Crude Oil Production, 1971–2009," http://www.capp.ca/publications-and-statistics/statistics/statistical-handbook.

83   Hawkes and Pollard, "Evolution of Canada's New Energy Policy," 162; Ronald Anderson, "Longer-Term Costs Flow from Cheap Oil," *Globe and Mail*, April 9, 1986, B2.

84   Matthew Fisher, "Chretien and Getty Chat about Katimavik and Oil Prices," *Globe and Mail*, April 2, 1986, A9; Patrick Martin, "Getty's Call Unsolicited, Yamani Says," *Globe and Mail*, April 9, 1986, A4.

85   Christopher Waddell, "Federal Aid to Be Given to the West," *Globe and Mail*, May 1, 1986, B1.

86   Larry Pratt, *Energy: Free Trade and the Price We Paid* (Edmonton: Parkland Institute, 2001), 16.

87   Hawkes and Pollard, "Evolution of Canada's New Energy Policy," 155–157. A natural gas agreement, negotiated after the Western Accord, endorsed market pricing for natural gas; a revamped frontier energy policy dropped the favouritism the NEP had shown to Canadian private and state-owned firms.

88   G. Bruce Doern and Brian W. Tomlin, *Faith and Fear: The Free Trade Story* (Toronto: Stoddart Publishing, 1991), 120–121.

89   National Energy Board, *Canadian Energy Supply and Demand 1985–2005* (Ottawa: Minister of Supply and Services Canada, 1986), 83. The federal Department of Energy, Mines, and Resources shared the NEB's pessimism.

90   National Energy Board, *Canadian Energy Supply and Demand*, 92.

91   Alberta Chamber of Resources, *Representative Costs for Mineable Oil Sands Projects* (Edmonton: Alberta Chamber of Resources, 1987).

92   The reference to stringent lending conditions was made in Alberta. Alberta Energy, *Energy Security for Canada: The Oil Supply Option* (Edmonton: Alberta Energy, August 1987), 5.

93   Alberta Chamber of Resources, Oil Sands Task Force, *Athabasca Oil Sands Opportunities for Economic Growth* (Edmonton: Alberta Chamber of Resources, August 1987), 11.

94   Alberta Chamber of Resources, *Athabasca Oil Sands Opportunities*, 13.

95   Alberta Chamber of Resources, *Athabasca Oil Sands Opportunities*, 16.

96   House of Commons, Standing Committee on Finance and Economic Affairs, *Minutes of Proceedings Standing Committee on Finance and Economic Affairs, 33rd Parliament, 2nd Session*, Issue no. 112 (September 23, 1987), 41–42.

97   House of Commons, *Minutes of Proceedings Standing Committee on Finance and Economic Affairs*, 42.

98   Payout in the Cold Lake system was defined as the point "when gross revenue exceeds cumulative operating costs, capital costs, gross royalty, and a 10% return allowance on unrecovered costs." See Richard Masson and Bryan Remillard, *Alberta's New Oil Sands Royalty System* (Edmonton: Alberta Energy, 1996).

99   Alberta, Saskatchewan, and Quebec, *Security of Supply: An Opportunity for Canada* (January 30, 1987), 10.

100 Alberta, Saskatchewan, and Quebec, *Security of Supply*.
101 Alberta Energy, *Energy Security for Canada*, 4 [emphasis in original].
102 Alberta Energy, *Energy Security for Canada*, 9–10.
103 According to National Energy Board statistics, the United States was the destination for 76 percent of Canada's total crude oil production over the 2013–2015 period.
104 Pratt, *Energy: Free Trade and the Price We Paid*, 14.
105 This provision is contained in Article 608 of the North American Free Trade Agreement.

3
Building Canada's Oil Factory: Reregulating the Tar Sands

"Venezuela ... was rapidly becoming just an oil factory. National sovereignty is a juridical concept, a legal abstraction. For it to become reality, a country must be able to have a fair degree of control over its own economic destiny, but this cannot be true in a country where the big economic decisions are completely in the hands of a dozen or so North American and British oil company directors."
—*Rómulo Betancourt,* Venezuela: Oil and Politics, *1979*

"This is fantastic, and close to what the industry was recommending."
—*Eric Newell, President of Syncrude Canada Ltd., 1995*

Introduction

Myth-making and misinformation figure importantly in conventional understandings of the contemporary history of the Athabasca tar sands. Central to such myths and misinformation is an unflattering portrait of the tar sands sector's financial health in the 1980s and 1990s. In 2007 the Canadian Association of Petroleum Producers (CAPP) argued that during those earlier decades Syncrude and Suncor were sickly. According to the myth-makers, the survival of Syncrude and Suncor was then very much up in the air. "Throughout the low-price era in the 1980s and 1990s," CAPP recollected, "both companies struggled for economic survival."[1] CAPP's inference was clear: if the federal and provincial governments had not reregulated the tar sands' fiscal regime in the 1990s, Syncrude's and Suncor's prospects and those of all tar sands operations and aspirations would have been very bleak indeed. Without reregulation, meaning the state's moderation of its royalty and taxation appetite, the sector would have died. Respected business news sources echoed CAPP's interpretation of history—David Ebner wrote that in the mid-1990s "the oil sands business was near dead" and government lightened the fiscal burden at that time in order to inject some much-needed vitality into the sector.[2] In 2007 a provincial Royalty Review Panel endorsed this history as well: "Oil sands royalties were set at a time when the very few participants in a fledgling industry were struggling."[3] Asked to reflect on the economic viability of the oil sands when she was federal Natural Resources Minister from 1993 to 1997, Anne McLellan noted that it wasn't clear then "that this was a profitable enterprise at all."[4]

This unflattering picture is a myth, an illusion. This understanding, politically useful though it undoubtedly has been for the tar sands industry, wildly exaggerates the fragility of Syncrude and Suncor in the late 1980s and early 1990s. Challenging this mythical interpretation begins this chapter's larger examination of the balance of political, technological, and economic factors responsible for the post-1995 boom in tar sands exploitation. This examination assigns particular importance to liberal renaissances in the international oil economy and domestic politics. Ideological and partisan considerations led governments to draft a very generous blueprint for building an oil factory in the tar sands. The generosity of that blueprint—manifested most powerfully in the "generic" royalty system Alberta introduced in 1997 and complementary federal tax changes—joins technological innovations as a driver of the post-1995 boom. Ideology drove the state to reregulate the fiscal and regulatory regime that companies such as Syncrude and Suncor were already profiting from. This sweetened fiscal regime, designed to attract new investors, succeeded beyond its creators' wildest ambitions. But this boom— its frenzied "wild west" character that dramatically increased the costs of tar sands projects—also sowed the seeds of future financial troubles for tar sands companies. The government measures the industry wanted so dearly may turn out to be serious threats to its long-term health.

Struggling to Survive?

Thoughts of a boom in any sector of Alberta's oilpatch were far from the minds of the province's oilmen and politicians after prices collapsed in 1986. Until the end of 1985 Saudi Arabia played a "swing producer" role in the global petroleum market; it had cut back oil production sharply in order to prop up world prices. Many OPEC cartel members took advantage of the Saudis' sacrifice by flagrantly exceeding their production quotas. By 1986, the Saudis had lost patience with this situation. No longer prepared to protect prices at the expense of lost market share, they opened the taps in order to restore their share of the market.[5] Petroleum prices plunged once the Saudis shifted to defending their production volume rather than world price. By July 1986, prices had collapsed to $10.91 per barrel, more than 50 percent lower than where they began the year.[6]

Unquestionably this collapse dealt a serious blow to the profitability of Syncrude and Suncor. In early 1986 Suncor was losing nearly six dollars on every barrel of synthetic crude oil it produced and was predicting a loss in its second quarter. Some thought was apparently given to shutting down its

Tar Island operations if global prices remained depressed.[7] Things were little better at Syncrude where the price collapse left the company barely breaking even.[8] These dreadful impacts of the crash of 1986, however, were very short-lived. Governments rushed into the tar sands to lend helping hands to Syncrude and Suncor. Ottawa excused the companies from paying the 10 percent petroleum and gas revenue tax on their synthetic crude oil production for the last eight months of 1986 at a cost to the national treasury of $35 million.[9] Alberta slashed the royalties due from Suncor for the last nine months of the year; the 12 percent royalty set on gross production was cut to 1 percent and cost the province approximately $23 million. Unlike Suncor, the profit-based nature of Syncrude's royalty agreement did not give the provincial government a production-based royalty to cut. Instead, Alberta chose alternative instruments to deliver financial relief to the tar sands' premier producer at that time. Syncrude intended a $4 billion expansion that, according to Syncrude's vice-president of finance and administration, wasn't economical in that environment. The province didn't want the consortium to abandon the project, so it gave Syncrude an $85 million interest-free loan to enable Syncrude to carry out engineering and feasibility studies for the proposed expansion.[10] In addition Alberta extended a $166 million standby loan to help Syncrude continue a $750 million expansion the joint venture had started before world prices collapsed.[11]

This state assistance, combined with a rebound in world prices in 1987 and significant operating efficiency improvements, helped to restore the bloom to tar sands production. Suncor was back in the black in the first half of 1987 on the strength of higher prices, increased tar sands production, and sharply lower operating costs. The company produced a record amount of synthetic crude oil during the first half of 1987; from 1985 to 1986 the firm slashed its operating costs by half—a staggering percentage—to $17.75 per barrel.[12] In the first six months of 1987 Suncor generated net earnings of $51 million as opposed to the $6 million loss it recorded over the same period in 1986.[13] Suncor's president reassured his shareholders their company was "far better equipped to cope with a low price environment" than it had been prior to the crash of 1986.[14] Musings about closing its plant were a thing of the past.

Syncrude, Suncor's larger neighbour, could tell a similar story of resilience. For Syncrude too, increasing production volumes and improving economies of scale were important keys to profitability. By 1987, after adopting new technology and improving the operation's production reliability, Syncrude had reduced its synthetic crude production costs to $15.35 per barrel; in 1979 those costs were $25.60.[15] Syncrude's production costs were getting closer and closer to those required to find and produce new conventional oil in Western Canada. Given such dramatic production cost improvements, Syncrude declared it was entertaining a massive $4 billion expansion, a proposal to nearly double the plant's production to 225,000 barrels per day by 1993. Just a 10 percent increase in the world price—to $22.50 per barrel—would prompt the company to look seriously at going ahead with the project.[16] Nearly 160 kilometres (100 miles) to the southeast, Imperial Oil also emerged from 1986 with a view to expand, not abandon, its Cold Lake heavy oil operations. It announced a $325 million investment to increase its production by 44,000 barrels per day; this expansion would increase its output by more than 50 percent.[17]

This general strategic orientation, realizing production and operational improvements, continued throughout the 1980s and into the 1990s. Syncrude's first public annual report, released in 1992, detailed the joint venture's success in attaining record production output of 60.3 million barrels in 1991 (more than 165,000 barrels per day). Although Syncrude's after-tax return on capital slipped to 6.1 percent from 9.1 percent in 1990, the firm was still able to claim its return ratio was three times better than the industry as a whole reported.[18] Table 1 demonstrates the successes Syncrude could claim in improving its operating performance and profitability between 1990 and 1996.

New production records were set in every year except 1996; between 1990 and 1996 Syncrude reduced its average unit operating costs by 21 percent to their lowest level ever recorded in the partnership's history. Claiming a rate of return on invested capital of 17 percent, Syncrude's owners were optimistic that, with oil in the US$20 range, their operation could remain,

Table 1   Syncrude Canada, Production and Financial Results, 1990–1996

	1990	1991	1992	1993	1994	1995	1996
Shipments	57.1	60.3	65.4	67.0	69.8	73.9	73.5
Revenue	1,510	1,386	1,493	1,410	1,519	1,758	2,137
Avg. crude oil price	26.25	22.82	22.83	21.20	21.64	23.80	29.08
Oper. cash flow	544	369	516	343	421	614	712
Earnings (after tax $)	240	157	218	106	158	265	368
ROCE (percent)	9.1	6.1	7.7	4.2	35.7	8.9	11.7

Shipments are in millions of barrels per year; revenue, operating cash flow, and after-tax earnings are in C$ millions; ROCE is return on capital employed.

Sources: "Syncrude Releases 1994 Results," *Business Wire*, May 16, 1995; "Syncrude Maintains Growth with 1996 Results," *Canada NewsWire*, February 5, 1997.

as Gwynn Morgan of Syncrude-partner Alberta Energy Company boasted, "one of the most profitable oil and gas operations in Canada."[19] J. P. Bryan, the CEO of Gulf Canada Resources and another co-owner of Syncrude, was even more ebullient: if real oil prices rose to $25 per barrel "Syncrude would become a gold mine."[20] But perhaps the strongest affirmation of Syncrude's profitability, then and into the future, came from Syncrude's chair Eric Newell. "In a low-price environment," Newell said, "we still make money. It's a steady, lower rate of return, like an annuity. But if the price goes up ... we just print money."[21]

Just upstream on the Athabasca River, Suncor boasted a similar record. With the exception of 1992, when a $238 million restructuring charge incurred to upgrade its tar sands operations pushed Suncor into the red, the post-1986 period should be viewed as one where the company consistently improved its production volumes, operating costs, and financial results. Suncor's success was widely recognized. In 1991, a Calgary consulting firm selected Suncor as the most successful integrated Canadian oil company.[22] Suncor's ability to deliver improved performance quarter after quarter drew accolades from the business press. Reports on its first quarter earnings announcement in 1994 were typical. Then its earnings rose by 70 percent year to year while the price for the benchmark crude oil West Texas Intermediate fell by $5 per barrel. The combination of record production levels and average cash costs of just $13.50 per barrel compensated for falling prices and produced exceptional financial results for the company.[23] It is not hard to appreciate why Rick George, Suncor's president, would conclude later in 1994 that "I do see that this is a great business to be in."[24]

In the 1990s, significant technological changes to mining techniques pushed operating costs lower and profitability higher. When Suncor incurred its $238 million restructuring charge, nearly a third of that amount was devoted to introducing the most significant change to tar sands mining since its inception. Suncor's huge bucketwheel excavators and conveyor belts were retired in late 1993 and replaced with electric power shovels and mammoth trucks capable of carrying hundreds of tons of bitumen-impregnated sands.[25] Syncrude soon followed suit. Looking back at this innovation 10 years later, Suncor's executive vice-president of oil sands operations noted how this change improved flexibility, reliability, and margins at his mine. "In fact," he concluded, "it practically guaranteed profitability over the normal range of oil prices."[26]

Hydrotransport was a second key technological innovation; Eric Newell identified it as "the key enabling technology."[27] Instead of transporting tar sands to processing facilities via unreliable conveyor belt systems, slurry pipelines were built to transport the sands from mines to the processing plant. Adding hot water to the raw bitumen and shooting it as slurry through these pipe-lines delivered several benefits. It enabled Syncrude to lower the temperature needed to extract the bitumen and thereby increase energy efficiency. Using hot water delivered the added benefit of starting the process of separating the bitumen from the sands in the pipeline well before the raw material reached the plant. Furthermore, this process reduced the significance of what had been an important economic constraint on expanding mining operations—the dis-tance between the mine and the bitumen upgrader.[28]

Cost reductions were also sought and realized for labour. Newell talks about the need at Syncrude to "redesign the work" and to involve the employees in this process. This redesigning went hand in hand with the technological changes taking place in the late 1980s and 1990s. Through this process Syncrude reduced its labour force from nearly 5,000 to less than 3,400 employees.[29]

Suncor, more publicly than any other tar sands producer, used the crash of 1986 as a lever to demand permanent, not just emergency, government measures to improve its fiscal health. The company got what it wanted. The previous chapter noted that a $150 million expansion was predicated in part on Suncor's move to a royalty structure based on the Cold Lake regime. Instead of a 12 percent royalty set on gross production, Suncor negotiated a shift to a profit-oriented, net revenue royalty regime. In 1987, Suncor's presi-dent declared the company would make a good profit under this new royalty arrangement with oil prices as low as $18 per barrel.[30] Officials in Alberta's energy department held similar views. They regarded the Cold Lake regime favourably. As noted in the previous chapter, this regime applied to most tar sands ventures by 1987. At an international heavy oil/tar sands conference, Alberta officials judged the province's royalty regime as one that treated industry fairly, perhaps generously:

> The evolution may not stop at this point but it will be difficult to make
> further changes to this royalty structure in order to improve the economics
> of a project. The pre-payout royalty is low and post-payout revenue-sharing
> is only consequential in the event the project is showing profits at a level
> not requiring enhancements.[31]

To government eyes Alberta had an attractive oil sands royalty regime in the late 1980s. Alberta's oil sands royalty system was "firmly established to provide a stable and responsive anchor during the often volatile economic climate experienced by this industry."[32]

Imperial Oil, the lead partner in the Syncrude consortium with a 25 percent interest and whose Cold Lake heavy oil operations were the first to benefit from the Cold Lake royalty regime, also saw the tar sands as a fundamentally important and profitable part of the company's future. In 1992, tar sands accounted for more than two-thirds of the company's net reserves (nearly one billion barrels). Heavy oil and tar sands production was key to compensating for the company's declining production of conventional oil.[33] That year Imperial's Syncrude share netted the company $60 million, or 30 percent of its net earnings.[34] The firm's confidence in the profitability of the Cold Lake operation was affirmed in November 1994 when it announced it would proceed with a $240 million expansion there to increase production to 127,000 barrels per day—a 41 percent increase.[35] A year later, Canada's largest petroleum company apparently had become "so devoted to oil sands that it has stopped exploring for conventional oil"; this unconventional petroleum resource, according to a senior company official, was Imperial's "future."[36]

The idea that Syncrude and Suncor, Alberta's premier tar sands producers, were struggling to survive in the 1980s and 1990s is laughable; it is a convenient myth. It has been used for more than a generation by tar sands principals and their boosters inside and outside of government to justify corporate demands for even more generous treatment than the state already had bestowed on these corporations. A more honest reading of the public record of this period leads to just the opposite conclusion. These companies, thanks to the combination of their own impressive operational and technological innovations and the state's fiscal regime and assistance, enjoyed a measure of health in this period many of their contemporaries could only wish would have been theirs.

The Liberal Renaissance

The state assistance lent to bolster the profitability of Syncrude, Suncor, and Imperial Oil was one part of the Canadian state's contribution to global efforts in the 1980s to reinvigorate the position of multinationals and OECD nations in the international petroleum economy. Since the early 1960s, the politics of that economy have been marked by clashes between statist and liberal forces. Statism's major successes in the 1970s were delivered in the form of more rent for producing countries and the nationalization of oil companies in the Middle East and Venezuela. These victories were painted on a canvas of surging OPEC production and slumping output from the lower 48 states of the US. Multinationals and OECD nations alike didn't take their loss of status well; they responded with efforts to change the market conditions that fuelled OPEC's "oil power." Their agreed-upon prescription was "the use of alternative fuels, the search for diversified sources of oil, and conservation."[37]

The discoveries of Alaska's Prudhoe Bay field in 1968, Norway's Ekofisk in 1969, and Great Britain's Forties field in 1970 helped the multinationals and OECD countries regain some of their standing and security in the global oil trade. By 1980 these three elephant fields alone were pouring more than two million barrels per day of new, non-OPEC production into the petroleum market.[38]

Alberta certainly wanted its tar sands to feature prominently in the West's efforts to reduce OPEC's influence. The provincial government eagerly hitched its tar sands wagon to efforts to attain what an American government official called "hemispheric self-sufficiency." For Exxon's chief economist these efforts were likened to a crusade; they were part of "the cause of Free World political and economic cooperation."[39] Premier Lougheed warned Albertans what might happen if the oil sands weren't exploited soon; if Alberta didn't develop the oil sands for these lofty purposes, other energy sources—nuclear and the Colorado oil shales—"could render obsolete, and as a useless asset, the Alberta oil sands…"[40] His administration's enthusiasm to get the tar sands in on this action could be seen in his environment, not energy, minister's musing about what a "most optimistic rate of development" in the oil sands would look like: 100,000 to 300,000 barrels-per-day plants coming on stream at the rate of nearly one per year throughout the 1980s and 1990s. "It is anticipated," Environment Minister William Yurko stated, "that the annual production of synthetic crude will reach three million barrels per day from approximately 20 plants by the year 2000."[41] Such an "optimistic" view of the future of oil sands development under a Lougheed administration may have escaped Peter Lougheed's memory when he criticized the Alberta government 32 years later for not developing the oil sands in an orderly manner.[42] Lougheed's ambitions in the 1970s could have been the script for the post-1995 rapid development of the tar sands by the Klein government that Lougheed panned.

As Canadian governments aided tar sands producers, liberal democracies elsewhere relaxed their fiscal regimes in order to accelerate non-OPEC production and boost corporate profits. The decline and then crash in world oil prices in the 1980s hit Norway hard. The collapse plunged Norway into its steepest recession since the Great Depression. Unemployment doubled; the trade balance went in the other direction; record deficits replaced record surpluses.[43] Norway's Labour government responded just as its Canadian centre-right counterparts did—by easing the government's financial take and industry's regulatory burden. Drilling bans imposed to promote environmental values were lifted. Royalties on new production from the country's continental shelf were cut to zero percent from a range of 8 to 14 percent.[44] Companies also were no longer required to pay the exploration costs of the Norwegian government and Statoil, the state-owned petroleum company. In 1990–91 corporate tax rates were cut to 28 percent from 50.8 percent (but a special petroleum tax of 50 percent was introduced to capture economic rent).[45]

Great Britain lurched even more radically toward the liberal, market pole after the election of Margaret Thatcher's Conservatives in 1979. She privatized the British National Oil Company and sold the government's shares in BP. Before 1985, the British government took 89.5 percent of North Sea petroleum revenues through a combination of royalties, a petroleum revenue tax, and corporate taxes. After changes made to the fiscal regime in 1983–84, the government's share sank to just 35 percent.[46] By 1993, when the government eliminated the petroleum revenue tax for new licences, Britain effectively stopped collecting any economic rent that could be claimed by the owner of offshore petroleum for assigning the rights to exploit that resource to corporations. Britain became the new model citizen for the liberal attack on the royalties that owners of petroleum might claim.[47]

This liberal renaissance in petroleum even seemed about to take root in the barren soil of Russia and Venezuela. There it wasn't falling oil prices that spurred the liberal turn but wider, more systemic economic crises. These crises prompted Russia and Venezuela to court the transnationals. The Soviet oil industry, as Bayulgen notes, historically had been subordinated to the Kremlin's view of what the state-run economy needed—cheap oil for industries and citizens alike. The state ignored the principles of sound petroleum management to realize this end. Petroleum reservoirs were managed poorly and too little capital was invested in technology; oil production plateaued in the early 1980s, peaked in 1987, and plummeted after the breakup of the Soviet Union.[48] Banned from the largest country in the world for 70 years after the October Revolution of 1917, many transnationals—often encouraged by their home countries—were eager to enter Russia. Conoco in the Arctic, Exxon and Shell in Sakhalin Island, and BP in West Siberia all hoped that the Russian book on nationalization and state control was closed forever.

For tar sands lobbying and policy-making in Canada, Venezuela likely was the scene for the most significant liberalization initiatives. Through the *Petroleum Nationalization Law of 1975*, Venezuela nationalized the oil industry in 1976 and created Petróleos de Venezuela (PDVSA) to hold the state's new assets. *Étatisme* had characterized Venezuelan oil policy and politics long before this nationalization. Its origins, ironically, rested with the international oil companies themselves. In the early twentieth century those companies sought to change the Venezuelan system of property rights since, like the American system, it gave landowners subsurface rights and the ability to inconvenience and frustrate their ambitions. They succeeded. Subsurface rights were stripped from landowners, and the state became the exclusive authority for dealing with foreign petroleum companies.[49]

Venezuela challenged the multinationals before any Middle East oil producer did.[50] The Hydrocarbon Law of 1943 established the 50/50 principle—petroleum income should be divided equally between companies and the state. Since the concessions alone couldn't deliver this equality, President Medina's government introduced a set of royalty and tax changes to obtain its share of the wealth. But, much to the outrage of the opposition Acción Democrática, the government paid a dear price for industry's acceptance of a heavier tax burden. The state extended the land tenures of the multinationals for an additional 40 years and leased more land to them in 1944 and 1945 than the companies had been able to gain access to in the previous 35 years.[51]

Another irony of Venezuelan oil history is that PDVSA, soon after it was created, pushed for liberalization. Its senior managers hoped to model the company after the multinationals; they wanted PDVSA to be like any other oil company and were jealous to preserve the state company's autonomy from the politicians. To these ends it internationalized its operations by moving into the refining business in the United States and Germany; its US purchase of Citgo brought with it a large network of retail service stations. The opposition in the Venezuelan parliament worried that PDVSA, just like the multinationals, would use this international presence as a transfer pricing opportunity, an opportunity to reduce its Venezuelan tax obligations.[52] In 1990, President Pérez appointed Andrés Sosa Pietri to lead PDVSA. Pietri wanted PDVSA to have the same amount of freedom as the company's private-sector counterparts; he wanted Venezuela to pull out of OPEC and join the International Energy Agency; and he believed private capital was PDVSA's ally and welcomed the prospect of forming "strategic associations" with multinationals to exploit the extra-heavy crude oil found in the Orinoco Belt.[53]

Economic crisis—born from out-of-control government spending, rapidly rising inflation and unemployment, and a bankrupt treasury—gave life to Pietri's dreams. Through *La Apertura Petrolera* ("the oil opening"), Venezuela once again welcomed foreign capital into the key sector of the Venezuelan economy. Association agreements—the extra-heavy oil dimension of *La Apertura Petrolera*—provided multinationals with a model they could use as leverage in their negotiations over the future of Alberta's tar sands. The Orinoco's extra-heavy oil, like Alberta's bitumen, requires extensive upgrading in order to become commercially valuable.[54] ExxonMobil, BP, Chevron, ConocoPhillips, Total, and Statoil all partnered with PDVSA in four extraction/upgrading projects (two projects were announced in 1993 and two in 1997). The projects called for more than US$15 billion in investment and were producing 650,000 barrels per day of synthetic crude oil by 2006.[55]

Given Venezuela's politics and past willingness to challenge multinationals, why would the world's leading oil companies jump back into Venezuela? First, there was the size of the prize. Estimates in the 1990s put the Orinoco's recoverable reserves at approximately 270 billion barrels of nonconventional oil.[56] Second were the fiscal terms. PDVSA lobbied the Venezuelan government to extend "unprecedentedly generous" financial arrangements to international oil companies to entice them to return.[57] The government's overtures prompted Conoco's executive vice-president of exploration and production to label Venezuela "an oilman's paradise."[58] For Sincor and Petrozuata, the first two extra-heavy oil projects PDVSA negotiated with Total, Statoil, and Conoco (now ConocoPhillips) in 1993, the regular royalty of 16.67 percent would be reduced for the first 10 years of the projects' lives to just 1 percent. These royalty terms were negotiated between 1993 and 1997. Two more upgrading projects, Cerro Negro and Hamaca, were finalized in 1997. The same royalty terms were extended to PDVSA's partners in these ventures: Mobil (now ExxonMobil) and Veba Oil (later purchased by BP) in the Cerro Negro project and Phillips (now ConocoPhillips in the Hamaca. The upgrading projects were also excused from paying the special oil corporate income tax rate of 67 percent; they only would be asked to pay the normal corporate rate of 34 percent.[59] The royalty terms the tar sands sector would secure in Alberta were first put on the drawing board in Venezuela.

PDVSA's multinational partners secured other important concessions in the Strategic Association Agreements. The agreements were to last for 30 to 35 years; PDVSA agreed to compensate the private investors if the Venezuelan government significantly damaged their earnings by actions such as increasing income tax rates; any disputes between the partners would be subject to international arbitration in New York using the rules of the International Chamber of Commerce.[60] With a petroleum paradise under construction in South America, the multinationals turned their attention to establishing a Canadian version in the boreal forest of northeastern Alberta.

The Missionary

A leading petroleum industry publication described him as a missionary; the federal minister of natural resources who embraced his sermon about the value of the oil sands called him a visionary. This was Eric Newell, who, in the early 1990s and near the peak of his career, led Syncrude and was the president of the Alberta Chamber of Resources. Newell's list of accomplishments and awards over the course of his career in petroleum is nearly as long as the northern Alberta winters he endured in Fort McMurray. They include the Order of Canada, Alberta's Order of Excellence, four honourary degrees, the 2003 Canadian Energy Person of the year, and a term as the Chancellor of the University of Alberta. He was the first chair of the board of directors of the Climate Change Emissions Management Corporation, a nonprofit corporation established in 2009 by the Alberta government to fund, in whole or in part, projects reducing greenhouse gas emissions. Few of Newell's contemporaries came close to matching his record at Syncrude when it came to balancing the goals of corporate profitability and social responsibility; in addition to promoting tar sands development he was a passionate advocate for education and for improving the life chances of Aboriginal peoples. His achievements testify powerfully to the sensibility, civic-mindedness, and doggedness he brought to his corporate and community leadership roles.

In 1991, the idea to create a vehicle to support and spread the message that Canada needed to massively exploit the tar sands was hatched in the Alberta Chamber's offices in Edmonton. Syncrude's Newell, a senior official from Alberta's energy department, and two officials from the Chamber reflected there on a disappointment—the shelving of the OSLO (Other Six Lease Owners) project. Ottawa, driven by a desire to reduce its deficit, announced in its 1990 budget it was withdrawing the $1 billion it had committed previously to the nearly $5 billion project.[61] Alberta was the most generous government contributor to the project and it refused to pick up Ottawa's tab. The shelving of OSLO was, in one sense, the final straw for Newell; it reaffirmed his belief that what he called the "megaproject mentality"—by which he meant lavishing government grants, loans, subsidies, equity positions, and other inducements on multibillion dollar projects—had to go. It also led Newell and his compatriots to reiterate, with more than a little frustration, that the Athabasca tar sands arguably represented the world's largest oil field and was effectively ignored. A self-deprecating Newell downplayed what he and his colleagues were about to agree on. "Without even knowing what we were saying," he said, "we have to create a National Oil Sands Task Force."[62]

Curiously, this declaration apparently was of little interest to the CAPP, for whom heavy oil or bitumen producers were arguably second-class citizens at that point in time. Instead, at Syncrude's urging, the Mining Association of Canada recommended the creation of a National Oil Sands Task Force in their brief to the national Mines Ministers meeting in September 1991. That recommendation needed the approval of those provincial and federal ministers. It came, but Jake Epp, the federal minister, was not there to see it approved and Epp's representatives said, according to Newell, "watch out, Jake, here they come again, the oil sands with their hands out." For the deacon of the tar sands industry, "it was the exact opposite. We understood by this time that we couldn't do it that way. What did we need to do to get people excited again about developing this resource and then, what are the barriers and then, what are the things we need to do to overcome the barriers. That was the logic."[63] For the next 16 months Newell worked, over the course of several meetings with Epp, to convince the minister that Newell's vision for the oil sands would not require the "handouts"—billions of dollars in government support—needed for a project like Hibernia to go ahead off the shores of Newfoundland. Epp ultimately was convinced but left it to his successor, Bill McKnight, to announce federal support for the industry initiative Newell had been championing—a National Task Force on Oil Sands Strategies. Its job would be to craft a vision of growth and develop a plan of action.[64]

In this respect the task force was part of what Fred Block called a structural mechanism of subsidiary importance, a technique of capital to exert direct influence on the state. In addition to lobbying and making campaign contributions, business may participate "in various private policy-making groups that have a powerful impact on the formulation of government policies."[65] We had already seen the Alberta Chamber of Resources play this role in the 1980s when it prepared a study of synthetic oil production costs for the provincial government. The National Task Force on Oil Sands Strategies reprised this earlier effort and far surpassed it when it came to the sophistication and comprehensiveness of its research and recommendations. Over a series of eight reports it covered subjects such as macro-economic benefits, taxation and royalties, technologies, marketing, and the environment; the Task Force plotted out the course tar sands producers wanted the federal and Alberta governments to follow. It would essentially recommend the reregulation of the tar sands sector.

Industry dominated this policy advisory group. This is clear from looking at the composition of the Task Force's six subcommittees. Industry chaired all six. It's stunning to note that no government members sat on the environment and regulatory subcommittee. None. They also weren't found on two other subcommittees: marketing and transportation and material/services and coalition building. Apparently government perspectives either weren't welcome or weren't needed on these subjects. The membership on all the other subcommittees was weighted heavily toward industry. The composition on the fiscal and socioeconomic subcommittee was 11 industry members to 4 government members. It was 10 to 2, again in favour of industry, on the government and communications subcommittee and 9 to 5 on the science and technology committee. Overall the six subcommittees contained 46 industry members and only 11 from government. Such a membership complexion predictably affected the Task Force's subsequent recommendations.

Newell spent a considerable amount of time—both before the Task Force was formed in 1993 and during the Task Force's life—travelling across the country and around the globe spreading the gospel about the strategic and economic importance of the oil sands. A handful of themes stand out from those travels. For Canadian audiences he first stressed that their national government had no vision of where the tar sands figured in the country's energy future—an important vacuum, given significant and irreversible declines in Canadian conventional oil production. Newell predicted that, by 2005, as little as one-third of Canadian demand would be satisfied from the country's conventional oil resources. This neglect would be tragic if not rectified, since the tar sands offered the most certain route to self-sufficiency. In a September 1993 speech to the Rotary Club of Edmonton, Newell emphatically made the case for linking Canadian self-sufficiency to exploiting the oil sands:

> As a country, we have a choice. We can secure our energy future, and thereby our economic future by developing the oil sands.
> Or, we can increasingly depend on Middle East oil and volatile Middle East politics, and lose the opportunity for a better future that is within our reach today.
> There's no question that oil will continue to be the world's major source of energy well into the next century. And in a turbulent world, oil self-sufficiency is a goal most countries would like to achieve...
> In Canada's case, we could switch to synthetic crude oil and be self-sufficient for the next 200 years if our oil sands were developed further. And, as conventional sources of oil continue to dry up, while consumption continues to rise, the need for such an alternative source becomes readily apparent.[66]

Newell had made this argument previously and persuaded Canadian editorial boards of its merits. The editorial board of the *Financial Post*, for example, embraced Newell's argument after he visited them in January 1993. "It's also time," they said, "for governments to sit down with oil sands producers to map out the fiscal regime they need to give Canada a secure supply of oil over the next decades."[67]

As Newell set out to increase the profile of the tar sands in the mind of the state, he was frustrated by Ottawa's refusal to see the tar sands' potential. The lack of appreciation Ottawa paid to the tar sands relative to the Hibernia offshore project galled him. He believed the federal government could get much more bang for its buck if it gave the oil sands a more favourable fiscal regime instead of devoting the billions in grants, loan guarantees, and equity it already had lavished on Hibernia.[68] Speaking about Syncrude, he said, "We're also still trying to overcome a public notion that we're still a project, yet we've produced 600 million barrels—the lifetime output of the Hibernia offshore field."[69] When Syncrude produced its 600 millionth barrel of synthetic crude oil in September 1992, Newell noted this "milestone is also greater than any other frontier or off-shore field in Canada ... And Syncrude has only produced a fraction of the oil contained on its lease."[70]

All tar sands principals were not as enthusiastic as Newell appeared to be about using the tar sands to realize Canadian self-sufficiency. Serving the American market, not the tiny Canadian one, would be the key to expanding tar sands production. Thus Imperial Oil's J. D. McFarland made no mention of Canadian self-sufficiency when he outlined his keys to a healthy future in the oil sands. McFarland stressed instead the importance of ensuring what free trade had affirmed—continued unrestricted access to the US export market.[71] Continentalism, not nationalism, animated his logic.

When the Task Force reported in May 1995, Newell had dropped the Canadian self-sufficiency position and had joined McFarland in singing from the continentalism hymnbook. By early 1995 the perceived threats, sentiments, and phrases that animated Newell's 1993 Edmonton speech were still paramount but they were delivered increasingly in a North American context. US conventional oil production, like Canadian production, had peaked in the early 1970s. "My fear," Newell told the 6th UNITAR International Conference on Heavy Crude and Tar Sands, "is that if this trend continues unarrested, then both our nations will lie twisting in the wind, at the mercy of Middle Eastern oil merchants."[72] The oil sands represented "the sleeping giant" that would deliver Canada and the United States from this danger; they were the ticket to continental energy supply security.

Later that spring, when he spoke at the release of the Task Force's report, some themes of the Canadian self-sufficiency message remained: the oil sands were strategic, they offered Canada a 200-year supply, their development would significantly reduce Canada's annual payments for and dependence on imported oil.[73] But this speech also revealed that Newell had converted to the continentalist energy gospel. The Task Force's market-based vision of future oil sands production and investment was premised clearly on meeting American petroleum demand. In Newell's words:

> Like virtually any business, the oil sands' growth will be market driven. We expect that export markets, mainly to the US Rocky Mountain region, the mid-West and the West Coast, will offer the largest opportunities to compete and expand our sales.
>
> An important factor in achieving increased exports and encouraging offshore capital will be the removal by government of long-term export restrictions. This will facilitate long-term planning and improve certainty on the part of both buyers and investors.

Industry needs open access to export markets which would permit better long-term planning and greater encouragement to foreign investors.[74]

If Newell's enthusiasm for Canadian self-sufficiency ultimately faltered, the same could not be said of a second theme he used to build a national following for his vision—the employment and economic gains to be realized from investing billions of dollars in the tar sands. Here Newell sought to acquaint political leaders—especially those from Ontario and Quebec as well as their publics—of the treasure chest that tar sands expansion could represent for them. Econometric studies commissioned by the Task Force maintained that 60 percent of the economic benefits of tar sands investments would be enjoyed outside of Alberta. Canada's manufacturing heartland in Ontario and Quebec would reap as many of the economic benefits of the Task Force's vision as Alberta would. The importance and value of the interprovincial or national economic linkages "Alberta" development generated were not news to Newell; much of the $1.5 billion Syncrude spent annually on operating costs was spent in Ontario and, to a lesser extent, in Quebec since that was where the "pots and pans" were made. "What we did ...," Newell recalled, "we actually got the data from Syncrude and Suncor and ... Esso and showed how much money was being invested in each MP's riding. I used to carry that around with me." When it came to the broader Canadian community, "people don't care whether it makes more profits for Imperial Oil or the owners but they sure do care about jobs and revenues to governments that can then finance social programs that we all value so highly as Canadians."[75]

When Newell unveiled the Task Force's report in May 1995 this jobs/revenue theme took pride of place. He essentially promised tremendous economic riches if oil sands development took the continentalist path. They constituted the "enormous prize" Canadians could secure from following the Task Force's vision. If the tar sands attracted $21 to $25 billion in investment by 2025, Informetrica estimated this would create 44,000 jobs—nearly twice the 1995 total—by 2020. Government coffers would bulge if these billions were poured into the tar sands. By 2025 the federal government's balance would improve by an estimated $58 billion; provincial balances would balloon by $39 billion, with 87 percent of that flowing to Alberta.[76]

The Canadian self-sufficiency theme had fallen from grace. "The opportunity to access new export markets," the Task Force concluded, "is a significant expansion opportunity for producers of oil sands crude oil and bitumen."[77] Those new markets and opportunities for growth were to be found in the United States. "In an uncertain world," it said, "the security of a major oil supply on the same continent, and in a stable geopolitical environment, could be of major economic value to the U.S."[78] While Canadian workers and governments would profit monetarily in the Task Force's world, this vision was blind to seeing the national strategic importance of the tar sands. That such a position could be taken in a world where secure access to oil was being linked more and more tightly to national security was arguably bewildering unless Canadian and American interests were seen as inseparable.

While the Task Force worshipped the marketplace, its ambitions demanded substantial government structural changes in order to pursue this multibillion-dollar bonanza. For Newell the fiscal system was "probably the most complex and most fundamental" of the development levers affecting the oil sands industry's prospects.[79] The existing fiscal system was an "impediment" to expansion in the tar sands; it needed a major overhaul. On the taxation front, the Task Force wanted the federal government to retain the 25 percent resource allowance and to allow tar sands developers to immediately write off their capital costs. On the royalty side, the Task Force wanted to establish a "generic" royalty regime, a regime that would treat all projects identically. It first wanted the provincial government to eliminate the 1 to 5 percent gross revenues royalty levied on tar sands production while projects were still in the cost-recovery stage of operations. No royalties should be paid to the resource owners until all of a project's costs plus a rate of return indexed to the Canadian long-term bond rate had been recovered. Then industry would agree to pay the provincial government a net royalty on production.

For their part, companies would relinquish the provision found in some royalty agreements to "uplift" capital and operating costs (by 1 and 10 percent respectively) as a simple way of accounting for overhead costs.[80] Furthermore, the Task Force recommended eliminating "royalty-free" gas—companies that used their own natural gas in processing the tar sands received a waiver on paying any royalties on that gas. But these corporate concessions were contingent on making changes to the fiscal system that would compensate for these lost benefits. To listen to Newell's speech and to read the Task Force's comprehensive report was to see a proposed generic fiscal regime dressed in the robes of efficiency, consistency, stability, equity, and balance; the days of seeking government handouts would be over.

The devil, as they say, is in the details. Cleverly, neither Newell's speech nor the Task Force's comprehensive report offered any details of this preferred generic fiscal regime. Those details were found in an appendix at the end of the report. That appendix recommended institutionalizing very generous fiscal provisions into the regime, provisions that, in some circumstances, could be at least as if not more generous than what government had doled out through "handouts" in the past. Financially, the most important plank in the Task Force's preferred position concerned what kind of petro-leum—higher value crude oil or lower value bitumen—the provincial government should use to calculate royalty payments. Since Suncor's birth, Alberta's oil sands royalties were calculated as percentages of crude oil prices. The Task Force wanted to end this. Instead, it proposed that Alberta's royalty "should be based upon the value of the first marketable product less [i]ts cost of production."[81] Essentially, industry wanted royalties to be calculated on the price of bitumen, not crude oil, minus all production costs.

The state of bitumen markets and pricing meant this change to calculat-ing royalties could deliver a windfall to tar sands producers. In 2005 CAPP bluntly told the US Securities and Exchange Commission that the bitumen market then was "immature and illiquid," an assessment at least as accurate to describing that market in 1995.[82] Bitumen has always traded at a discount, sometimes a very steep one, to the price of conventional crude oil. For example, CAPP told American regulators the average bitumen price at Cold Lake between 1997 and 2004 was just 51 percent of the price for West Texas Intermediate (WTI) oil.[83]

Switching the basis for calculating royalties from WTI prices to bitu-men prices could be very lucrative for integrated tar sands projects. This creates opportunities to reduce royalty payments through transfer pricing— "[T]he setting of prices for intra-group or company transfers of goods and services."[84] In a non-arm's length transaction, such as the Athabasca Oil Sands Project's Scotford upgrading operation where bitumen is purchased from mines owned by the project's partners, the opportunity arises for the company to charge itself less than market value for the product. This would reduce the royalties owed to the provincial government. More than 10 years after the Task Force recommended this fundamental change to the royalty system, a provincial government panel of independent experts concluded: "Bitumen prices are not as high as oil prices and therefore, the royalties they generate are lower. Bitumen has few producers, some of whom are also con-sumers in terms of their on-site, integrated upgrading facilities. That raises issues around internal transfer payments and an opaque market."[85]

The main text of the Oil Sands Task Force's comprehensive report was also silent when it came to identifying what specific net royalty rate (NRR) or percentage Alberta should charge. To identify this vital detail, you again needed to refer to the fiscal report appendix: "Industry members believe that a rate of NRR of 25 percent with a return interest allowance of LTBR plus 2 percent will provide the appropriate level of stimulus to oil sands develop-ment while providing a reasonable share to governments."[86] A 25 percent net royalty rate was less than the 30 percent net royalty then being custom-arily paid by Suncor and Imperial's Cold Lake project.[87] Again, the details industry preferred not to trumpet suggested that the Task Force hoped to institutionalize "handouts" into the generic fiscal regime. Industry wanted a more generous version of the fiscal regime Suncor and Syncrude had used to ride an impressive wave of prosperity over much of the previous decade.

The State Embraces the Sermon: Alberta

The federal and provincial governments agreed to the vast majority of the Task Force's recommendations. In fact, when analyzing the fit between the Task Force's recommendations and the governments' response, it would not be an exaggeration to suggest the Task Force effectively drafted the state's blueprint. The industry-dominated Task Force poured the foundations of the oil factory that would be built in northeastern Alberta. The province warmly received the essence of the Task Force's analysis and recommendations. The government accepted the view that the existing royalty system was ad hoc, that it was "an overall inharmonious royalty system," one that "led to uncertainty." Investors could not be "sure about the future royalty structure new investments or expansions might face."[88] Premier Klein sold the need for a generic "one size fits all" royalty regime as a prerequisite to increased exploitation of the tar sands. The premier said generic royalties "will provide the certainty that the task force said was required in planning oilsands projects." He went on to say that Alberta had "a maze of royalty agreements," and he agreed with the criticisms that Alberta was "not providing a level playing field for oilsands development."[89] Since the government followed the Task Force's script so closely, Newell's reaction was predictable; the premier's announcement was "fantastic."[90]

Paul Precht, a senior Alberta public servant and economist who was involved extensively with the Task Force, described the generic royalty regime as a "new royalty and tax treatment that was admittedly very generous." What is striking from his retrospective assessment of the Task Force was the absence of any apparent concern in the provincial government about capturing an adequate share of the economic rent the tar sands would generate. When it came to the economics subgroup of the Task Force, he suggested "the key things they were looking at there were, are there ways that we can structure royalties and taxes that can benefit this industry and can provide some of the stimulus we're looking for."[91] Patricia Nelson (then Patricia Black), the energy minister who delivered the new generic royalty regime, described the regime in very similar terms. "Well, that scheme was so solid," she said, "and it was built to attract investment. We knew if we got investment, then the long-term benefit would come from the corporate tax and the individual tax side. It was never intended to be a massive royalty grab."[92]

Bitumen prices, not crude oil prices, would provide the basis for calculating the royalties of companies following the new regime. Alberta presented no more than a semblance of toughness when it refused the Task Force's royalty holiday recommendation. Instead, industry would have to scrape together the cash to pay a minimum royalty of just 1 percent of gross revenue until all project costs were recovered. The government described this provision some years later as one whereby the state shared the up-front risk of developing the tar sands.[93] Project costs were defined generously; they included all research and development costs plus a return allowance on capital and operating costs equal to Canada's long-term bond rate. Once tar sands projects recovered their project costs, their royalty payments likely would increase, but only if a rate of 25 percent of net revenue would generate more revenue than a rate of 1 percent of gross revenue.

If the future of heavy oil and bitumen exploitation would be brighter in Venezuela than Canada, it wouldn't be because of an unfriendly fiscal landscape in Alberta. At the very least Venezuela's generous fiscal incentives to attract heavy oil investment needed to be matched by Alberta. Venezuela's liberalization made the tar sands sector's ambition to secure financial concessions in Alberta that much easier to realize. Patricia Nelson recounted Venezuela's importance in these words:

> And this is a true story, we were down in Venezuela, we had been invited down by Pedevesa to go down and see their Orinoco Project and talk to them, this was pre-Chávez. And, we were sitting there with the Pedevesa people and they were telling us that they had got their hands around what they thought was $60 billion of capital investment to go into their Orinoco project. And, I thought, oh my goodness me if they're getting that, we're going to get nothing. It's the same players we're trying to attract, and we're still arguing over the structure. So, I got out of the meeting. I said, "Get the plane. We're going home right now." So, we flew home that day and called everybody in and we finalized the generic royalty scheme right then and there, and we went to market with it.[94]

That the minister decided Alberta needed to mimic the Venezuelans suggests just how little importance the province gave to political stability as a political resource when negotiating with petroleum multinationals in the 1990s.

Alberta's enthusiasm for the Task Force's recommendations was also inspired by the ideological swing to the right the province took after Premier Klein's first provincial election win in 1993. The government was intent on divorcing itself from any semblance of the modest interventionist tendencies seen in the policies of the Lougheed and Getty administrations. The Klein administration's position was summarized by Finance Minister Dinning's declaration that Alberta was "getting out of the business of business." The Klein administration worshipped at the altar of market fundamentalism; lower taxes, fewer regulations requiring corporations to respect societal values, and a smaller civil service were key to its sermon. It was more than just coincidental for Patricia Nelson to use the phrase "we went to market with it" in her remarks about the generic royalty regime.

Energy Minister Nelson's first job after graduating with her Bachelor of Commerce degree from the University of Calgary was with Sun Oil. When interviewed for the Petroleum History Society's Oil Sands Oral History Project, Nelson was effusive in her praise for the oil sands industry and those in the industry she had the privilege to work with. A self-described "ticked-off taxpayer" and "very, very right-wing conservative," she felt that Don Getty's Progressive Conservative government wasn't interested at all in addressing the situation as she saw it: "We were spending out of control, we were in debt up to our eyeballs, and it was an outrageous situation in my view."[95]

The Dinning philosophy was second nature for the energy minister; she enthusiastically applied that perspective to her department. She was a disciple of the belief that society would be better off if government maximized the freedom of corporations to pursue their economic self-interest. When considering the design of the royalty system, she met privately with Newell (Syncrude), Dee Parkinson Marcoux (Suncor), and Howard Dingle (Imperial). She described their work together as work where alternative points of view to an industry/investment-first perspective weren't welcome: "And so, we sat down, and we hunkered down, and started to go through a program. And, of course, all the naysayers were lined up over there so we left them out of the room and we came in."[96] Industry voices, not government ones, appear to be what Nelson wanted to hear, what she admired most. To that end she invited members from all sectors of the energy industry to join her in an informal kitchen cabinet that met at her home on Saturday mornings. She relied heavily on those industry executives and was "eternally grateful to them" because they "were fundamentally key to helping with the change that we went through."[97]

Nelson's enthusiasm for getting government out of the way of the petroleum industry was reflected well in her ministry's first three-year business plan. That plan called for "clarifying and streamlining the regulatory framework and reducing the administrative burdens on industry."[98] In 1994 and 1995 the energy portfolio was a beehive of downsizing as it restructured its operations, merged central regulatory agencies, and cut staff and expenses. Industry applauded the minister's actions; her initiatives, to the CAPP, were "very positive moves."[99] Under Nelson's leadership, the Ministry of Energy's spending was cut sharply, in percentage terms more severely than the cuts made to total government spending. By the time Nelson left the portfolio in 1997, she had reduced the ministry's costs in current dollars to just 64 percent of what they had been in the 1992–93 fiscal year; by 1997 total government spending had been pared back to 83 percent of the 1992–93 amount.[100] Not surprisingly the ministry's administrative capacity dropped significantly during this period, too. On March 31, 1995, the ministry had 589 employees. Two years later the ministry's complement had fallen to 512—a 13 percent reduction.[101] Cuts made to the budget and staff of the Alberta Energy and Utilities Board (the product of the merger of the Energy Resources Conservation Board and the Public Utilities Board) also demonstrated the government's commitment to loosen the reins on industry. "Between 1992 and 1998," reported Marr-Laing and Severson-Baker, "funding for the EUB was reduced by 23% and staffing by 19%."[102]

"Performance measures" offer perhaps the strongest confirmation of the province's intent to ensure the growth of Alberta's petroleum industry took precedence over and above other policy directions. These measures were introduced as part of the government's commitment to bring a business planning approach to managing the affairs of state. In Energy, good departmental performance was synonymous with the performance of the petroleum industry. Oil and gas discoveries versus production, oil and gas production, employment in the oilpatch, oil and gas drilling activity, industry capital spending, energy exports, sale of petroleum agreements, and public safety—these were the yardsticks the government selected initially in order to measure departmental success. Public safety was the only measure that would not necessarily be fulfilled through petroleum sector growth. Nowhere to be seen in the department's first set of performance measures was any measure stipulating what share, through taxes and royalties, Alberta should claim from its petroleum bounty.[103] Investment, not rent, was the province's overwhelming concern.

Whether the previous "ad hoc" royalty regime really was hostile to investment was never seriously challenged before or after the premier announced his intention to revise the oil sands royalty system.[104] Neither the Liberals nor the New Democrats made the changes a serious issue when the required amendments to the *Mines and Minerals Act* were brought before the provincial legislature. Ken Nicol, the leader of the Liberal Official Opposition, congratulated the government on making these changes and supported the legislation. Only Pam Barrett, the leader of the two-member

New Democratic Party caucus, spoke against the legislation but did so only hurriedly, literally seconds before the amendments were passed by the legislature for the third and final time.[105] Nor did major provincial or national trade unions question whether government should follow the Task Force's vision and the high-paying jobs it would bring to Alberta; in fact, the Alberta Building Trades Council; the Canadian Labour Congress; the Communications, Energy, and Paperworkers Union of Canada; and the International Brotherhood of Boilermakers joined more than 300 members of the corporate community in being "Friends of the Oil Sands."[106] Virtually no voices in Alberta could be found speaking strongly against these changes to the fiscal terms of tar sands exploitation. Block suggested that one of the factors that delayed any significant challenge from a countermovement in the United States to market fundamentalism was a high level of elite unity.[107] When it came to the tar sands, Alberta exhibited just such a high degree of elite unity: government and opposition politicians, petroleum companies, and trade unions all wanted the state to reregulate the oil sands royalty regime to sweeten what already had been characterized as an attractive royalty system.

The attractiveness of what had become rather suddenly an insufficient fiscal regime is illustrated by an underappreciated dimension of the politics of the new generic royalty regime. It wasn't generic at all in the sense that the government didn't force it on any of the established tar sands producers. Syncrude and Suncor were in no rush to play on this new level playing field, and the government wasn't going to force them to switch. The terms of the established regime delivered benefits to them they wanted to maximize before they shifted to the regime that new entrants in the sector would follow. One size might fit all operators at some time in the future, but it wasn't going to fit all tar sands corporations immediately after the province reregulated the sector.

Under the terms of Crown Agreements with Alberta, Syncrude and Suncor deducted capital and other costs associated with expanding their operation from the revenues that would be the base for their royalty payments to the provincial treasury. Neither operator wanted to lose those benefits, and so they negotiated transition agreements with the government. In Syncrude's case, it negotiated a transition to cover the period from 1997 until 2003. During this period the government would give the consortium's partners an additional royalty credit of 43 percent on capital expenditures and a blended royalty rate of 25 to 50 percent of deemed profit subject to a minimum royalty of 1 percent of gross revenues.[108]

Suncor negotiated a longer transition. Suncor's transition agreement, normally referred to as an "option" in the company's annual reports, anticipated that the company would move its base tar sands operation to the generic bitumen royalty regime in January 2009. Until then it would continue to pay royalties based on its upgraded product, synthetic crude oil. During the transition, Alberta provided Suncor with additional deductions of up to $158 million per year for 10 years. This potential $1.58 billion deduction was related to Suncor's original investment, not to new investments. Furthermore, in the third year of the transition agreement Suncor's royalties, while still calculated on the price of its upgraded products, would be reduced. Suncor would pay 25 percent of revenues minus allowable costs or 1 percent of gross revenues. Suncor told its shareholders that it expected to pay only a 1 percent royalty to the government until 2010.[109] The old regime was treating Suncor well. Suncor was in no hurry to switch, especially if the province was of a mind to offer the company additional billions in deductions for royalty purposes. The provincial government, for its part, was content to let the established firms decide what was in their best interests. The companies were allowed to decide when it was in their best interests to embrace provincial reregulation of the financial terms of their activities.

The State Embraces the Sermon: Canada

The Task Force's recommendations landed in a thornier political thicket in Ottawa. Calls to reduce the federal income tax bill paid by tar sands companies were more disquieting in Ottawa's political atmosphere than they were in Edmonton. Accelerated capital cost allowances for calculating federal income tax were crucial to the Task Force. They would enable tar sands investors to recover their initial investments more quickly than otherwise was possible under Canadian tax law. Crucial, too, was ensuring that these beneficial tax provisions would apply to all tar sands operations—the in situ as well as the mining ones. With Jean Chrétien's Liberal government firmly set in deficit-cutting mode, it was harder to sell the idea of reducing federal taxes on major, often multinational, corporations. Officials in the Department of Finance certainly were opposed to using the tax system for this type of public policy purpose; so too was Finance Minister Paul Martin, unless a convincing economic—and political—argument could be mustered. According to Natural Resources Minister Anne McLellan, a related pressure concerned the federal government's waning commitment to megaproject developments, developments often dripping in red ink. For her the early to mid-1990s were extremely interesting and challenging years because of the conflicting pressures the federal government was under. On the one hand, Ottawa's basic philosophy was to get out of the business of participating in megaprojects, especially as a total or partial owner (Hibernia was an important exception here); on the other hand, the Oil Sands Task Force was asking

Ottawa to make tax changes to further what she described as the "mother of all megaprojects."[110]

In the March 1996 federal budget, Finance Minister Paul Martin delivered the tax changes the tar sands sector called for. According to McLellan, the finance minister had heard the convincing set of economic and political arguments he needed in order to increase the federal treasury's already generous treatment of the tar sands. For the natural resources minister, the Task Force developed a compelling case for the economic value of supporting further tar sands development. For McLellan "it does come down to whether I can convince Paul Martin that this is something that is important enough and that the homework has been done and the case is strong enough that he should be willing to push his officials in the Department of Finance over their objections to make the changes that would make this project ... happen."[111] For his part, the finance minister (and future prime minister) was open to the type of argument his rookie colleague from Alberta would make to him. Martin's openness to helping lay the federal portion of the fiscal foundation for an oil factory in northeastern Alberta may be seen, in part, in Eric Newell's memory of a conversation he had with the minister in Yellowknife:

> In fact Martin was very good to me. At a point, a critical point early on ... I met with him up in Yellowknife ... and I was amazed at how well that man understood the issue ... But, he told me there were ... two things I had to know about and manage for it to be successful. And one was that he says, "Look, I'm a businessman. I know a lot of things would make infinite good sense to you and me that we could never sell. You cannot have this thing come out looking like a handout to big business and he was in the middle of program cuts." ... The second problem was he had a problem with ... He was really upset at conventional oil and gas because he had a tax issue with them.[112]

Martin's receptiveness should also be seen in political terms. Promoting the tar sands could deliver future Liberal electoral success in Alberta. Martin, McLellan, and Prime Minister Chrétien all believed promoting the tar sands could expand the beachhead the Liberals had established in the 1993 election when Alberta elected four Liberals. According to McLellan, the oil sands offered a vehicle for correcting the political damage the National Energy Program did to the Liberals in 1980:

> But, Prime Minister Chrétien wanted to make sure that he sent a signal to Alberta and my appointment was part of that ... But, the Prime Minister, when he elected four Liberals in Alberta felt it was obviously important to

have an Alberta cabinet minister ... I think there was a predisposition to reassure Alberta and the industry that as a government we weren't going to do anything stupid because the industry was concerned ... I think certainly Paul Martin would agree that there was a desire to ... do something as long as they made sense ... that would help us politically in the future of Alberta.[113]

In Ottawa then, party-building was one of the motives encouraging the Liberals to participate in reregulating the oil sands. It joined the jobs and investment promised by the Task Force's vision to produce a powerful tonic to win over the support of cabinet and caucus for the tax changes made in 1996.

As both Newell and McLellan underlined, even if the Task Force had prepared an impressive case, this did not mean Ottawa would revise its tax regime. Hard lobbying had to occur in order to deliver change. Guy Boutilier, the young, energetic mayor of first Fort McMurray and then the amalgamated Regional Municipality of Wood Buffalo, took the Task Force's message to the Federation of Canadian Municipalities (FCM) and showed the mayors of Ontario's manufacturing heartland just how many employment and investment benefits would flow to their constituents if Ottawa embraced the Task Force's report. According to Newell, this helped make this vision a national issue and "that's why the FCM went to Paul Martin and said you should support it."[114] Boutilier also made a point of emphasizing to Sheila Copps, the federal Deputy Prime Minister and Minister of the Environment, how many jobs the Task Force's vision promised to deliver to the steelworkers in Copps's Hamilton constituency.[115] The Building Trades of Alberta, Alberta's peak association representing more than a dozen construction unions, "flooded the Prime Minister's Office with these ballot cards from all the workers saying support the oil sands task force because this is creating great jobs for us."[116] Suppliers of tar sands materials and equipment were identified and organized by federal constituency and urged to write to their MPs about the economic importance of the oil sands. Through the Canadian Manufacturers Association and the Canadian Exporters Association, Newell was able to draw in what would become two very important government allies for the Task Force—Industry Minister John Manley and Kevin Lynch, his Deputy Minister. Newell convinced them, in part through getting them to spend an afternoon at Syncrude's research and development facilities, that the tar sands business was a very high-technology enterprise and worthy of their support. Industry Canada went on to help Newell sell the Task Force's vision within the federal government.[117] Again this was a cause characterized by a very high level of unity among political and economic elites.

Environmental and/or nationalist arguments were not prominent in shaping the federal reaction to the Task Force's recommendations. Liberal Charles Caccia, arguably the most passionate champion for the environment any political party had in the 1990s, chaired the Standing Committee on Environment and Sustainable Development. The Committee's 1995 report to the government, *Keeping a Promise: Toward a Sustainable Budget,* had the petroleum sector in its crosshairs; it urged the government to reform the tax system since, by the state's own calculations, "the current federal tax system is biased in favour of such high-polluting energy sources as oilsands (20.8% tax benefit) ..."[118] Since the Committee also regarded the oil sands as "highly polluting," it recommended "[t]hat the federal government refrain from injecting any additional tax assistance into oilsands development."[119] For her part, Anne McLellan could not remember the Committee's report as being an important obstacle in the policy-making process, nor could she recall facing much opposition from Environment Minister Sheila Copps.[120] Nor did nationalist concerns regarding supplying petroleum to Canadian consumers figure in federal calculations about the wisdom of extending further tax advantages to the tar sands. The Liberal commitment in their 1993 campaign to try to renegotiate parts of NAFTA, including the Energy chapter, might have provided fuel for nationalist critics within the Liberal party to challenge support for the tar sands. McLellan could not remember this as part of the party's oil sands discussion. "I think that what did motivate us," she suggested, "was the fact that, if the Task Force was right, and their predictions around the reserves that this would provide energy security for us and the United States. I think what probably impressed us, on the energy security side, was that this was a huge resource if one could get it out of the ground profitably it would be an amazing asset for all of us."[121]

"An Era of Unprecedented Growth"[122]

The authors of the final report of the National Task Force on Oil Sands Strategies might have prided themselves for presenting their ambitions to build an oil factory in northeastern Alberta as the epitome of rationality. They sold their vision to governments as a "coordinated plan to foster indus-try efficiency and growth"; they imagined "a series of staged and logical developments over time—25 years." They promised that, by 2020, the strat-egy's "staged expansions" would generate anywhere from $21 to $25 billion in investments; oil sands production would triple.

These ambitions were quickly, easily met. In only nine years, from 1996 to 2004, investors poured an estimated $29 billion into new projects plus an additional $4.8 billion to sustain existing ventures.[123] In 14 years, not 25, tar sands production tripled; by 2015 Alberta produced more than four times the bitumen and synthetic crude oil it had generated in 1995. Appendix 1 illustrates this and shows that every year, starting in 2009, has seen a new production record set. The financial crisis of 2007, the crash in oil prices from the summer of 2008 until the spring of 2009, and the sharp post-2014 reduction in oil prices did little to slow down the boom in production. In June 2014 the CAPP predicted that by 2020, the end of the Task Force's timeline, tar sands production will be 3.06 million barrels per day—compared to the roughly 750,000 barrels per day that were dug and pumped out of Alberta's boreal forest in 1995.[124] Thousands of jobs—in construction, plant operations, manufacturing, and ancillary goods and services—were created, helping Alberta to boast either the lowest or second lowest provincial unemployment rate in Canada from 1996 to 2008. The Oil Sands Developers Group, a business association, told Rotarians in Fort McMurray in 2009 that more than 5,000 permanent project operations jobs had been created between 1998 and 2007, nearly twice the number to be found at the beginning of that decade. They claimed those jobs generated a further three local jobs and six national ones; none of this tally included the 27,500 construction workers then employed in the oil sands sector.[125]

It should be emphasized that world oil prices did not drive the first, late-1990s rush into this era of unprecedented growth. West Texas Intermediate (WTI) crude oil spot prices broke above $30 per barrel for only three months during the 1990s (the first three months after Iraq invaded Kuwait in August 1990). For 69 months in this decade WTI traded below $20 per barrel; it sank as low as $11.35 per barrel as the debilitating impact of the Asian financial crisis worked its way through the global economy. For the rest of this period, WTI traded between $20 and $30 per barrel.[126] The Gulf War, the collapse of Russian oil production after the dissolution of the Soviet Union, strikes in Nigeria, and cuts to OPEC production quotas couldn't generate any sustained momentum for higher oil prices. And if industry pundits believed oil prices were going to soar throughout much of the first decade of the twenty-first century, they kept those beliefs to themselves. The first wave of fortune seeking in Alberta's Athabasca tar sands after 1995 was technology- and policy-driven; it wasn't price-driven.

This wave of fortune seeking also wasn't particular rational. It more resembled a free-for-all than the promised "coordinated plan to encourage efficiency and growth." US Federal Reserve Board Chairman Alan Greenspan coined the phrase "irrational exuberance" in 1996 to describe investors overenthusiastically pushing stock market values higher and higher. "We as central bankers," he said, "need not be concerned if a collapsing financial asset bubble does not threaten to impair the real economy, its production, jobs, and price stability."[127] What began to take shape in Alberta was a "real economy" version of irrational exuberance, one with long-term risks to capital that policy makers ignored.

The rush to get a piece of the tar sands action may or may not have unduly boosted the stock market values of tar sands producers; it certainly and often dramatically escalated the costs of building and operating tar sands projects. Remember that, through the 1980s and into the 1990s, capital and operating costs in the tar sands were shrinking. In 2000, the NEB put estimated total supply costs for an integrated bitumen mining/upgrading project in a range between C$15 and $18 per barrel in 1997 dollars (C$21.36 and $25.64 per barrel in 2016 dollars).[128] Just six years later, the NEB reported these costs had essentially doubled—to between C$36 and $40 per barrel in 2005 dollars (or between C$43.33 and $48.14 per barrel in 2016 dollars).[129] The CAPP told a similar story; they argued against increases to the province's oil sands royalties in part based on the fact that capital costs had tripled from 2001 to 2007. When Suncor's Millennium project was completed in 2001, its final bill was $3.3 billion or $33,000 per daily barrel of plant capacity (the plant's capacity was 100,000 barrels per day). In 2007, the capital costs of a 100,000-barrel mining/upgrading operation had jumped to $10 billion or $100,000 per daily barrel.[130] Some of the staggering cost overruns seen during this period were: Athabasca Oil Sands Project expansion—$14.3 billion rather than the initial estimate of $3.5 billion (308% increase); Imperial Oil's Kearl Project—$12.9 billion instead of $8 billion (61% increase); CNRL's Horizon project phase I—$9.7 billion rather than $6.8 billion (43% increase). In its 2013 update to supply costs in the tar sands, the Canadian Energy Research Institute estimated it would cost about $14.85 billion or $129,122 per barrel of capacity to build a 115,000 barrels per day integrated operation.[131] The total supply cost at the point where upgraded bitumen would be ready to be shipped south by pipeline in this reference case scenario was $99.02 per barrel.[132] Irrational exuberance in the tar sands dramatically increased the costs, and potential economic risks, of participating in this boom.

It also turned on its head the expectations of where Alberta's bitumen would be upgraded. As Paul Precht and the Fort McMurray First Nations pointed out, in 2008 the ERCB believed that 73 percent of the growth in bitumen production would be upgraded in Alberta in 2014. In fact, only 27 percent of this new production was upgraded in the province. The explanation for this rests largely in the escalating costs that came with the boom. Competitive advantages to build upgraders in Alberta vanished in the wake of that escalation.[133] Government reregulated the tar sands sector in such a fashion that it crippled the expansion of upgrading, with the jobs and measure of diversification it would have supplied.

We cannot say whether the quadrupling of supply costs in just over a decade will constitute a mortal threat to tar sands capital sometime in the future. What we can say with certainty, though, is that the Canadian state, through the fiscal regime it constructed in the 1990s, helped conjure escalating project costs, more expensive break–even thresholds, heightened economic risks, and a less-diversified petroleum sector. In setting the terms for exploiting the tar sands, Canadian governments didn't adopt fiscal measures that encouraged, let alone demanded, fiscal discipline from tar sands companies. The regime shielded companies from much of the financial pain they should have felt from staggering cost overruns. Part of this shield appeared as Alberta's 1 percent royalty on gross project revenues until a project reached payout.[134] Cost overruns extended the length of time companies could operate under the umbrella of the province's minimal royalty; it delayed the day they might be required to pay higher royalties to the owners of the resource.[135] The federal government's accelerated depreciation allowance for oil sands projects also shielded companies from bearing damaging short-term consequences from cost overruns. Pigeon noted that the federal accelerated capital cost allowance provided "the full write-off of capital costs before a mine starts to pay income tax." Tar sands principals were able to fully recover all of their capital costs before they paid any federal income tax. It enabled those principals to protect the early income from their projects from government.[136] Cost overruns other industries couldn't write off for years were written off immediately in the tar sands. "While nobody is saying the fiscal benefits created the overruns," George Koch wrote, "they sure softened the impact."[137] The first half of Koch's assessment may be too generous.

Conclusion

Canada's mammoth oil factory in Alberta's Athabasca tar sands is built on fact and myth. The geological fact is that northeastern Alberta is a treasure chest that holds billions of barrels of petroleum. But from this fact a myth was constructed about why these treasures weren't being developed in the late twentieth century. The myth asserted that this tremendous opportunity hadn't been seized because the federal and provincial regulatory and taxation regimes made it impossible to profitably exploit the tar sands. This simply wasn't true. The financial reports of Suncor and Syncrude in the 1980s and 1990s plus the praise these firms received in the business press then plainly refute this contention.

Developments in the global petroleum economy and domestic politics, especially in Alberta, shaped government policy responses to this myth. Its exaggerations fit well with economic liberal policies elsewhere in the world crafted to respond to OPEC's increased influence. If Alberta wanted to play a role in the West's search for secure, stable petroleum production, then it too should follow the liberal path. If a heavy oil producer and competitor such as Venezuela was dropping royalty and taxation rates to secure tens of billions of dollars in investments from international capital, then Alberta needed to do the same. Venezuela, unlike the US oil shales, was a real threat to Alberta's position in the contest to increase production.

The idea of reregulating the tar sands in order to become "Venezuela North" found fertile soil in post-1992 Alberta. The Klein government, more than any other government in Canada, approximated the ideological orientation of the administrations of Margaret Thatcher and Ronald Reagan. This orientation inspired Klein's first energy minister, and Patricia Nelson used it to help bring a tar sands version of market fundamentalism to life. It didn't matter that, in the view of previous Progressive Conservative administrations, the fiscal terms of exploiting the tar sands were, at worst, fair. But as important as Nelson and her unabashedly pro-business mindset was, this expression of reregulation wasn't controversial in Alberta or Canada. There was a remarkable degree of elite unity about the wisdom of making the fiscal changes she initiated. Labour and opposition political parties joined business and government in forming a consensus that these changes must be made.

What unfolded in Alberta and Canada in the 1990s conformed well to the relationship between the state and capital in Venezuela that Betancourt described at the outset of this chapter. Market fundamentalism in the tar sands was facilitated by turning over de facto decision-making authority to industry—whether around the conference tables of the National Task Force on Oil Sands Strategies or the kitchen table of Alberta's energy minister. The regulatory changes governments subsequently introduced, such as accelerated depreciation allowances and lower royalty rates on bitumen—a less valuable commodity than synthetic crude oil—shifted risk off corporate shoulders and onto those of the state and taxpayers. The public treasury sacrificed the certainty of financial returns from resource ownership today for the possibility of returns in the future.

There can be no dispute that these regulatory changes, when married to corporate success in cutting operating costs, triggered a staggering flood of investment across northeastern Alberta. The billions of dollars that so quickly poured into building Canada's oil factory testifies to the investment success of the new fiscal regime. But, ironically perhaps, this stunning, unanticipated investment triumph produced a troubling set of issues for developing the tar sands. Alberta's reregulation, specifically the 1 percent royalty until payout, relaxed corporate discipline with respect to managing project costs. It contributed to dramatic escalations in those costs and supply costs; it thereby reduced the competitiveness and viability of tar sands operators in any future lower global oil price environment. Such soaring costs, compounded by a sharp rise in the Canadian dollar between 2001 and 2008, also deflated hopes that a boom in raw bitumen production would increase Alberta's capacity to upgrade bitumen into higher-value products. Given the vagaries of petroleum prices, it is far from certain that, for tar sands companies, this manifestation of market fundamentalism has contributed positively to "the order that they need for their own long-term accumulation of capital."[138] As the next chapter demonstrates, it certainly isn't the case that tar sands interests have constructed an order that treats nature well.

Notes

1   CAPP, *Oil Sands*, 40.

2   David Ebner, "Suncor, Syncrude May Feel Less Pain from Royalties Increase," *Globe and Mail*, September 27, 2007.

3   Alberta Royalty Review Panel, *Our Fair Share: Report of the Royalty Review Panel to the Hon. Lyle Oberg, Minister of Finance* (Edmonton: Department of Finance, 2007), 8.

4   Anne McLellan, interview by Adriana A. Davies, *Petroleum History Society Oil Sands Oral History Project*, Glenbow Museum, Calgary, Alberta, July 11, 2011, transcript, 10.

5   Yergin, *The Prize*, 746–51. Matthew Simmons offers a different explanation, the technical need to rest oilfields that had been overproducing, for the Saudi production cutbacks in the 1980s. See Matthew R. Simmons, *Twilight in the Desert: The Coming Saudi Oil Shock and the World Economy* (Hoboken, NJ: John Wiley and Sons, 2005), 65–67.

6   In January, the US refiner acquisition cost of imported crude oil was $24.93. See United States Energy Information Administration, "U.S. Crude Oil Imported Acquisition Cost by Refiners," https://www.eia.gov/dnav/pet/hist/LeafHandler.ashx?n=PET&s=R1300____3&f=M.

7   Dennis Slocum, "Profit Falls 87 Per Cent at Suncor," *Globe and Mail*, April 25, 1986, B1; "The chairman of Suncor of Canada, Mr. Bill Loar, has said his company may close its Alberta oil sands plant if world prices stay depressed," *Lloyd's List International*, April 29, 1986.

8   Diane Francis, "Canada's Ailing Oil Sands Plants Desperately Need Government Aid," *Toronto Star*, May 1, 1986, E3.

9   Waddell, "Federal Aid," 1986, B1.

10 Eric Newell, interview by Robert Bott, *Petroleum History Society Oil Sands Oral History Project*, Glenbow Museum, Calgary, Alberta, May 25, 2011, transcript, 16. "Alberta Cuts Royalties, Plans Expansion Loan for Oil Sands Plants," *Wall Street Journal*, April 29, 1986.

11   Bernard Simon, "Old Habits Die Hardest: Canada's Energy Policy," *Financial Times*, March 12, 1987; Derek Ferguson, "Tories vs. Tories over Alberta Oil," *Toronto Star*, January 8, 1987, A14. Initially Alberta offered to loan Syncrude $200 million for its expansion. However, the province's displeasure with Ottawa's refusal to increase its assistance to Syncrude led Alberta to reduce its loan by 17 percent—the percentage of the joint venture held by Petro-Canada, then a wholly owned state corporation.

12   Andrea Gordon, "Suncor Plans Step Up in Spending," *Toronto Star*, May 1, 1987, E5.

13   Alberta Chamber of Resources, *Athabasca Oil Sands Opportunities*, 5.

14   Gordon, "Suncor Plans Step Up in Spending."

15   Alberta Chamber of Resources, *Athabasca Oil Sands Opportunities*, 9.

16   Canadian Press, "Major Syncrude Project," B6.

17   Larry Welsh, "Canada Pushing Forward Heavy Oil and Tar Sands," *Reuter News*, August 3, 1987.

18   "Syncrude Canada Raises Profile with First-Ever Annual Report," *Toronto Star*, May 25, 1992, C5.

19   Claudia Cattaneo, "$3B Boost for Oilsands," *Financial Post*, November 25, 1997, 1.

20   William C. Symonds, "Congratulations—You Struck Sand," *Business Week*, December 18, 1995, 90.

21   Clyde H. Farnsworth, "Business Technology: Unlocking Oil in Canada's Tar Sands," *New York Times*, December 28, 1994.

22   Kenneth Kidd, "Pumping Profits," *Globe and Mail*, November 15, 1991, P21.

23   "Suncor Earnings Increase 70% in the Quarter," *Business Wire*, April 21, 1994.

24   Cathryn Motherwell, "Suncor to Pump $250-Million in Oil Sands: Report Says $21-Billion Needed over 20 Years," *Globe and Mail*, November 16, 1994, B1.

25   "Canadian Oilsands, Heavy Oil Adjusting to Tough Economics," *Oil and Gas Journal*, July 11, 1994.

26   Mike Ashar, "Canada's Oil Sands: A Globally Competitive Resource, Remarks by Mike Ashar, Executive Vice President, Suncor Energy Inc.," Conference on Energy in the North American Market: Innovation, Investment and a More Secure Future (Washington, DC: June 12, 2003).

27   Newell, interview, May 25, 2011.

28   Ashley Geddes, "Oilsands Task Force Eyes Future Expansion," *Financial Post*, May 25, 1995.

29   Newell, interview, May 25, 2011, 23–26.

30   Dennis Slocum, "Suncor Raises Commitment to Alberta Oil Sands Plant," *Globe and Mail*, July 21, 1987.

31   Paul Precht and Greg Stringham, "Fiscal Treatment of Oil Sands Development in Alberta," in *The Fourth UNITAR/UNDP International Conference on Heavy Crude and Tar Sands, Proceedings, Volume 1: Government, Environment (August 1988)*, ed. Richard F. Meyer and Ernest J. Wiggins (Edmonton: Alberta Oil Sands Technology and Research Authority, 1989), 119.

32   Precht and Stringham, "Fiscal Treatment of Oil Sands." Greg Stringham was the executive director for policy in the provincial Department of Energy in 1988. He subsequently moved from government to the CAPP in 1995. From 1998 until 2016 he was the Association's vice-president of markets and oil sands. He is now the President of GS3 Strategies, a Calgary-based consulting firm.

33 Donna Korchinski, "Drillers Turning to Alberta's Tar Sands," *Financial Post*, June 14, 1994.

34 John Southerst, "Through the Wringer," *Canadian Business*, August 1993.

35 "Newell's $21B Ambition: Syncrude Declares Tar Sands a 'National Priority,'" *Western Report*, December 5, 1994.

36 Symonds, "Congratulations—You Struck Sand."

37 Yergin, *The Prize*, 654.

38 Prudhoe Bay, Ekofisk, and Forties produced 871 million barrels of oil in 1980. See Norway Petroleum Directorate, *Annual Report 1980*, 213; United Kingdom Department for Business, Energy & Industrial Strategy, *Crude Oil and Petroleum: Production, Imports and Exports 1890 to 2015*, https://www.gov.uk/government/statistical-data-sets/crude-oil-and-petroleum-production-imports-and-exports-1890-to-2011; Alaska Department of Revenue, Tax Division, *Alaska Oil Production, Production History FY* 1959–2012*, http://www.tax.alaska.gov/sourcesbook/AlaskaProduction.pdf. Author's calculations.

39 Pratt, *Tar Sands*, 60–62.

40 Pratt, *Tar Sands*, 72.

41 W. J. Yurko, "Development of the Alberta Oil Sands," address to the Engineering of Canada Conference (Edmonton, Alberta: April 17, 1974), 29–30.

42 Jason Fekete, "Oilsands Plan Needed Now, Lougheed Says," *Edmonton Journal*, September 3, 2006, A3.

43 Oksan Bayulgen, *Foreign Investment and Political Regimes: The Oil Sector in Azerbaijan, Russia, and Norway* (Cambridge: Cambridge University Press, 2010), 191.

44 Daniel Johnston, *International Petroleum Fiscal Systems and Production Sharing Contracts* (Tulsa, OK: Penwell Publishing, 1994), 244.

45 Bayulgen, *Foreign Investment and Political Regimes*, 192. Economic rent may be defined as "the income remaining after the investor has recovered all project capital and operating costs, including a competitive return on investment." Auditor General of Alberta, *Annual Report of the Auditor General of Alberta 2006–2007* (September 2007), 98.

46 Johnston, *International Petroleum Fiscal Systems*, 255.

47 Bernard Mommer, *The New Governance of Venezuelan Oil* (Oxford Institute for Energy Studies: 1998), 38–40.

48 Bayulgen, *Foreign Investment and Political Regimes*, 126; Deborah Gordon and Yevgen Sautin, "Opportunities and Challenges Confronting Russian Oil" (Washington, DC: Carnegie Endowment for International Peace, May 28, 2013), http://carnegieendowment.org/2013/05/28/opportunities-and-challenges-confronting-russian-oil/g6x5.

49 Terry Lynn Karl, *The Paradox of Plenty: Oil Booms and Petro-States* (Berkeley: University of California Press, 1997), 78–79, 90.

50 Mexico offered the first and ultimate challenge to the multinationals when it nationalized their holdings in 1938.

51 Karl, *Paradox of Plenty*, 87; Rómulo Betancourt, *Venezuela: Oil and Politics* (Boston: Houghton Mifflin Company, 1979), 70–80.

52 Mommer, *New Governance of Venezuelan Oil*, 24–32; Thomas J. Pate, "Evaluating Stabilization Clauses in Venezuela's Strategic Association Agreements for Heavy-Crude Extraction in the Orinoco Belt: The Return of a Forgotten Contractual

Risk Reduction Mechanism for the Petroleum Industry," *University of Miami Inter-American Law Review*, 40, no. 2 (2009), 369–70.

53   Mommer, *New Governance of Venezuelan Oil*, 34–37; Leonardo Maugeri, *The Age of Oil: The Mythology, History, and Future of the World's Most Controversial Resource* (Westport, CT: Praeger, 2006), 171.

54   API gravity is the standard measure of the American Petroleum Institute for measuring the density of oil. The lower the number of the API gravity measure, the denser the oil and the more upgrading required in order to produce a synthetic crude oil. The API gravity of both the Orinoco's extra-heavy oil and Alberta's bitumen is less than 10 degrees. Conventional oil has an API gravity of at least 22 degrees. See Richard F. Meyer and Emil D. Attanosi, "Heavy Oil and Natural Bitumen—Strategic Petroleum Resources," US Department of the Interior, US Geological Survey Fact Sheet 70–03 (August 2003), http://pubs. usgs.gov/fs/fs070-03/fs070-03.html.

55   Osmel Manzano and Francisco Monaldi, "The Political Economy of Oil Contract Renegotiation in Venezuela," in *The Natural Resources Trap: Private Investment Without Public Commitment*, ed. Federico Sturzenegger and William W. Hogan (Boston: MIT Press, 2010), 439.

56   Peggy Williams, "The Orinoco," *Oil and Gas Investor*, Vol. 17, no. 11 (November 1, 1997). Only a small amount of those reserves were included in the proved reserves counted by organizations such as BP and the *Oil and Gas Journal*. BP nearly doubled Venezuela's proved reserves, to 172.3 billion barrels, in its 2010 statistical review of world energy. This near doubling was due to moving more of the Orinoco belt into the proved reserves category. Today, treating extra-heavy oil as proved reserves has catapulted Venezuela to the top of the world's proved oil reserves list. Its 298.3 billion barrels surpass Saudi Arabia's 265.9 billion barrels and Canada's 169.7 billion barrels. BP, *BP Statistical Review of World Energy June 2014*, http://www.bp.com/content/dam/bp-country/de_de/PDFs/brochures/ BP-statistical-review-of-world-energy-2014-full-report.pdf, 6.

57   Juan Carlos Boué, "Enforcing *Pacta Sunt Servanda*? Conoco-Phillips and Exxon-Mobil versus the Bolivarian Republic of Venezuela and Petróleos de Venezuela," *Centre of Latin American Studies, University of Cambridge* (Working Papers Series 2, No. 1), 8.

58   "Foreign Companies Racing to Get Piece of Venezuela's Oil Action," *Knight-Ridder Tribune Business News*, November 9, 1997.

59   Manzano and Monaldi, "Political Economy," 439–440. Mommer notes the delay in finalizing the royalty terms. Mommer, *New Governance*, 62. Marsh, citing Monaldi's doctoral dissertation, mistakenly claims that the Cerro Negro and Hamaca projects paid no royalties. Brandon Marsh, "Preventing the Inevitable: The Benefits of Contractual Risk Engineering in Light of Venezuela's Recent Oil Field Nationalization," *Stanford Journal of Law, Business and Finance* 13, no. 2 (Spring 2008).

60   Manzano and Monaldi, "Political Economy," 457–58. Previously, disputes were settled by Venezuelan courts as required by the Venezuelan Constitution and law. Mommer, *New Governance*, 48.

61   Tamsin Carlisle, "Arden Haynes: Man in the Middle," *Financial Post*, January 28, 1991, 7; Chastko, *Developing Alberta's Oil Sands*, 209.

62   Eric Newell, interview by author, October 5, 2006.

63   Eric Newell, interview by author, October 5, 2006.

64 "Canada and Alberta Announce Strengthened R&D Effort for Oil Sands and Heavy Oil," *Canada Newswire*, March 19, 1993.

65 Block, "Ruling Class Does Not Rule," 1977, 13.

66 Eric Newell, "Aboriginal Employment at the Athabasca Tar Sands," *Canadian Business and Current Affairs: Canadian Speeches* 7, no. 5 (September 1993).

67 "Oil Strategy Is Outdated," *Financial Post*, January 14, 1993, 14.

68 The Canadian Centre for Policy Alternatives reported that, between 1988 and 1992, Ottawa devoted approximately $3 billion to the Hibernia project through a combination of grants, loan guarantees, and an equity position. See John Jacobs, "CCPA-NS Presentation to the Public Review Commission on Oil and Gas Exploration off the Coast of Cape Breton" (January 2002), http://www.policyalternatives.ca/publications/reports/ccpa-ns-presentation-public-review-commission-oil-and-gas-exploration-coast-cap.

69 Elaine Verlicky, "Investors Stick with Their Oil-Sands Projects—One of the World's Richest Mineral Deposits," *Petroleum Economist*, January 13, 1993.

70 "Syncrude Sets New Oil Production Mark," *Canada Newswire*, September 18, 1992.

71 "Canadian Oilsands, Heavy Oil Adjusting to Tough Economics," *Oil and Gas Journal*, July 11, 1994.

72 "Development Strategy for North America," *Enhanced Energy Recovery and Refining News* 18, no. 8 (March 1, 1995).

73 Pat Daniel, another Oil Sands Task Force member and vice-president of Interprovincial Pipeline Ltd. (Interprovincial became Enbridge in 1998), warned on several occasions that imports would rise if governments did not adopt a fiscal regime encouraging oil sands development. See "Oil Sands Industry Seeks $2.8 Billion Tax Break," *Toronto Star*, May 20, 1995; Dan Rogers, "Canadians Seek Tax Relief to Develop Sands," *Journal Record*, June 7, 1995.

74 Eric P. Newell, "The Oil Sands: A New Energy Vision for Canada," Remarks by Eric P. Newell, President, Alberta Chamber of Resources at the Launch of the Report of the National Task Force on Oil Sands Strategies (Edmonton, Alberta: May 18, 1995).

75 Eric Newell, interview by author, October 5, 2006.

76 Newell, "Oil Sands."

77 National Task Force on Oil Sands Strategies, *The Oil Sands: A New Energy Vision for Canada* (Edmonton: Alberta Chamber of Resources, 1995), 14.

78 National Task Force on Oil Sands Strategies, *Oil Sands*.

79 Newell, "Oil Sands," 6. Science and technology was regarded as the second key lever since technological changes already had delivered important, significant improvements in profitability. The Task Force expected government to play a substantial role here too—but essentially only in the unprofitable basic research stage and in ensuring that the state's fiscal and regulatory frameworks encouraged industrial development.

80 If a firm reported operating costs of $100 million, then a 10 percent uplift would let that firm deduct $110 million for royalty calculation purposes.

81 National Task Force on Oil Sands Strategies, *A Recommended Fiscal Regime for Canada's Oil Sands Industry, Appendix C; Fiscal Report* (Edmonton: Alberta Chamber of Resources, 1995), 2.

82 Canadian Association of Petroleum Producers, "Submission: Bitumen Pricing Methodology for SEC Reserves Disclosure" (Calgary: CAPP, September 2005), 1.

83   Canadian Association of Petroleum Producers, "Submission: Bitumen Pricing Methodology," 5. Subsequently CAPP wrote to the Securities and Exchange Commission that, over the 2003–07 period, the average bitumen price as a percentage of West Texas Intermediate was just 44 percent.

84   Jonathan Law and John Smullen, eds., *A Dictionary of Finance and Banking*, 4th ed. (Oxford: Oxford University Press, 2008).

85   Alberta Royalty Review Panel, *Our Fair Share*, 79.

86   National Task Force on Oil Sands Strategies, *Recommended Fiscal Regime*, 2. NRR refers to net revenue royalty and LTBR refers to the Canadian government's long-term bond rate.

87   The terms of the Suncor and Imperial royalty agreements called for those firms to pay either 30 percent of net revenues or 5 percent of gross revenues— whichever was greater. Syncrude paid one-half of the project's net profit to Alberta as its royalty.

88   Masson and Remillard, "Alberta's New Oil Sands Royalty System," 5.

89   Sydney Sharpe, "'Generic' Oilsands Royalty Seen as Boost to Industry," *Financial Post*, December 1, 1995, 3.

90   Gary Park, "New Royalty Expected to Boost Oil Sands Production," *Platt's Oilgram News* 73, no. 232 (December 4, 1995).

91   Paul Precht, interview by Adriana Davies, *Petroleum History Society Oil Sands Oral History Project*, Glenbow Museum, Calgary, Alberta, January 29, 2013, transcript, 10, 12.

92   Patricia Nelson, interview by Brian Brennan, *Petroleum History Society Oil Sands Oral History Project*, Glenbow Museum, Calgary, Alberta, June 28, 2012, transcript, 9.

93   Alberta Economic Development, *Oil Sands Industry Update* (March 2004), 33.

94   Nelson, interview, 9.

95   Nelson, interview, 2.

96   Nelson, interview, 9.

97   Nelson, interview, 12.

98   Alberta Energy, *1994–1995 Annual Report*, 2.

99   "Alberta Energy Branch Restructuring Praised," *Financial Post*, February 16, 1994.

100 Alberta Energy, *1997/98 Annual Report*, 29.

101 The minister reduced her managerial class more significantly than her other salaried employees. The managerial ranks were trimmed by 20.6 percent over this two-year period. See Alberta Energy, *1995–1996 Annual Report*, 47; Alberta Energy, *1996–1997 Annual Report*, 53.

102 Thomas Marr-Laing and Chris Severson-Baker, *Beyond Eco-terrorism: The Deeper Issues Affecting Alberta's Oilpatch* (Drayton Valley, AB: Pembina Institute for Appropriate Development, February 1999), 17.

103 Even when the ministry identified "assessing and collecting the Crown's mineral resource revenue" as a core business in its 1996–97 annual report, it did not add a performance measure to indicate how well it executed this crucial function.

104 The Parkland Institute at the University of Alberta was an exception to this statement. In 1999, the Institute published *Giving Away the Alberta Advantage: Are Albertans Receiving Maximum Revenues from Their Oil and Gas?* (by Bruce Macnab,

James Daniels, and Gordon Laxer). In part, the study pointed to the sharp drop in oil sands royalties that followed the introduction of the generic regime in 1997 and argued that increasing the public's share of resource revenues would not cripple investment. The Institute did not participate, however, in what little public debate took place in 1997 when the changes were introduced.

105 Alberta, Legislative Assembly, *Hansard, 24th Legislature, 1st Session (1997)*, 520, 650, 800.

106 National Task Force on Oil Sands Strategies, *Final Report: A New Era of Opportunity for Canada's Oil Sands* (Edmonton: Alberta Chamber of Resources, 1995), 16–24.

107 Fred Block, "Polanyi's Double Movement and the Reconstruction of Critical Theory," *Revue Interventions économiques* 38 (2008), 9.

108 The royalty rate was blended to take into account whether production came from old leases or new leases. Canadian Oil Sands Trust, *2001 Annual Report*, 9.

109 Suncor Energy Inc., *2002 Annual Report*, 28.

110 Anne McLellan, interview by author, March 9, 2006.

111 Anne McLellan, interview by author, March 9, 2006.

112 Eric Newell, interview by author, October 5, 2006. The finance minister did not deliver good news to the conventional oil and gas industry in the 1996 federal budget. Finance Minister Martin tightened the eligibility rules for the flow-through shares issued by mining and petroleum companies. These shares allowed their owners to claim deductions and/or credits that otherwise would only be available to the company.

113 Anne McLellan, interview by author, March 9, 2006.

114 Eric Newell, interview by author, October 5, 2006.

115 Guy Boutilier, interview by Adriana A. Davies, *Petroleum History Society Oil Sands Oral History Project*, Glenbow Museum, Calgary, Alberta, December 12, 2012, transcript, 8.

116 Boutilier, interview.

117 Boutilier, interview.

118 Canada, Parliament, House of Commons, Standing Committee on Environment and Sustainable Development, *Keeping a Promise: Towards a Sustainable Budget: Report of the Standing Committee on Environment and Sustainable Development* (Ottawa: Canada Communication Group, 1995), 13.

119 Parliament, *Keeping a Promise*, 16.

120 McLellan, interview by author, March 9, 2006.

121 McLellan, interview by author, March 9, 2006.

122 This phrase is taken from National Energy Board, *Canada's Oil Sands*, 1.

123 Alberta Economic Development, *Oil Sands Industry Update* (Spring 2005), 15.

124 CAPP, *Crude Oil: Forecasts, Markets & Transportation*, i.

125 Jacob Irving, *Oil Sands: An Industry Overview* (Oil Sands Developers Group, January 28, 2009).

126 Monthly price data are from United States Department of Energy, Energy Information Administration, *Petroleum & Other Liquids: Cushing, OK WTI Spot Price FOB*, https://www.eia.gov/dnav/pet/hist/LeafHandler.ashx?n=pet&s=rwtc&f=m. According to the Federal Reserve Bank of Minneapolis's inflation calculator $20(US) in 1990 dollars equalled $35.74 in 2013; $30 (US) equalled $53.61. See https://www.minneapolisfed.org.

127 Alan Greenspan, "The Challenge of Central Banking in a Democratic Society," remarks by Chairman Alan Greenspan at the Annual Dinner and Francis Boyer Lecture of the American Enterprise Institute for Public Policy Research (Washington, DC: December 5, 1996), http://www.federalreserve.gov/boarddocs/speeches/1996/19961205.htm.

128 National Energy Board, *Canada's Oil Sands: A Supply and Market Outlook to 2015*, 35. The Bank of Canada's inflation calculator was used to convert the NEB's 1997 dollar estimates into 2016 dollars. Millington and Murillo define supply cost as "the constant dollar price needed to recover all capital expenditures, operating costs, royalties and taxes and earn a specified return on investment." Dinara Millington and Carlos A. Murillo, *Canadian Oil Sands Supply Costs and Development Projects (2012–2046)* (Calgary: Canadian Energy Research Institute, 2013), xiii.

129 National Energy Board, *Canada's Oil Sands: Opportunities and Challenges to 2015: An Update* (Calgary: National Energy Board, 2006), ix. The Bank of Canada's inflation calculator was used to convert 2005 dollars into 2016 dollars.

130 CAPP, *Oil Sands—Benefits to Alberta and Canada*, 12–15.

131 Millington and Murillo, *Canadian Oil Sands Supply Costs*, 18.

132 Millington and Murillo, *Canadian Oil Sands Supply Costs*, 32.

133 Fort McMurray First Nation, *Submission to 2015 Alberta Royalty Review Panel* (Assisted by Paul Precht Energy Economics Ltd.) (September 2015), 23–25.

134 Payout is reached when a project's revenues equal its total supply costs. It is when the project developer "has made profit equal to the capital and operating costs invested in the project, plus an allowance on those costs equal to the long term government bond rate." Alberta Royalty Review Panel, *Our Fair Share*, 60.

135 After payout was reached, projects were required to pay whichever of the following royalty rates were greater—either 25 percent of the project's net revenue (gross revenue minus allowable costs) or 1 percent of gross project revenue.

136 Marc-André Pigeon, "Tax Incentives and Expenditures Offered to the Oil Sands Industry" (Ottawa: Library of Parliament, January 27, 2003), 18.

137 George Koch, "Money Pit," *National Post Business*, July 2004, 70. Koch is now the partner and vice president of Merlin Edge Inc., a Calgary-based strategic marketing and corporate communications company.

138 Evans, "Is an Alternative Globalization Possible?", 280.

4

Landscape of Sacrifice: The Environmental Consequences of Reregulating the Tar Sands

"The Athabasca region itself is not a pristine wilderness. This is scrub land."
- *Clive Mather, President and CEO, Shell Canada, 2005*

"There is a perception painted by some of the environmental community that the oil sands development is proceeding at breakneck speed without regard for damage caused to the environment. This is not the case."
—*Greg Stringham, Canadian Association of Petroleum Producers, 2007*

Introduction

Valerie Kuletz offers a compelling account of the ecological ruin nuclear weapons research, testing, and waste storage delivered to the American west.[1] She coined the phrase "geographies of sacrifice" to describe those areas of the desert west where landscapes were sacrificed for uranium mining and nuclear weapons testing. Kolson Schlosser, in a study of how national security discourse shaped debate surrounding the Arctic National Wildlife Refuge (ANWR), borrows from Kuletz to represent ANWR environmentally as a "landscape of sacrifice."[2] This chapter explores the extent to which reregulating the tar sands turned Alberta's boreal forest into Canada's own landscape of sacrifice during the first decade of the tar sands boom.

Chapter One suggested that Polanyi's concept of the double movement may help in understanding contemporary tar sands politics and policy. Efforts to free markets and to increase business freedom, such as we detailed in the previous chapter, spark the birth of countermovements intent on checking the damage the excesses of self-regulated markets may inflict on their interests and values. Now we consider the place of ecological values in the reregulated tar sands regime and consider the development and effectiveness of an environmental opposition to tar sands development.

In his use of Polanyi's double movement to reconstruct critical social theory, Fred Block notes the importance of opportunities, capacity, and barriers to the ability of agents to challenge and successfully counter those who insist the market doesn't need state direction and constraint.[3] To understand the strength of the environmental countermovement to market fundamentalism in the tar sands, we focus first on the opportunities and barriers raised by political institutions. Tar sands projects require a range of permissions and permits from government; the accompanying regulatory and environmental assessment processes provide one gauge for measuring the presence and strength of an environmentally based opposition to exploiting the tar sands. Given the importance of institutional access and procedures to one's influence, we will be especially cognizant of the extent to which these processes privileged market interests over environmental ones.

Block emphasized the importance of ideological factors to understanding the relative weakness of the protective countermovement in American politics. The popularity of the free market ideal, the commitment of American elites to that ideal, and the activism of the religious right weakened the countermovement's response to dominant laissez-faire culture. We already have seen in the last chapter the relevance of the first two of Block's ideological factors to Alberta's embrace of the generic royalty regime for tar sands. As we'll see in this chapter, the ideological predispositions of regulators toward resource use should also be considered in accounting for the relative importance of environmental issues in the tar sands project approval process.

In examining the opportunities and barriers to environmental critiques of the tar sands, this chapter also asks the reader to appreciate that "all critiques are not created equal." Environmental critiques and actors have ideological predispositions that make them more or less hostile to laissez-faire; they may constitute more or less serious challenges to the laissez-faire policy agenda. Mark Dowie described American environmentalism in the early 1990s as the "polite revolution." The American environmental mainstream was polite, conservative, and compromising. In 1995 he wrote that "even in the face of irreversible degradation," compromise generally had become second nature to American environmentalism.[4] May the same be said about the environmental rebuttal to developing the tar sands? By 2004 nearly 2,000 square kilometres (772 square miles) of "planned regional disturbance" was underway or approved for the boreal forest north of Fort McMurray.[5] When it came to the tar sands—the resource the famous climate scientist Dr. James Hansen would later call "the biggest carbon bomb on the planet"[6]—did environmental critiques emerge during the first decade of the boom? Did they follow the path of compromise or confrontation and to what effect?

State Institutions: No Friends to Environmental Concerns

Alberta's history of resource exploitation is one where governments never tempered the exploitation of natural resources in the name

Figure 2 Tar Sands Operations, north of Fort McMurray, 1984

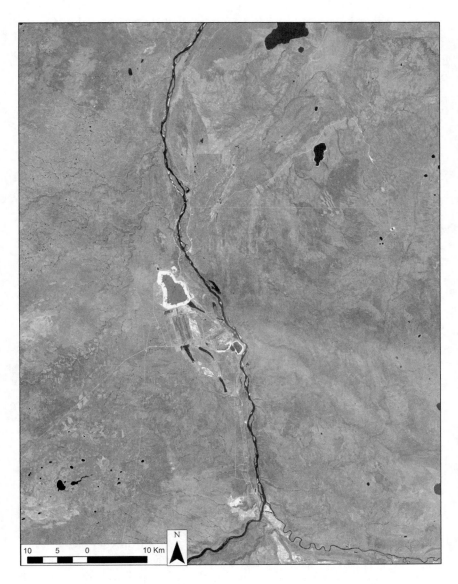

of the environment. This isn't to say that public servants in Alberta and in federal environmental ministries haven't urged their political leaders to privilege environmental considerations. They have, but that counsel simply fell on deaf ears. Tar sands development in the 1970s illustrates this well. Officials from both provincial and federal environment departments raised important, prescient questions and concerns about the environmental consequences of exploiting the tar sands. Alberta officials predicted that tar sands operations would be catastrophic for the boreal ecology.[7] Environment Canada's comments on Syncrude's initial environmental impact assessment warned that the consortium partners seriously underestimated the damage Syncrude would inflict on the northern landscape. To federal environment officials, Syncrude's environmental impact assessment "failed to appreciate the real scope of environmental concerns and ... also failed to address the question of environmental protection in either a realistic or an adequate manner."[8] But policy makers never insisted that industry's plans needed to be environmentally benign in order to proceed. William Yurko, Alberta's first environment minister, argued that exploitation of the tar sands should proceed despite the environmental knowledge and information gaps his officials had identified. Thus it is ironic that, as noted in the previous chapter, Environment Minister Yurko was excited about a possible tar sands development trajectory for the Lougheed administration in the 1970s little different from what has unfolded since the mid-1990s.

Throughout the 1980s and 1990s Alberta's environmental management capacity suffered. Drastic real cuts were made to provincial environmental, recreation, and culture functions during the 1980s.[9] Alberta Premier Ralph Klein, called "Canada's Reagan" and applauded for his tax and spending policies by the free-market Cato and Fraser Institutes, continued to make cuts throughout the 1990s.[10] Between the 1992–93 and 1996–97 fiscal years, the provincial environmental department's budget was cut by 29 percent; staff positions there were slashed by a comparable extent.[11] In the tar sands, ministers such as Patricia Nelson didn't really see the need for strict government environmental oversight since "the industry is harder on themselves than anybody else is."[12] The damage done to the province's environmental capacity was improved only marginally after Alberta eliminated its public debt and deficit, the rationale offered for the public service cuts of the 1990s. Over the first five fiscal years of the twenty-first century, environmental protection expenditures grew at an inflation-adjusted annual rate of just 4 percent.

Alberta's energy regulatory agency—the Energy and Resources Conservation Board (ERCB)[13]—didn't question the lack of political enthusiasm for contemporary understandings of conservation. Taking its cue from the Texas Railway Commission, the Board interpreted conservation in its early years to mean "the efficient use of natural resources, the development of these resources in such a way as to protect the interests of future generations, and the elimination of all economically avoidable waste."[14]

Dr. G.W. Govier, a Board member when he offered this view in 1950, would go on to become the Board's longest serving Chairman—serving in that position from 1962 to 1978. Govier's outlook on conservation had changed little by 1970, the year Alberta created Canada's first environment ministry. He said, "Our environment must be preserved but realism must prevail—we cannot frustrate the development and use of our energy resources."[15] This mindset on priorities remains very germane to understanding the contemporary tar sands regulatory process during the years considered here. It was seen most dramatically when regulators talked about "sterilization" in their assessments of tar sands project applications. Sterilization means leaving bitumen in the ground and not exploiting every last barrel. Projects should avoid or minimize such sterilization; sterilization in this one-dimensional administrative world is definitely not what bitumen exploitation could do to other resources or values. For example, in 2006 the Joint Federal-Provincial Review Panel that approved Albian Sands Energy's application to expand the Muskeg River Mine repeatedly used the term "sterilization" to refer to actions that would prohibit tar sands mining; the term was never used to refer to what exploiting the tar sands would do to other resources or other resource values. This narrow, blinkered view considered conserving culturally valuable archaeological sites as an option that would sterilize mineable bitumen deposits. The reverse relationship, that mining bitumen sterilized the heritage values contained in these sites, was never raised in these terms.[16]

Procedurally the natural order in Alberta was one where environmental voices struggled to be heard in energy regulatory processes. The state took a niggardly, stingy attitude toward allowing environmentalists to participate in the regulatory process pertaining to tar sands project applications. This orientation, with its bias in favour of development, animates Alberta's *Energy Resources Conservation Act*. The ERCB determined if applications to exploit the tar sands needed a public hearing. The Board's decision-making process offered very limited opportunities for third parties to participate when energy companies submitted applications to develop any petroleum project. Legal rights to offer evidence relevant to a project application and to make representations to the Board were established by section 26(2) of the Act. However, the statute only obligated the ERCB to extend these rights to persons who the Board felt might have their rights "directly and adversely" affected by the Board's decision on an application.[17] The ERCB determined what circumstances satisfied this "directly and adversely affected" test. Generally speaking, directly and adversely affected meant a person needed to have rights to lands that would be affected by a development application (such as actual occupancy, fee simple ownership, a grazing lease, or a rental agreement).

The ERCB's narrow interpretation of the "directly and adversely affected" test and the discretionary nature of public hearings was the bane of environmental participation in ERCB decision-making across the range of petroleum exploitation activities in Alberta for decades. A conservation organization such as the Alberta Wilderness Association (AWA), for example, rarely convinced the Board that its concerns over the health of Alberta's landscapes and ecosystems entitled the association to the legal rights found in section 26(2). On those rare exceptions when the ERCB granted the AWA standing under 26(2), it generally was because an individual member of the AWA had land rights that could be affected if the development application was approved.[18]

When environmental groups didn't enjoy standing under section 26(2), the ERCB might have allowed them to intervene in an application process by making a brief presentation to the Board. Crucially, any organization able to participate in this way was not allowed to cross-examine the project applicants; they also were not allowed to submit expert evidence of their own.[19]

With respect to tar sands applications, the vast majority of lands sought for development are Crown or public lands; private occupancy or use rights, other than for Canadian First Nations, don't exist on the vast majority of these lands. This has made it extremely difficult for environmental groups or other interested parties to gain access to regulatory/environmental assessment hearings on tar sands applications. The only environmental organization able to regularly satisfy the very restrictive "directly and adversely affected" test was the Oil Sands Environmental Coalition (OSEC). In the period considered here, OSEC was composed of the Pembina Institute, the Toxics Watch Society of Alberta, and the Fort McMurray Environmental Association. The coalition satisfied the directly and adversely affected test due to the Pembina Institute's legal interest in lands near the First Nations' community of Fort McKay—in the heart of the tar sands surface mining lease area. That interest was "a license to occupy lands on the Muskeg and Athabasca Rivers for recreational purposes, such as camping and boating."[20] The Institute's place in the public record as a persistent, continual environmental participant in regulatory proceedings rested in its ability to present this local and material interest to the ERCB.

The ERCB's status as an independent quasi-judicial agency meant its decisions could not be appealed politically. Neither the energy minister nor the provincial cabinet could overrule the Board. Requests for leave to appeal ERCB decisions on questions of jurisdiction or law could be directed to the Alberta Court of Appeal. When petroleum development ambitions became more and more focused on exploiting the bitumen found on Alberta's public lands, they were judged in a very closed process that was inhospitable to raising environmental concerns. This institutional bias is vital to understanding the relative absence of environmental groups from ERCB or Joint Panel hearings on tar sands projects.[21]

Integrated Resource Planning in Name Only: Sacrificing a Potential World Heritage Site

Some government processes certainly sounded like they would give serious consideration to environmental values. Integrated resource planning was one such process. In principle, integrated resource management offers a comprehensive, holistic, and inclusive approach to making land use decisions. Its positive qualities arise from the premise that all resources and all users will be considered before land use decisions are made. Alberta's integrated resource planning system had been praised as "almost a model land use planning system."[22] Unfortunately, in practice this almost model system was rarely used. The provincial government plunged ahead with massive territorial allocations to pulp, paper, and petroleum companies without first preparing integrated resource plans for the landscapes destined to surrender to industrialization. The idea of establishing protected areas to promote ecological values such as biodiversity was effectively precluded from consideration for most of the public lands in Alberta. Although integrated resource plans were used occasionally to deny or restrict some industrial dispositions from the late 1970s until the early 1990s, the implementation of this approach nonetheless generally was judged to be a failure.[23] By the mid-1990s even the semblance of practising integrated resource management vanished.[24]

The cynical nature of integrated resource planning in the Athabasca tar sands was punctuated repeatedly. Powell writes that, in the 1990s, regional integrated plans being developed in two areas of considerable relevance to tar sands exploitation—northeastern Alberta and the Peace River—were abandoned.[25] When Alberta's Energy and Utilities Board considered Syncrude's application to develop its Aurora Mine project in 1997, Environment Canada embraced the logic of integrated resource management in its comments. The federal department recommended to the Alberta regulators who were deliberating on Aurora "that all future oil sands developments should be considered on a regional cumulative effects basis."[26] Its message was reminiscent of what Canada's environment ministry had concluded about the original Syncrude project 20 years earlier. Environment Canada's 1997 message was that provincial regulators should recognize that behind the Aurora Mine stood another mining project proposal and another and another. The understanding of what constituted responsible environmental assessment had to recognize that a wave of industrialization was about to crest over the boreal landscape and consider that wave's cumulative impact.

The case of the McClelland Lake wetlands emphatically underlines the ultimately dismissive attitude Alberta took to integrated resource planning during the first decade of the tar sands rush. Ecologists and conservationists argued the area is a treasure, a boreal gem. A wetland composed of two beautiful patterned fens is the area's most outstanding aesthetic feature. Hundreds, perhaps thousands, of strings—narrow ridges of shrubs, black spruce, and peat—separate countless flarks—long, narrow, shallow pools of water. Over the centuries they have inscribed an intricate, fishnet-like pattern of flora and water on the landscape. [27] The Alberta Energy and Utilities Board said that the Alberta Wilderness Association described the McClelland wetland complex as a "world-class site;" the provincial regulator used the adjective "exceptional" to characterize peatland expert Diana Horton's description of the McClelland fen, a fen she felt had a beauty rivalling sites in the Canadian Rockies. [28]

The value of wetlands like McClelland Lake should be calculated in more than aesthetics. They perform a suite of vital ecological functions. The McClelland wetlands are home to more than 100 species of birds and to more than a dozen provincially rare plant species. Alberta Environment recognized these wetlands as one of the very few provincial ESAs (Environmentally Significant Areas) found between Fort McMurray and Wood Buffalo National Park. Its larger, North American significance rests in its importance as a waypoint for migratory birds that include the endangered whooping crane. To Richard Thomas, the author of the definitive ecological analysis of Alberta's taiga, the "McClelland fen is a potential World Heritage site."[29]

Before the tar sands rush began, the opinions of Horton and Thomas found strong support in government-sponsored reports and actions. In 1985, the Provincial Parks Department placed a protective notation on part of the McClelland Lake area to flag its recreational potential to other departments and industry. In 1990, a government-commissioned study identified a handful of environmentally significant areas in and around the McClelland Lake wetlands. The patterned fens were regarded as provincially significant; the Athabasca River valley was ranked as nationally significant. The ecological value of the area also enjoyed widespread endorsement from a wide spectrum of local and provincial groups—hunters, trappers, snowmobilers, birders, and other naturalists—groups who sometimes disagree intensely over how landscapes and wildlife should be managed. Responding to an invitation from the Alberta Wilderness Association, these interests came together in the 11-member Northeast Wild Alberta Coalition. The coalition urged government to extend legislated protection to the McClelland Lake wetlands and the surrounding Fort Hills by establishing an ecological reserve and a provincial park.

The coalition was formed in November of 1994, at roughly the mid-point of the four years it took to hammer out a subregional integrated resource plan for the Fort McMurray-Athabasca Oil Sands. The final product appeared to be a very significant environmental victory. In May 1996—one month before the Canadian and Alberta governments would issue their "Declaration of Opportunity" for tar sands development—the provincial cabinet approved the plan and its impressive-sounding management intent for McClelland Lake:

> To protect the natural landscape, which encompasses water, wildlife habitat, ecological and geological features, to ensure aesthetic, recreational, traditional and environmental values.[30]

Consequently, the guidelines in the plan prohibited exploiting the tar sands in the McClelland Lake wetlands, the Clearwater valley, and the McKay tributary adjacent to Fort McKay. Nowhere else in the 7,163 square kilometres (2,765 square miles) covered by this plan, other than in the immediate vicinity of Fort McMurray and the Gregoire Lake area, was surface mining prohibited. Other aspects of this subregional plan promised to protect the ecological resources located in the vicinity of McClelland Lake. The plan urged provincial departments to jointly review the nationally and provincially significant features identified in the larger area containing the patterned fens. It also urged the province to follow the intent outlined for the Fort Hills areas in a government protected areas study. Alberta Environment's boreal forest protected areas study identified McClelland Lake as "an excellent CPA (candidate protected area) worthy of a strenuous protection effort"—an unsurprising opinion since Richard Thomas authored the report.[31] It furthered confirmed the considerable interest shown in ensuring this roughly 200 square kilometre (77 square mile) area—less than 3 percent of the Fort McMurray-Athabasca Oil Sands area—would be spared from tar sands exploitation.

These optimistic developments were threatened first when the province rejected the nominations of the Fort Hills and McClelland Lake wetlands for legislated protection. Then, in just six months, the provincial government crippled the protective potential found in the 1996 integrated resource plan. At the request of TrueNorth Energy, the Canadian subsidiary of Koch Industries, the provincial cabinet amended the plan. TrueNorth requested the amendment in order to mine an additional one billion barrels of oil the company claimed lay beneath the wetland complex. The government obliged in June 2002; the recommended prohibition against surface mining and in situ operations in the McClelland wetlands was lifted. The amended Integrated Resource Management Plan (IRP) welcomed tar sands operations in parts of the wetlands; roughly 50 percent of the wetland complex would be destroyed under TrueNorth's shovel and truck operation. To the government, ripping apart half of a fragile, seamless ecosystem could be accomplished without compromising the remaining wetlands. It was never specified how this happy marriage of mining and ecological integrity could be realized or where any such radical approach had succeeded. This decision also reflected the concerns regulators expressed during True North's public hearings. Alberta's Energy and Utilities Board didn't want to "sterilize" tar sands resources by preventing their exploitation; according to the EUB's decision it was more acceptable to sterilize a potential World Heritage site.[32]

This attack on the substance of the original integrated resource management plan outraged environmentalists. They were just as furious at how the provincial government had manipulated the plan amendment process in order to "ram through" the crucial change sought by TrueNorth Energy. For example, the Alberta Wilderness Association complained that only four working days' notice of the first public information session was provided—with that notice coming in the form of a newspaper advertisement that failed to mention when or where the session would be held. One activist was left to muse, presumably with a healthy dose of understatement, that "[t]hey don't seem to want to make it easy to attend."[33] Any member of the public able to find out when and where the public information forum was going to be held had very few options to participate through this mechanism. The public sessions lasted just two days and were only held in Fort McMurray, a 435-kilometre (270-mile) drive from Edmonton.

The government declared that this brief, poorly advertised consultation was "an essential part of the amendment process." It's hard to believe that, with these characteristics, they felt it was essential to consider opposing voices to the proposed amendment. The character of the process was only one sign the government had decided to amend the plan to allow mining before the consulting began. The government provided background information to the public about TrueNorth's requested amendment. It noted that a new study questioned the uniqueness of the McClelland wetlands. The wetlands were just representative, not unique. But the government didn't tell the public who had paid for this new study. TrueNorth Energy, the company standing to profit from eliminating the original plan's protections, had largely bought and paid for this research. Alberta's failure to draw this significant detail to the public's attention speaks volumes about the government's pro-amendment bias. So too did the decision to allow TrueNorth Energy to promote its project as part of the public information sessions; so too did the decision not to hold any information sessions outside of the Fort McMurray area.

The ease with which the government reversed direction on the future of the McClelland wetlands was facilitated by changes in the province's administrative structure and its leadership. Environmental officials who might have made the case for protection were marginalized from the process. Perennial administrative reorganization is a constant in Alberta's environmental and resource management history. The environmental protection, land/forestry, and other non-petroleum natural resource management functions rested in one department, Alberta Environmental Protection, when the original integrated resource management plan was unveiled. When True-North Energy proposed its amendment, these functions were split between two departments, Alberta Environment and Alberta Sustainable Resource Development. Most significantly, Sustainable Resource Development, not Environment, was entrusted with the leading role in the IRP process. The administrative predisposition within Sustainable Resource Development favoured exploiting resources. In a previous incarnation as the Department of Forestry, Lands, and Wildlife, many of its bureaus had promoted the industrialization of most of Alberta's boreal forest in the late 1980s through a massive and generously state-sponsored expansion of the pulp and paper sector.[34] The department's head, Deputy Minister Dr. R. J. (Bob) Fessenden, had cut his industrial teeth in the tar sands where he spent four years leading Syncrude's efforts at planning landscape reclamation and environmental impact assessment. TrueNorth Energy's ability to take advantage of these administrative circumstances was not likely harmed by the knowledge and contacts Peter Kinnear, TrueNorth's Director of Government and Regulatory Affairs, acquired during his previous employment as provincial public servant and ministerial assistant. Kinnear's public sector experience included four years as executive assistant to Forestry Minister LeRoy Fjordbotten during the heyday of Alberta's pulp and paper boom. Then, after leaving Fjordbotten's office, Kinnear spent six years in a senior communications position with the provincial regulator of the petroleum industry, the Alberta Energy and Utilities Board.

When it comes to valuing ecological concerns during the first decade of the tar sands boom, the government served ample helpings of rhetoric but little real change. As Timoney and Lee pointedly observe, "A wit has commented: 'After all is said and done, all they've done is said.'"[35] That observation is reflected especially well in the place of integrated resource management and planning in exploiting Alberta's tar sands.

The Cumulative Environmental Management Association: Too Little, Too Late[36]

On April Fool's Day in 2004, Liberal MLA Don Massey asked Lorne Taylor, Alberta's environment minister, who was responsible for considering and managing the cumulative effects of coal-bed methane exploitation. Taylor's response seemed particularly apt for a day known for practical jokes. He offered a positive, rather upbeat, assessment of the Cumulative Environmental Management Association (CEMA). The Association was tackling environmental issues associated with the oil sands. It was working "quite well"; it was "trying to do some very creative and exciting things" with respect to managing oil sands-related environmental impacts.[37] Taylor's optimism seemed to confirm initial assessments of what CEMA could deliver. One account published soon after CEMA held its first meeting lauded its potential to manage the regional cumulative environmental effects of exploiting the oil sands. It was "a model initiative."[38] If a model initiative demanded substantive, timely action, CEMA was destined to be a spectacular failure.

The previous chapter noted how the state effectively privatized the policy process through the National Task Force on Oil Sands Strategies. That industry-dominated task force crafted the key elements of the tar sands strategy that the federal and provincial governments largely endorsed. CEMA was an environmental version of the National Oil Sands Task Force. Alberta's environment department called it an "industry-led multi-stakeholder group."[39] In November 2000 it boasted 41 members. Industry contributed 41 percent of these members; governments claimed 27 percent of its members; First Nations had 17 percent of the membership; environmentalists, with 15 percent of the CEMA membership, had the smallest representation.[40] The lion's share of funding for CEMA (approximately $3 million in 2001 and $5.5 million in 2005) came from industry; for the most part the provincial and federal governments offered in-kind support to the organization's activities.[41]

The seed of CEMA was planted in 1997 in the midst of a flurry of tar sands approvals and proposals. Provincial regulators had just approved Suncor's Steepbank mine; Syncrude's Aurora Mine was also approved; Petro-Canada announced its intent to proceed with the MacKay River in situ project; Shell Canada declared its commitment to develop the Muskeg River mining project. In the light of these projects and proposals, state agencies doubted whether the normal project-by-project approach to environmental assessment could handle well the likely pace and scope of tar sands exploitation. We already have noted that, in its submission regarding Syncrude's Aurora project, Environment Canada worried that environmentally assessing projects one at a time underestimated cumulative environmental effects. The Pembina Institute for Appropriate Development, the environmental group with the longest, most well-researched participation in tar sands regulatory/assessment hearings, echoed Environment Canada.[42]

During consideration of Syncrude's Aurora application by the Alberta Energy and Utilities Board (AEUB), Syncrude argued that the company and its fellows in the tar sands were sensitive and responsive to these concerns.[43] Syncrude told the AEUB that, left to their own devices, tar sands companies already had begun to coordinate between themselves the tasks of environmental assessment, monitoring, and planning.[44] The AEUB, in approving Aurora, also called for a regional approach to bitumen mining in order "to ensure optimal recovery and the protection of the environment."[45] The AEUB, although unwilling to delegate all of the responsibility to the companies for such matters, was sympathetic to Syncrude's assessment. Unlike the Environment Canada and Pembina Institute calls for a regional approach, the AEUB made it very clear it believed the tar sands companies should take the leading role. "The companies that will develop the resource," the AEUB said, "should lead the process. Government agencies representing the interests of the public should have a smaller yet influential role in ensuring those interests are protected in any eventual agreement."[46] To the AEUB, private industry should be the primary steward of the public interest.

Tar sands companies seemed to anticipate this opening for, as the AEUB was still considering Syncrude's application, they formed an industry-led organization to evaluate the cumulative effects of tar sands exploitation at the regional level. CEMA, which held its inaugural meeting in June 2000, was the ultimate fruit of that initiative. CEMA's record, as we will see now, demonstrated just how poisonous this fruit would be for the environment. This "model initiative" frustrated, rather than promoted, sustainable development.

CEMA was entrusted with implementing the Athabasca Regional Sustainable Development Strategy. This strategy, like the words of so many other Alberta sustainable development commitments, looked impressive at first glance. The strategy sought to establish "a framework for managing cumulative environmental effects and to ensure sustainable development in the Athabasca oil sands area"; it was called a pilot project for integrated resource management in the boreal forest.[47] Seventy-two environmental concerns were identified and prioritized.[48] When the strategy was unveiled in July 1999, it stated that management objectives for the five most urgent themes (of 14 identified) would be established within two years. It promised that these most urgent concerns would be tackled within three years.[49] This strategy sounded impressive enough to receive a bronze Premier's Award of Excellence; its authors were celebrated for developing "a strategy that will help resolve upcoming environmental issues."[50]

The provincial government handed over the crucial task of implementing the strategy to CEMA, an organization Minister Taylor made a point of saying wasn't "a government organization."[51] The Pembina Institute, a founding member of CEMA, regarded the organization as a policy maker.[52] In line with this expectation, CEMA's job was to formulate management objectives and options; their recommendations would be "reviewed and implemented" by regulators.[53] The federal-provincial review panel that assessed Shell Canada's Jackpine project also felt government had delegated environmental policy making to CEMA. The joint review panel expected "environmental management objectives and systems to be developed through CEMA and approved by government."[54]

CEMA's policy recommendations were the product of consensus; consensus decision making, in the words of a former executive director of CEMA, "makes for an easy sell for the government to act upon."[55] Some will see this consensus-based decision making as desirable. Actors from various sectors will collaborate and be able to resolve environmental problems without resorting to confrontational or adversarial options such as litigation.[56]

A second, less generous interpretation is preferred in these pages. It asserts that insisting on consensus is a convenient strategy for a reluctant regulator. We've already seen this reluctance and evidence that Alberta did not place great value on environmental stewardship. The government's miserly environmental protection budget, cuts to staff, and the AEUB's perennial refusal to consider broad socioeconomic and environmental concerns in its decision making all feed this suspicion.[57] From this vantage point, the state is more interested in appearing to treat its environmental stewardship responsibilities seriously; genuinely fulfilling those responsibilities is not important. In this circumstance government tries to maintain public confidence by stressing the merits of the nonconfrontational process itself; actual outcomes matter far less. Government deflected questions about substantive progress by emphasizing the need to respect the integrity of the consensus-based decision-making process. Snail-like progress, or no progress at all, in reaching substantive goals could be blamed on the difficulties of building trust among the participants, the problems of assembling expertise and gathering information, unrealistically optimistic decision-making deadlines, or just the enormity and complexity of the mandate. Perversely, process trumps the substantive goals the consensus-based process was conjured to realize—in this case an effective cumulative effects management regime.

This more critical interpretation is supported by CEMA's poor performance in realizing its goals and the government's failure to step in and regulate as if environmental stewardship was an important priority. Questions about CEMA's effectiveness could have been asked early. In 2001 the government's progress report on implementing the Regional Sustainable Development Strategy admitted that the strategy's timeline for setting management objectives for the most urgent themes would not be met. Not a single management objective had been set, but two new tar sands projects, the MacKay River and Christina Lake in situ projects, had been approved by the AEUB. Issue complexity, the desire to be thorough, and the "interactive nature of the partnership process" (whatever that meant) had made the strategy's substantive goals unrealistic.[58] Such factors meant the failure to meet the original targets was not really a failure at all; it was instead a "setback" or a "delay."

Reassuringly, the government reported that management objectives were likely to appear later in 2001. Several months later CEMA confirmed this would not happen. Not all of the management objectives for the most urgent themes would be forthcoming by then. The delivery of interim management objectives was now forecast to arrive sometime after the fall of 2001.[59] By August 2002, CEMA had approved only one management objective, for trace metals. Before Alberta Environment approved this recommendation, the AEUB had approved TrueNorth Energy's application to produce 190,000 barrels per day of bitumen from its Fort Hills property. Two other tar sands mines—Canadian Natural Resources Ltd.'s 270,000 barrels per day Horizon project and Shell Canada's 200,000 barrels per day Jackpine project—were about to apply for regulatory approval from Alberta and Canada. As project after project lined up for regulatory approval, hard questions about CEMA's worth should have been asked. Clearly what Alberta Environment called just a "delay" or "setback" in failing to set basic management objectives for the most urgent environmental themes was much more serious.

The revised timelines for producing management systems to fulfill the purposes of the Regional Sustainable Development Strategy, like many well-intentioned New Year's resolutions, came to nothing. One vital CEMA group, the Sustainable Ecosystems Working Group, dealt with its inability to define baseline conditions and set management objectives in a timely fashion by jumping to the task of identifying management tools. Logically, this put the cart before the horse. The Reclamation Working Group simply abandoned the effort to set management objectives. By late 2005, CEMA had sent just four recommendations to the government. Only two of those recommendations contained management objectives. No management objectives had been recommended for land or river water quality/instream river flows. From CEMA's creation in 2000 until that point in time, five tar sands projects in the Fort McMurray area promising to produce at least 750,000 barrels of bitumen per day had received the state's blessing; these projects would deliver that bitumen by ripping apart tens of thousands of acres of the boreal landscape. Given this record it is not surprising the provincial government only published one progress report on implementing the Regional Sustainable Development Strategy and stopped publishing *Sustainable Times*, a periodic update on CEMA, in July 2003. For a provincial government unwilling or unable to take its environmental stewardship responsibilities seriously, the less light shed on this policy failure the better. Keeping CEMA out of public sight would keep this industry-led policy-making institution, and the rapidly deteriorating ecological situation in the Athabasca tar sands region its inaction was contributing to, out of the public's mind.

The Pembina Institute and the Limits of the Reformist Critique

During the first decade of the tar sands boom the Pembina Institute, on its own and through OSEC in which it provided vital expertise and capacity, led the environmental critique of development. Pembina was undoubtedly the single best source of information on the environmental impacts of tar sands exploitation. Through publications such as *Oil Sands Fever*, the Pembina Institute emerged as Alberta's most-recognized environmental critic of unbridled tar sands growth.

In part, Pembina's importance as the flag bearer of environmental concerns was due to the biases of Alberta's regulatory institutions noted earlier. The "directly and adversely affected" test was difficult for Alberta environmental organizations to satisfy in sparsely inhabited public lands. It was virtually impossible to meet for national or international organizations that might have wanted to intervene in tar sands public hearings. According to the ERCB's rules of practice, individuals or groups interested in intervening needed to demonstrate to the Board that they possessed a right "that may be directly and adversely affected by a decision of the Board on the proposed application."[60] That right was tied to owning property in Alberta, residing in Alberta, or engaging in an activity in Alberta. Subsection 10(1)(c) of the ERCB's rules of practice stipulated that any person who filed an objection to an energy development application needed to indicate on their submission "the location of the land, residence or activity of the person in relation to the location of the energy resource that is the subject of the proposed application." The next subsection of the regulation required those who wished to intervene to provide "the name, address in Alberta, telephone number, fax number, if any, and if available, an e-mail address of the person."[61] These terms effectively barred individuals and organizations from outside the province from intervening before the ERCB unless they could establish some tie to lands in the immediate proximity of tar sands projects. The Pembina Institute's place in the public record as a persistent, continual environmental participant in regulatory proceedings was secured first by the ties to the land the organization established through its licence to occupy lands for recreational purposes.

Pembina's prominence was also secured by the Institute's philosophy and approach to environmental issues. Pembina is very mainstream and values conventional forms of political participation such as regulatory hearings and consulting with industry and/or government. You are much more likely to find Pembina's leaders in meetings with government and/or industry than in street demonstrations. Its reformist orientation toward environmental issues was reflected in the membership of the Institute's partners and clients of the Pembina's fee-for-service business. The money of governments, corporations, and petroleum companies was as welcome as that of foundations, nongovernmental organizations, and First Nations. All were seen as part of Pembina's vision for "a sustainable energy future."[62] During most appearances in hearings, Pembina and OSEC tried to be both critical and collaborative. Throughout this first decade they sought to reform development, not stop it. This stance was born of, in the coalition's words, "a long-standing practice of working pro-actively with oil sands proponents, in order to resolve issues when possible."[63] Or, as the Pembina Institute's Dan Woynillowicz put it:

> The relationship has evolved to one of mutual respect and an acknowledgement that it's better to engage in a dialogue about issues and concerns rather than just relying on the more conflict-based and controversial regulatory process which can lead to animosity and, at times, less pro-active or less progressive results.[64]

In public hearings, Pembina and OSEC generally intervened—not to oppose projects outright, but instead to urge government to attach environmental protection conditions to project approvals. A common demand was that tar sands operators be required to use the best available technologies in their facilities to reduce the emissions of greenhouse gases and other pollutants.

The regulatory process, the public hearings held to assess tar sands development applications, are relied on here primarily to evaluate the character and effectiveness of Pembina's reformist brand of environmentalism. Before looking at that record, it should be noted that Pembina certainly made participatory or procedural gains in institutions outside of the formal regulatory process. Through OSEC, Pembina played an instrumental role in developing CEMA and its consensus-based decision-making processes.[65] It opened communications channels with many tar sands companies; it ensured environmentalists had a seat at CEMA's various tables. OSEC's commitment to CEMA took many forms. OSEC was represented on CEMA's board,

CEMA's management committee, and four of CEMA's working groups.[66] But in light of CEMA's meagre list of accomplishments, such participatory or relationship-building gains delivered very little in terms of on-the-ground environmental mitigation; Pembina's assistance in building and then sitting at CEMA's tables certainly didn't slow down the pace of exploiting the tar sands.

Pembina's reformist philosophy, its willingness to accommodate large new tar sands projects, was displayed in regulatory hearings. A lack of stridency and a willingness to accommodate industry's vision marked its participation. From 1997 to 2004, government regulators approved seven tar sands mining operations.[67] These approvals promised to take bitumen and synthetic crude oil production to more than 1.4 million barrels per day. They would "disturb" tens of thousands of hectares of the boreal forest ("disturb" is the regulators' term for denuding the landscape of life). They would send skyward millions of tons of greenhouse gases and other pollutants. OSEC only categorically opposed the TrueNorth Fort Hills Oil Sands project (2002). In all of the other projects OSEC was a constructive, accommodating critic that worked with industry to identify areas of agreement and concern. The AEUB's language from its 1997 Suncor Steepbank mine decision characterizes well the importance OSEC attached to working with industry and the atmosphere OSEC helped create: "The Board also noted that the measures taken by Suncor and OSEC have reduced other public concerns and allowed for a cooperative approach for the review of the application."[68]

The tenor of Pembina's interventions changed somewhat between July and November 2006. Energy regulators held public hearings on three more projects over those months: Suncor's Voyageur upgrader project in July, Albian Sands Energy's Muskeg River Mine expansion in September, and Imperial Oil's Kearl mine project in November. OSEC called for the AEUB to reject the Voyageur and Kearl projects; however, the environmental coalition "took no position on the disposition" of the Albian Sands application.[69] By the time the Voyageur application was heard, the boom was so frenzied that even third-party supporters of tar sands such as the Regional Municipality of Wood Buffalo were asking regulators to slow down the pace of development. The Regional Municipality asked government to delay Voyageur until an inquiry into the socioeconomic consequences of tar sands development was conducted and infrastructure needs had been satisfied. Some First Nations—the Athabasca Chipewyan First Nation and Fort McKay First Nation—reached confidential mitigation agreements with Suncor that addressed their concerns. OSEC had tried to secure a similar agreement with Suncor but was, in the words of a Pembina analyst, "unable to extract a meaningful package of project specific mitigation from

Suncor." OSEC then uncharacteristically demanded the regulators deny Suncor's application.

Four months later OSEC categorically rejected Imperial Oil's Kearl Oil Sands Project. Pembina's executive director, Dr. Marlo Raynolds, called the company's approach to climate change "reckless."[70] Grounds for this damning charge rested in the company's estimate that once Kearl became fully operational its GHG emissions would be 3.75 million tons per year.[71] OSEC did not approach Imperial about negotiating a voluntary agreement to offset its project "based on their poor track record on environmental issues and stakeholder engagement."

The Albian Energy Muskeg River Mine expansion stands apart from the other two projects, not for the damage it would do to the boreal forest but for OSEC's position on this damage. The Muskeg River Mine expansion proposed to devour an additional 8,091 hectares (31.24 square miles) of the boreal landscape. This would bring the Muskeg River Mine's "disturbance footprint" to 12,474 hectares (48.16 square miles).[72] During operations, the expanded mine was predicted to annually emit 1.21 million tonnes (1.33 million US tons) of carbon dioxide equivalent gases.[73] OSEC didn't object to the project, based on an agreement with Albian Energy that addressed priority issues such as greenhouse gas emissions and terrestrial impacts.

Why did OSEC regard the Muskeg River expansion benignly while it condemned Kearl? It's hard to make the argument that expanding the Muskeg River Mine would not degrade the environment while the Kearl project would. It's hard to see how OSEC and Pembina, as organizations committed to protecting the ecological integrity of Athabasca tar sands region, could view Albian's Muskeg River Mine expansion as worthy of even the tacit approval that comes from not opposing a project. When OSEC denounced Imperial's Kearl project before the Joint Review Panel in November 2006 it stated:

> The Cumulative Environmental Management Association (CEMA) has not yet determined a maximum area of disturbance threshold for the region nor has it completed the development of reclamation certification criteria. As such, OSEC has significant concerns with the fact that decision-makers are allocating terrestrial resources to the oil sands industry in the absence of information on the region's terrestrial carrying capacity or demonstrated ability to reclaim lands affected by oil sands mining to certification standards.[74]

Later, OSEC recommended the Kearl project "be denied given that the current government resources appear incapable of delivering a regional cumulative effects management system that protects the public interest."[75]

The coalition's logic surely applied with equal force to the Albian Energy application, or to any application for more production from the tar sands. OSEC suggested as much in the statement of concern about the Muskeg River Mine expansion. Pembina's Dan Woynillowicz, writing for OSEC with respect to the additional 8,091 hectares now tasting the steel of Albian's shovels, stated that

> [t]o date, very little area directly affected by oil sands mining has been restored to land with equivalent capability to the pre-mining land, and no oil sands operations have yet received a reclamation certificate from the government of Alberta. Due to this track record, we are concerned with Albian Sands' plans to disturb such a large area and base their mitigation strategy on uncertain reclamation strategies and approaches.[76]

Woynillowicz's statement raised other serious environmental concerns difficult to reconcile with OSEC's decision not to take any position on the Albian application. None of the following points from OSEC's statement of concern arguably were addressed adequately in the Joint Review Panel's decision. OSEC was concerned about the permanent loss of wetlands, especially "the loss of irreplaceable peatlands." As well, Albian's tailings management technology was "unproven," and OSEC was "concerned about the high levels of uncertainty in their ability to successfully reclaim its in-pit tailings and create a viable, maintenance free and ecologically sustainable end pit lake." Most significantly, OSEC questioned the environmental baseline data used by Albian to assess the cumulative impact of its project. These data were inadequate enough to lead OSEC to "believe that insufficient environmental information is presented for stakeholders and regulators to develop an informed opinion on the appropriateness of the Project."[77] Notwithstanding these rather large question marks, the Albian project wasn't opposed by OSEC and Pembina.

Some might use Albian's contribution to GHG emissions to try to deflect my position that OSEC's tacit approval for the Muskeg River Mine expansion compromised the coalition's environmental protection commitment. Albian's voluntary agreement with OSEC talked about setting an emissions reduction plan in 2007 to reach meaningful GHG emissions reductions below business-as-usual levels. Notably, the company promised to analyze, but not necessarily accept, Pembina's preferred GHG emissions reduction goal—carbon neutrality by 2020. Albian also promised to consider factors such as stakeholder perspectives, federal policies, technological and offset options, emissions from alternative commercial supplies of oil, and the economics and cost of carbon in developing a GHG emissions reduction plan.[78]

As OSEC argued at the Kearl hearings, Albian's commitment "is the minimum standard for proponents of oil sands projects."[79]

Clearly Shell's original plan called for Albian's Muskeg River expansion's GHG emissions to be far below those of Imperial's Kearl project. Shell proposed that when Albian's expansion was operational its direct GHG emissions would amount to 1.21 million tonnes per year;[80] Kearl would emit 3.75 million tonnes per year. Albian's Environmental Impact Assessment (EIA) also estimated its "emissions intensity"—a phrase used to describe GHG emissions per unit of production. According to the emissions intensity yardstick, Albian's GHG emissions would be 28.8 kilograms (kg) of carbon dioxide equivalent per barrel of bitumen; Imperial's EIA projected the Kearl project's GHG emissions per barrel at about 40 kg per barrel—40 percent higher.[81] There's no doubt that Kearl would emit more greenhouse gases than the expanded Muskeg River operation.

But an Imperial-Albian comparison doesn't speak to the Muskeg River Mine expansion's projected GHG emissions intensity relative to that of the already existing mine; it also didn't address the aggregate or total GHG emissions from the expanded operations. With respect to emissions intensity, Albian's EIA stated that, on a per barrel basis, the GHG emissions from its expansion would be 28 percent higher than those of its original mine.[82] This significant difference was further magnified when the additional production from the Muskeg River expansion was considered. The expansion promised to send skyward more than twice the tonnage of greenhouse gases generated by Albian's established operation—7,776 tonnes, as opposed to 3,375 tonnes, per day. So, while OSEC may have preferred Albian's GHG impact relative to Imperial's, this didn't change a key fact. Unless major emissions reductions were delivered through OSEC's voluntary agreement with Shell, significantly more—not less—GHG emissions would enter the atmosphere courtesy of the Muskeg River expansion.

OSEC's responses to Kearl and the Muskeg River expansion may be explained in part by OSEC's success in negotiating this voluntary mitigation agreement with Albian Sands; Pembina didn't feel it was even worth trying to negotiate with Imperial on this front and may have dropped its opposition to Voyageur if negotiations had succeeded with Suncor. We will shortly consider just how much this mitigation agreement actually delivered, but before that another potential explanatory factor is considered—Pembina's financial connections to tar sands developers. Pembina's substantial financial relationship with the petroleum industry must be considered in explaining both the reformist character of Pembina's participation and the dramatically different treatment it meted out to Albian Energy and Imperial Oil.

Mark Dowie wrote in 1995 that American environmentalism was "both defined and limited by the philanthropy that supports it." Dowie argued that, whether this was bad or not, philanthropy could seriously restrict environmental group behaviour.[83] In Alberta, more than philanthropy is at issue when considering the character of Pembina's positions. Unlike environmental groups such as the Alberta Wilderness Association or the Canadian Parks and Wilderness Society, the Pembina Institute does not have charitable status under Canadian tax law. Consequently, the Institute's operations have been funded, to a considerable extent, by fee-for-service and consulting work. Some of this work was and is done for the companies that Pembina and OSEC critique before government regulators. In 2005, approximately two dozen firms or organizations connected to the petroleum industry could be counted among Pembina's 133 "funders, partners and clients." Even more significantly, this list included nearly all of the most important tar sands operators: Suncor, Shell, Petro-Canada (now part of Suncor), Nexen, Husky, Encana (now Cenovus), Devon, Deer Creek (now Total Petroleum), ConocoPhillips, and Canadian Natural Resources Limited. In 2007, Syncrude and Imperial Oil were the only tar sands producers with existing and approved tar sands mining operations not on this list.[84] Table 2 illustrates the financial importance of Pembina's fee-for-service and consulting services to corporations, governments, First Nations, and other nongovernmental organizations.

Table 2   Pembina Institute, Fee-for-Service Revenue in Millions of Dollars and as Percentage of Total Revenue, 2003–2012

	Fee for Service ($ millions)	Fee for Service (%)	Total Revenue ($ millions)
2003	1.753	68.4	2.550
2004	1.429	56.0	2.549
2005	1.755	50.8	3.453
2006	1.433	34.2	4.194
2007	1.611	37.2	4.328
2008	2.054	41.1	5.002
2009	1.959	37.7	5.203
2010	2.324	50.0	4.645
2011	2.726	59.0	4.620
2012	2.821	59.9	4.712

Source: Pembina Institute, *Annual Reports*, various years. The bulk of fee-for-service revenue came from consulting fees. Project grants were the other major source of revenue. These funds were described as: "Revenue from granting agencies for completing specific projects."

Corporate work presumably generates a significant percentage, either through fee-for-service or consulting work, of the Pembina Institute's total revenue. Marlo Raynolds, then Pembina's executive director, did not respond to requests in March and April 2007 for details about the percentage of its fee-for-service/consulting revenues coming from corporations or the specific amounts it received up until that point in time from Suncor and Shell. On November 28, 2007, Raynolds confirmed that both Suncor and Shell were clients of Pembina's Corporate Consulting group in 2005; he also revealed that "Suncor was a much more significant client (by a factor of 9 with regards to associated revenues)." He wouldn't reveal how much these companies paid to the Institute's Corporate Consulting group for its services.[85]

Pembina then had more than just the ecological integrity of the tar sands region to consider as it went about its business. It also had to consider how its actions would affect its business–client relationships with tar sands companies such as Shell and Suncor. Those considerations arguably influenced the respective positions taken on the Albian Energy and Imperial Oil projects. Pembina had an ongoing business–client relationship with Shell; it had no such relationship with Imperial Oil.

This business–client relationship also may have affected the timing and substance of Pembina's news releases in September 2006 about a tar sands development moratorium. On September 19, 2006, Pembina called for a moratorium on new oil sands project approvals. This was one day *after* the Albian Energy application hearings concluded and just a handful of days after OSEC took no position on whether regulators should approve the Muskeg River expansion.[86] Furthermore, in a September 14, 2006, media release about a Pembina presentation to a government consultation exercise, the Institute didn't publicize an aspect of that presentation that contradicted its position on the Albian Energy project. The release suggested that in that presentation Pembina's oilsands program director only called for a moratorium on the sale of new oil sands releases. In fact, he said: "We need to suspend new lease sales *and project approvals* until a regional plan is in place."[87] But to publicize the call for a suspension of new project approvals before the Albian hearings ended would have contradicted OSEC's position there; it also would not respect the positive relationship Pembina had with Shell.[88] Pembina's fee-for-service work for Shell should be considered in trying to understand OSEC's behaviour.

Another contributor to Pembina's decision not to object to the Muskeg River expansion project is its voluntary agreement with Albian Energy. This successful negotiation testifies to the value Pembina attached to developing positive relationships with many of the tar sands' most important players. It also reflected the Pembina philosophy of cooperation/accommodation with industry. From 1997 to 2004, OSEC or Pembina secured six voluntary agreements with tar sands miners.[89] These agreements varied in the extent to which they addressed the aquatic, atmospheric, and terrestrial impacts of tar sands mining. The value OSEC saw in these agreements prompted the coalition to request that the regulator "include the bilateral agreement as a condition of regulatory approval" or "formally recognize the agreement in any approval it might issue for the project."[90] The regulator declined all such requests. OSEC only opposed three projects between 1997 and 2006; in each case OSEC had not reached a voluntary agreement with the project proponent.[91]

These agreements are confidential. However, OSEC submitted its agreement with Albian Energy to regulators during the Muskeg River expansion hearings. It gives us a rare glimpse at the substance of a voluntary agreement and if it contained guarantees or loopholes. This agreement had loopholes and ambiguities and did not deliver the substantive benefits OSEC expected. The successful negotiation may help to explain why OSEC didn't oppose the project, but the agreement did little to mitigate the impact of Shell's mining operations.

The focus here is on greenhouse gas emissions. In the GHG emissions section of the Albian Energy/OSEC agreement the two parties proposed to "cooperatively address" environmental issues. For Pembina's Raynolds the agreement offered substantial environmental gains; the issue resolution document showed how Pembina could "raise the bar" since "[t]he commitments therein go beyond what is required by Alberta regulators."[92] The problem for Pembina, and more importantly for the climate, was that Shell didn't follow Pembina's interpretation of what this collaborative product demanded. OSEC's lawyers charged in 2009 that, with respect to both the Muskeg River agreement and the 2004 Jackpine agreement, "Shell Canada has failed to fulfill its commitments and agreements with OSEC regarding greenhouse gas emissions (GHGs)."[93] Raynolds accused the company of breaking the document's "binding agreements" to significantly cut greenhouse gas emissions. Simon Dyer, Pembina's oilsands program director, described Shell's actions as a "betrayal."[94]

Their outrage was understandable. The issue resolution document, after all, led OSEC to remove their objections to the expansion of the Muskeg River Mine. As such the voluntary agreement was crucial to Pembina's efforts to soften the impact of tar sands mining. But the language of the issue resolution document doesn't justify the outrage. The document had loopholes, ones that excused Shell from taking the strong, progressive actions to reduce greenhouse gas emissions that Pembina expected. The document stated that Albian/Shell would base its GHG reduction commitments on the following six inputs: "Full Cycle Analysis and most likely commercial alternative analysis," "emerging federal government policy," "stakeholder perspectives," "technology options and offset opportunities," "economics and cost of carbon," and "analysis of several long-term reduction goals, including carbon neutrality by 2020."[95] The document never ranked or weighted those six inputs.

When Shell shattered OSEC's expectations of how these factors should influence greenhouse gas management, the coalition demanded a rehearing of the Jackpine and Muskeg River Mine expansion applications. OSEC's demand was made as if Shell had committed to letting only one input, the full cycle analysis criterion, shape its greenhouse gas management and emissions.[96] OSEC didn't acknowledge what the voluntary agreement stated—that Shell would consider five other inputs as well. For its part Shell appeared to be giving much greater weight to emerging federal government policy than to full cycle analysis. And why not? There was nothing in the issue resolution document requiring Shell to privilege full cycle analysis over any other management plan inputs. Not surprisingly, governments did not order a rehearing into these projects. From the greenhouse gas emissions perspective, this issue resolution document didn't deliver. However, Shell's failure to deliver on Pembina's greenhouse gas emissions expectations did not appear to damage their overall relationship. Shell donated somewhere between $100,000 and $200,000 to Pembina in 2011 and contracted the Institute for fee-for-service work during that year.[97]

Conclusion

A "landscape of sacrifice"—that label seemed particularly apt as I flew over tar sands mining operations in the summer of 2006. As the Cessna climbed over the Clearwater River, leaving it behind to snake toward the Athabasca, the high price nature was paying for the spectacular growth of tar sands production loomed larger and larger from the surrounding horizons. The statistics I had read about—the thousands of square kilometres of forests and wetlands gobbled up by miners and the millions of tonnes of greenhouse gases and other pollutants sent into the atmosphere—now had faces. To the northwest a bright blue sky became a smudgy bluish-grey the closer it got to earth—a visual marker of the air pollution produced by the Syncrude, Suncor, and Shell operations. Hectare after hectare of clearcuts in the boreal forest lay in advance of expanding tar sands mines, delimbed aspens stacked like matchsticks. Deep in the vast open-pit mines, hidden well from anyone who goes on one of the sanitized land tours offered by Syncrude and Suncor,

Figure 3 Tar Sands Operations, north of Fort McMurray, 2016

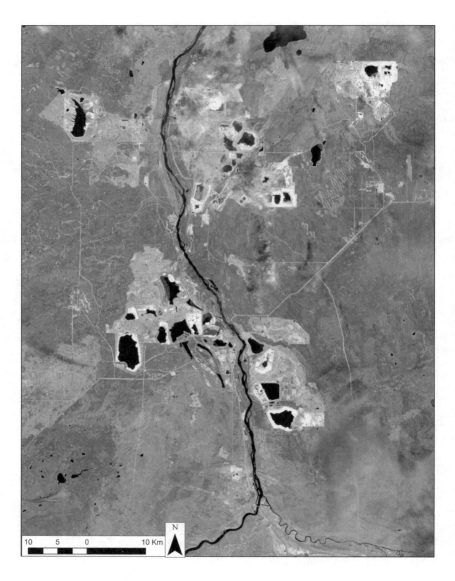

400-ton trucks scurried like ants at a picnic. Fed by mammoth 1,000 ton-plus shovels, they disgorged their nearly one-million-pound payloads of tar sands into crushers that, in turn, spit chunks of the sands out onto conveyor belt systems. Some of those systems were more than three football fields long. Tailings reservoirs, the toxic brew of pollutants and waste water left over from processing bitumen, already sprawled over more than 50 square kilometres of the landscape.[98] In a bit of tragic comedy, scarecrows in fluorescent orange suits—so-called bit-u-men—floated on oil barrels in the reservoirs and joined propane cannons mounted on the levees to try to scare waterfowl away from the tainted waters. Many of these reservoirs are little more than a block away from the Athabasca River, one contributor to the Peace-Athabasca delta, the largest inland freshwater delta in the world. If Alberta and Canada were doing anything to soften the environmental impact of exploiting the tar sands, they were doing a very good job at hiding it from the air.

This sad ecological state had many contributors. Institutional and ideological factors played complementary, reinforcing roles. Even before "Canada's Reagan" came to power in Alberta in 1992, the regulatory framework where energy development and environmental concerns might be balanced was decidedly tilted in favour of exploiting resources. Conservation in that framework had what in today's world is a quaint meaning—the efficient exploitation of petroleum resources. The difficulties public interest groups faced in gaining access to the regulatory process to raise environmental concerns about any petroleum development in Alberta pre-dated the ascendancy of neoliberalism and its Alberta incarnation. The inherited institutional setting provided a very friendly atmosphere for the scale of resource development unleashed by the technologies and policies of the 1990s. The ideological outlook of regulators toward resource development helped to guarantee that even state-sanctioned environmental protections—such as those initially established for the McClelland Lake wetlands—would be swept aside. Sterilization of the bitumen resource had to be avoided at all costs; every barrel of bitumen that could be economically extracted from a lease must be extracted. The Klein administration also did an excellent job in ensuring that those branches of the public service that might have objected to the environmental consequences were drained of the resources needed to make those objections well. If industry captained the process that led to changing the fiscal regime, it played an equally important role in ensuring that environmental policy forums such as CEMA didn't threaten the pace of development. Symbolic politics, the appearance of making environmental headway, best describes what CEMA contributed to during the first decade of the boom. These institutional and ideological factors helped to limit the strength of an environmental counter-movement to the frenzied pace of tar sands expansion.

To some extent the weaknesss of the environmental opposition to exploitation likely rests as well with the character of the Pembina Institute, the key player in that opposition. Pembina's desire to be polite, its desire to be collaborative, and its financial ties to the vast majority of the most important tar sands companies restricted and limited its critique. It was inconceivable for an organization that depended heavily for its survival on the work it did for industry to risk cutting off that vital source of income. Pembina's own ideological outlook helped to ensure the reformist nature of the environmental opposition. Through its preference to negotiate voluntary agreements with industry rather than try to organize a more uncompromising opposition, Pembina may have succeeded in securing some concessions from industry. But when those agreements failed to meet the Institute's expectations, it's fair to suggest that the nature of Pembina's opposition also legitimized the boom.

Finally, this chapter invited us to appreciate that the champions of market fundamentalism in the petroleum sector were not going to go gently into that good night when opposition emerged to their blueprint for exploiting the tar sands. Instead, they responded with a strategy designed to "counter, coopt, and compromise" their opposition. They joined government in ensuring that institutions such as CEMA wouldn't be able to let a concern with nature end their days of exploiting what lay beneath Alberta's boreal forests and wetlands. Also some, not all, hired environmental organizations and/ or negotiated with them over the industrialization of northeastern Alberta. The list of voluntary agreements industry signed with OSEC/Pembina was one fruit of those initiatives. But if those agreements were no more binding on industry than the Albian Energy issue resolution document, then nature remained at great risk as the boom swept over Alberta's taiga.

Notes

1   Valerie Kuletz, *The Tainted Desert: Environmental and Social Ruin in the American West* (New York: Routledge, 1998).
2   Kolson L. Schlosser, "U.S. National Security Discourse and the Political Construction of the Arctic National Wildlife Refuge," *Society and Natural Resources* 19 (2006), 3–18.
3   Fred Block, "Polanyi's Double Movement."
4   Mark Dowie, *Losing Ground: American Environmentalism at the Close of the Twentieth Century* (Cambridge, MA: MIT Press), 6.
5   The joint federal-provincial review panel into Canadian Natural Resources Ltd.'s Horizon project characterized the impact of oils sands mining this way. See Alberta, Alberta Energy and Utilities Board, *Report of the Joint Review Panel Established by the Alberta Energy and Utilities Board and the Government of Canada EUB Decision 2004-005: Canadian Natural Resources Limited, Application for an Oil Sands Mine, Bitumen Extraction Plant, and Bitumen Upgrading Plant in the Fort McMurray Area*, January 27, 2004, 56.
6   Elizabeth McGowan, "NASA's Hansen Explains Decision to Join Keystone Pipeline Protests," *Reuters*, August 29, 2011, http://www.reuters.com/article/idUS257590805720110829.

7   Pratt, *Tar Sands*, 102–3.

8   Pratt, *Tar Sands*, 107.

9   Allan Tupper, Larry Pratt, and Ian Urquhart, "The Role of Government," in *Government and Politics in Alberta*, ed. Allan Tupper and Roger Gibbins (Edmonton: University of Alberta Press, 1992), 50.

10 John H. Fund, "Learning from Canada's Reagan," *Wall Street Journal*, February 23, 1995.

11 Thomas Marr-Laing (with Gail MacCrimmon), *Downsizing, Deregulation, and Regionalization: The Weakening of the Alberta Government's Role in Environmental Protection* (Drayton Valley, AB: Pembina Institute, 1997), 1.

12 Nelson, interview, 15–16.

13 The name, but not the essential regulatory functions, of Alberta's petroleum industry regulator has changed periodically over the years. From 1938 to 1957 the regulator was called the Petroleum and Natural Gas Conservation Board. From 1957 until 1971 it was known as the Oil and Gas Conservation Board. It was renamed the Energy and Resources Conservation Board in 1971. In 1995 the ERCB was merged with the Public Utilities Board to form the Alberta Energy and Utilities Board. In 2008, this merger was dissolved and the ERCB once again became an independent regulatory agency. In 2012, the ERCB was renamed the Alberta Energy Regulator and its powers were expanded to include all environmental aspects of petroleum projects.

14 Dr. George Govier, member of the Conservation Board, quoted in Breen, *Alberta's Petroleum Industry*, xxix. In 1950, the Board's official name was the Petroleum and Natural Gas Conservation Board.

15 Quoted in Gordon Jaremko, *Steward: 75 Years of Alberta Energy Regulation* (Calgary: Energy Resources Conservation Board, 2013), 14.

16 Alberta Energy and Utilities Board and Canadian Environmental Assessment Agency, *Report of the Joint Review Panel Established by the Alberta Energy and Utilities Board and the Government of Canada, EUB Decision 2006-128 (Albian Sands Energy Inc.)* (Calgary: Alberta Energy and Utilities Board, 2006).

17 Alberta, *Energy Resources and Conservation Act*, section 26 (2), Revised Statutes of Alberta, 2000, Chapter E-10.

18 Such a situation allowed the Alberta Wilderness Association to enjoy these legal participatory rights in the Polaris Resources Ltd. application in 2003. This application proposed to develop a sour gas (poisonous hydrogen sulphide) well immediately adjacent to the Whaleback, a protected area in southwest Alberta. James Tweedie, an AWA member, owned land within the well's emergency planning zone and thus met the directly and adversely affected test. This enabled the AWA to appear as a witness and give evidence to the Board. The Board rejected this application. Alberta Energy and Utilities Board, *Polaris Resources Ltd. Applications for a Well Licence, Special Gas Well Spacing, Compulsory Pooling, and Flaring Permit Livingstone Field*, December 16, 2003, http://www.aer.ca/documents/decisions/2003/2003-101.pdf.

19 I would like to thank Shaun Fluker, Christyann Olson, and Richard Secord for helping me to try to understand standing and intervening before the ERCB. They are not responsible for any misinterpretations I may have made.

20 Oil Sands Environmental Coalition, *Submission by the Oil Sands Environmental Coalition regarding the Kearl Oil Sands Project* (October 12, 2006), 5, http://www.ceaa.gc.ca/050/documents_staticpost/cearref_16237/kr-0062.pdf.

21   If an oil sands proposal affected federal constitutional responsibilities (i.e., First Nations, fisheries, or migratory birds) a joint federal-provincial review panel would be convened under the terms of federal-provincial agreements for cooperating on environmental assessments. For joint reviews, the chair of the provincial regulator would appoint two of the three panel members (with the approval of the federal environment minister); one of those members would be the Joint Review Panel Chair. The federal environment minister would select the third member (with the approval of the provincial cabinet and the chair of the provincial regulator). The Joint Panel would carry out the responsibilities demanded by provincial and federal statutes. Oil sands applications were no less successful when reviewed by a joint review panel process as they were when considered by the ERCB alone.

22   The praise came from the Canadian Environmental Advisory Council and is quoted in Andrea B. Moen, *Demystifying Forestry Law: An Alberta Analysis* (Edmonton: Environmental Law Centre, 1990), 94.

23   Steven Kennett, *Integrated Resource Management in Alberta: Past, Present and Benchmarks for the Future (Occasional Paper #11)* (Calgary: Canadian Institute of Resources Law, 2002).

24   Brenda Heelan Powell, *Demystifying Forestry Law: An Alberta Analysis*, 2nd ed. (Edmonton: Environmental Law Centre, 2003), 97–98.

25   Powell, *Demystifying Forestry Law*, 98.

26   Alberta Energy and Utilities Board, *Application by Syncrude for the Aurora Mine (Decision No. 97-13)* (Calgary: Alberta Energy and Utilities Board, 1997), 15.

27   Testament to the spectacular visual impact of the McClelland Lake fen is offered by *National Geographic* magazine's decision to use Peter Essick's aerial photograph of the fen in the introduction to its March 2009 article on the tar sands. See Robert Kunzig, "Tar Sands Yield Millions of Barrels—But at What Cost?," *National Geographic* 215, no. 3 (March 2009), 34.

28   Alberta Energy and Utilities Board, *TrueNorth Energy Corporation Application to Construct and Operate an Oil Sands Mine and Cogeneration Plant in the Fort McMurray Area (Decision 2002-089)* (Calgary: Alberta Energy and Utilities Board, 2002), 35-36.

29   Richard Thomas, *Boreal Forest Natural Region of Alberta* (Edmonton: Alberta Environmental Protection, 1998).

30   Alberta Environmental Protection, *Fort McMurray-Athabasca Oil Sands Subregional Integrated Resource Plan* (Edmonton: Alberta Environmental Protection, 1996), 29.

31   Richard Thomas, *The Final Frontier: Protecting Landscape and Biological Diversity within Alberta's Boreal Forest Natural Region* (Edmonton: Alberta Environmental Protection, 1998), 252.

32   Concerns about sterilizing bitumen resources in the vicinity of McClelland Lake are found throughout the report approving the TrueNorth Energy application. Alberta Energy and Utilities Board, *TrueNorth Energy Corporation: Application.*

33   Alberta Wilderness Association, "Government Disregards Own Guidelines to Fast-track Policy Review. Changes Would Allow Oilsands Mining in Sensitive Wetland," news release, April 8, 2002, https://albertawilderness.

ca/wordpress/wp-content/uploads/20020408_nr_awa_mcc_government_
disregards_guidelines.pdf.

34   Larry Pratt and Ian Urquhart, *The Last Great Forest: Japanese Multinationals and Alberta's Northern Forests* (Edmonton: NeWest Press, 1994).

35   K. Timoney and P. Lee, "Environmental Management in Resource-rich Alberta, Canada: First-world Jurisdiction, Third-world Analogue," *Journal of Environmental Management* 63, no. 4 (2001), 63.

36   George Hoberg and Jeffrey Phillips consider CEMA in the context of the policy subsystem literature. See George Hoberg and Jeffrey Phillips, "Playing Defence: Early Responses to Conflict Expansion in the Oil Sands Policy Subsystem," *Canadian Journal of Political Science* 44, no. 3 (September 2011). The discussion in this chapter suggests several points that may distinguish it from Hoberg and Phillips. CEMA amounted to a de facto privatization of environmental policy making. The argument here also suggests that environmentalists legitimized CEMA's operations despite considerable evidence before 2005 that the institution was not making a positive contribution to addressing environmental issues. They willingly participated in a process that, year after year, showed no signs of seriously addressing environmental issues.

37   Alberta, Legislative Assembly, *Alberta Hansard, 25th Legislature, 4th Session (2004)*, April 1, 2004, 849.

38   Harry Spaling, Janelle Zweir, William Ross, & Roger Creasey, "Managing Regional Cumulative Effects of Oil Sands Development in Alberta, Canada," *Journal of Environmental Assessment Policy and Management* 2, no. 4 (December 2000), 525.

39   Alberta Environment, *Sustainable Times*, Issue 1 (April 2000), 1.

40   In 2007, these percentages were very similar. Of CEMA's 49 members 19 came from industry (39%), 14 from governments (29%), 10 from First Nations (20%), and 6 from environmental/hunter/trapper organizations (12%). By 2014, CEMA had grown to 60 members: 21 from industry (35%), 19 from government (32%), 12 from First Nations (20%), and 8 from the conservation community (13%).

41   Alberta Environment and Alberta Sustainable Resource Development, *Regional Sustainable Development Strategy for the Alberta Oil Sands Area, Progress Report, July 2001* (July 2001), 13. This report stated that the AEUB and the federal Department of Fisheries and Oceans funded some activities. Robert Nowosad, CEMA's Executive Director in 2005, provided the figures for 2005. Robert Nowosad, e-mail message to author, October 6, 2005.

42   Alberta Energy and Utilities Board, *Application by Syncrude for the Aurora Mine, (Decision No. 97-13)* (Calgary: October 1997), 15.

43   In 2002 the *Alberta Energy and Utilities Board Act* came into effect. The legislation amalgamated the Energy Resources and Conservation Board and the Public Utilities Board into one corporation, the Alberta Energy and Utilities Board. The ERCB continued to operate and to regulate the petroleum sector under this new corporate form.

44   Alberta Energy and Utilities Board, *Application by Syncrude for the Aurora Mine*, 27.

45   Alberta Energy and Utilities Board, *Application by Syncrude for the Aurora Mine*, 28.

46   Alberta Energy and Utilities Board, *Application by Syncrude for the Aurora Mine*, 34.

47   Alberta Environment, *Regional Sustainable Development Strategy, Progress Report*, 1, 8.

48   Alberta Environment stated that 72 issues was a low number of concerns. It then noted: "[t]his low number is a tribute to Alberta's highly effective environmental and natural resources management system and the high level of co-operation among stakeholders in the region." Alberta Environment, *Regional Sustainable Development Strategy for the Athabasca Oil Sands Area* (July 1999), 11.

49   A CEMA strategic planning workshop held in November 1999 decided to move three surface water quality issues into Category A. This increased the number of most urgent issues to eight.

50   Alberta Environment, *Sustainable Times*, Issue 2 (November 2000), 1.

51   Legislative Assembly, *Alberta Hansard*, April 1, 2004, 849.

52   James Mahony, "Alberta Government Makes Oilsands Policy Shift," *Daily Oil Bulletin*, October 27, 2005.

53   Alberta Environment, *Regional Sustainable Development Strategy, Progress Report*, 7.

54   Alberta Energy and Utilities Board and Canadian Environmental Assessment Agency, *Report of the Joint Review Panel Established by the Alberta Energy and Utilities Board and the Government of Canada (Decision 2004-009)*, February 5, 2004.

55   Robert Nowosad, e-mail message to author, October 6, 2005.

56   Alberta Environment, *Regional Sustainable Development Strategy, Progress Report*, 1.

57   Shaun Fluker contends that the AEUB's behaviour sprung from an unnecessarily narrow interpretation of the regulator's obligations under section three of the *Energy Resources Conservation Act*. See Shaun Fluker, "The Jurisdiction of Alberta's Energy and Utilities Board to Consider Broad Socio-Ecological Concerns Associated with Energy Projects," *Alberta Law Review* 42, no. 4 (2005). Such an unnecessarily narrow interpretation was entirely consistent with the regulator's view of its primary mandate—to facilitate the development of the province's petroleum resources.

58   Alberta Environment, *Regional Sustainable Development Strategy, Progress Report*, 12.

59   Alberta Environment, *Sustainable Times*, Issue 4 (October 2001).

60   Alberta, *Energy Resources Conservation Board Rules of Practice (Alberta Regulation 252/2007)* (Edmonton: Queen's Printer, 2010), Subsection 10(1)(a).

61   Alberta, *Energy Resources Conservation Board Rules of Practice (Alberta Regulation 252/2007)*, Subsections 10(1)(c) and 10(1)(d).

62   The phrase is taken from the Pembina Institute, *Annual Report 2004*, 16.

63   Oil Sands Environmental Coalition, "Submission in the Matter of a Joint Panel Review," (October 12, 2006), 6. The OSEC made this submission to the joint review panel examining the Kearl Oil Sands project application made by Imperial Oil.

64   Pay Dirt Pictures, *Making the Unconventional Conventional*.

65   This description of the OSEC's view of CEMA was written by the AEUB and appeared in Alberta Energy and Utilities Board, *TrueNorth Energy Corporation*, 53.

66   April 7, 2009 Letter from Karin Buss, Counsel, Ecojustice to The Honourable Jim Prentice, Energy Resources Conservation Board, and Canadian Environmental Assessment Agency, re Joint Panel Report and EUB Decision

2004–009; Shell Canada Limited: *Applications for an Oil Sands Mine, Bitumen Extraction Plant, Cogeneration Plant and Water Pipeline in the Fort McMurray Area, February 5, 2004/Joint Panel Report and EUB Decision 2006–128*; Alberta Energy and Utilities Board and Canadian Environmental Assessment Agency, *Report of the Joint Review Panel EUB Decision 2006–128: Albian Sands Energy Inc., Application to Expand the Oil Sands Mining and Processing Plant Facilities at the Muskeg River Mine*, December 17, 2006, 12–13.

67 These mining projects were Syncrude's Aurora (1997), Suncor's Steepbank (1997), Suncor's Millennium (1999), Shell's Muskeg River (1999), TrueNorth's Fort Hills (2002), Shell's Jackpine (2004), and Canadian Natural Resources Ltd.'s Horizon (2004).

68 Alberta Energy and Utilities Board, *Application by Suncor Inc. Oil Sands Group for Amendment of Approval No. 7632 for Proposed Steepbank Mine Development, (Decision No. 97–1)*, 3.

69 Alberta Energy and Utilities Board, *Joint Review Panel Report on Muskeg River Mine Expansion*, 20.

70 Pembina Institute, "Imperial Oil Reckless Regarding Global Warming Implications of Kearl Oilsands Mine," media release, November 15, 2006, http://www.pembina.org/media-release/1336. ExxonMobil, then the petroleum industry's leading climate change denier, is the majority shareholder of Imperial Oil. ExxonMobil owned 69.6 percent of Imperial Oil's common shares in 2013. Imperial Oil, *Annual Financial Statements, 2013*, A45.

71 Imperial Oil Resources Ventures Limited, *Kearl Oil Sands Project—Mine Development (Regulatory Application)*, vol. 5, *Air and Water (July 2005)*, 2–166/67.

72 Albian Sands Energy Inc., *Application for Approval of the Muskeg River Mine Expansion Project:* Volume 1, *Project Description* (Shell Canada Limited, April 2005), 18–19.

73 Albian Energy Inc. (Albian) and Oil Sands Environmental Coalition (OSEC), *Issue Resolution Document for the Proposed Muskeg River Mine Expansion Project* (August 21, 2006), in Oil Sands Environmental Coalition, *OSEC Hearing Submission Regarding Albian Muskeg River Mine Expansion Project, EUB Application No. 1398411, EPEA Application No. 004–20809 and Water Act File No. 60330* (August 25, 2006), 2.

74 Oil Sands Environmental Coalition, *Submission in the Matter of a Joint Review Panel (Kearl Oil Sands Project)*, 28.

75 Oil Sands Environmental Coalition, *Submission in the Matter of a Joint Review Panel (Kearl Oil Sands Project)*, 57.

76 Letter from Dan Woynillowicz, Pembina Institute for Appropriate Development for the Oil Sands Environmental Coalition to Director, Northern Region, Alberta Environment, and Shauna Cartwright, Alberta Energy and Utilities Board, re Albian Sands Energy Inc.—EPEA Application No. 004-20809 (Muskeg River Mine Expansion), EUB Application No. 1398411 (Muskeg River Mine Expansion), and Water Act File No. 60330 (Muskeg River Mine Expansion), August 2005, 2.

77 Letter from Dan Woynillowicz re Albian Sands Energy Inc.—EPEA Application No. 004-20809 (Muskeg River Mine Expansion), EUB Application No. 1398411 (Muskeg River Mine Expansion), and Water Act File No. 60330 (Muskeg River Mine Expansion), August 2005, 2–3.

78 Oil Sands Environmental Coalition, *Submission in the Matter of a Joint Review Panel (Kearl Oil Sands Project)*, 15.

79 Oil Sands Environmental Coalition, *Submission in the Matter of a Joint Review Panel (Kearl Oil Sands Project)*.

80 The project would emit an additional 597,000 tons of greenhouse gases per year indirectly as a result of electricity purchases.

81 Albian Sands Energy Inc., *Muskeg River Mine Expansion Project*, vol. 2, *Air Quality, Noise and Environmental Health* (April 2005), 3–126; Imperial Oil Resources Ventures Limited, *Kearl Oil Sands Project—Mine Development*, vol. 5, *Air and Noise* (July 2005), 2–167.

82 The original Muskeg River Mine emitted 22.5 kg CO_2E (carbon dioxide equivalent) per barrel.

83 Dowie, *Losing Ground*, 41.

84 In 2007, Syncrude had seven partners. Three of them, Petro-Canada, Nexen, and ConocoPhillips, were listed on the Institute's list of funders, partners, and clients.

85 E-mail from Marlo Raynolds to author, November 28, 2007.

86 Pembina Institute, "Government Must Rein in Disorderly Development, Balance with Environmental Protection," media release, September 19, 2006, http://www.pembina.org/media-release/1286.

87 Alberta Oil Sands Consultations Multistakeholder Committee, *Peace River Hearings: Transcripts*, September 14, 2006, 15–16 [emphasis added].

88 I asked Dr. Raynolds to explain how Pembina could request a moratorium on oil sands development just days after not taking a position on the Muskeg River Mine expansion project. He suggested that Pembina had "been calling for a cessation of new oil sands project approvals since 2005." Marlo Raynolds, e-mail message to author, November 28, 2007. I believe Dr. Raynolds is mistaken. The media release Dr. Raynolds used to make his claim made no mention of a moratorium; neither did the ENGO declaration that was the subject of the media release. See Pembina Institute, "Canadian Environmental Groups Issue Declaration on Oilsands Development," http://www.pembina.org/media-release/1166; "Managing Oil Sands Development for the Long Term: A Declaration by Canada's Environmental Community," December 1, 2005, http://www.pembina.org/reports/OS_declar_Full.pdf.

89 The agreements were with Syncrude (1997: Aurora project), Suncor (1997: Steepbank project), Suncor (1999: Millennium project), Shell (1999: Muskeg River project), Shell (2004: Jackpine project), and Canadian Natural Resources Ltd. (2004: Horizon project).

90 OSEC requested that its agreement with Suncor regarding the Millennium mine be a condition of regulatory approval; it requested the regulator formally recognize these agreements in the Jackpine and Muskeg River Mine expansion hearings.

91 The three projects were TrueNorth's Fort Hills project (2002), Suncor's Voyageur project (2006), and Imperial's Kearl project (2006).

92 Raynolds, e-mail message to author, November 28, 2007.

93 Karen E. Buss, "Letter to the Honourable Jim Prentice," 6.

94 Pembina Institute, "Shell Breaks Global Warming Promise for Oilsands Projects," media release, April 8, 2009, http://www.pembina.org/media-release/1808.

95 Albian Energy and Oil Sands Environmental Coalition, *Issue Resolution Document for the Proposed Muskeg River Mine Expansion Project.*

96 Karen E. Buss, "Letter to the Honourable Jim Prentice," April 7, 2009.

97 Pembina Institute, *Annual Financial Report 2011*, 3.

98 Woynillowicz, Severson-Baker, and Raynolds, *Oil Sands Fever*, 30–31. By 2011 this area had more than tripled to 182 square kilometres. See Carolyn Campbell, "Birds and Tar Sands Tailings Ponds: Ever Safe to Land?," *Wild Lands Advocate* 22, no. 2 (April 2014), 10. The most recent published figures from Alberta's Department of Environment and Parks do not report beyond 2013. In 2013, the total active oil sands tailings area amounted to 220 square kilometres. See Alberta Environment and Parks, "Total Area of the Oil Sands Tailings Ponds over Time," http://osip.alberta.ca/library/Dataset/Details/542.

5
First Nations: Resistance and Compromise

"So long as the future for oil is good, the future for Fort McKay is good."
                                    —*Chief Jim Boucher, Fort McKay First Nation, 2005*

"We're talking about the survival of the Athabasca River, but more than
that this is about the survival of our people."
                                    —*Pat Marcel, Elder, Athabasca Chipewyan First Nation, 2007*

Introduction

Popular commentary about Alberta's tar sands is sprinkled liberally with
hackneyed phrases and caricatures. This claim generally applies to the common understanding of the relationship between Canada's Aboriginal peoples
and the exploitation of the tar sands reserves of northeastern Alberta. That
understanding is narrow and blinkered. It privileges a pro-environment/
pro-traditional lifestyle view of Aboriginal peoples' priorities; it claims that
First Nations in the region so value the customs and practices associated
with the "bush" economy and a traditional lifestyle that we should see these
peoples as consistent, implacable opponents of the industrial juggernaut that
pulverizes Alberta's boreal forests. This view has merit. Sometimes it portrays
quite well the positions of the Mikisew Cree First Nation (MCFN) and the
Athabasca Chipewyan First Nation (ACFN). These First Nations, living at
the epicentre of the boom, challenge tar sands companies and government
for exploiting the tar sands. Those actions and policies have compromised
their members' health. An environmental ethic is linked intimately to those
words. They criticize the protagonists of industrialization for the ecological
damage the tar sands economy has delivered to northeastern Alberta. Both
the human health and ecological dimensions of this critique animate the
words of Pat Marcel, the Athabasca Chipewyan Elder.

But the First Nations' opinion about the tar sands economy today is not
monolithic; to imagine a consensus about the tar sands' place in the lives
and prospects of Aboriginal peoples is to conjure an illusion, a myth. It's
naive to believe a single, monolithic Aboriginal perspective on exploiting
natural resources exists; it's naive to believe Aboriginal peoples, any more
than the wider society they are a part of, agree there is one gospel when it
comes to what to do with the bitumen resting beneath their ancestral lands.

Greg Poelzer made this general point when he examined the positions First Nations communities and their state actors took with respect to three cases where resource production and environmental protection values interact: James Bay hydro, Clayoquot Sound logging, and clearcut logging on the Stoney Reserve.[1] The Alberta government's eagerness to lease the rights to rip up the boreal forest to extract bitumen presented First Nations with a stark choice. They could categorically oppose development or they could try to adapt to and benefit economically from the oil-soaked future governments and industry envisioned for traditional Aboriginal lands. Fort McKay First Nation Chief Jim Boucher's perspective is this second one.

Descriptively, this chapter suggests the First Nations, perspective is more complicated than many believe. The most familiar narrative likely will be found in the sampling of Aboriginal critiques of what the tar sands are doing to First Nations communities and their traditional lands. The second view, one showing that First Nations in the northeast have also reaped important material benefits from the tar sands boom, is seen less frequently. Today's First Nations' outlook sees resistance and compromise jostle for primacy.

The "pro-oil sands" leaders in First Nations communities affect the complexion and temper the strength of the Aboriginal contribution to the countermovement that has made the tar sands its target. This chapter also demonstrates again that, while opposition to the free market champions of Canada's oil factory may arise spontaneously, those elites don't stand idly by and let that opposition damage their creation. Elite hegemony, as Peter Evans reminds us, "depends on combining consent with coercion."[2] In the case of First Nations, we will see that, from the early days of the Syncrude project, elites tried to manufacture Aboriginal consent for their ambitions. Several corporate practices sought to secure this consent from First Nations. First, companies have lent Aboriginal communities assistance to conduct environmental assessments of tar sands projects. They have contributed financially to creating some of the much-needed administrative capacity First Nations required to cope with and assess the flood of projects released by government decisions in the 1990s. Second, corporations have also offered Aboriginal peoples junior partnerships in exploitation; this is seen in the birth of Aboriginal energy services entrepreneurs and firms that now do billions of dollars of business with the companies who mine and extract bitumen from Aboriginal traditional lands. Third, confidential "impact and benefits" agreements between business and First Nations communities are also designed to build consent. Although these agreements, like those between OSEC and petroleum companies, are "somewhat mysterious" due to their confidentiality, they likely deliver financial and economic benefits to First Nations and address these communities' environmental and cultural concerns.[3] The regulatory approval of Shell's Muskeg River Mine in 1999, for example, noted that Shell and the Fort McKay First Nation signed an agreement "that addressed issues around education, economic development, employment opportunities, retention of culture, and physical infrastructure."[4] The political benefits of these agreements for corporations and governments rest in their potential to make Aboriginal objections to projects disappear or to significantly temper First Nations' resistance to the elites' vision for what boreal lands in the northeast should be sacrificed for.

First Nations' Concerns and Objections: Developing a Scientific Critique

Discoveries of microcores and microblades at the Beyza site in the Athabasca tar sands region suggest the ancestors of today's First Nations may have been living in northeastern Alberta 4,000 years BP (Before Present; used in radiocarbon dating). Tar sands production sprawls across the traditional territories of several Aboriginal cultural groups: the Athabasca Chipewyan, the West Woodland Cree, and the Athapaskan Beaver and Slavey.[5] Shell's Albian Sands joint venture protected the Quarry of the Ancestors archaeological site despite the fact this meant that 683,000 cubic metres of bitumen ore "would potentially be sterilized."[6] Other archaeological sites, however, have been destroyed by tar sands mining. Today, five government-recognized First Nations are found in the Regional Municipality of Wood Buffalo; together they number nearly 7,000 registered members (see Table 3).

Table 3 First Nations in the Regional Municipality of Wood Buffalo, Alberta (October 2016)

	Registered population	Number of reserve areas	Reserve area (hectares)	Primary community
Mikisew Cree First Nation	3,082	9	5,119.2	Fort Chipewyan
Athabasca Chipewyan First Nation	1,206	8	34,767.1	Fort Chipewyan
Fort McKay First Nation	851	5	14,886.0	Fort McKay
Fort McMurray #468 First Nation	760	4	3,231.7	Anzac
Chipewyan Prairie First Nation	928	3	3,079.7	Chard

Source: Indian and Northern Affairs Canada, "First Nation Profiles," http://fnp-ppn.aandc-aadnc.gc.ca/fnp/Main/index.aspx?lang=eng.

First Nations' concerns about and objections to the tar sands is a major theme in contemporary media coverage of projects and pipelines. For example, dozens of media outlets reported a 2016 announcement by the Treaty Alliance Against Tar Sands Expansion. This alliance of 50 First Nations and Tribes from British Columbia, Manitoba, New Brunswick, Ontario, Quebec, Minnesota, North Dakota, and Washington State declared their unconditional opposition to the tar sands; they were collaborating to stop all tar sands transportation projects in their territories.[7] In the late 1990s, media coverage suggested the scale and intensity of concerns were much smaller than they are today. Media coverage of hearings into tar sands projects was scarce; recognition therein that there was no room for traditional Aboriginal pursuits on lands committed to projects such as Suncor's Steepbank Mine or Syncrude's Aurora Mine was virtually nonexistent. What coverage there was of a First Nations' perspective pointed to the tension between the bush and modern economies. "We look at the industries as a positive thing economically," said Fort McKay's environmental director Pete Ladouceur. "We'd be fools not to get involved. But on the environment side," he added, "it's different." Dorothy McDonald, chief of the Fort McKay First Nation for much of the 1980s, saw the provincial government as turning a blind eye to the environment and her people: "They protect the industries, not the land, water, or people. The almighty dollar is what's important."[8] Elders were frustrated by losing old ways of living, accelerated by tar sands development. Youth, on the other hand, saw opportunities. "They want the fast cars and boats," Ladouceur said. "They don't practice traditional ways."[9]

Table 4 presents a record of the participation of three First Nations in oil sands regulatory hearings. One contributor to the lack of media coverage of First Nations and the tar sands in the latter half of the 1990s might be the relative absence of the Mikisew Cree, Athabasca Chipewyan, and Fort McKay First Nations from those hearings. The CNRL Horizon Mine application in 2004 was the first to see all three of these First Nations intervene. Since then they have intervened regularly.

Judging from regulatory decisions, the first interventions by First Nations were general; they weren't, as the Energy and Utilities Board said about the ACFN's 1997 Steepbank Mine submission, "specific."[12] First Nations' concerns deepened, however, and became more specific as the boom gathered pace. When the ACFN intervened at the Muskeg River Mine hearings in 1999, it drew the regulator's attention to "unnatural foaming of the river water, discoloured river ice, and deformed and tainted fish."[13] The Mikisew Cree submitted a very extensive, technically sophisticated evaluation of CNRL's Horizon project. Water was their most significant concern about the project. A healthy traditional way of life could not be pursued without

Table 4 Regulatory Interventions/Confidential Agreements with Oil Sands Mining Companies, Mikisew Cree First Nation, Athabasca Chipewyan First Nation, and Fort McKay First Nation, 1997–2013

	Mikisew Cree First Nation		Athabasca Chipewyan First Nation[10]		Fort McKay First Nation	
	Intervention in Regulatory Hearing	Confidential Agreement with Company	Intervention in Regulatory Hearing	Confidential Agreement with Company	Intervention in Regulatory Hearing	Confidential Agreement with Company
Syncrude Aurora (1997)	No	No	No	No	No	No
Suncor Steepbank (1997)	No	No	Yes	No	No	No
Suncor Millennium (1999)	No	No	Yes	Yes	No	No
Shell Muskeg River (1999)	No	No	Yes	No (but Shell funds EIA participation)	Yes	Yes
True North Energy Fort Hills (2002)[11]	No	No	No	No	Yes	Yes
CNRL Horizon (2004)	Yes	Yes (two months after the hearing)	Yes	Yes	Yes	Yes
Shell Jackpine (2004)	Yes	Yes	Yes	Yes	Yes	Yes
Suncor Voyageur (2006)	Yes	Partial	Yes	Yes	Yes	Yes
Shell Albian Sands (2006)	Yes	Partial (Envt); Still objects	Yes	Yes	Yes	Yes
Imperial Kearl (2007)	Yes	Partial	Yes	Yes	Yes	Partial
TOTAL Joslyn North Mine (2011)	Yes	Yes	Yes	Yes	Yes	Yes
Shell Jackpine Expansion (2013)	Yes	Yes	Yes	No	Yes	Yes

Source: Alberta, Oil Sands Mining Application Decision Reports, 1997–2013.

sufficient water from the Athabasca River. They insisted they already were trying to cope with lower than normal flows of water and that the thirst of tar sands plants for water would magnify those negative impacts. Like the concerns of the ACFN five years earlier, water quality too rested at the heart of their worries.

Human health concerns also were prominent at the Horizon hearings. Mikisew Cree Elders "reported serious worries about a large number of deaths in a short period of time in Fort McKay and Fort Chipewyan from a range of different ailments." The Fort McMurray Medical Staff Association supported their observations; the Elders' testimony suggested to the Association "that [A]boriginals appear to be particularly susceptible to life-threatening diseases, such as cancer and immune system problems."[14]

Such concerns did not receive the public attention they deserved until 2006 when Dr. John O'Connor, Fort Chipewyan's fly-in doctor, publicly called for Health Canada to investigate what he believed were abnormally high rates of cancers and immune diseases in such a small community.[15] O'Connor's concerns arguably never received the government's serious attention—except in the negative sense that Health Canada filed a complaint with Alberta's College of Physicians and Surgeons, claiming he was spreading "undue alarm" among the people of Fort Chipewyan.[16] Alberta's Cancer Board repudiated O'Connor's suspicions just four months after he made them when the Board participated in the EUB hearing on Suncor's Voyageur project. The Board rushed to judgement—its own review wasn't based on complete sets of data for 2004 or 2005.[17] The incompleteness and hastiness of the Board's analysis led O'Connor to stand by his initial position and reiterate the need to undertake a comprehensive study of the health of Aboriginal peoples in the region.[18] The tar sands, in his view, presented a profound health threat to First Nations.

O'Connor's views were no more convincing to government regulators in 2006 than the appearance and testimony of First Nations before the EUB had been earlier. In both the Horizon and Jackpine hearings, the EUB would go no further than recommending that federal and provincial health authorities "consider undertaking" a regional health study in the Fort Chipewyan area focused on the Aboriginal population.[19] In the Jackpine hearing, the MCFN pointed to the possibility that Shell might help fund a community health study; note, though, the crucial qualifications to Shell's commitment:

> MCFN's agreement with Shell included a commitment by Shell to contribute funding to a baseline health study of the Fort Chipewyan population, provided that the study was conducted independently and with appropriate

scientific rigour and *provided that other oil sands developers and/or governments agree to participate in the funding of the study.*[20]

The alarm sounded by O'Connor, and government's reluctance to take it seriously, seemed to stiffen the opposition of some First Nations to further bitumen development. In June 2007 the MCFN recommended a moratorium on issuing "any further licenses, permits, or approvals with regard to any and all activity in the Athabasca oil sands region or what the Mikisew Cree recognize as its traditional territory."[21] Health concerns were one reason offered for this recommendation. Others were insufficient consultation; lack of consideration for Aboriginal and treaty rights; absence of a cumulative effects assessment of development in the region; failure to establish a precautionary, scientifically sound instream flow needs framework for the lower Athabasca River; outstanding treaty land entitlement issues; and uncertainty regarding reclamation requirements and standards.

Another branch of this Aboriginal scientific critique of the tar sands boom appeared in 2007 when the Nunee Health Board Society released Dr. Kevin Timoney's report on water and sediment quality in Fort Chipewyan. Timoney concluded that existing high levels of arsenic, mercury, and polycyclic aromatic hydrocarbons (PAHs) appeared to be rising.[22] In late May 2008 the people of Fort Chipewyan finally thought they heard what they wanted: the Alberta Cancer Board announced it would lead a comprehensive study (with Health Canada's participation) into the incidence of cancer in Fort Chipewyan.[23]

Perhaps Timoney's study was the straw that broke the state's opposition to conducting the health investigation the local community had been demanding. Another event's potential importance, however, should not be overlooked. On May 6th, Suncor convened a community meeting in Fort Chipewyan. There the company revealed that contaminated water from the company's 40-year-old Tar Island tailings pond was seeping into groundwater and toward the Athabasca River at a rate of 67 litres per second or nearly six million litres per day. These research findings, sponsored in part by Suncor, had been disclosed in a conference presentation the previous November, just a few days before Timoney's report was released.[24] At the very least, this qualified the government's consistent message that there was no evidence to suggest that the tailings ponds affected water quality in the Athabasca River.[25]

Regardless of what combination of factors pushed the state to act, the government study satisfied neither the consultative nor the methodological expectations of Fort Chipewyan's First Nations. In July 2008 ACFN Chief Allan Adam charged that the Cancer Board had failed to consult at all with his community about conducting the study. First Nations officials took the extraordinary step of rejecting the study's findings before they were released. MCFN Chief Roxanne Marcel claimed the draft study was identical to the one the community had rejected as incomplete and insufficiently comprehensive two years previously. "They just didn't include us," said Steve Courtoreille, the Chair of the Nunee health authority in Fort Chipewyan. "Bottom line, I haven't seen the team come up here. They haven't come to the community to actually meet with the [E]lders or to get some feedback from the community."[26]

The study's results, released in February 2009, did not confirm Dr. O'Connor's suspicions. But it also didn't soothe community concerns. The Cancer Board concluded that, between 1995 and 2006, only two of the six cases O'Connor suspected of being cholangiocarcinoma, an extremely rare bile duct cancer, were confirmed cases of that cancer. Two confirmed cases over that period did not exceed statistical expectations. But the overall number of confirmed cancer cases over this 12-year period was higher than expected (51 confirmed cases vs. 39 expected cases). Furthermore, the incidence of some specific cancers—biliary tract cancers, soft tissue cancers, and cancers of the blood and lymphatic system—also was higher than expected. The study didn't address the issue of what relationship might exist between cancer risks in Fort Chipewyan and environmental exposures such as those related to pulp mills, tar sands operations, and abandoned uranium mines. Five independent experts reviewed the study and generally agreed with its conclusions.[27]

Since it didn't confirm O'Connor's suspicions, the 2009 Cancer Board study didn't help his case before Alberta's College of Physicians and Surgeons. The College decided that O'Connor, despite receiving support from both the Alberta and the Canadian Medical Associations, made "inaccurate" or "untruthful" public statements regarding his claims about cancer in Fort Chipewyan. The College's investigation, one never made public, also concluded that O'Connor "obstructed" Health Canada and the Alberta Cancer Board when they attempted to investigate his claims.[28] But neither the College nor the public health officials who lodged the complaint felt the public interest would be furthered by punishing the physician. "The message that Dr. O'Connor and others may take from this review," said the College, "is the need for advocacy to be fair, truthful, balanced, and respectful."[29] Some might see a chilling effect in the College's reprimand; it may discourage physicians from following O'Connor's lead in the future.

First Nations' Concerns and Objections: The Constitutional Critique

Canada's constitutional and legal provisions regarding Aboriginal and treaty rights—like free trade agreements and like the structure of regulatory/

environmental assessment processes—constitute an institutional face that may smile or frown on exploiting the tar sands. Section 35(1) of the *Constitution Act, 1982* recognized and affirmed the existing Aboriginal and treaty rights of Canada's Aboriginal peoples.[30] A long and growing list of cases is constructing a framework for how the duty to consult and accommodate, a key constitutional duty toward First Nations, should be interpreted. The 1990 case of *R. v. Sparrow* affirmed a duty to consult with Aboriginal peoples and established that key terms in Section 35(1) such as "existing" and "recognized and affirmed" should be interpreted generously and liberally.[31]

Two cases, *Haida Nation v. British Columbia (Minister of Forests)* and *Mikisew Cree First Nation v. Canada (Minister of Canadian Heritage)*, are key decisions regarding what the duty to consult demands from the state on lands subject to an Aboriginal land claim and on treaty lands respectively.[32] Treaty lands are the lands at the centre of the Athabasca tar sands area. These decisions offer political resources for First Nations who object to the tar sands, but they also qualify the value of these resources. They establish, for example, that the state has a duty to consult that cannot be delegated to industry or other third parties. But they also establish that consultation doesn't demand Aboriginal consent. In *Mikisew Cree First Nation v. Canada (Minister of Canadian Heritage)*, a case concerning treaty rights on surrendered lands in northeastern Alberta, Justice Binnie's decision recognizes that the Crown's "assurances of *continuity* in traditional patterns of economic activity" were key to the successful negotiation of Treaty 8.[33] But other language denies, or at least downplays, the importance of guaranteeing continuity. Both Indian and white negotiators are said to have recognized in 1899 that the treaty promised transition when it came to Indian practices on the land; treaty language "could not be clearer in foreshadowing change." Justice Binnie concluded that neither side believed the treaty was "a finished land use blueprint"; instead it signalled "the advancing dawn of a period of transition."[34] Views such as these led him to reject the Mikisew Cree's presupposition "that Treaty 8 promised continuity of nineteenth century patterns of land use."[35] The continuity Justice Binnie affirms at one point in his judgement becomes transition away from traditional pursuits at another point in the judgement.

First Nations constitutional challenges to tar sands approvals only appeared nearly 20 years after the boom started and 10 years after the Mikisew Cree won in *Mikisew*. In 2012 the ACFN filed a notice of questions of constitutional law with the Federal-Provincial Review Panel established to consider the expansion of Shell's Jackpine mine. The focus was on the constitutional duty to consult and accommodate and whether the provincial and federal governments had fulfilled that duty. The ACFN argued that Shell's project had potentially adverse consequences for their treaty rights since Canada and Alberta had failed to adequately perform their duty to consult and accommodate. The ACFN asked the panel not to authorize the project until the Crown corrected this situation. They also asked the Panel to, alternatively, do one of two things: defer a decision on the project until such time as the duty had been discharged or recommend to the federal minister of environment that the project's adverse impact on ACFN treaty rights couldn't be justified until governments had fulfilled these duties.[36]

The Panel, after considering written and oral submissions, concluded it didn't have the jurisdiction to answer the constitutional questions posed. The Panel's statutory authority didn't expressly authorize it to consider the adequacy of Crown consultation.[37] The ACFN asked the Panel to adjourn the hearing so it could ask the Alberta Court of Appeal for leave to appeal the Panel's decision. The Panel refused. After the hearings concluded, the ACFN went to the Court of Appeal to seek leave to appeal the Panel's decision regarding the First Nation's constitutional law questions. The Court of Appeal dismissed that application; subsequently, the Supreme Court of Canada refused to grant the ACFN leave to appeal the Alberta Court of Appeal's decision.[38] The Joint Review Panel approved the Jackpine mine expansion on the grounds that, in light of the significant economic benefits associated with the project, the project was in the public interest despite the significant adverse environmental impacts the project would also deliver.

The ACFN then asked the Federal Court of Canada to overturn the federal environment minister's December 2013 approval of the Jackpine expansion. The First Nation repeated the thrust of the constitutional law argument it wanted the Joint Review Panel to consider: the Crown had breached its duty to consult and accommodate. The ACFN argued the consultation was rushed, too short, not transparent enough, and insufficiently attentive to the ACFN's concerns and to the cumulative effects of the project. It also claimed government neglected commitments to the ACFN that were supposed to be fulfilled as part of the consultation process; it further alleged that government broke its promise to consider accommodations after the Joint Review Panel submitted its report.[39]

Justice Tremblay-Lamer relied on the standard of reasonableness to assess the adequacy of the Crown's efforts to discharge its constitutional duties. Here the fact that more consultation could take place didn't necessarily make the amount of consultation that had taken place unreasonable. The Justice accepted the Review Panel's conclusions that the project would deliver "significant adverse environmental effects" and that the cumulative effects of Jackpine plus all the other development in the region "would likely result in significant harm to Aboriginal rights and the environment."[40]

Nonetheless, the Justice rejected every ACFN submission. The consultation was not rushed—it had lasted for more than six years and, in the Justice's view, was ongoing. During that time the government and Shell had provided funding to facilitate the First Nation's participation in the process; the ACFN had filed more than 6,000 pages of submission, had marshalled witnesses, and had presented its views at dozens of meetings.[41] She identified a list of measures—all indicating the ACFN's views were "seriously considered." Government had modified the original project; the ACFN's interests were reflected in numerous recommendations from the Review Panel; many of those recommendations became conditions the project needed to meet. "I fail to see," Justice Tremblay-Lamer wrote, "what more could be done to ensure meaningful consultation."[42] The Justice had the same view of whether the Crown had upheld its honour with respect to accommodating the Athabasca Chipewyan: "Canada accommodated the ACFN's concerns by imposing a long list of conditions binding Shell. I do not believe that the duty to accommodate required Canada to adopt all of the mitigation measures that the Panel recommended."[43] Perhaps the only positive the Athabasca Chipewyan First Nation could take from this judgement was that Justice Tremblay-Lamer didn't rule on the sufficiency of the provincial government's performance of its duty to consult and accommodate.

Compromise: The Other Face of the First Nations' Relationship to the Tar Sands

The failure to advance constitutional arguments against the tar sands earlier may be explained in part by the willingness, or resignation, of First Nations to compromise and adapt to the boom. The ACFN's request that the Jackpine Panel consider questions of constitutional law wasn't the first time First Nations made such a request; it was, however, the first time a First Nation pursued it to its logical conclusion in the courts. Both the ACFN and the MCFN declared they were going to raise questions of constitutional law during the 2010 Joint Review Panel hearings into Total's Joslyn Mine project. The Mikisew Cree presented a damning list of complaints about consultation and accommodation issues to the Panel. They asserted that Treaty 8 harvesting rights had been seriously infringed by tar sands exploitation. The First Nation's lawyers maintained these infringements could not be justified according to the *Sparrow* test because

– consultation had been "inadequate and incomplete,"
– consultation had "not been carried out in good faith or with any genuine intention of understanding, addressing or remediating the concerns" of the beneficiaries of Treaty 8, and

– government had offered "no meaningful accommodation" to the MCFN
with respect to protecting habitat, minimizing the cumulative harm
of oil sands projects on the Mikisew Cree way of life, or balancing the
interests of the Mikisew Cree and the Crown.[44]

The MCFN changed their position one day into the Total hearings. The
First Nation reached an agreement with the company. With this agreement
in hand, the MCFN withdrew its objections to the project as well as its
notice of intent to raise a constitutional law question.[45]

The ACFN constitutional submission to the Joslyn hearings, like that of
the Mikisew, presented a compelling portrait of the importance of traditional lands to Aboriginal culture, identity, and way of life. The waters of the
Athabasca were the "lifeblood" of this territory. The proposed Joslyn mine
represented yet another project promising to reduce the amount of land
available for the meaningful exercise of Treaty 8 rights. The brief urged the
Panel not to approve the mine because it "would have profound impacts
on traditional resources in the Regional Study Area and further diminish
the land base and resources available to support the meaningful exercise of
ACFN's Treaty Rights."[46] When the hearings began, the ACFN too withdrew their objections to the project and their intent to raise constitutional
questions.[47] They too reached an agreement with the company addressing
their concerns.

These First Nations' adaptations to development through company–First
Nations agreement are unique because of this constitutional dimension. Table
4 makes it very clear that company–First Nations agreements were anything
but unique. Beginning with the CNRL Horizon project in 2004, the MCFN
and the Fort McKay First Nation reached agreements in all seven mining
projects that obtained regulatory approval. The ACFN had six agreements
to its credit over this period. In the seventh case, the Jackpine expansion, the
ACFN looks like it drew a line in the sands and went to court instead.

Through these agreements Mikisew Cree leaders compromised their
people and their future to the developing pattern of industrial expansion
in their territories. By the time the Jackpine mine expansion was approved
in 2013, First Nations occupied an ironic or paradoxical position—
concerned about cumulative effects of exploiting the tar sands but refusing
to object to a specific project that would increase those cumulative effects.
This irony is captured in the Mikisew Cree's submission to the Jackpine
Mine panel:

> Shell has addressed the Project-specific concerns of MCFN associated with
> these projects to MCFN's satisfaction. MCFN remains concerned about

> issues related to cumulative effects of development in the Athabasca region
> and with issues related to Crown consultation. In light of Shell's efforts
> to address Project-specific concerns, MCFN hereby withdraws its State-
> ments of Concern dated September 26, 2008 filed in connection with the
> Projects…
>
>   For greater clarity, MCFN does not object to the regulatory approval of
> the Projects.[48]

For much of the period considered here, the First Nations' profile in oil
sands regulatory proceedings sits at odds with the mainstream opinion of
how First Nations and their supporters view exploiting the tar sands. That
conventional view stresses the vociferous, categorical, opposition of First
Nations to this exploitation because of what it's doing to human and environmental health. It's a view excluding a reality where, through confidential,
negotiated settlements with tar sands companies, some affected First Nations
temper or withdraw their objections to specific projects. The conventional
view expects to see Chief Allan Adam of the Athabasca Chipewyan First
Nation sitting beside Neil Young when the music icon talks about his *Honour the Treaties* tour—his 2014 campaign to shed more light on how exploiting the oil sands affects Treaty rights and the environment.[49] It expects to
see George Poitras, a former chief of the Mikisew Cree First Nation, invite
film director James Cameron to tour the tar sands.[50] The conventional view
expects Cameron to say: "The way I look at it … it's the indigenous people
that step up and say, 'We speak for nature.' Because that's their culture, that's
what they believe and feel."[51] Accordingly, we shouldn't be surprised to learn
that, while Cameron was getting a first-hand look at the tar sands, Poitras
was in Washington, DC, to help lobby the Obama administration against
TransCanada's Keystone XL tar sands pipeline.

But this conventional view doesn't prepare us to learn that Poitras's lobbying and Cameron's visit took place at exactly the same time the Mikisew
Cree reached a settlement with Total E&P and withdrew their objections
to the Total Joslyn North Mine project.[52] If Total E&P Canada ever proceeds with building this mine on what the company calls its "Joslyn asset,"
it will consume more than 220 square kilometres (85 square miles) of the
boreal forest in order to produce 100,000 barrels of bitumen per day for
20 years.[53] The conventional view also doesn't necessarily prepare us to
learn that George Poitras, who launched a "bloody oil" anti-tar sands tour
in Europe and questioned whether it was worth exploiting petroleum if
oil and gas harmed human health, became the Chief Executive Officer of
the Mikisew Cree First Nation. As CEO, Poitras has responsibilities with
respect to impact benefit agreements between industry and his First Nation
and in managing the dividends the First Nation receives from the Mikisew

Group of Companies. Such dividends are largely generated by the fact that First Nations companies, as we will soon see, are extensively involved in the "bloody oil" business. The conventional view also doesn't prepare us to read Chief Adam alluding to impact benefit agreements signed between his people and the tar sands companies when he's answering questions at a press conference with Neil Young.[54]

First Nations: Partners in Exploiting the Tar Sands

This tension, this diversity in opinion and actions, shouldn't surprise. To see these two positions as inconsistent may be, as Neil Reddekopp suggests, to see an illusion. For First Nations faced with poverty and the death of their traditional way of life, Reddekopp argues it's not unprecedented to address the most serious crisis (poverty, vanishing way of life) at the cost of ignoring or magnifying other challenges (environment and human health).[55] Or, as Gabrielle Slowey suggests, the Mikisew's pragmatism, their realization that a traditional livelihood was impossible, didn't require them to lose their indigenous identity if the core values of that identity could animate the First Nations' economic development strategies.[56] But can they find a middle ground? This question is central to the lives of First Nations during the tar sands boom.

Warming to a more "industrialization-friendly" position is not difficult to understand considering the per capita income situation of Aboriginal peoples in northern Alberta in the late 1990s. The Fort McKay First Nation stood out then as one of the region's "wealthy" Aboriginal communities. But its wealthy status was relative; it came from comparing Fort McKay with other northern Aboriginal communities. The average income of people living in Fort McKay in 1996 was $16,325—more than any other northern Alberta First Nations community. It was, however, 38 percent below the Alberta average. The vast majority of Indian reserves and settlements in northern Alberta could not even claim a per capita average income level equal to 50 percent of the Alberta average.[57]

Some First Nations leaders came to view the tar sands not as a curse but rather as a blessing to a brighter future. Fort McKay First Nation's Chief Jim Boucher stands out in this respect. Industrialization and environmentalism combined to destroy the traditional lives of Chief Boucher's people. First came the Great Canadian Oil Sands project. It wreaked "horrific" damage on Fort McKay's traditional lands. Then there were the environmentalists and their fur boycott in Europe. It was the second nail in the coffin of the traditional lifestyle in Boucher's community.[58] Adapt or die—those were the only options Boucher felt were open to his people. "On a whole," Chief

Boucher maintained in 2005, "I would say that the opportunities and the benefits far outweigh the risks associated with the environmental degradation of the land."[59] Or as he told the American Broadcasting Company in 2008, "If it wasn't for the oil sand [sic], we wouldn't have a new economy. So, to be pragmatic and practical about it, the alternative is to sit there and do nothing and collect welfare, or to be a part of the economy. And I'd rather be part of the economy than to let our people be there collecting welfare."[60]

The Mikisew Cree leadership to the northeast of Fort McKay shared Boucher's outlook. The Fort McKay First Nation opened the doors of a small contracting business in 1986, just around the time the MCFN was about to settle its Treaty Land Entitlement negotiations with Canada and Alberta. After this settlement, the MCFN sought to rectify its absence from the region's resource economy and regarded participating in exploiting the oil sands "as a way to optimize its economic potential."[61]

Capital played a vital, arguably proactive, role in encouraging First Nations to partner in the tar sands economy. It had done so since the start of the Syncrude project in the 1970s. Some senior executives in the tar sands sector recognized early in the history of exploiting their treasure that it was in their interests to involve Aboriginal peoples in the industrialized future they intended for boreal Alberta. The 1970s had opened controversially for Aboriginal/government-business relations. The federal government's 1969 proposal to abolish the *Indian Act* sparked a firestorm among Aboriginal peoples. This response was at least as intense in Alberta as elsewhere in Canada. Led by Harold Cardinal, the Indian Association of Alberta responded to the federal proposal with charges that Ottawa intended nothing less than the cultural genocide of Aboriginal peoples through assimilation.[62] In 1973 the Supreme Court of Canada issued a landmark ruling in *Calder et al. v. Attorney-General of British Columbia*.[63] There the Court split evenly on the crucial question of whether the Nisga'a people had Aboriginal title to the traditional territories they had never ceded to the Crown. Three judges agreed with the Nisga'a; Nisga'a title had never been extinguished by treaty or by legislation. Although the Nisga'a lost the case, they didn't lose on the grounds they did not have title to their lands. In Canada's north, Aboriginal peoples who had never ceded their lands to the Canadian state were concerned about what the Mackenzie Valley natural gas pipeline proposals would do to their homeland. Mr. Justice Thomas Berger was appointed in 1974 to conduct a wide-ranging inquiry into these proposals.[64] In Quebec, Cree and Inuit peoples fought against the massive hydroelectricity projects planned for the James Bay area; their struggles produced the *James Bay and Northern Quebec Agreement*, the first modern comprehensive land claim settlement in Canada.

These concerns and unrest, with the problems they could pose for exploiting natural resources, help explain Syncrude's introduction of its Aboriginal Development Program in 1974, four years before the consortium produced its first barrel of synthetic crude oil.[65] Rather than shelve its development ambitions, the consortium would encourage First Nations to share and profit from those ambitions. This program was the first step Syncrude took on its journey to becoming, for a time, the Canadian company with the largest complement of Aboriginal employees. The program focused on five components: employment, education, business development, support for community projects such as community and Elders' centres, and environmental protection.[66] In addition to establishing the company's first policies and targets for Aboriginal recruitment, the agreement introduced cultural awareness courses for supervisors and support/counselling services for Aboriginal employees.[67] Two years later, the Syncrude Indian Opportunities Agreement was signed. This 10-year agreement furthered Syncrude's commitment to hire First Nations workers who met Syncrude's employment standards and to assist in upgrading the skills of Aboriginal peoples who didn't meet those standards. Politically, this agreement's important value could be seen by the fact the Indian Association of Alberta, a harsh critic of Ottawa's 1969 White Paper, joined the company and the federal government in signing the agreement.[68]

In the 1990s, Syncrude expanded its support for Aboriginal people who wanted a piece of the tar sands action. The support came in the form of venture capital-like financing and sole source, no-bid contracts with Aboriginal firms. "We needed a network of trusted suppliers," Syncrude's Robert Loader told a Senate committee, "and so we made a limited number of sole source awards and sometimes restricted bids to Aboriginal suppliers and contractors. Although we do not finance businesses, we have been known to come up with some creative arrangements to help jump-start ventures until they are running and profitable."[69] Slowey writes of the assistance Syncrude lent to the Mikisew Cree in the 1990s to help that First Nation get into the market for tar sands services. The company helped launch 2000 Plus Limited Partnership in 1991.[70] This partnership, named to reflect the MCFN leadership's desire to get as many of their people as possible off social assistance by 2000,[71] grew quickly in the 1990s and by decade's end was doing business with other tar sands companies such as Suncor and Shell Canada.[72] Syncrude also was a talent scout, looking for individuals in First Nations communities with entrepreneurial promise who supported growth in the tar sands. Syncrude favoured David Tuccaro, a very successful entrepreneur in northeastern Alberta, and supported his purchase of Neegan Development from the MCFN. Syncrude evaluated the company for Tuccaro and suggested strategies he could use to increase Neegan's income and the efficiency of the company's operations. In the words of one Syncrude official, the company's assistance "essentially got things off the ground and Dave went on to build Neegan into a profitable and reputable company."[73] When Syncrude's Steve Jani appeared before Alberta's Oil Sands Multi-Stakeholder Consultation Panel in 2006, he told them how proud his employer was of the testimonials Syncrude received from Aboriginal suppliers and the help the company gave to the Aboriginal business community to "take control over its destiny." Syncrude had helped that community "be a major contributor to, and beneficiary of, the continued growth of the oil sands industry."[74]

By the dawn of the twenty-first century, approximately 13 percent of Syncrude's workforce was Aboriginal and the company had done more than $350 million in business with Aboriginal companies since 1984.[75] In 2011, 8.6 percent of the Syncrude workforce, 492 employees, were self-identified members of First Nations. In that year, Syncrude procured more than $140 million in goods and services from Aboriginal businesses. This brought the consortium's total Aboriginal business spending to more than $1.7 billion since 1992.[76] In 2009, Suncor declared it too had crossed the $1 billion threshold; $367 million of that spending came in 2007–08 alone.[77] Suncor, lagging behind Syncrude, was left to joke in the local newspaper how it intended to best Syncrude when it came to reaching the $2 billion mark.[78] That milestone was passed in 2012.[79] Looking at the tar sands sector generally, CAPP's vice-president oil sands said Aboriginal firms had earned more than $8 billion from contracts with oil sands companies prior to 2014; in 2012 those businesses generated more than $1.8 billion.

With respect to community and cultural development, tar sands companies gave more than $20 million in 2011 and 2012 to Aboriginal communities "for school and youth programs, celebrations, cultural events, literacy projects, and other community programs."[80] The $500,000 Shell Canada contributed to the construction of the Mikisew Cree First Nation Elders Care Centre in November 2012—support coincidentally announced just over one month after the MCFN withdrew its objections to Shell's Jackpine mine expansion project—is a specific example of the type of community development some tar sands companies help finance. This $12 million centre, the first to offer assisted living and palliative care in northeastern Aboriginal communities, received $5 million in donations from tar sands companies; the federal and provincial governments didn't contribute a dime.[81]

Such corporate efforts, and the numbers they have produced, are laudable. There's also no doubt about the passion some senior tar sands executives such as Syncrude's Eric Newell brought to efforts to hire Aboriginal workers and contract with Aboriginal firms. But these initiatives weren't altruistic.

They should be seen as part of the "counter, coopt, and compromise" strategy business adopted in the face of a nascent countermovement. In 1999, the Senate Standing Committee on Aboriginal Peoples heard that Syncrude didn't view its programs "so much as a helping hand as an investment in our future." Loader described contributing to the future of the Aboriginal community as "a fringe benefit."[82] Most importantly, First Nations had no input into what type of development and how much industrialization would take place in northeastern Alberta. They were noticeably absent, for example, from the National Task Force on Oil Sands Strategies. When Jim Carter said Syncrude's fundamental objective was to help Aboriginal people "take charge of their future,"[83] he might have added that government and industry had already drafted the blueprint for that future. First Nations were welcome, with his company's help, to join them in industrializing Alberta's boreal forest if they chose to.

For its part, the government of Alberta made it clear that, while tar sands employment or contracts for First Nations were positive, First Nations participation as owners of subsurface petroleum rights was a heresy. Alberta was adamantly opposed to including lands from the Athabasca tar sands area in any Treaty Land Entitlement agreement with the Mikisew Cree that would give First Nations ownership rights to the tar sands. Alberta's intransigence on this point effectively scuttled a preliminary agreement in the early 1970s between Ottawa and the Mikisew to transfer 45,280 acres (18,324 hectares) of provincial lands to the First Nation. Alberta balked because those lands contained tar sands. Alberta only warmed to settling the treaty entitlement nearly a decade later when the Mikisew Cree relinquished any claim to the tar sands. Notes taken during negotiations on May 6 and 7, 1982, report that Alberta would transfer 24,000 acres (9,712 hectares) to the MCFN; it also agreed to transfer mineral rights—other than rights to the tar sands—in this territory to the First Nation.

By embracing the tar sands, Jim Boucher and other chiefs have put more money, much more money, into the pockets of some of their constituents. Statistics Canada's figures show the people of Fort McKay have made staggering income gains during the tar sands boom relative to Albertans generally and to their circumstances in the mid-1990s. If above-average income in a community is the metric of "the good life," then more and more people in Fort McKay live it. Table 5 presents data from Statistics Canada's 2011 National Household Survey. In the Fort McKay Indian Band area the average income in 2010 of the Aboriginal identity population was $66,110. This was nearly 30 percent more than the provincial average income of $50,956. In inflation-adjusted dollars, this was more than a 300 percent increase from the average income reported for Fort McKay in 1996.[84]

Table 5   Average Incomes, Alberta and Aboriginal Identity Populations in Fort McKay Indian Band Area/Census Division No. 16, 2010

	Alberta	Fort McKay	Census Div. No. 16
Male	$64,260	$65,602	$88,214
Female	37,439	66,593	43,714
Both sexes combined	50,956	66,110	67,007

Source: Statistics Canada, *2011 National Household Survey* (Aboriginal Identity Population in Fort McKay First Nation, Indian Band Area; Aboriginal Identity Population in Census Division No. 16; Alberta Population). The specific Statistics Canada URLs for this data are found in footnotes 85 and 86.

Contrary to the overall Alberta picture, it's Aboriginal women, not men, who earned the largest average incomes. And, at $66,593, their average income was an eye-popping 78 percent higher than the average for Alberta women ($37,439). The average income of Aboriginal men in Fort McKay also was greater than the average for all Alberta men but only marginally so ($65,602 vs. $64,260). More than 12 percent of Aboriginal people in Fort McKay earned more than $100,000 per year; nearly 10 percent earned more than $125,000 per year. Both percentages are higher than those recorded for all Albertans.[85]

Have the members of other First Nations communities in the Athabasca tar sands area seen their average incomes skyrocket? Table 5 suggests that, generally speaking, the Fort McKay story is more typical than not when it comes to measuring the material effects on First Nations communities of developing the tar sands. The incomes of Aboriginal peoples throughout the Athabasca tar sands area have benefited tremendously from exploiting the tar sands. Census Division No. 16 sprawls across northeastern Alberta; it includes Fort McMurray and the other key residential communities in the region for all five First Nations of the Athabasca Tribal Council (the Council these First Nations are affiliated with): the communities of Anzac, Janvier, Fort McKay, and Fort Chipewyan. The 2011 National Household Survey data show the average incomes of the Aboriginal identity population aged 15 years and over in northeastern Alberta to be considerably higher, at the very least, than the provincial averages. Thirty-one, 37, and 17—these are the percentages by which the average incomes of the total Aboriginal identity population, Aboriginal males, and Aboriginal females exceed the respective provincial averages.[86]

This is not to suggest the five First Nations of the Athabasca Tribal Council have shared equally in the financial rewards that have come from building an oil factory on their ancestral lands or that all Aboriginal residents have benefited materially from the boom. Members of the Chi-pewyan Prairie First Nation and the Fort McMurray #468 First Nation have not gleaned the same financial benefits as Fort McKay. The average income in 2010 of the Chipewyan Prairie Aboriginal identity population was only $24,528, 52 percent below the provincial average. That year the income picture of the Fort McMurray #468 First Nation was better, but still far below the provincial average. The average income there of the Abo-riginal population over 15 years of age was $36,945, 27 percent below the provincial mean.[87] Given that the Mikisew Cree and Athabasca Chipew-yan First Nations constitute nearly two-thirds of the total population of Athabasca Tribal Council First Nations (see Table 3), it is likely their mem-bers, like Fort McKay's Aboriginal population, are profiting handsomely from the tar sands boom.

The material importance of the Aboriginal–tar sands relationship forged in the post-1995 boom is visible in other ways as well. One measure rests in the vitality of the Northern Alberta Aboriginal Business Association. Its 249 members include 102 full members, businesses with their head offices in the Wood Buffalo region that have at least 51 percent Aboriginal owner-ship. Syncrude helped create this association in 1993, and all major tar sands companies are associate or industry members of the organization.[88]

One of the striking features of this association and the Aboriginal corpo-rate profile more generally is the considerable place state enterprise, in the guise of corporations owned by First Nations governments, enjoys. For the Fort McKay First Nation its "national" company is the Fort McKay Group of Companies. According to Chief Boucher, Fort McKay's flagship began modestly in 1986 and had grown by 2004 to include 10 companies employ-ing roughly 300 people and generating $100 million annually in sales.[89] Gordon Jaremko reported that, in 2007, band members received annual divi-dends of between $3,000 and $4,000 from the First Nation; these dividends came from Fort McKay's state enterprises.[90] In 2012, Jim Carbery, the Fort McKay Group of Companies' CEO, told an energy security forum his stable of firms was doing nearly $200 million of business every year with petro-leum companies.[91]

Chief and Council members of the Fort McKay First Nation profit handsomely, some might say excessively, from the commercial successes the Fort McKay Group of Companies have had in the tar sands. Band policy regarding the salaries of Chief and Council states that "the sum of all salaries to Chief and Council cannot exceed 3% of total revenues in any one year."[92] In the 2013–14 fiscal year Chief Jim Boucher received a salary of $644,441 for his service; his total remuneration amounted to $704,800. This amount was more than three times the $217,750 the premier of Alberta collected

in that year.[93] The annual salary of each Fort McKay First Nation council-
lor was $316,270; with honoraria and other remuneration their total annual
income ranged between $359,000 and $368,952.[94] The First Nation's audi-
tors reported that the $2,067,098 paid to Chief and Council did not violate
band policy.

Fort McKay's state enterprise profile is typical of other First Nations
in northeastern Alberta. All members of the Athabasca Tribal Council
court tar sands and petroleum-related jobs and business. The Chipewyan
Prairie Dene First Nation Group of Companies has done this largely
through forming joint ventures.[95] Since 1987, Christina River Enterprises
has operated as the corporate arm of the Fort McMurray #468 First
Nation. Led by Steve Jani, a former Syncrude Aboriginal relations team
leader identified above, the firm's ventures are oriented heavily toward the
petroleum sector.[96]

Most significantly, even First Nations now firmly linked in the public
mind with opposing tar sands exploitation, such as the Mikisew Cree and
the Athabasca Chipewyan, have developed long-term, profitable commercial relationships with the energy and tar sands sectors. Before the tar sands
boom started, the Mikisew Cree First Nation concluded it needed a healthy
stake in the tar sands sector. From a modest start of eight employees in 1991
working for the firm 2000 Plus, Mikisew Cree business interests employed
nearly 200 people by 1995.[97] The Mikisew Energy Services Group (MESG)
is the First Nation's key operational face in the tar sands. It describes itself
as "a major participant in the resource development sector for the oil sands
industry" and includes Syncrude, Suncor, and Shell Albian Sands among
its clients.[98] MESG's circumstances in 2012, aiming for $65 million in gross
revenues and employing between 300 and 600 people, justifies such self-
description.[99] In addition to MESG, the Mikisew Group of Companies
in 2012 included six other wholly owned companies: Mikisew Industrial
Supply, Mikisew Sport Fishing, Super 8 Fort McMurray, Fort Petroleum,
Mikisew Fleet Maintenance, and Mikisew Property Development. It also
was a partner in two joint ventures.[100] The Group's vision is "to become a
major service provider in the maintenance and construction for Oil and Gas
Industry in North (sic) Alberta" and its mission, in part, is described as "[m]
aximizing utilization of [A]boriginal workforce and providing training and
employment opportunities to Mikisew members."[101] The first incarnation of
Mikisew Industrial Supply, Mikisew Slings and Safety Ltd., depended crucially on Suncor for its birth and early success.[102] The profitability of these
ventures depends heavily on a vibrant tar sands sector. Even members of the
Mikisew Cree First Nation who do not work in a tar sands-related business
are reminded of the importance of exploiting bitumen to their material

well-being through semi-annual dividend cheques they receive courtesy of the Mikisew Group of Companies.[103]

The Athabasca Chipewyan First Nation also has deep economic roots in Alberta's bitumen-soaked sands now. Its commercial beginnings were as modest as those of the Fort McKay and Mikisew Cree First Nations. Denesoline Environment opened its doors to seven employees in the early 1990s; 200 employees were crossing its threshold in 2002 and the firm was doing nearly $2.7 million of waste management, janitorial, and equipment cleaning business with Syncrude.[104] Slowey suggests that Syncrude's assistance in establishing this Chipewyan enterprise arose from Cree/Chipewyan competition for the jobs created through 2000 Plus. The Mikisew Cree firm focused its "hiring on the Cree band and the Chipewyan weren't getting access to any opportunities."[105] Syncrude, surprised by accusations from the Chipewyan that they weren't supporting that First Nation, then helped Denesoline get off the ground. All of the product lines offered by ACDEN, the acronym for the Athabasca Chipewyan First Nation's state enterprise and the successor of Denesoline Environment, are connected to the petroleum industry.[106] ACDEN, headquartered in a stunning building in Fort McMurray that conforms to Gold Level LEED (Leadership in Energy and Environmental Design) standards, generates approximately $250 million annually in revenues.[107] Garry K. Flett, ACDEN's president and CEO, opens a company promotional video by suggesting that the many admirable sustainability features of ACDEN's headquarters illustrate well the company's commitment to sustainability in all its affairs:

> To me, this eco-friendly building represents our commitment to the environment. We practice what we preach in all elements of our business and this building is a direct reflection of that.[108]

His view differs little from what you will read Steve Williams, Flett's counterpart at Suncor, say in his 2013 sustainability message.[109] It's the sort of language and imagery you expect from any chief executive of a corporation that depends heavily on exploiting the tar sands to maintain its health and profits.

Building First Nations' Organizational Capacity ... with Strings Attached

The timing of First Nations' entry and participation in the regulatory process is explained at least partially by First Nations' institutional or organizational capacity. Not participating in the regulatory process, especially given the technical demands of hearings, may be rooted in the fact that First Nations simply didn't possess the requisite resources. First Nations' acceptance of tar sands projects between 1997 and 2003 noted earlier, then, may be traced to an inability to supply the expert testimony regulatory processes demand.

But the sophistication of the Mikisew Cree's intervention in CNRL's 2003 Horizon application signalled a turning point in both the frequency and the technical quality of First Nations' interventions. CNRL's financing of it is crucial to understanding the technical sophistication of the Mikisew's intervention. CNRL's $155,000 cheque likely went a considerable distance to help the Mikisew build or retain the expertise needed to assemble the arguments presented to the Joint Review Panel.

CNRL's substantial contribution to the Mikisew Cree points to the fact that industry, and governments to a lesser extent, chose to help First Nations improve their organizational capacities to cope with development. The first step in this direction was taken in 1998. The Athabasca Tribal Council and the Athabasca Regional Issues Working Group, an industry association composed overwhelmingly of companies with direct interests in exploiting the tar sands, began to discuss the need for First Nations to build capacity in order to deal with the anticipated blitzkrieg of resource development in the Athabasca tar sands.[110] In 1999, the two parties signed a three-year capacity-building agreement.[111] Both Alberta and Canada supported this agreement, with Indian and Northern Affairs Canada (INAC) committing up to $750,000 to help support the economic development activities the Liberal government in Ottawa regarded as key to First Nations' self-sufficiency.[112]

Federal support for this capacity-building initiative reflected and complemented Ottawa's more general enthusiasm during this period to promote Aboriginal entrepreneurship. The latter was illustrated in northeastern Alberta, for example, by Ottawa's contribution in 2000 of $1.75 million to assist the Fort McKay First Nation's interest in participating in the Athabasca Oil Sands Project. INAC Minister Nault linked this federal assistance to strong public support for the value of government efforts to promote First Nations' self-sufficiency.[113] The self-reliance theme figured prominently, as well, in Fort McKay First Nation's Chief Jim Boucher's enthusiastic assessment of what the Fort McKay/Shell Canada Business Agreement would mean for his constituents.[114] This shared enthusiasm between Ottawa and Fort McKay for exploiting the tar sands was also shared by both Liberal and Conservative administrations. In 2007, Stephen Harper's minority Conservative government adopted the Fort McKay First Nation Oil Sands Regulations. These regulations furthered Fort McKay's interest in developing a tar sands mine on Fort McKay Indian Reserve No. 174C. The regulations embraced much of the provincial regulatory regime existing at that time.

The effort to substantially increase the capacity of First Nations to assess regulatory applications and participate in the state's tar sands approval regime took a second, crucial step in 2003. Then 15 companies, the vast majority of them from the energy sector, joined the three levels of government and the Athabasca Tribal Council (ATC) in signing the All-Parties Core Agreement. Over the Agreement's three-year term, industry agreed to provide more than $4 million to First Nations to assist them in efforts to continue to assemble the organizational capacity needed to address industrial activities in the northeast. Jim Boucher, then the president of the ATC, enthused that "[i]ndustry's commitment to this agreement will enhance our ability to build strong economies and self-sustaining communities … We look forward to a continued productive working relationship in the implementation of our resource development strategy."[115] The federal government renewed its previous financial commitment to the ATC to promote this type of capacity building; it offered an additional $1.2 million over the three-year term of the agreement "to continue to support ATC's role as a partner" in exploiting the oil sands.[116]

Corporate sponsorship and financing of First Nations' Industry Relations Corporations (IRCs) was a key feature of this agreement. Each First Nation community in the Athabasca tar sands area received $230,000 to "create an Industry Relations Corporation and create the capacity for each community to deal with Industry and the impacts of industrial development."[117] To Lisa King, Director of the Athabasca Chipewyan First Nation Industry Relations Corporation, the IRC was intended "to serve as the principal means of communication between industry and the ACFN" and to address project referrals the provincial government would give the AFCN. Prior to the creation of the IRC there was "no capacity in the ACFN band office to deal with these matters." She described the money from industry to deal with project referrals as "minimal."[118]

These welcome corporate and government contributions were far from altruistic. Strings were attached. They came with expectations regarding how First Nations would use this newly created capacity; adapting to petroleum industrialization was key here. First Nations should use their newfound organizational capacity to adapt their ambitions to the growth of the tar sands industry. The Liberal government's use of the word "partner" in its news release is instructive. It reinforced the direction the federal government signalled First Nations should take when the first agreement was signed in January 2000. Then Minister Nault said, "The whole objective is to create an Aboriginal economy."[119] First Nations were framed in the ATC/All Parties Core Agreement as something akin to junior partners in exploiting the tar sands, a position First Nations leaders such as Jim Boucher appeared willing, if not eager, to accept as part of their drive for community self-sufficiency. The Standards of Consultation outlined in the agreement make it very clear signatories were expected to manage their relationships in a nonconfrontational way. The Core Agreement stands, then, as more than just an important milestone in the development of First Nations capacity to engage with tar sands companies. It also announced an important compromise regarding the future of industrialization in the Athabasca tar sands. The results section underlined the compromising intent of the First Nations/corporate relationship forged in the Core Agreement. It read:

> The value of results is measured by:
> - an increase in the number of agreements negotiated between First Nation communities and industrial proponents; and
> - an increase in First Nation access to industrial development opportunities, including, but not restricted to, training, education, employment and contracting; and
> - an increase in capacity to consult and build understanding between Industry and First Nation communities.[120]

The Core Agreement represented a fundamental choice by the leadership of First Nations about how to respond to exploiting the tar sands. But it's important to appreciate how constrained First Nations' responses could be to what unfolded. Much of the canvas for industrializing northeastern Alberta had already been painted. Government's complete disinterest in managing the boom helped close the door to conceptualizing and developing other economic possibilities. In the post-1995 land rush to secure tar sands leases, First Nations, in the blink of an eye, found their treaty lands fenced in by tar sands mining operations and proposals. In a very real sense, First Nations were presented with a fait accompli by the state—these lands, lands that may have mattered in order to pursue traditional practices, became nothing more than tar sands leases. There is only one state-sanctioned use for these lands—to extract the bitumen needed to produce synthetic crude oil.

With respect to outcomes, Heather Kennedy, then Suncor's vice-president for employee and community relations, offered a glowing assessment of what this agreement had accomplished by 2006. The agreement, created in "an atmosphere of respect and cooperation," produced "such a wide range of positive outcomes."[121] These agreements, however, didn't necessarily give First Nations sufficient capacity to deal adequately with the administrative avalanche generated by the tar sands boom. John Rigney, the manager of an ACFN residential construction project in 2006, described for the Alberta Court of Queen's Bench just how limited the First Nation's technological capacities were three years after the Core Agreement was signed. None of the staff regularly used e-mail or the Internet. This was due first to the fact that until 2008, the band office relied on snail-like, frustrating, and expensive dial-up Internet services. Rigney also felt ACFN staff "were not computer savvy and did not have the skill set to use the internet and email."[122]

In *Athabasca Chipewyan First Nation v. Alberta (Minister of Energy)*, the ACFN argued the combination of insufficient staff, information, and expertise meant the First Nation neither appreciated the intent of a new provincial Internet tool nor had the resources to use it promptly and effectively. *Aboriginal Community Link* was an Internet portal designed exclusively for the use of Aboriginal communities. The site posted, among other information, lands the Department of Energy was offering to lease for tar sands development. The Department claimed it offered Alberta's First Nations "the earliest possible access to information on land postings that may be of interest to them."[123]

Lisa King claimed the ACFN viewed *Aboriginal Community Link* very differently. "We understood," she swore under oath, "that the thrust of the Aboriginal Community Link was to find business opportunities."[124] The ACFN never understood that the new web-based process was intended to replace the already existing provincial process for referring potential lease lands to the attention of the First Nation. In 2006, the ACFN IRC only had two staff members, a director and an environmental specialist. They "were overwhelmed and understaffed" when it came to dealing with the number of consultation referrals they were receiving from industry; even though they had some computer skills they "were not very familiar with the internet opportunities." This combination of factors meant that, for two years, the ACFN never used the *Aboriginal Community Link* website. After a new hire at the IRC the First Nation was able to access the website; that access never took place until November 2008. By that point in time *Aboriginal Community Link* wasn't very useful for the ACFN since "with very few exceptions, all of the oil sands leases in our traditional territory had already been sold."[125]

Alberta's courts rejected the ACFN's claims that the First Nation had not received adequate notice or been consulted adequately regarding the leasing of tar sands lands in the ACFN traditional territories. Justice D.R.G. Thomas concluded that the ACFN was "out of time" to contest the leases it was concerned about. The Alberta Court of Appeal agreed.[126]

Conclusion

This chapter argues that an underappreciated complexity characterizes the views Aboriginal peoples hold regarding exploiting the tar sands.

The popular view, fittingly offered by a famous Hollywood director, portrays Aboriginal peoples as uncompromising protectors of Mother Earth.[127] Here I tried to show that, as much merit as that opinion has, it ignores a longstanding and growing commitment from some First Nations in the northeast to the very pattern of industrialization that poses immense threats to Mother Nature's ecological integrity. Near the beginning of this chapter the Treaty Alliance Against Tar Sands Expansion was mentioned. None of its members are from the Athabasca tar sands area; none are from Alberta. First Nations do not speak with one voice when it comes to the worth of exploiting the tar sands.

If First Nations could rewrite the policy history of northeastern Alberta, circumstances likely would look very different today. They can't. Government and the tar sands industry wrote that history and authored the public policies First Nations must fit their lives into. They have lived lives of both resistance and compromise as J. Howard Pew, Ernest Manning, Peter Lougheed, Ralph Klein, and transnational petroleum companies unveiled their blueprints to industrialize the boreal forest.

Given their history and attachment to the land sacrificed for oil, Alberta's First Nations were likely candidates to figure prominently in the development of a countermovement against the wholesale dedication of northeastern Alberta to the tar sands economy. If they had not been impoverished when the tar sands boom commenced, they might have been able to invest in the administrative capacity to develop a more noticeable, more effective ecological critique of development. Without administrative capacity they remained quite silent and compliant in the early days of the boom; they found it very difficult to do what is expected of members of a countermovement—ask the state why their voices and interests are subordinated to those of capital. When industry and government offered funding to develop specific administrative capacity to address the tar sands, that cash came with strings attached. First Nations had to respect the rules of the tar sands game—projects would be approved and the most First Nations could hope for was jobs and perhaps some environmental conditions to temper the sacrifice of the boreal landscape for petroleum.

The actions of tar sands companies here illustrate how those who benefit from market fundamentalism will try to tame those tempted to join a countermovement. Helping First Nations understand company plans, paying for First Nations' environmental assessments, building cultural and Elders' centres, offering impact and benefits agreements, and fostering the birth and growth of a tar sands-dependent Aboriginal business sector should be seen through this lens. Their strategy of "counter, coopt, and compromise" has enjoyed considerable success.

The future of the tar sands economy may depend importantly on which, if either, of the voices of resistance and compromise triumph. The Canadian constitution may become an important political resource as this future unfolds. So far Aboriginal rights guarantees haven't led the courts to order significant substantive accommodations regarding the potential infringements of treaty rights. Here I wonder if First Nations' strategies since the late 1990s ultimately will prove to be counterproductive to securing those substantive accommodations. Time after time First Nations, after securing confidential benefit agreements with the agents who tear up the taiga, have withdrawn their objections to gigantic projects only to say they remain concerned about the cumulative effects of development on and around their traditional lands. Ecologically speaking, this behaviour surely undermines First Nations' claims to nature stewardship. Recently the Supreme Court in *Grassy Narrows First Nation v. Ontario (Natural Resources)* reaffirmed the position articulated in *Mikisew*. First Nations will have a potential action for treaty infringement if the Crown's taking up of lands leaves First Nations without a meaningful right to hunt, fish, or trap.[128] If that day comes in Treaty 8 lands due to tar sands development (if that day hasn't come already), will it matter in the courts that First Nations, by withdrawing objections to projects such as Kearl and Jackpine, facilitated the very pattern of industrialization that compromises those rights?

Notes

1   Greg Poelzer, "Aboriginal Peoples and Environmental Policy in Canada: No Longer at the Margins," in *Canadian Environmental Policy: Context and Cases* (2nd ed.), ed. Debora L. VanNijnatten and Robert Boardman (Don Mills, ON: Oxford University Press, 2002). Ellen Bielawski notes similar tensions in her account of the coming of diamond mining to Dene lands in the Northwest Territories. Ellen Bielawski, *Rogue Diamonds: Northern Riches on Dene Land* (Vancouver: Douglas & McIntyre, 2003), 91–92.

2   Evans, "Is an Alternative Globalization Possible?," 279.

3   Brad Gilmour and Bruce Mellett, "The Role of Impact and Benefits Agreements in the Resolution of Project Issues with First Nations," *Alberta Law Review* 51, no. 2 (2013), 387.

4   Alberta Energy and Utilities Board, *Shell Canada Limited: Muskeg River Mine Project, Decision 99–2* (1999), 10.

5   Angela Younie, "Prehistoric Microblade Technology in the Oilsands Region of Northeastern Alberta: A Technological Analysis of Microblade Production at Archaeological Site HiOv-89" (master's thesis, University of Alberta, 2008), 16.

6   Alberta Energy Utilities Board, *Report of the Joint Panel, EUB Decision 2006-128, December 17, 2007*, 82. The use of the verb "sterilize" here is telling; Shell estimates 4.3 million barrels of bitumen are beneath the Quarry.

7   Treaty Alliance Against Tar Sands Expansion, "First Nations and Tribes Sign New Treaty Joining Forces to Stop All Tar Sands Pipelines," news release, September 22, 2016, http://www.treatyalliance.org/wp-content/uploads/2016/09/TAATSE-PR-Treaty-Signing-EN-FINAL.pdf.

8   Bryant Avery's special report on Fort McKay for the *Edmonton Journal* stands out as an exception to the general tenor of First Nations' oil sands media coverage. See Bryant Avery, "Fort McKay Writes Off Gov't, Will Deal with Plants Directly; Surviving in the Land of Giants," *Edmonton Journal*, March 22, 1997, E1.

9   Bryant Avery, "Way of Life Sees Drastic Changes," *Edmonton Journal*, March 22, 1997, E4. On the presence of both the economic and environmental concerns in First Nations opinion, also see Marie Burke, "Metis Concerned about Expansion," *Windspeaker* (February 1999), 39.

10   The Athabasca Chipewyan were called the Athabasca Fort Chipewyan First Nation when they intervened during the 1997 Suncor Steepbank application.

11   In 2014, after several mergers and partnerships, Suncor owned the largest share of and is the operator of the Fort Hills project. The owners are Suncor (40.8%), Total (39.2%), and Teck (20.0%).

12   Alberta Energy and Utilities Board, *Application by Suncor Inc. Oil Sands Group for Amendment of Approval No. 7632*, 3.

13   Alberta Energy and Utilities Board, *Shell Canada Limited Application, (Decision 99-2)* (1999), 33.

14   Alberta Energy and Utilities Board, *Report of the Joint Review Panel, EUB Decision 2004-005*, 71.

15   Canadian Broadcasting Corporation, "Cancer Rate in Fort Chipewyan Cause for Alarm: Medical Examiner," March 10, 2006, http://www.cbc.ca/news/canada/edmonton/cancer-rate-in-fort-chipewyan-cause-for-alarm-medical-examiner-1.609695; Andrew Nikiforuk, *Tar Sands: Dirty Oil and the Future of a Continent* (Vancouver: Greystone Books, 2008), 89–92.

16   Canadian Broadcasting Corporation, "Oilsands-Area Hamlet Supports Whistleblower MD," 5 March 2007, http://www.cbc.ca/news/canada/oilsands-area-hamlet-supports-whistleblower-md-1.636759.

17   Canadian Broadcasting Corporation, "Cancer Rates Not Higher in Fort Chipewyan, Investigation Concludes," July 19, 2006, http://www.cbc.ca/news/canada/edmonton/cancer-rates-not-higher-in-fort-chipewyan-investigation-concludes-1.575738.

18   Canadian Broadcasting Corporation, "Local Doctor Doubts Report on Fort Chipewyan Cancer Rates," July 25, 2006, http://www.cbc.ca/news/canada/calgary/local-doctor-doubts-report-on-fort-chipewyan-cancer-rates-1.600942.

19   Alberta Energy and Utilities Board, *EUB Decision 2004-005*, 72; Alberta Energy and Utilities Board, *EUB Decision 2004-009*, 87–88. William Marsden was wrong to claim the regulators granted approval to these two projects "with the condition that they fund a baseline health study of the population of Fort Chipewyan." William Marsden, *Stupid to the Last Drop: How Alberta Is Bringing Environmental Armageddon to Canada (and Doesn't Seem to Care)* (Toronto: Alfred A. Knopf Canada, 2007), 188. No such condition was part of the respective regulatory approvals.

20   Alberta Energy and Utilities Board, *EUB Decision 2004-009*, 86 [emphasis added].

21 Mikisew Cree First Nation, "Response to the Multi-Stakeholder Committee Phase II Proposed Options for Strategies and Actions and Submission to the Government of Alberta for the Oil Sands Strategy," (June 2007), 65.

22 Kevin P. Timoney, "A Study of Water and Sediment Quality as Related to Public Health Issues, Fort Chipewyan, Alberta" (on behalf of the Nunee Health Board Society, Fort Chipewyan), December 2007, https://sites.ualberta. ca/~swfc/images/fc-final-report-revised-dec2007.pdf.

23 Canadian Broadcasting Corporation, "'Comprehensive' Review of Fort Chipewyan Cancer Rates Announced," May 22, 2008, http://www.cbc.ca/ news/canada/edmonton/comprehensive-review-of-fort-chipewyan-cancer-rates-announced-1.720133.

24 Jim Barker, Dave Rudolph, Trevor Tompkins, Alex Oiffer, Francoise Gervais, and Grace Ferguson, "Attenuation of Contaminants in Groundwater Impacted by Surface Mining of Oil Sands, Alberta, Canada," paper presented to the International Petroleum Environmental Conference, Houston, Texas, November 6–9, 2007, http://www.cec.org/sites/default/files/submissions/ 2006_2010/9182_10-2-rsub-appendix_v-_uwaterloo_suncor_leakage.pdf. Two important qualifications should be noted here: the paper argued that most seepage is collected and returned to the tailings pond, and the average flow of the Athabasca River at Tar Island was 860,000 litres per second.

25 On May 15, 2008, Environment Minister Rob Renner responded to Alberta Liberal Party Leader David Swann's question about groundwater contamination of the Athabasca River by saying: "Again, Mr. Speaker, I've answered this question many times over. The answer again is the same. There is no evidence to indicate that there is any impact on the Athabasca River as a result of leaching or leaking or emissions from tailings ponds associated with activity in the oil sands." Alberta, Legislative Assembly, *Alberta Hansard, 27th Legislature, 1st Session (2008)*, May 15, 2008, 762.

26 Canadian Broadcasting Corporation, "Fort Chipewyan Rejects Alberta Cancer Board Study," November 10, 2008, http://www.cbc.ca/news/canada/ edmonton/fort-chipewyan-rejects-alberta-cancer-board-study-1.752332.

27 Dr. Yiqun Chen, *Cancer Incidence in Fort Chipewyan 1995–2006* (Alberta Cancer Board, 2009); Alberta Health Services, "Fort Chipewyan Cancer Study Findings Released," news release, February 6, 2009, http://www.albertahealthservices. ca/news/releases/2009/Page500.aspx.

28 Katherine O'Neill, "Report Casts Doubt on MD's Claims about Alberta Reserve's Cancer Rates," *Globe and Mail*, November 8, 2009.

29 O'Neill, "Report Casts Doubt."

30 Canada, *Constitution Act 1982*, s. 35(1). This subsection reads: "The existing aboriginal and treaty rights of the aboriginal peoples of Canada are hereby recognized and affirmed."

31 Peter W. Hogg, *Constitutional Law of Canada, 2007 Student Edition* (Scarborough, ON: Thomson Canada, 2007), 613–14.

32 *Haida Nation v. British Columbia (Minister of Forests)*, 3 S.C.R. (2004), 511.

33 *Mikisew Cree First Nation v. Canada (Minister of Canadian Heritage)* at para. 47 [emphasis in original].

34 *Mikisew v. Canada* at para. 27.

35 *Mikisew v. Canada* at para. 32.

36   Woodward and Company Lawyers LLP, "Athabasca Chipewyan First Nations—Written Submission to Participate in the Hearings and Notice of Question of Constitutional Law," (Document #465), October 1, 2012, Jackpine Mine Expansion, Canadian Environmental Assessment Agency, http://www.ceaa-acee.gc.ca/050/documents-eng.cfm?evaluation=59540&page=3&type=0&sequence=0.

37   The complete reasons for the Panel's decision are found in Alberta Energy Regulator, *Report of the Joint Review Panel Established by the Federal Minister of the Environment and the Energy Resources Conservation Board, Decision 2013 ABAER 011: Shell Canada Energy, Jackpine Mine Expansion Project* (Calgary: Alberta Energy Regulator, 2013), 355–70.

38   Alberta Energy Regulator, *Decision 2013 ABAER 011: Shell Canada Energy, Jackpine Mine Expansion Project*, 14–15.

39   *Adam v. Canada (Environment)* (2014) FC 1185, paras. 26 to 30.

40   *Adam v. Canada (Environment)*, at para. 11.

41   *Adam v. Canada (Environment)*, at para. 74.

42   *Adam v. Canada (Environment)*, at para. 86.

43   *Adam v. Canada (Environment)*, at para. 91.

44   Prowse Chowne LLP, "Notice of Question of Constitutional Law Filed by Prowse Chowne LLP on Behalf of Mikisew Cree First Nation," Document #252, September 3, 2010, pp. 25–26, Joslyn North Mine Project, Townships 94–96, Ranges 11–13 West of 4th Meridian, Canadian Environmental Assessment Agency. This and other documents cited this way pertaining to the Joslyn North Mine Project were supplied by the Department of Fisheries and Oceans (the responsible agency for this CEAA assessment) on a CD.

45   Prowse Chowne LLP, "Letter from the Mikisew Cree First Nation Regarding Their Agreement with Total E&P Joslyn Ltd." Document #296, September 22, 2010, Joslyn North Mine Project, Townships 94–96, Ranges 11–13 West of 4th Meridian, Canadian Environmental Assessment Agency.

46   Prowse Chowne LLP, "Letter from the Mikisew Cree First Nation," 4.

47   Alberta Energy Resources Conservation Board, *Report of the Joint Review Panel Established by the Federal Minister of the Environment and the Energy Resources Conservation Board, Decision 2011-005: Total E&P Joslyn Ltd., Application for the Joslyn North Mine Project* (Calgary: Energy Resource Conservation Board, 2011), 7, 13.

48   Melody Lepine, "Letter from Mikisew Cree First Nation (MCFN) to Alberta Environment and Water—Withdrawl [sic] of Mikisew Cree First Nation (MCFN) Statement of Concern—Jackpine Mine Expansion and Pierre River Mine Projects (see Reference CEAR #21)," October 2, 2012, http://www.ceaa-acee.gc.ca/050/documents/p59540/81960E.pdf.

49   Kelly Cryderman, "Not on an 'Anti-Tar-Sands Crusade', Neil Young Says," *Globe and Mail*, January 19, 2014, https://www.theglobeandmail.com/news/national/neil-young-concludes-anti-oilsands-concert-series-with-show-in-calgary/article16398977/#dashboard/follows/.

50   Isha Thompson, "Mikisew Cree Activist Garners International Attention," *Alberta Sweetgrass* 17, issue 9 (2010), http://www.ammsa.com/publications/alberta-sweetgrass/mikisew-cree-activist-garners-international-attention.

51   Hanneke Brooymans, "Cameron Gets First Look at Oilsands," *Edmonton Journal*, September 28, 2010, A1.

52   Hanneke Brooymans, "Mikisew Cree Withdraw Constitutional Challenge of Mining Project," *edmontonjournal.com*, September 23, 2010; Pembina Institute, "US Decisions on Tar Sands Imports Will Impact First Nations Communities, Leaders Say," media release, September 22, 2010, http://www.pembina.org/media-release/2087.

53   On May 29, 2014, Total announced that, because of escalating costs, it was putting the Joslyn North Mine Project on hold indefinitely. Carrie Tait, "Total Shelves $11-Billion Oil Sands Mine," *Globe and Mail*, May 30, 2014, B1; Total E&P Canada, "Our Partners in Canada," http://ca.total.com/en-us/list-of-partners?&xtmc="Joslyn%20asset"&xtnp=0&xtcr=1#nid2477.

54   Cryderman, "Not on an 'Anti-Tar-Sands Campaign.'"

55   Neil Reddekopp, "Theory and Practice in the Government of Alberta's Consultation Policy," *Constitutional Forum constitutionnel* 22, no. 1 (2013), 59.

56   Gabrielle Slowey, *Navigating Neoliberalism: Self-Determination and the Mikisew Cree First Nation* (Vancouver: UBC Press, 2008), 64.

57   Ian Urquhart, "A Modest Proposal?: Diversity and the Challenge of Governance in Northern Alberta," *The Northern Review* 25/26 (Summer 2005), 96; the only other average income data reported in the 1996 Census for predominantly Aboriginal people living in Census Division No. 16, Alberta (the division including Fort McMurray and the Aboriginal communities affected by developing the Athabasca Oil Sands area) was for Janvier. The average income there in 1996 was $14,654, 44 percent lower than the provincial average of $26,138. See Statistics Canada, "1996 Census, Electronic Area Profiles," http://www12.statcan.ca/english/census96/data/profiles/Geo-index-eng.cfm?TABID=5&LANG=E&APATH=3&DETAIL=0&DIM=0&FL=A&FREE=0&GC=0&GID=0&GK=0&GRP=1&PID=35782&PRID=0&PTYPE=3&S=0&SHOWALL=0&SUB=0&Temporal=1996&THEME=34&VID=0&VNAMEE=&VNAMEF=&D1=0&D2=0&D3=0&D4=0&D5=0&D6=0.

58   Shaun Polczer, "First Nation's Chief Has Gone from Fighting Oil Industry to Embracing It," *Calgary Herald*, November 9, 2006, A20; Jim Carbery, CEO of the Fort McKay Group of Companies, reiterated this at a forum in 2012 at Florida International University. Regarding environmentalists, he said that while the First Nation and environmentalists were taking on oil sands companies, "the trapping industry was being attacked by celebrities around the world and year by year, the price of fur dropped so that it was not economically feasible to earn a living by trapping." Jim Carbery, "Fort McKay," presentation to Global Energy Security Forum, Florida International University, February 21, 2012, 8, http://energyforum.fiu.edu/events/2012/canadian-oil-sands/jim-carbery.pdf.

59   Paul Haavardsrud, "Environmental Tug-of-War Clouds Oilsands Future," *Calgary Herald*, October 25, 2005, A8.

60   ABC News, "Hunting for Oil Canada," *Nightline*, July 28, 2008, transcript.

61   Slowey, *Navigating Neoliberalism*, 66.

62   Indian Association of Alberta, *Citizens Plus: Alberta Red Paper* (Edmonton: 1970); Harold Cardinal, *The Unjust Society: The Tragedy of Canada's Indians* (Edmonton: M. G. Hurtig, 1969).

63   *Calder et al. v. Attorney-General of British Columbia*, [1973] S.C.R. 313.

64   Canada, *Northern Frontier, Northern Homeland: The Report of the Mackenzie Valley Pipeline Inquiry*, 2 volumes (Ottawa: Minister of Supply and Services Canada, 1977).

65   Slowey suggests that agreeing to help Aboriginal people find work in Syncrude was one of the conditions for the government assistance originally lent to the consortium. Slowey, *Navigating Neoliberalism*, 59.

66   *Proceedings of the Standing Senate Committee on Aboriginal Peoples*, 36th Parliament, 1st Session, 23 (March 16, 1999) (evidence of Robert Loader, Manager, Aboriginal Affairs, Syncrude Canada Ltd.). In 2002, Syncrude President and Chief Operating Officer Jim Carter added corporate leadership as a sixth component. See "Breaking New Ground: Syncrude's Partnerships with Aboriginal People," Speaking Notes for Jim Carter Resource Expo 2002: Business Agreements for Profit, Calgary Alberta, December 3, 2002.

67   Syncrude, "Submission to the Oil Sands Multi-Stakeholder Consultation Panel—Fort Chipewyan, AB," October 4, 2006.

68   Harold Cardinal's approval of the agreement may be seen at "Syncrude Signs Two Agreements Providing Jobs, Grants for Indians," *Gazette (Montreal)*, July 5, 1976, 26. The Indian Association of Alberta never followed the "hardline policy" Pratt suggested Cardinal was considering if native peoples did not win an adequate share of resource wealth. Pratt, *Tar Sands*, 114.

69   *Proceedings of the Standing Senate Committee on Aboriginal Peoples*, 23 (March 16, 1999).

70   Slowey, *Navigating Neoliberalism*, 67.

71   Miriam Jorgensen and Rachel Starks, *Forwarding First Nation Goals Through Enterprise Ownership: The Mikisew Group of Companies*, paper prepared for Aboriginal Leadership and Management, The Banff Centre (written August 2012, released April 2014), 6, http://nni.arizona.edu/application/files/2314/6179/0332/2014-4_mikisew_case_study.pdf.

72   Slowey, *Navigating Neoliberalism*, 67.

73   Gabrielle A. Slowey, "The Political Economy of Aboriginal Self-Determination: The Case of the Mikisew Cree First Nation" (PhD dissertation, University of Alberta, 2003), 180, http://www.collectionscanada.gc.ca/obj/thesescanada/vol2/001/nq88048.pdf.

74   Syncrude, "Submission to the Oil Sands Multi-Stakeholder Consultation Panel." Steve Jani, who made Syncrude's submission as the company's Aboriginal Relations Team leader was the CEO of Christina River Enterprises, the business arm of the Fort McMurray No. 468 First Nation, in June 2015.

75   *Proceedings of the Standing Senate Committee on Aboriginal Peoples*.

76   Syncrude, *Pathways: Aboriginal Review 2012*, http://www.syncrude.ca/assets/pdf/Syncrude-Pathways-2012.pdf.

77   Suncor, "Suncor Sees Possibilities, Outlines Environmental Goals in Sustainability Report," June 18, 2009, http://www.suncor.com/newsroom/news-releases/1088547.

78   Roland Cilliers, "Aboriginal Association Marks $1B in Suncor Business," *Fort McMurray Today*, May 27, 2009.

79   Suncor, "Suncor Energy Releases 2013 Report on Sustainability," news release, July 17, 2013, http://www.suncor.com/newsroom/news-releases/1741591.

80   "CAPP Says Industry Working to Establish Mutually Respectful Relationships: An Interview with CAPP's Greg Stringham," *Alberta Oil*, April 9, 2014, http://www.albertaoilmagazine.com/2014/04/establishing-mutually-respectful-relationships-capp-greg-stringham/.

81   Maria Church, "Fort Chipewyan Celebrates Opening of Elders' Care Centre," *Northern Journal*, May 19, 2014, http://norj.ca/2013/10/fort-chip-elders-care-centre-to-open-by-spring/. The following oil sands companies made contributions to the Centre: Shell Canada ($1,000,000), Imperial Oil ($1,000,000), Cenovus ($750,000), Syncrude ($500,000), Suncor ($500,000), Husky Energy ($500,000), Canadian Natural Resources Ltd. ($250,000), and Total E&P (undisclosed amount from the confidential Impact Benefits Agreement signed with the Mikisew Cree First Nation).

82   *Proceedings of the Standing Senate Committee on Aboriginal Peoples.*

83   Carter, "Breaking New Ground."

84   The estimate of the increase in inflation-adjusted dollars was made using the Bank of Canada's inflation calculator, which uses consumer price index data. See http://www.bankofcanada.ca/rates/related/inflation-calculator/.

85   Statistics Canada, 2013, Fort McKay First Nation, Indian Band Area, Alberta (Code 630467) (table), National Household Survey (NHS) Aboriginal Population Profile, *2011 National Household Survey*. Statistics Canada Catalogue no. 99–011-X2011007. Ottawa: November 13, 2013. http://www12.statcan.gc.ca/nhs-enm/2011/dp-pd/aprof/details/page.cfm?Lang=E&Geo1=BAND&Code1=630467&Data=Count&SearchText=Fort%20McKay&SearchType=Begins&SearchPR=01&A1=All&Custom=&TABID=1; Statistics Canada, 2013, Alberta (Code 48) (table), National Household Survey (NHS) Profile, *2011 National Household Survey*. Ottawa: September 11, 2013. Statistics Canada Catalogue no. 99–004-XWE, http://www12.statcan.gc.ca/nhs-enm/2011/dp-pd/prof/details/Page.cfm?Lang=E&Geo1=PR&Code1=48&Data=Count&SearchText=Alberta&SearchType=Begins&SearchPR=01&A1=All&B1=All&GeoLevel=PR&GeoCode=48.

86   Statistics Canada, 2013, Division No. 16, CDR, Alberta (Code 4816) (table), National Household Survey (NHS) Aboriginal Population Profile, *2011 National Household Survey*, Statistics Canada Catalogue no. 99-011-X2011007. Ottawa: November 13, 2013. http://www12.statcan.gc.ca/nhs-enm/2011/dp-pd/aprof/details/page.cfm?Lang=E&Geo1=CD&Code1=4816&Data=Count&SearchText=Division%20No.%2016&SearchType=Begins&SearchPR=01&A1=All&B1=All&GeoLevel=PR&GeoCode=4816&TABID=1.

87   In the Chipewyan Prairie First Nation the average income of Aboriginal males was $27,163 and that of Aboriginal females was $21,608. In the Fort McMurray #468 First Nation these respective average incomes were $43,835 and $27,586. Statistics Canada, 2013, Chipewyan Prairie First Nation, Indian Band Area, Alberta (Code 630470) (table), National Household Survey (NHS) Aboriginal Population Profile, *2011 National Household Survey*, Statistics Canada Catalogue no. 99-011-X2011007. Ottawa: November 13, 2013. http://www12.statcan.gc.ca/nhs-enm/2011/dp-pd/aprof/details/page.cfm?Lang=E&Geo1=BAND&Code1=630470&Data=Count&SearchText=Chipewyan%20Prairie%20First%20Nation&SearchType=Begins&SearchPR=01&A

1=All&Custom=&TABID=1; Statistics Canada, 2013, Fort McMurray #468 First Nation, Indian Band Area, Alberta (Code 630468) (table), National Household Survey (NHS) Aboriginal Population Profile, *2011 National Household Survey*, Statistics Canada Catalogue no. 99-011-X2011007. Ottawa: November 13, 2013. http://www12.statcan.gc.ca/nhs-enm/2011/dp-pd/aprof/details/page.cfm?Lang=E&Geo1=BAND&Code1=630468&Data=Count&SearchText=Fort%20McMurray%20#468&SearchType=Begins&SearchPR=01&A1=All&Custom=&TABID=1.

88   Natural Resources Canada, "CSR Case Study: Syncrude Canada Ltd. Earning Its Social License to Operate" (Canada: Natural Resources Canada, 2004), 8, https://www.commdev.org/userfiles/files/1077_file_syncrude_e.pdf; "Northeastern Alberta Aboriginal Business Association," www.naaba.ca/site/naaba_members?mode=listing&pg=9.

89   William K. McIntosh, "Building Sustainable Relationships: A Compendium of Leadership Practices in Aboriginal Engagement and Sustainability," Canadian Business for Social Responsibility, 2005, 15–16.

90   Gordon Jaremko, "Fort McKay Becoming Power Hub: Aboriginal Vision Guides $9.7–Billion Project Horizon with New Town, Jobs," *Edmonton Journal*, December 29, 2004, G1; Dianne Meili reported in 2007 that, "[e]ach band member is awarded substantial payouts from profits brought in by the Fort McKay Group of Companies owned and managed by the band." Meili, "Oilsands Boom Creates Uneasy Wealth in the North," *Alberta Sweetgrass: The Aboriginal Newspaper of Alberta* 14, no. 6 (May 2007), 4.

91   Carbery, "Fort McKay," 10.

92   Jim Boucher and George Arcand Jr., *2014 Management Discussion and Analysis, Fort McKay First Nation, Alberta,* September 15, 2014, http://fnp-ppn.aandc-aadnc.gc.ca/fnp/Main/Search/DisplayBinaryData.aspx?BAND_NUMBER_FF=467&FY=2013-2014&DOC=Schedule%20of%20Remuneration%20and%20Expenses&lang=eng.

93   Alberta, Legislative Assembly, "MLA Remuneration—Effective April 1, 2014," http://www.assembly.ab.ca/lao/hr/MLA/MLA%20Remuneration%20April%202014.htm.

94   Financial Statements Fort McKay First Nation, Schedules of Salaries, Honoraria, Travel Expenses and Other Remuneration, Year Ended March 31, 2014, http://fnp-ppn.aandc-aadnc.gc.ca/fnp/Main/Search/DisplayBinaryData.aspx?BAND_NUMBER_FF=467&FY=2013-2014&DOC=Schedule%20of%20Remuneration%20and%20Expenses&lang=eng.

95   Chipewyan Prairie Dene First Nation Group of Companies, "Companies," http://cpgroupofcompanies.com/companies/.

96   Christina River Enterprises, "Partnerships," http://christinariverenterprises.ca/partnerships/.

97   MM Limited Partnership, "The Mikisew Energy Services Group," http://www.mesg.ca/pages/company.htm; Slowey, "Political Economy of Aboriginal Self-Determination," 175.

98   MM Limited Partnership, "Mikisew Energy Services Group." According to the Partnership's website: "The corporate philosophy revolves around the entrenchment of sustainable resource development within the traditional lands of aboriginal people."

99   Jorgensen and Stark, *Forwarding First Nation Goals*, 6.
100 Jorgensen and Stark, *Forwarding First Nation Goals*, 6–8.
101 MM Ltd Partnership, "Mikisew Energy Services Group."
102 Michelle Dacruz, "First Nations Partner with Suncor in Business," *Fort McMurray Today*, October 4, 2002, A8; Mairi MacLean, "This Job Requires Heavy Lifting: Mikisew Cree Put Heart in Slings," *Edmonton Journal*, September 27, 2002, F1.
103 Jorgensen and Stark, *Forwarding First Nation Goals*, 11.
104 Nancy LeBlond and Sasha Brown, "Training Options That Would Increase Employment Opportunities for Local People in Resource Extraction Projects in Northern Communities: Final Report," Prepared for Manitoba Research Alliance on Community Economic Development in the New Economy, November 2004, 18, http://mbresearchalliance.files.wordpress.com/2012/11/32land_reclamation_rev.pdf; Carter, "Breaking Ground," 3. Carter mistakenly refers to the company as Denesolene Environmental.
105 Slowey, "Political Economy of Aboriginal Self-Determination," 179.
106 "ACDEN: The Strategic Service Provider," http://www.acfnbusinessgroup.com/.
107 Angela Sterritt, "Athabasca Chipewyan First Nation Makes the Best of Oil Money," April 2, 2014, http://www.cbc.ca/news/aboriginal/athabasca-chipewyan-first-nation-makes-the-best-of-oil-money-1.2579126; the facility is showcased in the video ACDEN, "ACDEN New Facility Walkthrough," YouTube video, 6:15, uploaded May 23, 2013, http://www.youtube.com/watch?v=ut8H1Hq2hBw.
108 "ACDEN New Facility Walkthrough."
109 Suncor, "Report on Sustainability 2013: CEO Message," http://sustainability.suncor.com/2013/en/about/ceo-message.aspx.
110 In July 2008, the Regional Issues Working Group changed its name to the Oil Sands Developers Group. In 2011, industry concluded that the Oil Sands Developers Group "needed a renew focus on socio-economic issues and to be strategically aligned with other industry advocacy structures that exist under the Canadian Association of Petroleum Producers." As of October 2013, the new organizational face of this renewed focus is the Oil Sands Community Alliance. Oil Sands Community Alliance, "About OSCA," http://www.oscaalberta.ca/about-osca/; Oil Sands Community Alliance, "The Oil Sands Developers Group Changes Name as It Aligns Focus on Socio-Economic Issues," press release, http://www.oscaalberta.ca/wp-content/uploads/2015/08/FINAL-Press-Release-for-transition.pdf.
111 Alberta Chamber of Resources, *Learning from Experience: Aboriginal Programs in the Resource Industries* (Edmonton: Alberta Chamber of Resources, January 2006), 59; Athabasca Tribal Council, "Industry Capacity Building Agreement," August 4, 1999, http://atc97.org/finance-administration/industry-capacity-building-agreement.
112 Glenn Luff, "Corporate Alberta and First Nations Meet to Promote Economic Partnership," *Grassroots: Aboriginal Business in Alberta* (Ottawa: Minister of Indian Affairs and Northern Development, Spring 2001), 4, http://publications.gc.ca/collections/Collection/R12-14-2001-1E.pdf; "Athabasca Tribal Council Inks Historic Oil Sands Deal," *Globe and Mail*, March 16, 2001, C6.

113 Jim Starko, "Alberta Economic Development Projects Receive Ministerial Kick-Off," *Grassroots: Aboriginal Business in Alberta* (Ottawa: Minister of Indian Affairs and Northern Development, Spring 2001), 6.

114 Starko, "Alberta Economic Development Projects."

115 Syncrude, "Industry Signs Agreement with Athabasca Tribal Council," news release, January 9, 2003. Thirteen of the 15 corporate signatories identified in the news release were from the energy sector. Alberta–Pacific Forest Industries and ATCO Group of Companies were the exceptions.

116 Indian and Northern Affairs Canada, "Minister Nault Signs Capacity Building Agreement with Athabasca Tribal Council to Promote Natural Resource Industry Partnerships," *Canada NewsWire*, January 9, 2003.

117 *ATC/All Parties Core Agreement, Schedule D: Community Industry Relations Corporations* (October 2, 2002), 1–2.

118 "Affidavit #1 of Lisa King," Court document related to *Athabasca Chipewyan First Nation v. Alberta (Minister of Energy)*, 2009 CarswellAlta 1640, [2010] 2 W.W.R. 703, 13 Alta. L.R. (5th) 352, 46 C.E.L.R. (3d) 258.

119 Athabasca Tribal Council, "ATC, Industry and Federal Government Sign Ground-Breaking Agreement," January 24, 2000, http://atc97.org/finance-administration/federal-government.

120 *ATC/All Parties Core Agreement*, 2.

121 Alberta Chamber of Resources, *Learning from Experience: Aboriginal Programs in the Resource Industries* (Edmonton: Alberta Chamber of Resources, January 2006), 60.

122 "Affidavit #1 of John Rigney," Court document related to *Athabasca Chipewyan First Nation v. Alberta (Minister of Energy)*, 2009 CarswellAlta 1640, [2010] 2 W.W.R. 703, 13 Alta. L.R. (5th) 352, 46 C.E.L.R. (3d) 258.

123 Alberta, *Alberta's First Nations Consultation Guidelines on Land Management and Resource Development*, 3, http://www.aboriginal.alberta.ca/documents/First_Nations_and_Metis_Relations/First_Nations_Consultation_Guidelines_LM_RD.pdf.

124 Affidavit of Lisa King.

125 Affidavit of Lisa King.

126 *Athabasca Chipewyan First Nation v. Alberta (Minister of Energy)*, 2009 ABQB 576; *Athabasca Chipewyan First Nation v. Alberta (Minister of Energy)*, 2011 ABCA 29.

127 Brooymans, "Cameron Gets First Look."

128 *Grassy Narrows First Nation v. Ontario (Natural Resources)*, 2014 SCC 48 (2014) 2 SCR. 447, at para. 52.

6
Prison Break? The Political Economy of Royalty Reform

"Caracas on the Bow River."
—*Steve Larke, Peters & Co., September 2007*

"I made a commitment and I delivered. Future generations of Albertans will receive a fair share from the development of their resources."
—*Premier Ed Stelmach, October 2007*

Introduction

When the year 2007 dawned, there were reasons to think that change in the relationship between the Alberta provincial government and the tar sands sector was afoot. January welcomed a new premier—Ed Stelmach—to captain Alberta's ship of state. Premier Stelmach decisively defeated former treasurer Jim Dinning and rookie Member of the Legislative Assembly F. L. (Ted) Morton in the previous December's second round of voting for the leadership of the Progressive Conservative party. One of Premier Stelmach's first decisions would put the petroleum sector under the financial microscope. In February, Stelmach established a panel of independent experts to investigate Alberta's petroleum and taxation policies "to ensure Albertans are receiving a fair share from energy development."[1] As we see in the next section, this panel's mandate, and its open, transparent approach to fulfilling it, veered sharply from the course Premier Klein had set in Alberta.

The Stelmach government's royalty review offers a good opportunity to examine whether or not the new leadership of the Progressive Conservatives would and could challenge the generous fiscal regime that the Klein government's version of market fundamentalism had instituted in the 1990s. It offers us the opportunity to see if this new administration would try to escape from the imprisoning impact Lindblom believes the market imperative has on public policy in liberal democracies.[2] Lindblom doesn't suggest that policy changes are impossible in market-oriented societies, but he says very little about the political resources and conditions needed to engineer a prison break.

Alberta arguably possessed valuable political resources as it revisited the division of petroleum royalties in 2007. Most importantly, the province's bitumen resources were increasingly recognized and coveted at the turn of the twenty-first century. It was a time when oil appeared to be an increasingly scarce resource. Some credence was given to the possibility of "peak oil"—to the possibility we would run out of petroleum within a generation. Colin Campbell and Jean Laherrère boldly predicted that, barring a global recession, world production of conventional oil likely would peak sometime during the first decade of this century.[3]

In an atmosphere of presumed scarcity, Alberta had what very few jurisdictions could offer the petroleum industry: plentiful undeveloped petroleum resources, political stability, a skilled and educated workforce, and, perhaps most importantly of all, no requirements for the private sector to partner with state corporations. In 2011, national or state oil companies controlled roughly 90 percent of global oil reserves and approximately 75 percent of global oil production.[4] Without that state presence, Alberta was a very attractive locale for transnationals to do business and try to counter the weight of national oil companies in the international oil economy. The Alberta Federation of Labour, in its presentation to the Royalty Review Panel in 2007, argued these sorts of assets gave Alberta "all the cards" and real "bargaining power" when it came to negotiating with tar sands companies. The AFL called on the government to use that power and renegotiate the terms of development to increase the public treasury's share of economic rent by increasing royalties, to increase the amount of bitumen upgrading done in Alberta, and to entertain the unthinkable—establish a state petroleum corporation.[5]

Could Alberta then shake off the shackles, gilded as they might be, of the market? Could Alberta adopt a royalty system that offended corporate sensibilities about how the economic rent generated by exploiting the tar sands should be divided between the state and industry? Chapter Three argued that post-1995 changes made to the province's oil sands royalty system constituted an important catalyst for the tar sands boom that began soon after. Rapidly rising world oil prices, what some may like to suggest produced the billions of dollars in tar sands investments, weren't crucial to explaining the boom. Where those spectacular price increases proved especially important, however, was with respect to debates about the amount of money the Alberta government should collect through its royalty system. The ascent of oil prices that began in 1998 and accelerated dramatically in 2002 both rekindled and intensified the debate in Alberta politics over the royalty system. The focus of this debate was significantly different from the debate of the mid-1990s. Then the public wasn't included in the debate; royalties were raised and debated from an investment stimulus perspective. By the middle of the first decade of the twenty-first century, the royalty system was being

discussed and questioned from the "fair share" perspective Premier Stelmach had embraced. Were Albertans, the owners of the province's natural
resources, receiving their fair share of the tar sands–related bounty through
the provincial government's royalty system? Since economic rent belongs
to the owner of the resource, was the provincial government capturing an
appropriate amount?[6]

The Politics of Leadership Succession and Petroleum Royalties

As we saw in Chapter Three, very few questioned the provincial government's assertion in the 1990s that oil sands royalties needed to be changed in
order to make investments in the tar sands profitable. When the occasional
criticism of Alberta's petroleum royalty systems arose, such as in the Parkland
Institute's 1999 study *Giving Away the Alberta Advantage*, it was far too often
dismissed unfairly as just ideological or "simple-minded."[7] But questions
about whether the public was collecting sufficient economic rent through
its royalty regimes were not just being asked by the "left-leaning," "simple-minded" staff of Parkland. Less than a year after the Parkland critique,
Alberta's Department of Energy stated privately that, on the one hand, it did
not see a need to increase petroleum royalties, but it also said that, with oil
trading around "windfall price levels" of $30 per barrel, such high oil prices
suggested a need for government to give additional thought to the public/
industry shares of petroleum rents.[8] Here was the seed for the Alberta auditor general's 2007 observation that energy department officials didn't believe
Alberta had been collecting enough rent since 2000.[9]

In 2000, the average monthly price for West Texas Intermediate oil
traded on the NYMEX in Chicago was C$45.60 per barrel; the similar price
for Canadian heavy or Western Canada Select (WCS) oil at Hardisty was
C$36.75. By 2005, the NYMEX average monthly price for WTI stood at
C$69.35 while the average monthly price for WCS had risen to $50.71 per
barrel.[10] These respective increases of 52 percent and 38 percent in current
dollars attracted the attention of the opposition parties in the Alberta legislature. They consistently demanded that the energy minister, Greg Melchin,
tell them what these price increases actually delivered to Alberta taxpayers. Opposition members and the energy minister alike talked about a "fair
share" of nonrenewable resource revenue. Melchin assured the House that
Albertans were getting a fair share through the royalty system; opposition
party members were skeptical. New Democrat MLA David Eggen called
for a royalty hike to capture some of the "windfall profits" he said petroleum companies were reaping as prices climbed higher and higher; Egg-
en's party leader, Brian Mason, called for a Royal Commission on oil sands

development, one that would re-examine royalty rates. Liberal MLA Hugh MacDonald, perhaps the most dogged critic of the government's royalty arrangements, repeatedly asked Melchin who was advising the government on royalties, what reports the government had commissioned on this subject, and why the government's take through royalties in 2004 (19 percent) fell short of the government's own target range (20–25 percent). Albertans, MacDonald claimed, wanted a full public review of the province's royalty regime.

The energy minister refused to budge. He defended the government's administration of energy as one that struck a balance between securing a fair share of resource revenue through royalties, taxes, lease payments, and rentals for taxpayers and ensuring "we're attractive to investors, both conventional and unconventional sources alike."[11] Customarily in Alberta politics, the opposition's demands for a public review of the royalty system would have ended there, with the minister's refusal either to supply the information they sought or to act on the demand for some type of public review. This session of the Alberta legislature was different, though. It marked the last session in which Premier Ralph Klein led the Progressive Conservative Party. Klein had suffered a surprising rebuke to his leadership at the March 2006 Progressive Conservative Party convention. Only 55.4 percent of party delegates supported Klein in a leadership review vote; the rest wanted to elect a new party leader. It was truly "a crushing setback."[12] With Klein headed for the exits, the opportunity to strike out in different policy directions arose for those who aspired to replace him.

On the royalties issue, all eight candidates in the Progressive Conservative leadership race sang from the same song sheet. They all promised to conduct a royalty review of one kind or another if party members elected them to be the next premier of Alberta.[13] Former Treasurer Jim Dinning, whose first place position after the first ballot justified the widespread belief he was the front runner in the race to replace Klein, promised a transparent review of the royalty systems for oil sands, conventional oil, and natural gas. Ted Morton, the candidate with the strongest appeal to those furthest to the right in the party, finished second on the first ballot. He doubted whether Albertans were receiving a fair share when oil sands companies paid only the pre-payout rate of 1 percent and promised to review that situation. Ed Stelmach, who placed a rather distant third on the first ballot with half the votes of Dinning, also promised to review the oil sands royalty system and also doubted whether the existing system should be retained. Only the top three finishers on the first ballot were allowed to run in the second, final ballot. Much to the surprise of the pundits, Stelmach capitalized on his strong support in northern Alberta, the endorsements from three of the candidates forced to drop out, and his status as a compromise candidate between Dinning and Morton. Stelmach swept to victory.[14]

When Ed Stelmach won the party leadership and premiership, he announced that one of his first tasks would be to establish an independent review of Alberta's royalty regimes. He pledged to establish an independent expert panel that would hold public hearings on the issue. Economists, oil and gas industry experts, and those with knowledge about how to maximize value-added processing of natural resources would be sought for the panel.[15] To his credit, Premier Stelmach delivered on that promise. In February 2007, he appointed an independent panel of six experts to evaluate the province's petroleum royalty regimes. Reporting to the finance minister, the panel was created as part of the finance minister's mandate to "conduct a public review to ensure Albertans are receiving a fair share from energy development through royalties, taxes and fees."[16] The public, transparent character of this review distinguished it sharply from the private deliberations of the National Oil Sands Task Force that fathered the generic royalty regime in 1997. This transparency and accessibility also distinguished the Royalty Review Panel from virtually all of the consultations or studies undertaken during the Klein years. Public hearings would be held in four cities, the transcripts of those hearings would be published on the Internet, and all submissions to the Royalty Review Panel would be considered public information and published there as well.

Those who hoped for the public to receive a greater share of the available economic rent might have been disappointed to hear what Finance Minister Dr. Lyle Oberg said when he announced the panel's creation. He sounded very much like former Energy Minister Melchin when he defended the status quo and deflected the opposition's demands for information and action. Oberg said the goal of the royalty framework should be to ensure Albertans received "a fair return on the province's natural resources while maintaining an internationally competitive system that allows the Alberta economy to continue to prosper."[17] They also might have been concerned or suspicious to read the welcome the panel received from CAPP. Canada's leading petroleum organization looked forward to the review of Alberta's petroleum royalty regimes because it would give industry the opportunity to explain the value and importance of the established regime. "I see it," said CAPP's Greg Stringham, "as a good education opportunity."[18] When Pierre Alvarez, CAPP's president, subsequently made a presentation to the review panel, he told its members that he saw "great value in getting all the current information out to Albertans."[19] Hearing these welcoming words might have made some wonder if those who had worried or issued warnings about the idea of reviewing royalties during the leadership race were just a little paranoid.

Shell Canada's oil sands chief had said then that the royalty structure was one of the keys to the economics of its oil sands investments; Canadian Natural Resources Ltd.'s president flatly claimed the company's Horizon project wouldn't have been started without the 1997 royalty changes. The existing royalty regime had facilitated oil sands investments. "Don't screw it up" was Petrobank Energy's pointed advice to those who wanted to replace Premier Klein.[20]

Once the Royalty Review Panel was appointed, Stringham, CAPP's vice-president responsible for markets and oil sands, underlined his association's pleasure with the makeup of the panel. He believed that its six members, drawn from the private resource sector and academia, had the expertise needed to offer the best advice to government about the future of petroleum royalties. He made it very clear in remarks to a second, oil sands-focused consultation committee that royalties issues should be the primary, and preferably the exclusive, domain of the Royalty Review Panel. The chair of this second committee, the Oil Sands Multistakeholder Committee, invited Stringham's thoughts on why this committee, with representation from environmental organizations, First Nations, and municipalities as well as government and industry, shouldn't touch the oil sands royalty question. CAPP's vice-president was glad to oblige. Referring to the Royalty Review Panel, he said:

> What I am saying is that that panel of experts with all the input that they will be receiving on the short-, medium- and long-term outlook for the financial side of it is probably best dealt with in that forum. We don't want to duplicate the effort that's going forward. They have been tasked directly with that and have the expertise from their backgrounds to be able to deal with the technicalities associated with a very complex system. That doesn't mean that there may not be something that you need to address generally, but when it comes to the overall, definitely they are the experts in that area.[21]

As the industry would discover five months later, CAPP's confidence in the Review Panel's expertise was misplaced.

Establishing the Public's "Fair Share": The Alberta Royalty Review Panel

When industry appeared before the Panel it endorsed the status quo. Alberta's royalty regimes were fine, they said; the regimes should be embraced because they served the long-term interests of Albertans well. CAPP's presentation invited the Panel to conclude that, given the contemporary price and cost environments faced by tar sands ventures, the oil sands royalty system was "fair and appropriate."[22] Pierre Alvarez reminded those who favoured oil sands royalty increases because light oil prices had increased dramatically since 2001 to look at the extent to which costs had escalated. Using a Syncrude-like project proposal from 1997 as his model he argued that

> [t]he factors which have improved the economics such as higher prices
> and lower income tax rates, have been more than offset by the sum of [a]
> variety of factors which have impaired the economics of that same project.
> The net result is that a project of similar size and scope being contemplated
> at the introduction of the generic royalty regime is in no better condition
> today. So since the royalty regime was appropriate then, it remains equally
> appropriate today.[23]

He didn't suggest that, as was noted in Chapter Three, the pre-payout features of the 1997 royalty regime did little to promote financial discipline in project owners. The idea the royalty regime itself could impair the economics of an tar sands mine was heresy.

In contrast to CAPP, municipalities, non-energy interest groups, and the public were virtually unanimous in demanding changes. The Regional Municipality of Wood Buffalo, the municipality most affected by exploiting the tar sands, favoured royalty increases and also sought the Panel's support for its call for Alberta to dedicate a predictable annual percentage of tar sands royalties to Wood Buffalo and other municipalities shouldering the burden of supplying the public infrastructure and services demanded by the explosive growth in tar sands investments.[24] The Pembina Institute recommended various options to maximize the revenue Albertans would receive from this resource; the Institute's vision saw government receiving approximately 70 percent of the available economic rent through royalties and taxes and saving at least 50 percent of that rent in a long-term savings fund.[25] The Alberta Federation of Labour came out swinging against the generic regime's "infamous" 1 percent royalty and the "sweetheart deal" tar sands companies were getting.[26] The AFL argued it would be reasonable for the public to capture anywhere between 70 and 80 percent of the available economic rent.[27]

The Royalty Review Panel's final report, *Our Fair Share*, embraced some of this more critical view of the status quo. The Panel bluntly and straightforwardly made one essential point that, out of hand, rejected the foundation of the industry's argument. Albertans, the owners of the province's oil and gas resources, were not receiving their fair share through the government's royalty regimes. Royalties and taxes could be increased without jeopardizing the health of the petroleum economy. The Panel recommended significant changes to the natural gas, conventional oil, and oil sands royalty regimes. For oil sands, the Panel recommended a suite of royalty and taxation changes. It did not, however, call for any increase in the pre-payout 1 percent base royalty levy. Given the high, up-front costs of tar sands ventures, the Panel felt the 1 percent levy was justified. Producers would be guaranteed that in the pre-payout period royalties would not affect significantly their ability to recover their investments, an especially important consideration in the event world oil prices fell precipitously. The important changes would come, for the most part, after payout. Then companies would continue to pay the 1 percent base royalty plus a 33 percent net revenue royalty.[28]

The Panel's recommendations would immediately increase Alberta's overall share by 20 percent. In 2010, the proposed changes would generate an additional 26 percent for the provincial treasury. The Panel projected its recommendations would increase revenue by 37 percent more in 2016 than would be gathered under the terms of the established royalty system.[29] In the long term the revenue impact of the Panel's recommendations would be hardest on players in the tar sands. Immediately, the provincial revenue increase from the tar sands only would amount to 7 percent. But in 2010 the Panel's proposals would produce a 38 percent increase, and in 2016 oil sands royalties would be 51 percent greater than what the 1997 regime would deliver. The Panel's recommendations to increase the provincial share of tar sands revenues reflected the belief that the international political economy of petroleum had changed markedly—because of both the steady upward march of world oil prices and the royalty/taxation changes many jurisdictions had made to capture some of these price increases. In a new global environment where governments around the world were demanding more from petroleum companies, the revenue shares delivered by the generic regime were no longer judged suitable.

The proposed introduction of an Oil Sands Severance Tax (OSST) was one recommendation that would affect tar sands ventures over their entire lives. Arguably the Panel felt the strongest about the OSST. This tax would inject a measure of world oil price sensitivity to the overall fiscal regime. The OSST, to be levied on all bitumen production, was "an absolutely essential component of a 'fair' royalty system for Albertans."[30] This tax initially would be levied on gross bitumen production revenues where the price of bitumen would be pegged at 40 percent of the value in Canadian dollars of WTI crude oil. The OSST rate was a sliding rate; it would increase with WTI prices to a maximum of $120 per barrel. The tax would be zero when WTI was less than $40 per barrel, 1 percent at $40 per barrel, and would increase by 0.1 percent for every $1 increase in the price of WTI (1 percent for every $10 increase). A ceiling of 9 percent would be reached when oil hit or went beyond $120 per barrel. Significantly, the proposed OSST, unlike the base royalty, would not be an eligible cost for calculating payout, net revenues, or income subject to corporate income tax.

The Panel also felt very strongly that a bitumen pricing formula, a Bitumen Valuation Methodology (BVM), was required in order, among other things, to address transfer pricing concerns. There was some urgency attached to the Panel's recommendation that Alberta hire "a truly independent, un-conflicted, world-renowned and highly experienced advisor" to develop a permanent BVM, one that obviously would not necessarily be equal to the interim 40 percent formula suggested above. This advisor was expected to consult widely and study how other jurisdictions approached this or analogous issues. But this consultation was not intended to give tar sands producers any veto power in the process; their consent to a permanent BVM should not be required.[31]

The Panel was nothing if not well informed about royalties. It reached its conclusions and recommendations after consulting a wide range of information. First, it considered the submissions from Albertans, petroleum companies, and other interest groups. Second, the Panel considered studies prepared by leading oil and gas consulting firms such as Cambridge Energy Research Associates and Wood Mackenzie; it also relied on data from Alberta Energy. Furthermore, the Panel retained Dr. Pedro van Meurs, a well-recognized, well-respected expert on global petroleum fiscal systems. Van Meurs was commissioned to prepare a comparative study of fiscal systems to guide the Panel's recommendations. During the Panel's public meetings, van Meurs was a darling of the petroleum industry. His 1997 comparative study on government/industry shares of petroleum rents was cited favourably by industry during the hearings. Industry used that study to argue that Alberta ranked very high when it came to the government's take.[32] But, to industry's chagrin, the up-to-date work van Meurs did for the Panel, work the industry did not have access to and was unable to comment on, demonstrated that exactly the opposite situation

> is now unequivocally true: the situation has changed dramatically since 1997 and based on the current situation, Alberta's Government Take ranks very low against competing jurisdictions, especially in the oil sands arena.[33]

The recommendations flowing from these various sources resonated well and powerfully with Albertans. Public opinion stood firmly behind the panel's call to increase the public's share of resource rents. An overwhelming majority of Albertans surveyed by Leger Marketing—88 percent—did not believe they were getting their fair share of revenue from the province's

petroleum bounty. A majority of 51 percent strongly agreed with that position; only 4 percent strongly disagreed. Two-thirds wanted Premier Stelmach
to follow the advice of the Panel's chair and implement its recommendations
in their entirety. They wanted the additional 20 percent recommended by the
Panel, and there were not, as one might have expected, significant differences
in the public sentiment in Calgary compared to the rest of Alberta. Furthermore, Albertans were not overly concerned that higher royalties would lead
industry to abandon the province. Fifty-four percent refused to believe that,
if royalties were increased, petroleum companies would try to harm Alberta
by changing their investment strategies and commitments.[34]

The Panel's recommendations received an important boost from the fall
2007 report of the auditor general. In late August 2006, Auditor General Fred
Dunn heard one of many references Energy Minister Melchin made during
that legislative session to the ongoing nature of his department's review of
royalty programs. Dunn told Edmonton journalist Sheila Pratt that when he
heard a reference to an ongoing review he wanted to see it.[35] The auditor
general was interested because, as Melchin's answer in the legislature made
very clear, even small changes to royalty programs, what Melchin called "the
tinkering kinds of questions," could involve hundreds of millions of dollars.

Dunn's 2007 audit of Energy's royalty review system was alarming in
several respects. First, as the opposition had alleged in the legislature, the
rapid rise in petroleum prices had reduced the province's share of royalties
below the target range anticipated by the royalty systems. More than just a
"tinkering" amount of revenue was at stake here. Dunn concluded that, for
at least three years, the Department of Energy had estimated it could have
collected an additional $1 billion from energy companies. Importantly, the
department believed this money could have been collected "without stifling
industry profitability."[36] Second, none of the critical issues the department
had identified during its ongoing review had been addressed publicly. The
size of the gap between what officials collected and what they felt the industry could contribute remained a secret. So too did the reasons the provincial
government didn't make changes to the royalty systems.

The problems identified by the auditor general didn't arise due to administrative shortcomings in the energy department. Generally, department officials "produced quality analysis." For example, with respect to the tar sands,
officials had been concerned about the bitumen-based royalty system since
at least the year 2000. Basing royalties on bitumen raised

> a transfer pricing issue, where oil sands producers pay royalty based on a
> non-arm's-length price for their produced bitumen. This issue affects royalty
> calculation, fair share calculations, and revenue forecasting.[37]

If companies could avoid purchasing bitumen through arm's-length transactions, as they did for the bitumen they produced and then used within their integrated upgrading operations, they had opportunities to undervalue bitumen. Undervaluing bitumen meant fewer dollars for the treasury, for the owners of the resource. "To give perspective," the auditor general said, "in 2005 the Department estimated that by 2010 as much as $1 billion per year of royalty revenue could be at risk."[38] The auditor general's statement was the type of understated perspective one might expect from the stereotypical chartered accountant.[39] Bitumen valuation, although it had been on the oil sands business unit's desk since 2000, still had not been resolved. As noted earlier, this also was an issue of concern to the Royalty Review Panel.[40]

Responsibility for neither publicizing these circumstances nor taking action on them rested most certainly with the energy minister and the premier. It might also have rested with the most senior levels of administration in the energy department. The political response to the analyses of departmental officials, at the very least, was unsympathetic. Neither successive energy ministers nor the premier saw any need for change. A 2004 internal departmental Royalty Review, for example, advised the energy minister to consider adjusting net oil sands royalty rates at high prices.[41] He didn't. This recommendation was repeated in a 2005 departmental Royalty Review; again, no action was taken. The minister told the auditor general he didn't proceed because he was not satisfied his department had done enough work on these issues in order to support such a change to the status quo.[42] In 2006, the energy department concluded that the government should implement a bitumen valuation methodology in order to prevent additional royalty losses. Again, the minister declined to proceed. It's an open question whether the premier would have endorsed these changes if the minister had accepted them and tried to move them forward in the policy process. In 2006, by which time Energy had repeatedly presented analyses supporting changes to the province's royalty systems, Premier Klein steadfastly rejected any talk of revisiting royalty rates. When petroleum royalties were a focal point for debate in 2006, Klein was asked about the government's reviews of Alberta's royalty systems. Had the energy department reviewed the royalty systems and concluded, as Energy Minister Melchin maintained, that the province already was receiving its fair share of petroleum resource revenues? Klein, not one to blink at offering an outlandish quote, did not disappoint here: "I don't know if it was completed or not, nor do I give a tinker's damn whether it was completed or not ... I've always been satisfied that our royalty regime is proper and right ... We do get our pound of flesh."[43]

Industry Strikes Back

Industry, faced with the Royalty Review Panel's recommendations, the auditor general's report, and a public craving a greater share of economic rent, was shocked. Murray Edwards, vice-chairman of the board of directors of Canadian Natural Resources, called the recommendations "draconian."[44] Greg Stringham delivered CAPP's immediate reaction to the Royalty Review Panel: "It's way bigger than we thought—it is a wholesale change to the entire royalty system."[45] This was not the message industry expected to hear from the experts it had earlier applauded as those who should be entrusted with the task of reviewing the royalty regime. At times the anger and sense of betrayal pouring out of corporate boardrooms and from the pages of the business press took on absurd proportions. Allusions to Hugo Chavez's socialist Venezuela, authoritarian Central Asian republics, or just plain madness were as popular in Calgary's oilpatch and the business press as Smithbilt hats during the Calgary Stampede. "Albertastan," "Caracas on the Bow," "the Bolivarian Republic of Alberta"—these were some of the terms used to suggest what Alberta would become if the Stelmach government adopted the Panel's recommendations.[46]

Industry—individually and through CAPP—immediately went on the counterattack. Yesterday's panel of experts went from darlings to pariahs overnight. CAPP's once-trusted experts had authored a "flawed" report.[47] CAPP questioned the research skills and abilities of the Panel; it claimed the Panel's conclusion that Alberta's royalties were low, comparatively speaking, was based only on the study prepared by van Meurs, that now-fallen darling. Stringham said CAPP could not "understand how the panel can assume that these recommendations wouldn't affect activity levels, investment and future jobs in making their projections for future revenue increases."[48]

Some panel members were incredulous at these charges and allegations. Evan Chrapko, a chartered accountant and successful software entrepreneur, noted the Panel considered "all the industry's data, including what they tell their investors and what they file with the authorities as to costs and so on."[49] Sam Spanglet, panel member and former Shell Canada executive who had profited personally from the tar sands boom, bluntly told his former colleagues to stop whining about the proposed increases and to focus their energies on cost control strategies.[50] Encana, Canada's largest natural gas producer, was one of the first major petroleum companies to warn it would cancel investments in Alberta if all of the Panel's recommendations were implemented. It promised, in full-page advertisements taken out in major newspapers, to cut its planned 2008 capital investment budget in Alberta by approximately $1 billion, supposedly a 30 to 40 percent cut to its pre-Panel intentions. Such a dramatic cut would be concentrated in the company's natural gas division; the company wrote this would have far-reaching, very damaging consequences for "working Albertans." Encana promised darkly that its spending cuts "would mean extensive job losses across the industry" and "over the long term, well-paying permanent jobs will not materialize across Alberta." Encana President Randy Eresman sought to convince the public just how badly he would feel if this course of events was forced on his company: "We would greatly regret seeing these job opportunities evaporate. We are Albertans. We care about the people of Alberta and we hope we won't have to make these choices."[51]

Less apocalyptic, but nonetheless powerful, warnings were sounded about what the Panel's recommendations would mean for the commercial future of the tar sands. First Energy Capital warned that, under the Panel's proposed royalty and severance tax system, it was likely that future projects would be reevaluated, at the very least, and perhaps delayed or cancelled. The Calgary investment dealer speculated that as much as $28 billion in future capital investment could be lost, costing the Alberta economy 11,000 jobs. If capital spending in the tar sands faced a 10 percent annual cut, an additional 8,000 jobs would not materialize annually.[52] CNRL, developer of the Horizon oil sands project, supported this view in its own rebuttal of the Panel's analysis. Phrases such as "severe curtailment of future development," "lower employment levels," "decreasing government revenues," and "lower economic activity and job losses" were sprinkled liberally throughout the company's rebuttal. With respect to the Horizon project, CNRL underlined that, while nearly completed and already initiated phases of the project would be completed, future expansions "would likely be cancelled due to the Panel's proposals."[53] Petro-Canada wrote an open letter to Premier Stelmach. It joined the others in seeing "material flaws" in the Panel's analysis and in suggesting that a capital strike might appear over the horizon if the government embraced too enthusiastically the Panel's recommendations. "If the report were enacted as is," wrote Petro-Canada's President and CEO Ron Brenneman, "we believe investing in Alberta would be severely impaired given prices today and those reasonably expected in the future."[54] Albertans would lose in both the short and the long term. For the tar sands, Brenneman contended the oil sands severance tax ignored the higher risk and costs of developing the oil sands. It was simply "not appropriate for oil sands investments." Again, implementing the severance tax would kill investment in Alberta. The severance tax would make in situ projects, the future of exploiting the oil sands, "simply uneconomic." Prices would need to be sustained at more than $100 per barrel for in situ projects "to make sense with the proposed changes."[55] Nexen used its third-quarter conference call to comment in part on the Royalty

Review Panel. It played the disinvestment card. "We have concerns with the Panel's recommendations and if these changes are implemented," said Kevin Reinhart, Nexen's Vice-President for Corporate Planning and Business Development, "our global portfolio of opportunities provide us with many choices to invest capital where overall returns are most attractive for our shareholders."[56] Charlie Fischer, Nexen's President and CEO, later said that if the company's margins were growing, it certainly could afford to pay more in royalties. But, like Petro-Canada's Brenneman, he was very opposed to the oil sands severance tax; it was "egregious" and would cause "some severe problems."[57]

These public ultimatums, analyses, and rebuttals, with their warnings about the damage to investment, employment, and growth the Panel's counsel would bring, were not the only tactics used by the petroleum industry to strike back against the Royalty Review Panel report. Alberta graciously greeted industry outrage with a calming promise—it would start a second "de facto" round of consultations with the industry and the public. The focus of this round, one that took place despite the premier's recognition that "the formal consultation is over," would be on the Panel's recommendations. Deputy Premier Ron Stevens would be a liaison with industry; other Albertans, be they individuals or groups, were not offered face-to-face meetings with key ministers—they were invited to offer their comments online or by telephone.[58] For his part, Energy Minister Mel Knight promised: "We are going to continue to consult in an open manner, both with industry and with Albertans."[59]

Industry took advantage of this second opportunity to consult in two ways. First, it took advantage of its special standing and met frequently with Deputy Premier Stevens. Sixty industry representatives met with Stevens in the five weeks between his appointment and the release of the government's decisions on its royalty frameworks. Stevens's suitors included the presidents and/or chairs of ConocoPhillips Canada, Encana, Imperial Oil, Nexen, Petro-Canada, Suncor, Synenco, and Talisman—all companies with operations or land positions in the tar sands. Other companies with interests in the tar sands—Murphy Oil, Shell Canada, and Suncor—sent other senior management personnel. Pierre Alvarez, the president of CAPP, also personally lobbied Stevens through this private consultative process the government arranged for industry.[60] No independent experts from outside of government were invited to evaluate the veracity and merit of industry's complaints and arguments.

Second, at least some companies contacted their employees and contractors and urged them to contact their MLAs or the government website created to receive comments from the public about the Royalty Review Panel's work. Encana, for example, phoned at least some of its contractors to urge them to speak out against the Panel's work. Canadian Natural Resources e-mailed its employees and contractors urging them to do the same. CNRL's e-mail invited its employees/contractors to use the government website as well as contacting MLAs and cabinet ministers (a list of all MLAs in the legislature was included as an appendix to the e-mail). "The panel's recommendations," advised CNRL's president, "have created a significant risk to future government revenue along with the employment of thousands of people and the viability of businesses that support Canadian Natural Resources as we explore for and produce energy resources in Alberta."[61] In the battle for public support, many corporate messages were dotted with references to compromise and balance; companies did "detailed and diligent" reviews before they responded to the Panel's recommendations.[62] They were reasonable. The Panel, on the other hand, was unprofessional; its recommendations were careless and dangerous. By stressing employment, investment, and growth, the petroleum industry played the cards expected of them in the accounts of Lindblom and Block.[63] Albertans, so this argument went, should brace themselves for calamity if government changed the royalty regime.

Alberta's 2007 Oil Sands Royalty Changes: Draconian or Reaffirming?

Premier Stelmach responded to the Panel's recommendations and the industry's lobbying with a new royalty framework on October 25, 2007—a day when WTI was trading at just over $92 per barrel.[64] The framework inspired two general commentaries immediately following its release. First, some interpreted it as a compromise between the Panel and industry. Here industry's full court pressure on government had borne fruit. Several aspects of the new royalty framework belied Premier Stelmach's insistence the framework wasn't such a compromise.[65] For example, the royalty changes would not take place immediately, as recommended by the Panel; they would begin in 2009. Overall, the new royalty package promised to deliver the 20 percent increase in revenues recommended by the Panel, with a significant difference: the timing of the increase—the Panel recommended an immediate 20 percent increase while the government's increase would not be seen until 2010 (by which point the Panel's proposals were projected to deliver a 26 percent increase). With respect to tar sands, the success of the industry's blitz of Deputy Premier Stevens appeared first in the government's rejection of six of the Panel's 11 tar sands recommendations and then in an additional significant modification to the bitumen valuation recommendation.[66]

Compromise also may be seen in how the government dealt with the Panel's royalty and OSST recommendations. On the one hand, government rejected the OSST. Industry detested this recommendation the most; the Panel seemed to value the severance tax proposal more than other oil sands recommendations since it was "absolutely essential" to a fair royalty system. On the other hand, government also rejected the Panel's most industry-friendly position. This was its support for continuing the requirement that producers should pay the 1 percent base royalty only until payout. Rather than inject oil price sensitivity into the fiscal regime through the OSST, the government chose to incorporate price sensitivity into both the pre- and post-payout royalty terms. The 1/25 percent formula set by 1997's generic regime would remain in place until oil rose above C$55 per barrel. Above $55 the pre-payout base royalty on gross production revenue would rise in steps to a ceiling of 9 percent at $120 (or more) per barrel.[67] The net revenue royalty would rise from 25 to 40 percent over this same price range.[68] The government predicted its changes would garner $470 million more from tar sands producers than they would have paid under the terms of the generic regime. The Panel's proposed changes would have generated $666 million more for the provincial treasury in 2010.[69]

The second type of commentary, popular with the sirens in the business press, saw the royalty changes as a renewed attack on the driving force of the Alberta economy. With several dollops of hyperbole, the petroleum columnist from the *National Post* suggested Alberta's proposals were "usurious"; through them Premier Stelmach endorsed "mediocrity" and introduced "a new anti-oil industry era." "It's a deal," wrote Claudia Cattaneo, "that places Alberta alongside the hydrocarbon-rich Banana Republics of this world where deals are ripped up and promises broken."[70] Deborah Yedlin suggested the premier may not have understood how markets functioned and asked rhetorically if, through comments made about changing established Crown agreements with Suncor and Syncrude, the premier was using "the sort of threatening language that is freely used in parts of the world run by demagogues and dictators?"[71] Gwynn Morgan, the retired CEO of Encana, weighed into the debate with comments typical of the tar sands sector's reaction. The new royalty framework was a serious blow to the tar sands; Stelmach's initiative shocked the industry. "New project decisions in the oil sands," Morgan suggested, "will have to factor a much higher government take in a business already replete with risk."[72] Canadian Oil Sands, the largest partner in the Syncrude joint venture, hinted that the government was following electoral, not economic, logic. Voter demands prompted the government to deliver more revenue to them through a "significant increase" in royalties. Those demands pushed the government off the trail of "pursuing the fuller potential of the resource through higher industry investment, which generates several times more in value through economic activity, employment and other benefits than do royalties." Marcel Coutu, the president and CEO of Canadian Oil Sands, thought he saw the spectre of disinvestment beginning to loom over the tar sands:

> Furthermore, by reducing our industry's profitability, these changes likely will reduce oil sands activity. Some projects may no longer proceed on the same timetable, if at all, and some of the lower-grade oil sands resource, which form part of every project, may never be recovered due to a now higher economic threshold.[73]

Syncrude would do its best to "persevere."

It might look as if the Stelmach government engineered a prison break if the new royalty framework betrayed the tar sands industry. It might look as if the government used its possession of scarce commodities such as petroleum and political stability to impose terms of development the industry universally opposed. This conclusion would be incorrect. It underestimates the degree to which tar sands producers secured changes that insulated themselves from royalty increases. A handful of investment dealer assessments may be used to sketch this alternative, less generous view of what the province's oil sands royalty changes say about the power of government to challenge tar sands producers in public policy-making. Tar sands producers were not affected materially by the royalty changes in this picture. First Energy Capital reported that the net asset value (NAV) impact of the gas, conventional oil, and oil sands royalty changes on Suncor, the company most dependent on tar sands production, actually would be less than that on any of the more diversified companies with tar sands exposure. It estimated the impact on Suncor's NAV to be only minus 2 percent. That isn't to say that dramatic changes were predicted to be in store for the other major players in the tar sands and the Alberta petroleum industry. They weren't coming there either. First Energy Capital estimated the following NAV impacts: Talisman Energy (−3 percent), Nexen (−3 percent), Petro-Canada (−3 percent), Encana (−4 percent), Imperial Oil (−4 percent), Canadian Natural Resources Ltd. (−6 percent), and Husky Energy (−6 percent). Furthermore, First Energy Capital emphasized that capital cost controls and oil price assumptions would have a greater impact than the royalty changes on the returns of future oil sands projects.[74] "Moreover," the investment dealer concluded, "we do not see these changes as being material enough for management deciding whether or not to proceed with the large scale projects currently being progressed."[75] If disinvestment and a capital strike followed, it wouldn't be due to the material consequences of the government's changes.

CIBC World Markets reached a similar conclusion after running the terms of the new oil sands royalty system through their analysts' generic tar sands model. At US$70 oil they estimated their hypothetical project would generate an internal rate of return (IRR) of 13.4 percent and a NAV per barrel produced of $2.79. The new royalty framework would reduce the project's IRR to 13.1 percent and its NAV to $2.57 (a 7.8 percent drop)—hardly grounds for the hand wringing exhibited by the likes of Gwynn Morgan. Tar sands ventures, to remain potentially attractive investments, would require a long-term crude price of approximately US$65.[76]

Even Tristone Capital, a sharp critic of any royalty increases, noted that the impact on an integrated mining operation would be "relatively moderate." Tristone calculated that the IRR at $70 oil would be virtually identical under either the 1997 generic regime or the new royalty framework. At $100 oil, the IRR would be just over 19 percent, compared to just over 20 percent under the generic regime.[77] The company's recommended investment strategy was to buy integrated producers if the market sold off in response to the government's changes. In fact, Suncor, the company most leveraged to synthetic crude oil production from tar sands mining, saw its stock price remain virtually unchanged—at a near record level—the day after the government's announcement. Alberta's "usurious" oil sands royalty changes were a non-event in the stock market.

Another compelling argument demonstrating the marginal impact of the government's changes may be taken from the work of Dr. André Plourde, economist and Review Panel member. Plourde used a simulation model to explore the net returns to tar sands producers and governments from three royalty/tax regimes: 1997 generic, 2007 generic, and the 2007 New Royalty Framework. Corporate income tax changes explain the utility of introducing the 2007 generic category. While provincial royalties remained constant from 1997 to 2007, both Alberta and Ottawa reduced their corporate tax rates significantly. The combined federal/provincial corporate income tax rate in 1997 was 44.62 percent; in 2007 that combined rate was 28.5 percent. Another important change that reduced the overall royalty/tax burden of tar sands producers between 1997 and 2007 concerned the deductibility of royalties. In 2007, royalties paid to Alberta were deductible when calculating federal and provincial taxable income; they weren't deductible in 1997.[78] The return to producers was significantly higher in 2007 than in 1997 due to those federal and provincial corporate income tax reductions and changes. At US$70 per barrel oil, Plourde's base case showed that mining producers according to the 2007 generic regime captured 47.7 percent of net present value. This was 12.5 percent more than these operations would have secured under the fiscal terms of the 1997 generic regime at that oil price. In the case of tar sands mining, the federal government's share of net present value fell from 24.2 percent to 16.2 percent; the Alberta government's share fell from 40.7 to 36.1 percent. According to Plourde's analysis, the new royalty framework essentially returned the total producer and government shares to very close to what they were in the 1997 generic regime. Actually, tar sands producers under the new royalty framework would be slightly better off than under that 1997 deal Eric Newell described as being "fantastic." Miners would pocket 37.8 percent of a project's net present value at US$70 oil; under the 1997 generic regime they would have collected 35.2 percent.[79] The essential outline of Plourde's picture, like that drawn by investment dealers, is one where the government's changes to royalties cannot be viewed credibly as either an attack on industry or even a serious compromise.

Conclusion

In 2008, André Plourde presented an early version of his 2010 article on the petroleum fiscal system in Alberta. At that time his subtitle read "From 1997 … to 1997." It summarized so very well how little the royalty changes of 2007 actually altered the financial bargain struck between government and the tar sands sector in 1997. Clearly, the royalty and policy changes ushered in by the Stelmach government in the fall of 2007 did not constitute a prison break. The government advertised its changes as an "historic, new royalty regime."[80] Historic it was, but only in the sense of confirming the historic relationship between the state and tar sands producers in Alberta. The relationship remained one where foreign multinationals and major Canadian petroleum companies towered over government.

The petroleum industry, stunned by the challenge to its privileged position authored by the Alberta Royalty Review Panel, responded in ways that fit well with the expectations of Lindblom's understanding of the relationship between business and government. Tar sands producers played their growth, investment, and employment cards, and the provincial state folded. It also underlines how we should expect business to resist any changes to market fundamentalism-inspired policy they feel will harm their understanding of their interests. The architects of potential countermovements must overcome both the structural and the ideological foundations of business influence. This will be particularly challenging in a setting such as Alberta where petroleum is so central to the immediate material well-being of the population.

Was a prison break, even of the modest proportions suggested by the Alberta Royalty Review Panel's recommendations, possible? I think so, but only if the state was prepared to recognize it possessed important, but neglected, political resources. Perceptions of oil's growing scarcity, Alberta's political stability, a well-educated Canadian labour force, and the province's proximity to the American market offered politicians important bargaining levers they could have used to increase the public's share of petroleum rents more significantly. But if the state is to take advantage of these resources, at the very least it will have to take off the ideological blinders that have guided the course of petroleum exploitation in Alberta since the mid-1990s. Those blinders, first worn by the Klein administration, dictated that when it comes to the tar sands an unfettered market should rule. According to this idea of political leadership unfettered, market-dictated growth—regardless of its social, environmental, or economic costs—is the best path for the province to follow. This mindset, one that cheapens the state, encourages the more passive approach to economic rent collection seen here. It believes that wealth belongs in the coffers of those given the privilege to exploit the tar sands, not in the public's treasury. It also encourages the state to approach the environmental challenges of exploiting the tar sands in the ways detailed in the next two chapters.

Notes

1   Alberta Finance, "Expert Panel to Examine Alberta's Royalty Regime," news release, February 16, 2007, http://alberta.ca/release.cfm?xID=21056C B7A4991-EBE3-078B-B875B4E7E86EBE6A.

2   Lindblom, "The Market as Prison."

3   Colin J. Campbell and Jean H. Laherrère, "The End of Oil," *Scientific American* (March 1998), 78–83.

4   Silvana Tordo with Brandon S. Tracy and Noora Arfaa, *National Oil Companies and Value Creation* (World Bank Working Paper No. 218) (Washington, DC: World Bank, 2011), xi.

5   The Alberta Federation of Labour's list of bargaining resources consisted of: a globally sought after resource, political stability, proximity to the US market, and the absence of national oil companies. Gil McGowan, President, Alberta Federation of Labour, "AFL Presentation to Alberta Royalty Review Panel," Calgary, Alberta, May 23, 2007.

6   Economic rent was defined previously. See footnote 45 in Chapter Three.

7   The *Globe and Mail's* main news story on the Parkland study describes the institute as "left-leaning." See Steven Chase, "Klein Giving Away Alberta Oil, Gas Riches: Study Think-Tank Finds Province Collects Less Royalties, Taxes than Two Other Peers," *Globe and Mail*, November 10, 1999, B1; the "simple-minded" slur is found in Matthew Ingram, "Royalty Critique Doesn't Add Up," *Globe and Mail*, November 16, 1999.

8   Auditor General of Alberta, *Annual Report of the Auditor General of Alberta 2006–2007*, 106, 120.

9   Auditor General of Alberta, *Annual Report of the Auditor General of Alberta 2006–2007*, 123.

10 These per barrel prices are calculated from the data for 2000 and 2005 published by Natural Resources Canada. See Natural Resources Canada, "Selected Crude Oil Prices Monthly—2000," http://www.collectionscanada. gc.ca/webarchives/20071116044435/http://www2.nrcan.gc.ca/es/erb/prb/english/view.asp?x=476&oid=523; Natural Resources Canada, "Selected Crude Oil Prices Monthly—2005," http://www.collectionscanada.gc.ca/webarchives/20071120173540/http://www2.nrcan.gc.ca/es/erb/prb/english/view.asp?x=476&oid=1008.

11 Alberta, *Hansard 26th Legislature, 2nd Session*, April 4, 2006, 707.

12 Jason Fekete and Tony Seskus, "Tories Desert Klein: Premier 'Shocked' Party Has Turned Against Him," *Calgary Herald*, April 1, 2006, 1.

13 "Where the Leadership Contenders Stand: The Herald Examines Candidates' Positions on Six Key Policy Issues," *Calgary Herald*, November 25, 2006, A17.

14 For an analysis of this leadership selection contest, see David K. Stewart and Anthony M. Sayers, "Leadership Change in a Dominant Party: The Alberta Progressive Conservatives, 2006," *Canadian Political Science Review* 3, no. 4 (December 2009).

15 Bob Weber, "Alberta's Premier Designate Fleshes Out Plan for Oilsands Royalty Review," Canadian Press, December 13, 2006.

16 Alberta Finance, "Expert Panel to Examine," news release.

17 Alberta Finance, "Expert Panel to Examine," news release.

18 Weber, "Alberta's Premier Designate Fleshes Out Plan"; see also Jason Fekete and Renata D'Aliesio, "Oilsands Royalties Put Under Review: Industry Welcomes Move," *Calgary Herald*, December 14, 2006, D1.

19 Alberta Royalty Review Panel, *Meeting transcripts, Calgary, May 22, 2007* (mimeo.), 9.

20 Gordon Jaremko, "Is Alberta's Treasury Extracting a Fair Share?: Oil Price Has Tripled Since Compact Made to Jumpstart Oilsands Investment," *Edmonton Journal*, September 16, 2006.

21 Alberta Oil Sands Consultations Multistakeholder Committee, *Phase Two, meeting transcripts, Calgary, morning session, April 23, 2007*, 81–82.

22 Alberta Royalty Review Panel, *Meeting transcripts, Calgary, May 22, 2007* (mimeo.), 17.

23 Alberta Royalty Review Panel, *Meeting transcripts, Calgary, May 22, 2007* (mimeo.), 16.

24 Alberta Royalty Review Panel, *Meeting transcripts, Fort McMurray, June 5, 2007* (mimeo.), 173–74.

25 Alberta Royalty Review Panel, *Meeting transcripts, Calgary, May 22, 2007* (mimeo.), 244. Pembina offered three options for the Panel's consideration. All options kept the pre-payout royalty at 1 percent of gross revenues. The first option increased the post-payout royalty from 25 to 55 percent. The second option recommended a three-tier structure—1 percent until payout, 30 percent of net revenues post-payout until a company recovered an additional 10 percent on its investment, and from that point thereafter 60 percent of net revenues. The final option introduced an environmental tax of $40 for every tonne of carbon dioxide emitted by a project as well as a post-payout royalty of 40 percent of net revenues.

26   Alberta Royalty Review Panel, *Meeting transcripts, Calgary, May 23, 2007* (mimeo.), 9, 11.

27   Alberta Royalty Review Panel, *Meeting transcripts, Calgary, May 23, 2007* (mimeo.), 15.

28   Under the generic regime companies would pay either 1 percent of gross production revenues or 25 percent of net revenues, whichever amount was greater. For the Panel, the 1 percent base royalty could be used as a deduction in determining net revenues.

29   Alberta Royalty Review Panel, *Our Fair Share*, 17.

30   Alberta Royalty Review Panel, *Our Fair Share*, 13.

31   Alberta Royalty Review Panel, *Our Fair Share*. The Panel made other oil sands recommendations not discussed here. They were: treat environmental fees or taxes as eligible costs for revenue/royalty calculation purposes, introduce a 5 percent tradable royalty credit to encourage bitumen processing in Alberta, eliminate the Accelerated Capital Cost Allowance (ACCA), clarify the cost rules with respect to projects and eligible costs, do not offer any grandfathering provisions, eliminate the ability of some heavy oil producers to have their operations treated as if they were oil sands operations, and bring forward in time the point at which oil sands lease holders were required to pay escalating rentals of the properties they said they intended to exploit.

32   Of the 324 fiscal systems evaluated by van Meurs in his 1997 report, Alberta's oil sands regime ranked 79th (where the number one ranking indicated the system offering the industry the largest take). He characterized the oil sands regime as a four-star system, one that was favourable to investors (69 systems received a five-star—very favourable—ranking). See PennEnergy, "Online Research Center: Worldwide Fiscal Systems Improve for Investors, Favor Oil over Gas," January 1, 1998.

33   Alberta Royalty Review Panel, *Our Fair Share*, 23.

34   Tony Seskus, "A Bigger Piece of the Pie," *Calgary Herald*, October 3, 2007.

35   Sheila Pratt, "An Audit Too Far: The Stelmach Government Pledged Accountability—Until Fred Dunn Discovered Their Billion-Dollar Giveaway," *Alberta Views* 13, no. 8 (October 2010). The article is incorrect in suggesting this was the first time the government admitted to an ongoing review of royalty programs. As Melchin said to Knight, "As I've said on numerous occasions, this is part of the ongoing review that the Department of Energy does with respect to royalty programs." Alberta, *Hansard 26th Legislature, 2nd Session*, August 24, 2006, 1687.

36   Auditor General of Alberta, *Annual Report of the Auditor General of Alberta 2006–2007*, 91.

37   Auditor General of Alberta, *Annual Report of the Auditor General of Alberta 2006–2007*, 120.

38   Auditor General of Alberta, *Annual Report of the Auditor General of Alberta 2006–2007*.

39   Frances Miley and Andrew Read, "Jokes in Popular Culture: The Characterization of the Accountant," *Accounting, Auditing & Accountability Journal*, Vol. 25, No. 4 (2012).

40   Auditor General of Alberta, *Annual Report of the Auditor General of Alberta 2006–2007*, 114.

41 Auditor General of Alberta, *Annual Report of the Auditor General of Alberta 2006–2007*, 107.

42 Auditor General of Alberta, *Annual Report of the Auditor General of Alberta 2006–2007*.

43 Jason Fekete, "Tory Candidates Skeptical of Alberta Royalties Review," *Calgary Herald*, July 13, 2006, A5.

44 Tony Seskus and Lisa Schmidt, "Tories to Hear Review Gripes," *Calgary Herald*, September 21, 2007.

45 Graham Thomson, "'It's Way Bigger Than We Thought,' Says CAPP," *Edmonton Journal*, September 19, 2007.

46 Claudia Cattaneo and Jon Harding, "Royalties Hike Would Kill 'Golden Goose,'" *National Post*, September 20, 2007; David Ebner and Norval Scott, "Energy Stocks Plunge After Call to Raise Royalties," *Globe and Mail*, September 19, 2007; John Partridge, "US Market Pundit Flees 'Socialist' North," *Globe and Mail*, September 19, 2007; Paul Sankey and Ryan Todd, "Oil Sands Royalty Review: The Bolivarian Republic of Alberta" (Global Markets Research, Deutsche Bank, September 28, 2007).

47 CAPP, "Royalty Panel's Report Flawed; Industry Committed to Working Constructively with Government," news release, September 24, 2007.

48 "Oilpatch Plans Offensive Against Alta Royalty Review Report," Canadian Press, September 24, 2007.

49 Jeffrey Jones, "Royalty Panel Member Fires Back at Critics," Reuters, September 28, 2007.

50 Tony Seskus, Jason Fekete, and Lisa Schmidt, "Royalty Report Rattles Stocks; Oilpatch Issues Warning; I Won't Be Bullied: Premier; Klein 'Fears' for Oilsands," *Calgary Herald*, September 20, 2007.

51 Encana, "EnCana Plans to Cut about $1 Billion from 2008 Alberta Investments If Royalty Panel Report Adopted in Full," news release, September 28, 2007. See https://www.encana.com/news-stories/news-releases/details.html?release=609981.

52 First Energy Capital, "Job Losses Quantified—A Look at the Alberta Royalty Impact," October 10, 2007.

53 Canadian Natural Resources Limited, "Canadian Natural Resources Limited Expresses Concerns over the Royalty Review Panel Report," news release, October 9, 2007, 3. See http://www.cnrl.com/upload/media_element/131/01/1009_royalty_review.pdf.

54 Petro-Canada, "Petro-Canada's Letter to Alberta Premier Regarding Royalty Review Recommendations," news release, October 3, 2007.

55 Petro-Canada, "Petro-Canada's Letter to Alberta Premier."

56 Thomson Financial, *Thomson StreetEvents, Conference Call Transcript NXY—Q3 2007 Nexen Earnings Conference Call*, October 24, 2007 (mimeo.).

57 Thomson Financial, *Thomson StreetEvents, Conference Call Transcript NXY*.

58 Alberta, "Province to Capture Feedback on Royalty Recommendations," news release, September 25, 2007. See http://alberta.ca/release.cfm?xID=221663DDF2206-A43B-D590-E8244B31BFA13C82. The *Globe and Mail* suggested that Deputy Premier Stevens would "publish a report on his discussions." No such report, other than a list of industry representatives consulted, was ever produced. See David Ebner, "Report Finds Alberta Still a Bargain, Even with Higher Royalties," *Globe and Mail*, September 26, 2007.

59 Claudia Cattaneo, "20% Hike in Royalties Would Cost US $26B," *Financial Post*, September 26, 2007.

60 Alberta Justice, "Royalty Review Industry Liaison Meetings" (mimeo., n.d.).

61 Canadian Natural Resources Limited, "RE: Royalty Report to Alberta Government," memorandum to employees and contractors, September 26, 2007 (mimeo.).

62 Canadian Natural Resources Limited, "Canadian Natural Resources Limited Expresses Concerns," 3.

63 Lindblom, "The Market as Prison"; Block, "The Ruling Class Does Not Rule."

64 WTI traded for US$92.09 on the spot market when Premier Stelmach announced his new framework. See United States Department of Energy, "Cushing, OK WTI Spot Price FOB (Dollars per Barrel)."

65 Jason Fekete and Tony Seskus, "Stelmach Under Fire," *Calgary Herald,* October 26, 2007.

66 The government did not commit to hiring the type of independent authority the Panel championed. It also would continue to rely on the market for bitumen to set some prices and seems to have opened the door to a much more extensive consultation with industry than what the Panel envisaged.

67 The base royalty was set to rise by 0.12308 percent for every dollar increase in the price of oil.

68 The net revenue royalty rate increment was set at 0.23077 percent for every dollar increase in the price of oil.

69 For newspaper commentary arguing that the new royalty framework should be seen as a compromise, see Don Braid, "Sorry, Mr. Stelmach, This Is One Big Compromise," *Calgary Herald,* October 26, 2007, and Graham Thomson, "Game of Numbers, and Semantics," *Edmonton Journal*, October 26, 2007.

70 Claudia Cattaneo, "A Slap in the Face for Alberta," *National Post*, October 26, 2007.

71 Deborah Yedlin, "Anxiety Hangs over Oilpatch; It's Hard to Conclude Stelmach Got It Right," *Calgary Herald*, October 26, 2007.

72 Gwynn Morgan, "Populism Tramples Principle in Alberta," *Globe and Mail*, October 29, 2007.

73 Canadian Oil Sands Trust, "Canadian Oil Sands Discusses Royalty Changes," news release, October 26, 2007, http://www.newswire.ca/fr/news-releases/canadian-oil-sands-discusses-royalty-changes-534540301.html.

74 First Energy Capital, "Integrated & Large Caps: Better to Boil Your Bitumen!," October 26, 2007. The reference to "boil your bitumen" foreshadows the report's conclusion that producers who upgrade bitumen into synthetic crude oil are better candidates for investment than bitumen-only producers.

75 First Energy Capital, "Oil Sands—A Totally Bitumen Deal!," October 26, 2007.

76 CIBC World Markets, "Equity Research Industry Update—The New Alberta Oil Sands Royalty Regime," October 26, 2007.

77 Tristone Capital Inc., "Energy Investment Research—Conventional Oil Hammered, Oil Sands Hit, and Where's the Clarity on Conventional Gas?," October 26, 2007, 23.

78 André Plourde, "On Properties of Royalty and Tax Regimes in Alberta's Oil Sands," *Energy Policy* 38, no. 8 (2010), 4654.

79 Plourde, "On Properties of Royalty and Tax Regimes, 4660.

80 Alberta, "Premier Stelmach Delivers Historic, New Royalty Regime for Alberta," news release, October 25, 2007, http://alberta.ca/release.cfm?xID=22384D8D0CC20-9549-7D32-2CF5FDADC70214D2.

7
Taking Environmental Issues Abroad: Toxic Tailings, Dead Ducks

"Alberta's oilsands opponents have a new emblem—hundreds of ducks coated and killed in oily toxic sludge."

—Calgary Herald, *2008*

"A stringent regulatory system governs tailings management in Alberta."

—*Government of Alberta, 2015*

Introduction

By 2005 the reregulated, unrestrained vision of tar sands development was triumphant. Regulators had approved more than 1.2 million barrels per day of new bitumen mining production from 1997 to 2004. Between 1996 and 2006, petroleum companies invested an estimated $34 billion in the tar sands—$9 billion more than what the National Task Force on Oil Sands Strategies had hoped would be committed by 2020.[1] No branch of the Canadian state, no political party, no constituency within civil society offered a serious and effective challenge, either singly or in combination with others, to this investment frenzy.

For nearly 10 years this tremendous expansion of what public commentary soon would increasingly label "dirty oil" essentially was ignored by environmental organizations outside of Alberta. In 1993, Greenpeace announced an international campaign to phase out fossil fuels by the end of the twenty-first century. This campaign was a "top priority" for Greenpeace, and its Calgary campaign manager swore Greenpeace would urge governments to stop all financial assistance to the oil sands.[2] Media coverage between this announcement and the end of 2004 suggests Greenpeace paid little more than lip service to protesting the race to exploit the tar sands. A "campaign" against Suncor that amounted to a few days of protest in March 2000 in Edmonton illustrates the ephemeral character of Greenpeace's actions against the tar sands.[3] While a Toronto spokesperson could tell the *New York Times* that Greenpeace wanted "a halt to the expansion of all tar sands projects," he couldn't point to many actions backing up that call.[4] The point to emphasize is how sporadic and low-key the Greenpeace efforts were. Greenpeace didn't take advantage of the plentiful opportunities the mid- to late 1990s offered for protesting tar sands exploitation in Alberta's boreal forest.

A somewhat similar story could be told about the National Resources Defense Council (NRDC), the self-described "most effective environmental action group" in the United States.[5] It wasn't until 2002 that the NRDC explicitly objected to the environmental costs of exploiting the tar sands. The NRDC/Sierra Club of Canada report *America's Gas Tank: The High Cost of Canada's Oil and Gas Export Strategy* devoted some attention to tar sands production, focusing primarily on their greater greenhouse gas emissions relative to conventional oil production.[6] By 2002, tar sands projects were gobbling up tens of thousands of hectares of Canada's taiga. It is stunning to anyone at all familiar with wilderness preservation issues in Alberta to read in this report about petroleum's threats to wilderness in the Bighorn and Castle areas of Alberta but not to see one critical word raised about the similar threats that exploiting the tar sands posed to the boreal forest.

This chapter describes the sea change that took place in the environmental critique of the tar sands, which started to transform into a transnational critique in the late spring of 2006. Its transnational character manifested itself in two ways: actors and strategies. Transnational and foreign actors such as Greenpeace and NRDC, who had been absent to that point, began to mobilize against the tar sands. Given how barren Alberta's political landscape was to planting and nurturing an environmental critique, the new players directed a great deal of their energies to using the media to try to convince consumers and legislators in the US and Europe to boycott or outlaw "dirty oil" from the tar sands. A fledgling global countermovement against the tar sands emerged out of the failure of domestic interests to dent the unconditional support the Canadian state extended to the tar sands rush. The goal in the next two chapters is to describe this opposition and evaluate its impact. Did it temper the state's unreserved enthusiasm for the reregulated, unrestrained vision of resource exploitation? Did it soften the environmental footprint of the tar sands? Two issues are used to explore these questions. In this chapter we examine the global spotlight that was about to shine on one of the tar sands' toxic legacies—tailings reservoirs that by 2007 were estimated to cover more than 100 square kilometres (42 square miles) of the boreal landscape; by 2013 these reservoirs and their associated infrastructure sprawled over 220 square kilometres (84 square miles).[7] The next chapter focuses on climate change.

Mr. Smith Goes to Washington

The global transformation of the environmental critique received an important assist, ironically, from the attention-seeking mindset of the provincial government. Alberta had lobbied for years to get American politicians and consumers to recognize the importance of tar sands petroleum to US national security concerns. These efforts first paid off in December 2002, when the *Oil & Gas Journal*, for the first time, included Alberta's oil sands in its list of global proven crude oil reserves.[8] Its decision to add 175 billion barrels of bitumen to Canadian reserves catapulted Canada to second place (180 billion barrels) behind only Saudi Arabia (259 billion barrels) on the journal's "estimated proven reserves" list.[9] Subsequently, the US Energy Information Agency (EIA) endorsed this change in its *International Energy Outlook 2003*.[10] Finally, the American government and industry were paying attention to Alberta's bitumen.

This recognition, and the boom that by 2002 was well underway, was not enough for Alberta's politicians. The annual Smithsonian Folklife Festival struck the Alberta government as an opportunity to cement or further the recognition of the tar sands' importance to America's appetite for secure oil. Alberta pursued this opportunity with the Smithsonian Institution in 2005 and was invited to participate in the 2006 Festival. As Ed Stelmach, then the province's minister of intergovernmental relations, told the Legislature, the Smithsonian's invitation showed "we are getting our word out."[11] It is quite surprising this invitation never received any serious media attention until more than a year later in the late spring of 2006.

Alberta's participation in the Smithsonian Folklife Festival was inspired by insecurity and hubris. The insecurity rested in the belief that Alberta, like the comedian Rodney Dangerfield, "don't get no respect" for its importance as a supplier of petroleum to the United States. Most Americans didn't recognize then, and probably still don't today, that Canada is the single most important foreign source of petroleum to the US.[12] If the United States was, as President Bush suggested, addicted to oil, then Canada was now the most important supplier of its fix. This lack of recognition galled Alberta's political class. Even if the territorial limits of further tar sands expansion were looming, Alberta still wanted the respect it felt it deserved from being America's most important foreign supplier of petroleum.

Murray Smith, Alberta's representative to Washington, personified the government's hubris. Before Smith's appointment to head the Alberta office in the American capital, he had served as the province's energy minister and was a former petroleum industry executive. For Smith the phrase "rational objections to rapid oil sands development" was an oxymoron. His enthusiasm to highlight the tar sands during the Folklife Festival suggests a total blindness to the environmental criticisms Alberta's high-profile appearance at the festival might invite in a city not known for an absence of reporters looking for a story. Smith thought it wise to ensure the gigantism associated with exploiting the oil sands was not lost on anyone who saw the tar sands display on the National Mall during the festival. To this end he recommended the exhibit offer festival attendees the chance to see a baby brother, what Smith called "a Tonka Toy," of the 400-ton trucks that carry bitumen payloads weighing as much as one fully loaded Boeing 747.[13] Smith described himself as "the truck guy from day one."[14] He explained his enthusiasm this way:

> When we linked with the Smithsonian Folklife Festival one of the visual impacts that I thought was so important to this town was an earth mover because Washington is such a big town. There is the Washington Monument, the Lady Liberty, so I figured a big yellow truck that moves earth at the rate of 400 tonnes per load would be a very strong impact on the national mall.[15]

If one wanted to have a "very strong impact" on environmentalists, the exact opposite from what prudence would counsel, it is hard to imagine a better strategy than Smith's. Environmental groups (ENGOs) seized on Alberta's ostentatious display to hammer both the Smithsonian's decision to feature Alberta in the festival as well as the substance of the Alberta display. The festival was a media coup for ENGOs. The *Wall Street Journal*, *Washington Post*, *Reuters*, *Platt's Oilgram News*, *Toronto Star*, *Globe and Mail*, and Alberta's major dailies were among the print media running stories featuring the environmental critique of Alberta's enthusiasm to exploit the tar sands. The NRDC led the charge against Alberta's participation in the festival. NRDC claimed that, despite the presence of more than 120 Alberta artists and other participants not affiliated with petroleum, Alberta's presence on the National Mall was "a one-sided focus on the tar sands." Susan Casey-Lefkowitz, then the NRDC's Director of Canada Projects, declared: "Our objection is that Alberta is using the Smithsonian Folklife Festival as a jumping off point for an all-out lobby to secure more American involvement in the tar sands development."[16] NRDC responded to Alberta's provocation by inviting Alberta environmentalists, including the Pembina Institute, and First Nations to Washington to offer their very different narrative on the tar sands than what "the truck guy" preferred.[17]

"The Press Is the Enemy"[18]

The Smithsonian episode signalled significant additions to or shifts in the environmental politics of the tar sands. Markets became an important focus. The media became a more important political resource. Activists tried to use the media to impress foreign consumers, legislators, and financiers about the damage tar sands production was doing to the land and those who depended on it. Seven years before Shannon Phillips, as Minister of Environment and Parks, would get her opportunity to show how the centre-left New Democratic Party would improve the environmental performance of the tar sands, she produced a show on the tar sands for Al-Jazeera. Reflecting on that experience, she contended that "[t]he fate of the oil sands lies with the global marketplace and, ultimately, global media."[19] Events of the past decade certainly underline the international media's importance as a battleground for the clash between the tar sands' proponents and opponents.

Greenpeace should receive a healthy portion of the credit for generating the international media attention the tar sands received. Arguably the world's most recognized environmental organization, Greenpeace owes a major debt for its recognition in the public mind to the attention its actions receive from the world's media. From its first nonviolent direct action, sailing to Alaska's Aleutian Islands in 1971 to protest US nuclear tests there, Greenpeace has framed many of its protests in ways news directors find irresistible. Greenpeace came to Alberta in 2007 and, under Mike Hudema's direction, quickly garnered considerable press attention through its direct actions. Greenpeace activists rappelled from the ceiling of Edmonton's Convention Centre to hang the banner "$telmach: the best Premier oil money can buy" during the annual premier's dinner in 2008; they chained themselves to tar sands mining equipment and scaled upgraders to unfurl banners.[20] Greenpeace's chutzpah certainly succeeded in putting the media spotlight on the tar sands operations of companies such as Syncrude, Suncor, and Shell.[21] In 2008, Jason Chance, the executive assistant to Energy Minister Mel Knight, told Shannon Phillips that he felt international media coverage of the oil sands unfairly tarred the province and the industry. In foreshadowing his minister's refusal to grant an interview request from Al-Jazeera English, he told Phillips: "You try something completely different from the rest of the international media, then, and do a balanced story for a change."[22] Criticisms of the tar sands also inspired several high-profile advertisements from American ENGOs, sometimes with the collaboration of their Canadian counterparts and First Nations, placed in publications such as *CQ Roll Call, Variety*, and *USA Today*.

Members of First Nations in northeastern Alberta joined the Indigenous Environmental Network (IEN) and travelled to the United Kingdom to spread the message of the tremendous damage tar sands mining was doing to the health of the boreal lands and the people. George Poitras, a former Chief of the Mikisew Cree First Nation and former consultation coordinator with the MCFN's Industry Relations Corporation, likened exploiting the tar sands to genocide. Poitras wrote in the *Guardian*:

> My people are dying, and we believe British companies are responsible.
> My community, Fort Chipewyan in Alberta, Canada, is situated at the heart
> of the vast toxic moonscape that is the tar sands development. We live in
> a beautiful area, but unfortunately, we find ourselves upstream [sic] from
> the largest fossil fuel development on earth. UK oil companies like BP, and
> banks like RBS, are extracting the dirtiest form of oil from our traditional
> lands, and we fear it is killing us.[23]

Awareness-raising tours in the United Kingdom; protests at and submissions to the annual meetings of companies such as BP, Royal Bank of
Scotland (RBS), and Royal Bank of Canada; meetings with members of the
United States Congress; efforts to attract support from celebrities such as
James Cameron, the director of *Avatar* and *Titanic*, were key elements of the
very media-focused campaign the IEN waged against the tar sands in the
first decade of the twenty-first century.[24]

The belief grew in the provincial government that the international
media were the enemy, that their reporting wasn't balanced. This prompted
Premier Stelmach to respond with a media campaign of his own in April
2008. The Alberta "brand" needed a makeover due to the bruising it was
receiving internationally. Negative perceptions of Alberta needed to be challenged. To this end the province launched a three-year, $25 million adver-
tising and marketing campaign to develop, in the words of a government
memo, a "brand that will work to reinforce a positive, accurate picture of
Alberta, and to increase awareness of our province as a great place to live,
work, invest and visit."[25] Premier Stelmach's communications director left
no doubt that the critical attention the international media paid to the tar
sands was the catalyst for this three-year intiative. Paul Stanway said, "We
have to produce clean energy—that's Job 1 ... But Job 2 is to tell the world
that we're producing clean energy. I don't think we can leave that job to
Greenpeace and the Sierra Club."[26] To Liberal David Swann, this strategy of
the Public Affairs Bureau, which he called the "government's propaganda
arm," was "blatant greenwashing."[27] Liberal leader Kevin Taft suggested the
government, rather than solve the environmental problem posed by the tar
sands juggernaut, chose instead to "pretend the problem away" through its
multi-million-dollar advertising campaign.[28]

Alberta Environment Minister Rob Renner responded to such charges
by reprising a well-rehearsed Progressive Conservative tune.[29] Alberta was
the first jurisdiction in North America to pass climate change legislation,
he said. Furthermore, Alberta's climate change plan was realistic, achievable,
and would "result in very real reductions in CO_2 that can be substantiated and will be substantiated."[30] Renner's first three claims couldn't be

disputed; that can't be said about the claim the province was making real greenhouse gas emissions reductions (this is discussed in more detail in the next chapter). In fact, what made Alberta's 2003 Climate Change legislation both realistic and achievable was its failure to make *any* real reductions in greenhouse gas emissions. Alberta's legislation promised seemingly ambitious reductions in greenhouse gas emissions intensity (intensity equals the amount of greenhouse gases emitted relative to each barrel of oil produced or relative to the size of the Alberta economy). A May 2002 plan for action established the goals for the legislation of 2003. The plan called for greenhouse gas emissions relative to provincial GDP in 2020 to be 50 percent below 1990 levels. This sounded impressive, superficially more impressive than Kyoto's call for Canada to produce a 6 percent cut in emissions relative to the same year. But, as Matthew Bramley so clearly pointed out, since the intensity benchmark is based on the size of the economy, emissions intensity reductions can occur while the total tonnage of greenhouse gases emitted into the atmosphere actually increases. Between 1990 and 2000, a decade where Alberta didn't have a climate change policy, emissions intensity fell by 13 percent but absolute emissions rose by 30 percent.[31] Substantively, but not rhetorically, Alberta's climate change policy promised to continue this trend. Total emissions would increase; emissions intensity would decrease. The promise of continued economic growth gave the lie to the government's claim that "[t]he reduction in emissions intensity should translate into an absolute reduction in emissions."[32] To suggest here that Alberta's legislation and climate change plan were failures assumes that "very real reductions" required sending fewer, not more, tonnes of CO_2 skyward. Or, in Bramley's words: "The environment only 'cares about' absolute emissions; it is oblivious to GDP."[33]

Dead Ducks, Tarred Images

Mother Nature delivered these new media-focused critics a great, if sad, opportunity in late April 2008. The opportunity came in the form of a spring snowstorm that dumped 37 centimetres (14.6 inches) of snow on Fort McMurray in the fourth week of the month—an unusually heavy amount of snow for April. Hundreds and hundreds of ducks, perhaps due to a combination of precipitation, exhaustion, and flying for days without food, sought rest and refuge on what they thought was an inviting lake. It wasn't. The open water they landed on was instead the toxic, bitumen-infused waters of Syncrude's Aurora Settling Basin. On April 28, an anonymous caller tipped off a provincial wildlife biologist in Fort McMurray that migrating waterfowl were landing on the two square miles covered by Syncrude's tailings reservoir. Their migration ended there. A mat of bitumen, "several inches thick, viscous and cohesive with the consistency of a frothy roofing tar," trapped the waterfowl and dragged them to the bottom of the pond.[34]

Dozens of newspaper stories were published about this incident in May 2008.[35] When Imperial Oil CEO Bruce March described this event as "tragic," one might be forgiven for wondering if he was referring to what was then thought to be hundreds of ducks that died or to what those deaths would mean for the provincial government and his fellow tar sands companies.[36] For Alberta, the timing of this tragedy couldn't have been worse. Deputy Premier Ron Stevens was spending some of the province's $25 million rebranding money in Washington, DC. There he was pitching the benefits of the tar sands to American legislators. He was telling members of Congress and the executive branch that:

> partnering with Alberta to develop the oil sands in an environmentally sustainable manner is far better, both in terms of energy security and environmental protection, than penalizing oil sands products and increasing imports from unstable and at times environmentally irresponsible overseas sources of crude.[37]

News of ducks dying by the hundreds in a tar sands tailings pond didn't strengthen the credibility of Stevens's claim that, when it came to environmental sustainability, Alberta had a "wonderful story" to tell or that the only "environmentally irresponsible" sources of crude were from outside North America.[38] As news of Syncrude's dead ducks spread from Wall Street to Kalgoorlie in the outback of western Australia, corporate and provincial spokesmen fought a rearguard action. They claimed such an incident had never happened before; Syncrude also blamed Mother Nature—her "unusually heavy snow" the week before prevented the company from deploying its propane cannons and effigies to deter birds from landing on the settling basin (the effigies are sometimes referred to as Bit-u-men).[39]

One of the casualties in the media's rush to be the first to report breaking news stories is interrogating or investigating the accuracy of the information interviewees pass on to reporters.[40] This observation certainly applied to the duck incident. Government and corporate efforts to blame the weather and to insist this had never happened before were not questioned by the media. The closest that reporters came to suggesting the public might want to regard those claims with some skepticism was to report that Greenpeace, First Nations, and the opposition Liberals called for a public inquiry into what happened. Greenpeace's Mike Hudema hoped such an inquiry would produce the "truthful answers, hard questions, and meaningful action" needed to understand why the ducks had died in the Aurora tailings reservoir and to prevent it from happening again.[41]

Those who trusted the message that the state and Syncrude told to the media should have been shaken by what Judge K.E. Tjosvold concluded when he found Syncrude guilty of breaking federal and provincial laws more than two years later. Without good historical information it would be impossible to know if the late April incident was unique. Judge Tjosvold didn't believe the historical data existed. He challenged the assertion that the company's bird deterrent program was necessarily effective. He found "no evidence of a methodical or comprehensive system of monitoring to produce a thorough census."[42] And, while the late April snowstorm may have made deploying deterrents more difficult, why did Syncrude wait until then to place deterrents? Judge Tjosvold's ruling offers an alternative theory of the crime, one where the priority of ensuring effective deterrent measures were in place shrank over the years. Other tar sands miners took action well before the April snowstorm hit the region. Albian Sands, mining bitumen just south of the Aurora lease, began to deploy deterrents on March 24, 2008; land cannons were set up on April 3rd. Suncor started its cannon deterrents on April 8th. In past years Syncrude too had put its deterrents in place earlier. In 2001, Syncrude had deployed them by April 9th. But between 2001 and 2008 the numbers of personnel, trucks, and deterrents committed to deterring birds from landing on Syncrude's tailings ponds fell significantly.[43] Perhaps more dedication by Syncrude to its bird deterrent efforts would have tempered or prevented the deaths of 1,606 ducks on the Aurora tailings pond in April 2008.

Nearly a year later the story broke in Edmonton that Syncrude, Alberta, and the federal government hadn't told the public the truth about the extent of what happened on the Aurora tailings reservoir. More than 1,600 ducks, not 500, died in the Aurora incident of 2008. Government and industry spokespersons alike insisted their hands were tied when it came to telling the truth about the number of waterfowl that had perished. Syncrude acted as if the company needed the permission of Crown prosecutors to tell the truth, to say that more than three times as many ducks had died than they claimed originally and throughout 2008.[44] Government spokespersons claimed that, counterintuitively as it might sound to a layperson, they couldn't tell the truth in 2008 because an accurate total might have jeopardized, not assisted, an ongoing investigation.[45] While there may have been a compelling legal reason for this silence, keeping this news quiet unquestionably delivered political benefits to the tar sands industry and its regulators. Silence played well to the fear in government and industry offices about how the media, especially the international media, would broadcast bad environmental news from Alberta's tar sands. The last thing the protagonists of exploiting the tar sands needed, given the pummelling they already were taking in the media in the spring and summer of 2008, was the release of information that tar sands waste had killed many, many more waterfowl.

The Bitumen Triangle: Industry, Government, and Universities Unite to Tell a Better Story

What tar sands companies, like their partners in government, desperately needed was a strategy to improve their reputations. Public relations, as in 2002–03, were key to that strategy. Companies and industry associations complemented Alberta's advertising campaign with communication strategies of their own. Syncrude published full-page newspaper advertisements apologizing for killing the 500 (1,606) ducks and promised to make changes to ensure this "sad event" never happened again. The company also promised to meet the public's expectations regarding the "responsible development" of the oil sands.[46]

Contrition wasn't, however, industry's only reaction. The tar sands sector also complained that the media weren't treating them fairly; the industry was misunderstood. Marcel Coutu, perhaps ironically the CEO of Canadian Oil Sands—the largest shareholder of the contrite Syncrude—believed there was an "unbalanced view" of oil sands companies and that the sector needed "to pick up the ball and tell our side of the story."[47] To this end, CAPP launched an educational website to help the public learn more about the tar sands and how the industry was developing them.[48] Defenders of the tar sands now took more seriously a disconcerting possibility—their development aspirations could suffer badly if they didn't address the public's concerns.[49]

A communications partnership between the petroleum industry and the governments of Canada and Alberta was key to efforts to improve the international reputation of the tar sands industry. People around the world needed to be told that a reregulated tar sands sector wasn't the pariah some environmentalists and First Nations were making it out to be. Some light on the strength and orientation of this public relations partnership is shed by government documents Greenpeace Canada obtained through Canada's *Access to Information Act*.[50] In April 2009, Natural Resources Canada (NRCan), Department of Foreign Affairs and International Trade (DFAIT), the Government of Alberta, and CAPP partnered to hold two days of meetings and outreach in Washington, DC. The roundtable portion of the program "examined oil sands in the United States context and how best to address the increasingly negative portrayal of Canada's industry, both in political circles and in the public arena, through the use of coordinated engagement."[51]

NRCan Deputy Minister Cassie Doyle told the roundtable that its participants needed to develop a pro-oil sands campaign that was as sophisticated as that crafted by the anti-tar sands lobby. She urged them to develop common facts, to focus on a common message, and to commit to a coordinated engagement strategy. Her department was pushing two main messages: first, the oil sands were a strategic continental resource, and second, government and industry were working hard to address environmental issues. David Collyer, CAPP's president, agreed on the need to ensure that messages were complementary. The Canadian government's summary of this roundtable said: "Collyer agreed that alignment on messaging was key as we cannot be seen to be misrepresenting our data given that we are held to a much higher standard than the ENGO community." He also wanted to see greater emphasis placed on technology in this joint defence or promotion of the oil sands. This chorus—that technology would cure the environmental ailments of exploiting the tar sands—had been sung many times before.[52] CAPP had started to devote more attention in its messaging to "a few emerging technologies which offer *potential* for addressing some of the industry's environmental issues" [emphasis added].

The Washington roundtable, despite being concerned over the escalating media critique, offered little new when it came to communicating about the tar sands. It stressed time-honoured themes of tar sands politics. Americans would appreciate the security bonus that came with Canadian oil once they realized just how important Canadian supplies were to satisfying the US addiction to oil. American politicians and consumers could be persuaded that environmentalists exaggerated the tar sands ecological footprint or simply weren't telling even partial truths. Technology would be the saving grace for the boreal ecosystem and the climate impacts of mining the boreal lands for petroleum.

In early 2008, when the ducks that died on Syncrude's Aurora tailings pond were still alive in southern wintering grounds, CAPP already had decided to make the tar sands environmental impact its major communications focus in 2008.[53] Federal and provincial politicians, in the aftermath of the Syncrude incident, invoked instability in the Middle East and the premium on the cost of crude from there as powerful reasons for Americans to fuel their cars with gasoline from Canadian crude.[54] Alberta's energy minister was adamant that technology would save the day: carbon capture and sequestration technology held the key to reducing Alberta's emissions. "We know the technology works," Mel Knight said. "It's a solid piece of business, and we're about to embark on applying it on a large scale."[55]

The April 2009 meeting created an industry/government steering committee to facilitate ongoing coordination among the participating interests.[56]

The seriousness with which industry took its communication challenge is suggested by the establishment of an Oil Sands CEO Communications Task Group. Its members represented the vast majority of tar sands production. All members of the group were expected to be represented at a June 2009 meeting with Kevin Lynch, the Clerk of the Privy Council.[57]

Nearly a year after the Washington roundtable, CAPP hosted a meeting in Calgary on oil sands outreach and communications. At the meeting CAPP presented a renewed strategy to the deputy ministers of NRCan, Alberta Energy, and Alberta Environment in which the Oil Sands CEO Communications Task Group would be "upping its game" when it came to outreach and communications. CAPP proposed to stress that environmental issues were being addressed and that both government and industry had the right attitude. Coordination between Canada, Alberta, and tar sands companies was a key message CAPP wanted governments to embrace. Deputy Minister of NRCan Doyle underlined the federal government's long-term commitment to work with industry on communications. Apparently CAPP and the deputy ministers also discussed including a certain kind of environmental group in this renewed strategy: "Improved NGO participation was also discussed by bringing in less strident groups."[58]

The third leg of this bitumen triangle came from willing partners in Alberta's universities. They too would play an important role in delivering a more industry-friendly message to the public. In a CAPP television advertisement Dr. David Lynch, dean of engineering at the University of Alberta, sang the praises of new technologies. He delivered the upbeat message about technology's promise—exactly the kind of message that CAPP's Collyer wanted to see more of. Against the backdrop of CAPP's textual message—"New ideas are making a difference"—Dean Lynch told his television audience how "quite energized" people were to hear that the University of Alberta had more than 1,000 researchers working on one major topic—"the responsible development of our oil sands." Technology was the key to responsibility. Nothing could be further from the truth, he insisted, than to believe people weren't working on the environmental challenges of oil sands development.[59]

Lynch's optimistic, reassuring message conformed well with the mandate of the Canada School of Energy and Environment (CSEE), a nonprofit corporation established in 2008 as a partnership between the Universities of Alberta, Calgary, and Lethbridge. Ostensibly the CSEE was born to fulfill the vision articulated in a 2004 Memorandum of Understanding between these universities. These postsecondary institutions would collaborate and share information with a goal of furthering "investment in energy innovation to ensure an abundant supply of environmentally responsible energy for the continuing prosperity and social well-being of Canadians."[60] Designated as a prestigious federal Centre of Research Excellence and Commercialization in the 2007 federal budget, the CSEE received $15 million in federal funding.[61]

Bruce Carson, the CSEE's executive director, squashed any hope that the CSEE would interpret the "environmentally responsible energy" mandate broadly or liberally. Before coming to the CSEE, Carson had had careers in law and politics. His legal career ended badly. In 1983, Carson was convicted of two counts of theft over $200. He was sentenced to 18 months in prison for those crimes and was released on parole later that year. The Law Society of Upper Canada disbarred him for his crimes. Carson's political career began in 1993, three years after he was convicted for a second time and sentenced to 24 months-probation for committing three counts of fraud under the *Criminal Code of Canada*. For nearly 10 years he served as director of policy and research for the Conservative Party leader in the Canadian Senate. Between 2002 and 2004 Carson worked for the Ontario Progressive Conservative Party. After the 2004 federal election, an election in which he helped craft the Conservative Party platform, he became Opposition Leader Stephen Harper's director of policy and research. When the Conservatives won a minority government in the January 2006 election, Carson joined the Prime Minister's Office in Harper's administration, first as a legislative assistant and then, after a promotion, as a senior advisor to the prime minister. Although he left the government in November 2008, he came back in January and February of 2009 to work on the federal budget.[62]

Nicknamed "The Mechanic," Carson started his job with the CSEE in August 2008, well before he left the PMO, and was "available full time at the end of the year"—a claim contradicted by his work on the federal budget.[63] He was regarded as the consummate political insider in Ottawa.[64] That reputation, plus his close relationship with Prime Minister Harper, helped stoke the enthusiasm of the leaders of Alberta universities to appoint him as executive director of the CSEE. Bruce Heidecker, the chair of both the CSEE and the University of Alberta Board of Governors, told the CBC radio program *Edmonton AM* that the size of Carson's Rolodex certainly was considered when the universities offered Carson the position. University of Alberta President Indira Samarasekera had no doubt that, under Carson's leadership, the CSEE would make a major contribution to the success of the "major turning" the global community faced with respect to energy and the environment.[65]

His CSEE employers lost their enthusiasm to comment about their star recruit when they were questioned about the circumstances responsible for Carson's resignation in disgrace from the school in March 2011.[66] Soon after his resignation Carson was charged with influence peddling.[67] Charges were laid because of the elderly Carson's efforts to help his 22-year-old girlfriend, a former escort, secure federal government contracts for water filtration equipment.[68] As salacious and scandalous as this chapter in Carson's life was, Dr. David Keith, recruited by the University of Calgary to be an academic leader of the CSEE, believes the real scandal rests elsewhere. That scandal was the muzzling of a debate about energy and climate change. The muzzling was engineered by Carson and his contacts in government and industry. Keith alleges that soon after Carson became executive director, he used "his academic post to further the interests of the Conservative government and a narrow segment of the petroleum industry."[69] The school was far from being a neutral centre for hearing the entire range of opinion on the energy/ environment nexus—what Keith suggests he had been told to expect. Carson ensured it would be a handmaiden for the petroleum industry. Carson's intent and allegiances might be deciphered with hindsight from his inaugural message in the CSEE's *Annual Report 2009–10*. The CSEE took actions "[t]o become relevant to the energy production industry and to discern the research and scientific needs of industry" and "[t]o interact on a regular basis with government departments relevant to energy and environment issues."[70]

If Carson's intent wasn't clear from those words, his actions made it very clear that he saw himself as a faithful member of the choir assembling to sing the tar sands' praises to the world. Carson was in the room when CAPP hosted the March 2010 meeting of industry and federal/provincial deputy ministers. The previous year he had chaired an oil and gas working group made up of CAPP and the deputy ministers of environment from Alberta, Saskatchewan, and Canada.[71] CAPP made it clear in its comments on a draft working group document that it had only two outstanding concerns: the group shouldn't single out the oil sands and it should pay attention to competitiveness. Neither Mike Beale, a senior official in Environment Canada who was "heavily involved" in federal climate change policy-making, nor Carson seems to have had any difficulty in accommodating CAPP's concerns.[72] Industry was very involved in drafting this document; it wasn't forced on them. No counterweight from the environmental perspective was involved.

For Carson, the goals of industry, government, and Alberta universities were one—develop and communicate strategies to defend the oilpatch from international criticism. Carson viewed the CSEE as just another political resource to be used to further that end. The symmetry Carson imagined to exist between what he did as a think-tank boss and what he did as a government advisor is confirmed by how he represented his attendance at the first meeting of the Major Economies Forum on Energy and Climate in 2009.

To his university employers, he said he attended this inaugural meeting as the executive director of the CSEE; to the Canadian American Business Council, he claimed he attended that forum as an advisor to the federal Conservative environment minister.[73]

As detailed in RCMP documents pertaining to Carson's influence-peddling trial, Carson also co-chaired the nonprofit Energy Policy Institute of Canada (EPIC) while he was the executive director of the CSEE. The Energy Institute's "nonprofit" label is misleading in an important sense. All of its members were energy corporations or industry associations; 19 of its 37 founding members had deep roots in the petroleum industry; those 19 founding members from the petroleum sector contained virtually all of the major tar sands producers; membership in the Policy Institute cost $50,000 per year for two years.[74] One of EPIC's objectives with respect to crafting a national energy strategy, according to Thomas D'Aquino—former chair of EPIC and leader of the Business Council on National Issues/Canadian Council of Chief Executives from 1981 until 2009—was "to build public sensitivity, that being newspapers and special purpose magazines."[75] Carson and petroleum industry veteran Gerry Protti were the key architects of the initiative EPIC developed between 2009 and 2011.[76] David Emerson, who took over D'Aquino's duties in November 2009, described Carson as the "mind and pen" of the Institute. So impressed was Doug Black, EPIC's president, with Carson's work on developing a national energy strategy proposal EPIC could take to governments that he increased Carson's $60,000 annual honourarium by another $10,000 or $20,000.[77] Between December 2009 and March 2011, Carson received $160,000 from EPIC for his services to the Institute.[78] Such were the monetary rewards that came to Carson for being EPIC's "secret sauce" when it came to making progress with governments on the Institute's vision for a Canadian energy strategy.[79] But after his legal difficulties came to light, this secret sauce wasn't mentioned when the Energy Policy Institute of Canada served its Canadian energy strategy fare to Canadians in 2012.[80]

Directive 074 and the Politics of Tailings Ponds Reclamation

So many of the phrases identified in the previous section that were used by government, industry, or university officials—"coordinated engagement," "responsible development," "unbalanced view," "emerging technologies"— essentially asked the public to be patient and to believe industry and regulators had been doing and would continue to do their best to mitigate the environmental impact of the tar sands. Their response to international criticism was better communication. Did they respond in other, more substantive ways to the media criticisms they faced? If toxic tailings ponds were killing wildlife, did government propose stricter policies and regulations to reclaim these toxic waters?

Since Great Canadian Oil Sands began mining and processing bitumen on Tar Island in 1967 the regulation of tailings had been lax; the Pembina Institute described tailings management as voluntary.[81] While mining applications always promised to convert liquid tailings into some type of landscape, they always failed to meet the targets they set for themselves. Government did not penalize them for these shortcomings.[82] The historical laxity of government regulations concerning any aspect of reclamation is suggested by the province's own reclamation data. Alberta reported that, as of December 31, 2013, more than 89,000 hectares were "affected" by oil sands mining.[83] Only 104 hectares, less than 0.0012 percent of those affected lands, had been certified as reclaimed; this sliver of certified reclaimed land is virtually invisible on the provincial government's colourful chart depicting the status of the boreal lands subject to oil sands mining.[84] This percentage jumps to 6 percent if permanently reclaimed land awaiting certification in 2013 is included. This 6 percent, however, is marginally lower than this category of land was in 2012. Lee Foote, a University of Alberta expert on wetlands reclamation, thinks it's unlikely the wetlands that are forecast to be destroyed by surface mining will be replaced with wetlands; his research also suggests there isn't any known technology/process able to purify the more than 840 billion litres of wastewater in the tailings reservoirs of mines in a time frame that's meaningful to those who live in the tar sands region today.[85]

Directive 074 from the Energy Resources Conservation Board seemed to respond substantively to the concerns about tailings ponds and their reclamation. While government regulators were loath to link this February 2009 provincial measure to the Aurora tailings reservoir incident, the reputational damage Alberta suffered after that episode provided a strong political incentive for the government to take action sooner rather than later. Alberta regulatory staff had been directed in July 2004 to establish tailings management performance criteria by March 2008, a deadline the regulator didn't meet.[86] Presumably the directive should be seen as evidence of the commitment the new chair of the ERCB felt should characterize the regulator. "It's through our actions, I think," Board Chair Dan McFadyen suggested, "that we continue to demonstrate our independence and credibility."[87]

Directive 074's rules for reducing the amounts of tailings produced by processing bitumen had been proposed in June 2008, just a handful of weeks after the Aurora incident. As you'd expect, these reductions, along with timelines for transforming toxic liquid ponds into terra firma, were discussed with industry; the draft tailings management directive was posted to the ERCB's website and individuals and industry commented on its substance; First Nations joined the ERCB, industry, and government departments at a September 2008 workshop to gather information and hear concerns. The ERCB chair promised that, with these new rules, "for the first time Albertans will have certainty on how tailings from tar sands projects will be stored, converted, and reclaimed."[88] The directive called for the operators of tar sands mines to reduce the volume of fluid tailings by meeting increasingly stringent targets for the percentage of dry fines captured. Fines refer to minuscule mineral solids; they are no larger than the diameter of a strand of hair. Twenty percent of mine tailings needed to be dry by July 2011, 30 percent by July 2012, and 50 percent by July 2013 and thereafter.[89] Tailings reservoirs needed to be transformed into something more than just a sink for collecting the liquid waste of tar sands. Called "dedicated disposal areas" in the directive, they needed to be established to ensure their deposits were solid enough to be "trafficable." Unlike quicksand, these reclaimed sands needed to support weight. Annual criteria were set and disposal areas were required to be ready for reclamation no later than five years after a miner stopped pouring liquid tailings into its reservoir(s).

Industry didn't welcome the new regulation. The Oilsands Developers Group, an industry association representing all the major operators, characterized the measure as "pretty challenging" and one that would be "difficult" for its members. Suncor said it expected to satisfy the regulator's demands but it wouldn't be easy.[90] The Pembina Institute greeted the directive with some support but also with some suspicion or skepticism. On the one hand, how could the environmental group not support the idea that the long-term storage of liquid tailings should be eliminated? But the ERCB's enforcement record didn't inspire confidence that the directive would be successful. The ERCB regulation also didn't move Pembina off its position that the ERCB should not approve new projects until proven solutions to tailings were evident.[91] Greenpeace shared this view but was more strident when it came to demanding that Alberta do something about the hundreds of billions of litres of toxic tailings already blighting the boreal landscape.[92] Pembina's worries that the directive might lack teeth was countered by the ERCB. A spokesman for the regulator asserted:

> And the most important thing is that these targets will be enforceable. So by 2011, if companies are not meeting our requirements, we can take enforcement against them. That means everything from increasing their inspections right through to shutting facilities to refusing to approve any upgrades or improvements. This has teeth.[93]

The pulling of Directive 074's teeth began soon after it was issued. By the end of September 2009, nine tailings management plans had been submitted to the ERCB. Only two of those submissions proposed to meet the directive's standards and deadlines for capturing fine tailings and for creating a surface that would bear traffic. Only one complying submission, from Suncor for its Millennium and North Steepbank Mines, applied to operating mines.[94] The proposed plan for Imperial Oil's Kearl project stuck by what the federal and provincial governments had accepted when they approved the project in 2007. Imperial believed implementing its consolidated tailings process in 2023, as originally planned, met "the intent of the Tailings Directive by reducing the long term storage of fluid tailings."[95] The plan was silent on when its tar sand tailings waste would be solid enough to withstand the weight and levels of traffic prescribed by the ERCB. Because the miner obviously proposed to miss the ERCB's timeline, Imperial said it was evaluating commercial and developing technologies to reduce the percentage of fluid tailings in storage pursuant to Directive 074.[96] Canadian Natural Resources Ltd. declared that commercially viable fine tailings technologies simply didn't exist. Pilot tests of new technologies might be promising but "no commercially proven method for fluid tailings dewatering yet exists."[97] It proposed to implement more advanced fines capturing technologies "as soon as practical."[98] Canadian Natural wanted to be excused from meeting any of the deadlines set out in the directive. Accordingly, and likely guided by the conviction the ERCB's requirements were impossible to meet, CNRL set 2015 as its target date for meeting the yearly fines capture percentages stipulated by Directive 074; the proposed target date for satisfying the cumulative fines capture requirement was 2025.

CNRL's exemption request referred to Section 3 of the ERCB directive. There the regulator opened the door to "project-specific" circumstances that could affect how the directive was applied to bitumen miners. The submissions of mining projects could "identify any project-specific constraints that may have a bearing on meeting the requirements."[99] The regulator recognized operators might need flexibility when it came to implementing the best-suited technologies and techniques for any particular mining project. This flexibility created the possibility that the tough talk from the ERCB about enforcement would be nothing more than that—tough talk. The regulator approved all of the submitted 2009 tailings management plans, whether or not they intended to deliver the outcomes and respect the timeline set by the ERCB.

The ERCB's lenience produced a regulatory landscape that can only be described as a hodge-podge. It didn't contain the promised universal or industry-wide tailings management standards. Suncor, by accepting the directive's schedule of performance demands, was expected to capture 20 percent of the fines in its oil sands feed by June 30, 2011, and 30 percent by June 30, 2012. Table 6 illustrates how the expectations for Suncor were significantly higher than those for its peers; fines capture requirements varied widely across tar sands miners.

Such wide variations in the commitments made to the regulator largely evaporated when it came to corporate success in drying out fluid tailings by 2011–12. Suncor's commitments, pleasing as they would have sounded to the ERCB, couldn't be kept. Instead of capturing the promised 20 percent of fines in 2010–11, Suncor only captured 10.7 percent; the next year's performance was worse and the company missed its 30 percent target by an even larger amount. As Table 7 shows, by the end of the second year of operations under the tailings management directive, a fines capture percentage of 8.8 percent was the best any mining operation could deliver, a far cry from the 30 percent the ERCB believed every mining operation could and should meet.

Table 6 Fines Capture Requirements for Oil Sands Mines/Miners, Percentages of Oil Sands Feed, 2010–11 and 2011–12

Mines/Miners	2010–11	2011–12
Suncor	20.0	30.0
Syncrude Mildred Lake	9.2	12.0
Shell Muskeg River	8.5	23.5
Shell Jackpine	9.5	15.5
Syncrude Aurora North	0.0	0.0
CNRL Horizon	0.0	0.0

Source: Alberta, Energy Resources Conservation Board, *2012 Tailings Management Assessment Report, Oil Sands Mining Industry, June 2013*, 4.

Table 7 Fines Capture Performance for Oil Sands Mines/Miners, Percentages of Oil Sands Feed, 2010–11 and 2011–12

Mines/Miners	2010–11	2011–12
Suncor	10.7	8.5
Syncrude Mildred Lake	17.7	8.8
Shell Muskeg River	1.9	8.8
Shell Jackpine	0.0	0.0
Syncrude Aurora North	0.0	0.0
CNRL Horizon	0.0	0.0

Source: Alberta, Energy Resources Conservation Board, *2012 Tailings Management Assessment Report, Oil Sands Mining Industry, June 2013*, 4.

Directive 074 was intended to be a prescription to help heal the tarnished environmental reputation of the tar sands sector and its government regulators. By the summer of 2013, it looked like it wasn't going to deliver substantive or reputational gains. Tar sands miners were several football fields away from reaching the tailings management goalposts the government set after the Aurora incident of 2008. Despite the global pressure to address toxic tailings reservoirs, an historically lax, even absent, regulatory approach to tailings management instead wrote a prescription for policy failure. That's what Directive 074 became. For nearly 40 years, government and industry gave little serious attention to stopping the growth of tar sands tailings reservoirs. Industry was long on promises to reclaim tailings in its development applications and government was short on pushing the regulatory envelope to demand research, and then action from companies to manage tailings in ways to reduce their blight on the landscape. The dreadful, damaging international spectacle created by 1,606 dead birds created a powerful political demand for action. But, after decades of neglect, the government's response to this outcry raised unrealistic expectations; while companies spent millions and millions of dollars, and committed billions, in their rush to come up with tailings management solutions the government's regulatory bar and timelines were beyond their reach.[100] As one geotechnical engineer said of Suncor's promising tailings reduction technology, "that technology was rushed to full-scale production."[101] While the politics generated by the growing international critique may have demanded that rush, the ERCB's 2013 assessment of tailings management in the industry showed how poorly that and other technologies performed under commercial conditions. The ERCB reported in that assessment that its expectations, and those of industry, were "optimistic." This optimism became the rationale for why the provincial regulator didn't take any of the sometimes tough-sounding enforcement actions the board had outlined more than four years earlier. Instead, the ERCB hinted that enforcement actions *might* be taken after the regulator released its second tailings management assessment report in 2015. "If operators do not meet their tailings management performance expectations," the regulator said, "the ERCB will assess enforcement options at that time."[102]

That time never came. A second assessment report, if it was ever prepared, was never released. Instead, March 2015 saw the Alberta Energy Regulator (AER) confirm Directive 074's failure. The AER suspended the directive. Simultaneously the provincial government released a new tailings management framework document replete with generally soothing, sometimes exaggerated, statements about the province's commitment to environmentally sustainable development of the oil sands. The government, from the shadow of its failure to enforce Directive 074, insisted that Alberta managed tailings with "(a) stringent regulatory system."[103] The newest blueprint added to "an already strong legislative and regulatory system," a system "providing overarching direction to guide the *appropriate management* of fluid tailings in the mineable oil sands area."[104] Implicitly, Directive 074's expectations and standards no longer constituted "appropriate management." The government discarded the regulator's requirement that tailings reservoirs be ready for reclamation within five years of the end of a mine's life; instead the framework expected miners to prepare their tailings reservoirs for reclamation within 10 years of that closing. Unlike the suspended Directive 074, the new framework wouldn't demand miners deliver specified percentages of dry fines by specified dates. The Regulator didn't propose to hold operators to annual targets (not that the ERCB actually used Directive 074 to hold miners accountable for the objectives of their tailings management plans); instead the AER proposed a much more flexible regulatory timeline and an approach tailored to the specific circumstances of each mining venture. It appears to be much more sympathetic to what companies told governments they practically could do. Annual performance targets were discarded; universal requirements for all operators wouldn't be established. Rather than stipulate what operators needed to accomplish from one year to the next, the Regulator recommended an approach where companies would identify the volumes of fluid tailings they would pump into reservoirs and plans for how to realize reductions in fluid tailings over time. The requirement was that tailings reservoirs should be reclamation-ready within 10 years of the reservoir's retirement. In this revised approach to tailings management, thresholds will be set for the volumes of fluid tailings. If volumes increase beyond a management plan's thresholds, industry will be expected to correct the situation. Such an increase would also initiate a management response from the Regulator. In late 2015, these recommendations were part of a draft directive designed to replace the discredited Directive 074.[105] This directive was implemented by a new government in 2016 and is considered in Chapter Nine.

As government and industry continued to struggle with tailings management, the volume and sprawl of tailings reservoirs continued to grow apace. From 2008 (the year of the Aurora incident) until 2013, the provincial government estimated the footprint of these reservoirs grew by 69 percent, from 130 square kilometres to 220 square kilometres (85 square miles). The volume of fine fluid tailings held within these structures grew by an estimated 33 percent over these five years, from 732 million cubic metres to 975.6 million cubic metres.[106] This reality emphatically underlines how mistaken Alberta's Premier Alison Redford was to suggest to a Brookings Institution audience in April 2013 that tailings ponds would soon disappear from Alberta's boreal landscape.[107]

The Institutional Framework

Mounting global criticism of the tar sands' environmental consequences also inspired the state to make defensive changes to its decision-making processes. These institutional changes made it even more difficult for what CAPP's Collyer had identified as the "less strident groups" to voice environmental critiques in the regulatory process. Government was firmly opposed to seeing any legitimacy in those critiques or to incorporating them into tar sands policy. These defensive institutional changes were both interpretive and legislative; combined, they further diminished environmental opinions in Alberta's tar sands regulatory process.

On the interpretive front, in 2009 Alberta Environment officials decided to interpret language in provincial legislation in a fashion making it very unlikely, if not impossible, for even moderate opponents of rapid tar sands expansion to participate in one aspect of government policy-making. In addition to regulatory approval from the ERCB/AER, a tar sands project requires authorizations under the province's *Environmental Protection and Enhancement Act* and *Water Act*. According to these laws, persons "directly affected" by an application could file statements of concern with the provincial government regarding projects. This created the opportunity to raise questions about a company's plans. Those who filed such statements had a legal right to appeal to Alberta's Environmental Appeals Board. Then, if the Regulator authorized a project, as it always did, a directly affected person could appeal that authorization to the Environmental Appeals Board.[108]

Historically, Alberta's environment department regarded the Pembina Institute as a directly affected person under this legislation. That changed in 2009. Tailings reservoirs were at issue then. The Oil Sands Environmental Coalition tried to file a statement of concern about how Syncrude proposed to manage the tons of tailings produced by its Mildred Lake mining operation. A briefing note prepared for Alberta's deputy minister of environment said that OSEC no longer would be regarded as a directly affected person. Provincial officials turned their backs on their previous decisions that the OSEC met the directly affected test. The reason for this about-face was simple—the coalition objected to developing the tar sands. The OSEC was no longer as collaborative and cooperative as it had been previously. The briefing note flagged two examples of this uncooperative spirit. First, the OSEC withdrew completely from the Cumulative Environmental Management Association (CEMA), the advisory group that—as argued elsewhere here—had accomplished next to nothing in managing the cumulative effects of tar sands exploitation in nearly 10 years. Second, the Pembina Institute published "negative media on the oil sands." The provincial ministry took these actions to mean the OSEC was "now less inclined to work cooperatively."[109] The environmental coalition's different, more hostile attitude demanded a different, less accommodating administrative response. The ministry began to regularly deny applications from OSEC to file statements of concerns over applications for authorizations under the *EPEA* and the *Water Act*.

The briefing note speaks authoritatively to how provincial officials reinterpreted legislative provisions in order to marginalize environmental opposition even further. As Justice R. P. Marceau noted when he ruled against the government in *Pembina Institute v. Alberta (Environment and Sustainable Resource Development)*, a decision the government did not appeal, this reinterpretation flouted principles of natural justice. "In my view the entire process in this case is so tainted by the 'Briefing Note,'" he wrote, "that in arriving at my decision, I need only refer to the applicants' contention that the Director breached the principles of natural justice by taking into account improper and irrelevant considerations."[110] Marceau wrote that, since government determined the eligibility to file a statement of concern according to whether the actor was cooperative or had published negative media about the oil sands, "the reasons are fatally flawed."

For their part, Premier Alison Redford and her Environment and Sustainable Development Minister, Diana McQueen, were unapologetic. The premier claimed her government had the prerogative to decide the Pembina Institute couldn't file a statement of concern; the environment minister claimed her officials behaved properly. Both Premier Redford and Minister McQueen spoke as if Justice Marceau had ruled in the government's favour, not the reverse. They reacted as if they didn't appreciate or respect the rule of law and the separation of powers between the executive and legislative branches of government.[111]

Provincial legislative changes made in 2012 increased the inhospitality of Alberta's institutional setting to those with environmental concerns about the tar sands. The *Responsible Energy Development Act* (REDA) ushered in these changes. The law repealed the *Energy Resources Conservation Act* and replaced the ERCB with the Alberta Energy Regulator (AER or the Regulator). Environmentalists were immediately concerned about the REDA's transfer of regulatory responsibilities away from Environment officials to the AER. The Alberta Energy Regulator, not the Ministry of Environment and Sustainable Resource Development, would be responsible for applying the terms of the *Environmental Protection and Enhancement Act*, the *Water Act*, and the *Public Lands Act* to petroleum development in Alberta. Environmentalists saw little in the administrative history of petroleum regulation in Alberta to suggest that, notwithstanding government rhetoric, this transfer of authority from an agent of the Crown to a corporation would serve environmental values well.[112]

Increased politicization of the new regulator compounded this concern. The AER is several steps further removed than the ERCB was from the ideal of an independent, quasi-judicial agency. Politicization appears as increased ministerial control and direction of the AER. The provincial cabinet appoints hearing commissioners, those who decide the fate of petroleum development projects, but these commissioners are not appointed for a fixed term. Contrary to the principle of administrative independence, they serve at the pleasure of the politicians who appoint them. The energy minister's authority to direct commissioners to follow government policy when they exercise their powers further compromises the norm of administrative agency independence. If this political straitjacket wasn't tight enough, the new law also gave the provincial cabinet the authority to tell hearing commissioners what factors they must consider when making decisions. "The well-informed person," Shaun Fluker concluded, "viewing the matter realistically and practically, can only conclude there is no independent hearing process at the proposed Alberta Energy Regulator."[113]

Speaking to other specifics of the new law, Cindy Chiasson, then the executive director of the Environmental Law Centre (Alberta), concluded it would curtail and limit Alberta's environmental regulatory processes.[114] First, it narrowed the test for standing. The "directly affected" test found in the *Environmental Protection and Enhancement Act* and the *Water Act*, a test we have seen the courts already decide was used to discriminate against environmental groups, was replaced by the narrower or stricter "directly and adversely affected" test with respect to petroleum developments. Second, the Environmental Appeals Board would no longer hear petroleum-related appeals under the *Environmental Protection and Enhancement Act* and the *Water Act*. Instead, the AER would review its own decisions; self-review replaced review by an independent, quasi-judicial agency. More pointedly, Alberta's new appeal process for petroleum-related development smacks of police departments policing themselves when it comes to allegations of impropriety.

Fluker echoes and extends Chiasson's concerns about what the *Responsible Energy Development Act* meant for the treatment of environmental concerns in Alberta regulatory policy. The very limited statutory rights to public hearings that landowners had under the *Energy Resources Conservation Act* were stripped away by the new legislation. In fact, no actor other than an energy company has a statutory right to a public hearing under Alberta's new regulatory regime. This was confirmed once the rules and regulations of the REDA were set. The rules "contain no legal right to a hearing for landowners or the public in general and if anything the Rules speak more to denying hearings or the ability to otherwise participate before the Regulator."[115] Whether or not a public hearing will be held regarding any petroleum project is left entirely to the discretion of the Regulator. Whether or not a party will be allowed to intervene if the Regulator decides to conduct a public hearing also is entirely at the discretion of the regulatory agency. The factors the AER will consider in deciding whether to allow an intervention are decidedly unfriendly. The most important factor here may prove to be a new demand of potential interveners—whether they, like those who seek a hearing, can show they meet the "directly and adversely affected" test. Fluker suspects that groups and organizations (such as those concerned about the environmental impacts of exploiting the oil sands) will have to demonstrate that a majority of their members may be directly and adversely affected by the project they're concerned about. "The overall message here is that interventions are generally not welcome," he wrote, "and public interest groups need not apply at all!"[116]

Shifting the focus from the provincial to the national level, the federal government that stressed the importance of better communication about the tar sands merits also jumped with both feet onto the Alberta-style institutional bandwagon in 2012. A key federal regulatory responsibility in the tar sands is approving and regulating petroleum pipelines. Through the National Energy Board (NEB), the federal government exercises sole jurisdiction over the construction and operation of interprovincial and international petroleum pipelines. In 2012, Natural Resources Canada Minister Joe Oliver made some extraordinary claims about "environmental and other radical groups." They threatened "to hijack our regulatory system to achieve their radical ideological agenda."[117] The federal Conservative government was determined not to let these groups disrupt or delay resources development. To this end Ottawa amended the *National Energy Board Act* and repealed the *Canadian Environmental Assessment Act*. The NEB had used quite a liberal test when it came to deciding who could make arguments to Board members. The NEB would "consider the objections of any interested person."[118] The Board interpreted "interested person" in a way respecting the principle that serious members of the public should be able to participate in its deliberations. Minister Oliver's amendments to the *National Energy Board Act* included a stricter participatory test. The amendments were similar to what Alberta's playbook contained. The NEB must "consider the representations of any person who, in the Board's opinion, is *directly affected* by the granting or refusing of the application, and it may consider the representations of any person who, in its opinion, has relevant information or expertise."[119] Minister Oliver's "radical groups" would have a more difficult time overcoming this more stringent obstacle to participating in NEB hearings.

The government also amended the *National Energy Board Act* to set a 15-month time limit on considering applications. After 15 months the NEB must make a recommendation to the federal cabinet. The Conservative government's changes also gave the cabinet the authority to overrule the NEB and approve any pipeline proposal the Board may reject. Previously, the cabinet could only deny an application approved by the NEB. These amendments clearly privileged efforts to exploit the tar sands.

Simultaneous changes were made to the federal environmental assessment regime. They also underlined the Conservative government's commitment to raise institutional hurdles to conservationist participation in Canadian policy-making. The *Canadian Environmental Assessment Act* was repealed and replaced with the *Canadian Environmental Assessment Act, 2012*. The new Act ushered in restrictions to public participation similar to those found in the *National Energy Board Act* amendments. The repealed legislation was generous in identifying legitimate parties to an environmental assessment process. An interested party was defined as "any person or body having an interest in the outcome of the environmental assessment for a purpose that is neither frivolous nor vexatious."

The 2012 legislation was stricter in several respects. First, the law now restricts interested parties to persons. Second, determining who is an interested party is assigned to the federal agencies responsible for conducting environmental assessments or to the review panels created to assess projects. Finally, to be an interested party a person must be "directly affected by the carrying out of the designated project" or have "relevant information or expertise." Furthermore, in addition to narrowing the definition of who could be an interested party, the federal government narrowed the range of tar sands projects potentially subject to a federal environmental assessment. Most future development in the tar sands will not occur through mining operations; instead it will be driven by in situ projects, projects that today use great amounts of natural gas to generate steam to allow deep, very thick, or viscous bitumen deposits to flow into extraction wells. With a stroke of the pen the federal government declared that in situ projects could not trigger a federal environmental assessment.[120]

Conclusion

In the late spring of 2006 the character of environmental opposition to the tar sands began to evolve. New actors, foreign and transnational ENGOs, made connections with and/or joined Canadian opponents of the tar sands and pressured government and industry to slow down or stop the tar sands juggernaut. These new actors brought new strategies to the tar sands opposition. Greenpeace, often through the direct actions it was famous for, tried to put the environmental ruin of exploiting the tar sands in the media spotlight. Organizations partnered to run advertisements in prominent US media to alert the public and consumers to the unchecked industrialization of a Canadian Pandora through exploiting the Avatar Sands. Other new participants, such as the NRDC, brought their lobbying skills to the opposition and endeavoured to convince local, state, and national political leaders that they should shun the sands. The Aurora tailings reservoir incident was a political resource and vehicle for these groups to use.

In this more media-focused contest for the hearts and minds of the public and consumers, the state responded in kind. If ENGOs and First Nations were going to spend tens of thousands of dollars on ads in *Variety* and *Hollywood Reporter*, then Alberta would spend millions on its own advertising campaign to sing the praises of the province. For the state and industry, notwithstanding tragic "accidents" like the waterfowl deaths in April 2008, the substance of the tar sands environmental story was fine. The problem wasn't with the substance but rather with the telling of the story of what was happening on the forest floor and in the wetlands of northeastern Alberta. People needed reassurances, not stricter regulations and stronger enforcement actions. The public needed to hear and embrace this positive message, not the misinformation ENGOs were peddling. Joined by Alberta's universities, the state and industry forged a bitumen triangle aimed at soothing the public with better environmental communications, not better environmental policy. Directive 074 confirmed this. Reassuring messaging and timid, failed policy walked together. This partnership offered nothing to mitigate the toxic legacies of the tar sands tailings reservoirs that continued to grow on the landscape.

Fred Block, citing Polanyi, noted that "the exercise of state power fundamentally shapes the relative strength of different social actors."[121] Directive 074 illustrated the extent to which the exercise of state power was impervious to reform in the light of challenges such as the Aurora incident. It affirmed the precepts of market fundamentalism in Alberta. Reregulation would not respond to the new environmental critique so as to diminish the structural power of the tar sands industry. This affirmation also came through changes the state made to the institutional framework regulating the environmental dimension of exploiting the tar sands. Concerns about the future of nature in the boreal landscape were met with actions designed to marginalize and freeze out those concerns. The state and industry weathered the storm of the Aurora tailings reservoir incident much better than the waterfowl did.

Notes

1   Alberta Employment, Immigration and Industry, *Oil Sands Industry Update* (December 2006), 21.
2   "Fossil Fuels Targeted," *Financial Post,* April 28, 1993.
3   "Greenpeace Opposes Suncor Refinery Planned for Australia," *Asia Pulse,* March 7, 2000; "Greenpeace Protests Oil-Sands Expansion," *Globe and Mail,* March 7, 2000, A6.
4   James Brooke, "Canada Is Unlocking Petroleum from Sand: Digging for Oil," *New York Times,* January 23, 2001, C1.
5   Natural Resources Defense Council, "Finances and Annual Report," https://www.nrdc.org/finances-and-annual-report.
6   Natural Resources Defense Council and Sierra Club of Canada, *America's Gas Tank: The High Cost of Canada's Oil and Gas Export Strategy* (2002).
7   Alberta, Environment and Parks, "Total Area of the Oil Sands Tailings Ponds over Time."
8   Marilyn Radler, "Worldwide Reserves Increase as Production Holds Steady," *Oil & Gas Journal* 100, no. 52 (December 23, 2002); the Alberta government's lobbying efforts are described in Gary Park, "Alberta Wants Oil Sands Included in Global Crude Oil Reserves," *Petroleum News* 7, no. 32 (August 11, 2002).
9   At the end of 2014, Canada ranked third in total proved reserves of oil (172.9 billion barrels). This is due to the recognition of Venezuela's mammoth unconventional oil reserves as proved reserves. At 298.3 billion barrels, Venezuela now is the nation with the largest amount of proved reserves; Saudi Arabia, with 267 billion barrels, sits in second place. BP, *BP Statistical Review of World Energy June 2015* (64th edition), http://biomasspower.gov.in/document/Reports/BP%20statistical%20review-2015.pdf.
10 United States Department of Energy, Energy Information Administration, *International Energy Outlook 2003,* https://www.eia.gov/outlooks/archive/ieo03/index.html.
11 Alberta, Legislative Assembly, *Alberta Hansard, 26th Legislature, 1st Session (2005),* May 2, 2005, 1186.
12 A public opinion commissioned by Alberta and released on the eve of the Festival suggested that only four percent of American voters recognized Canada as the most significant supplier of crude to the U.S. Thirty-eight percent of respondents believed Saudi Arabia was the largest supplier. See Alan Freeman, "Mr. Klein Goes to Washington with Oil Message; Festival Aimed at Raising Awareness," *Globe and Mail,* June 28, 2006, B9.
13 Tim Harper, "US Capital Faces Alberta Invasion; Province Kicks Off Massive Two-Week Lobbying Blitz," *Toronto Star,* June 26, 2006, A2.
14 Alan Freeman, "Alberta's Gift to Culture," *Globe and Mail,* June 7, 2006, R1.
15 "Alberta Tries to Break into US Psyche," *Upstream,* March 24, 2006, 24. Smith's reference to the Lady Liberty likely was a reference to the Statue of Freedom that sits atop the dome of the US Capitol.
16 Harper, "US Capital Faces Alberta Invasion." See also Jacqueline Trescott, "The Truck Stops Here: Energy Exhibit Rankles Environmentalists," *Washington Post,* June 8, 2006, C01.

17 Pembina Institute, "Alberta Oilsands Development Takes Centre Stage at Smithsonian: Canadian and US Environmental Groups Bring Environmental Costs into the Spotlight," media release, June 27, 2006, http://www.pembina. org/media-release/1250. Interestingly, less than a week after the festival concluded, the Oil Sands Environmental Coalition intervened in the public hearings on Suncor's Voyageur project. There the OSEC adopted a more moderate position than what the NRDC had taken at the Folklife Festival. If the regulator imposed "stringent conditions that ensure actions to minimize greenhouse gas emissions," Pembina appeared willing to let the project proceed. See Pembina Institute, "Suncor Project Should Not Go Ahead As-Is: Energy Utilities Board Must Set Tough Limits on Greenhouse Gas Emissions," media release, July 13, 2006, http://www.pembina.org/media-release/1256.

18 Richard M. Nixon in *Nixon by Nixon: In His Own Words*, HBO (August 2014).

19 Shannon Phillips, "Head in the Sands," *Alberta Views* 11, no. 10 (December 2008). Phillips was elected to the provincial legislature in 2015 and was appointed the Minister of Environment and Parks and Minister Responsible for the Status of Women in the New Democratic Party government led by Premier Rachel Notley. The surprising NDP win in 2015 ended the 44-year Progressive Conservative dynasty.

20 "Greenpeace Activists at Ed Stelmach's Fundraising Dinner," YouTube video, 3:09, posted by Greenpeace Canada, April 24, 2008, https://www.youtube. com/watch?v=c3K2QF_-zuI; "Stop the Tar Sands—Shell Albian Sands Mine Action," YouTube video, 2:00, posted by Greenpeace Canada, October 7, 2009, https://www.youtube.com/watch?v=rKZKmHvmo74.

21 Some of Greenpeace's actions between 2007 and 2010 are listed in David Berry, "The Disobedient Albertans," *Alberta Views* 13, no. 5 (June 2010).

22 Phillips, "Head in the Sands." Environmental groups also joined together, sometimes with First Nations, to take out full-page advertisements in prominent American publications to slam the oil sands.

23 George Poitras, "Canada's Bloody Oil," *Guardian*, August 24, 2009, http://www. theguardian.com/commentisfree/2009/aug/24/climate-camp-canada-oil-tar-sands. Fort Chipewyan actually is downstream from the existing tar sands operations.

24 Jess Worth, "'Bloody Oil': Canadian First Nations Internationalize Their Struggle Against the Most Destructive Project on Earth," *New Internationalist*, Issue 427 (November 1, 2009); Rob Edwards, "RBS in Battle with the Cree First Nation over Dirty Oil Development Project on Tribal Lands," *Herald Scotland*, April 18, 2010.

25 Jason Markusoff, "Alberta's Image Getting Makeover to Battle Its Environmental Rep," *Edmonton Journal*, April 24, 2008, B8.

26 Markusoff, "Alberta's Image." Several days later Premier Stelmach defended the strategy in almost exactly the same words when he answered a question from Liberal David Swann. The premier wanted to ensure that people got the "correct information" about Alberta. He said further: "I can tell you that I'm not going to rely on that group or Greenpeace or Sierra Club to spread the misinformation not only in this province and this country but around the world." Alberta, Legislative Assembly, *Alberta Hansard, 27th Legislature, 1st Session (2008)*, April 29, 2008, 288.

27   Markusoff, "Alberta's Image."

28   Markusoff, "Alberta's Image."

29   The Progressive Conservative government's initial climate change policy is described and critiqued in Ian Urquhart, "Alberta's Land, Water, and Air: Any Reasons Not to Despair?," in *The Return of the Trojan Horse: Alberta and the New World (Dis)Order*, ed. Trevor W. Harrison (Montreal: Black Rose Books, 2005), 149–51.

30   Legislative Assembly, *Alberta Hansard*, April 29, 2008, 288.

31   Matthew Bramley, *An Assessment of Alberta's Climate Change Action Plan* (Pembina Institute for Appropriate Development, September 2002), 3.

32   Alberta Environment, *Albertans and Climate Change: A Plan for Action*, (Edmonton: May 2002), 11.

33   Bramley, *An Assessment of Alberta's Climate Change Action Plan*, 4.

34   *R. v. Syncrude Canada Ltd.*, 2010 ABPC 229, para. 2. Judge K.E. Tjosvold of the Provincial Court of Alberta suggested the combination of factors mentioned in this paragraph may have forced the ducks to land on the Aurora Settling Basin. See para. 16.

35   Paul Nelson, Naomi Krogman, Lindsay Johnston, and Colleen Cassady St. Clair, "Dead Ducks and Dirty Oil: Media Representations and Environmental Solutions," *Society and Natural Resources* 28.

36   Prime Minister Harper and Alberta Environment Minister Renner called the deaths a tragedy. See Scott Haggett, "Oil Sands Duck Deaths Tragic, Imperial CEO Says," *Reuters News*, May 1, 2008.

37   Alberta, "Washington Mission Aims to Build on Alberta-US Relations: Stevens to Stress Environmental Stewardship in Oil Sands Production," news release, April 23, 2008, http://alberta.ca/release.cfm?xID=233637BF323A2-EABD-EFD8-8048078D8B29257A.

38   "500 Fowl Symbols Tarnishing Alberta," *Edmonton Journal*, May 1, 2008, A18; Jim Macdonald, "Only Five Ducks Saved from Syncrude Tailings Pond, 500 Perish in Oilsands Wastes," *Canadian Press*, April 30, 2008.

39   Ian Austen, "Canadians Investigate Death of Ducks at Oil-Sands Project," *New York Times*, May 1, 2008, 2; "Ducks Doomed in Canadian Sludge Lake," *Kalgoorlie Miner*, May 1, 2008, 8.

40   Howard Rosenberg and Charles S. Feldman, *No Time to Think: The Menace of Media Speed and the 24-hour News Cycle* (New York: Bloomsbury, 2008).

41   Jim Macdonald, "Alta Minister Rejects Public Inquiry into 500 Dead Ducks in Oilsands Tailings Pond," *Canadian Press*, May 5, 2008; Jennifer Fong, "Greenpeace Wants Inquiry into Duck Deaths; Province's Investigation Too Close to Industry, Environmental Body Says," *Vancouver Sun*, May 6, 2008, A4.

42   *R. v. Syncrude Canada Ltd.*, [2010], ABPC 229, para. 34. Shaun Fluker wrote four illuminating blog posts on this case at ablawg.ca. The one dealing with the verdict in the case is Shaun Fluker, "The Case of the 1600 Dead Ducks: The Verdict Is In—Syncrude Guilty under the Migratory Birds Convention Act," *ABlawg.ca* (blog), June 30, 2010, http://ablawg.ca/2010/06/30/the-case-of-the-1600-dead-ducks-the-verdict-is-in-syncrude-guilty-under-the-migratory-birds-convention-act/.

43   *R. v. Syncrude Canada Ltd.*, [2010], ABPC 229, para. 22 to 34.

44   Jeffrey Jones, "Update 1—Syncrude Duck Deaths Now Triple Initial Tally," Reuters, March 31, 2008.

45   Hanneke Brooymans, "Syncrude Duck Deaths Kept Quiet; Province Aware 1,606 Ducks Killed on Tailings Pond, Not 500 Originally Reported to Public," *Edmonton Journal*, April 1, 2009, A1.

46   Lisa Arrowsmith, "Oil Sands Giant Says 'Sorry' for Dead Ducks," *Globe and Mail*, May 3, 2008.

47   Jeffrey Jones, "Analysis—Talk Is Cheap, Skeptics Say of Oil Sands Message," *Reuters News*, June 24, 2008.

48   http://www.canadaoilsands.ca; that website is now http://www.oilsandstoday.ca.

49   Jon Harding, "US Mayors Target 'Dirty Oil;' Oilpatch Website Takes On Critics," *Calgary Herald*, June 24, 2008, A1.

50   Canada, *Access to Information Act* (R.S.C., 1985, c. A-1).

51   Ken England, e-mail message to Elaine Feldman, May 6, 2000. This e-mail message was contained in Greenpeace Canada, "ATIP—Notes of April 23 CAPP-DFAIT Workshop," https://docs.google.com/a/ualberta.ca/file/d/0B_0MqnZ4wmcMWTNjOTcxMUh2d00/edit?pli=1.

52   Nelson et al. noted that technological innovation was the most popular solution to the tailings ponds issue in the three years of newspaper articles they studied. See Nelson et al., "Dead Ducks and Dirty Oil," 353.

53   Claudia Cattaneo, "Oilpatch New International Whipping Boy; CAPP Aims to Debunk Impact of Inaccuracies," *Financial Post*, February 19, 2008, FP 3.

54   Rob Gillies, "Will Canada's Oil Boom Be an Environmental Bust?," Associated Press, August 24, 2008.

55   Norval Scott, "Environmentalists Target Oil Sands Investors," *Globe and Mail*, September 16, 2008.

56   The committee members were Sue Kirby (Assistant Deputy Minister, Natural Resources Canada), Mike Ekelund (Assistant Deputy Minister, Alberta Department of Energy), Greg Stringham (Vice-President of Markets and Fiscal Policy, CAPP), and Jason Tolland (Counsellor—Energy and Environment, Embassy of Canada, Washington, DC).

57   The Clerk of the Privy Council is arguably the most influential public servant in the federal government. Mr. Lynch was familiar with the tar sands. During his tenures as Associate Deputy Minister and Deputy Minister of Industry Canada between 1992 and 2000, the National Oil Sands Task Force had sought Industry Canada's support for tar sands development.

58   Paul Khanna, "Summaries of the Deputy Minister Meetings with Industry and the Alberta Government on Oil Sands Outreach and Communications, March 16, 2010" (March 25, 2010), https://drive.google.com/a/ualberta.ca/file/d/0B46zsDD7Xqu3NzIxNmVhYmEtMTQoNCooNzVkLTk0ZDgtMGJiYThm NzA1ZWQz/view?pli=1.

59   Once available to the public at the YouTube links listed here, these videos now are private. Dr. David Lynch, P.Eng., Dean of Engineering at University of Alberta, https://www.youtube.com/watch?v=IVelcaGxUHU (uploaded on June 12, 2011). In the longer version of the CAPP video from which this 30-second commercial was taken, Lynch predicted: "In the oil sands in the next twenty years I see entirely new breakthrough technologies being implemented, technologies like the extraction of oil sands without using water..." Dr. David

Lynch, P.Eng., Dean of Engineering at University of Alberta, https://www. youtube.com/watch?v=555YXq4jyX8 (uploaded on September 2, 2011), accessed October 30, 2015. The longer video once available on CAPP's website, http://www.oilsandstoday.ca/reports/pages/videosvignettes.aspx, has been removed.

60   Canada School of Energy and Environment, *Annual Report, 2009–10*, 10.

61   The 2007 federal budget called the CSEE the Canada School for Sustainable Energy. Canada, *The Budget Plan*, "Knowledge Advantage, Chapter 5—A Stronger Canada Through a Stronger Economy," in *The Budget Plan* (2007) http://www.budget.gc.ca/2007/plan/bpc5d-eng.html.

62   Royal Canadian Mounted Police, Commercial Crime Section, *Information to Obtain a Production Order*, Police File # 2012–1046508, https://drive.google.com/a/ualberta.ca/file/d/0B6wfH8hIAchFbEF4c2NsazlXVUE/view.

63   Canada School of Energy and Environment, *Annual Report 2009–10*, 7.

64   Gerry Protti, Vice Chair of the Energy Policy Institute of Canada, when interviewed by the RCMP as part of the Carson influence-peddling investigation, told the police that Carson "seemed to know everyone in Ottawa and understood the Ottawa scene very well" and that he had "a tremendous set of contacts in the federal government." See Royal Canadian Mounted Police, *Information to Obtain a Production Order*, 19.

65   "Long-Time Politico Brings Expertise to Alberta-Led Centre of Excellence," *Folio* 45, no. 23 (August 15, 2008).

66   For a scathing indictment of Alberta's universities' lack of due diligence in Carson's hiring see Todd Babiak, "No Answers Coming as to How Tainted Political Fixer Got Job," *Edmonton Journal*, April 9, 2011, A5.

67   In November 2015, Carson was found not guilty of those charges. CBC, "Bruce Carson, Former Harper Aide, Not Guilty of Influence-Peddling," November 17, 2015, http://www.cbc.ca/news/politics/bruce-carson-not-guilty-influence-peddling-1.3322811.

68   Carson was subsequently found not guilty of influence-peddling. The judge found that Indian and Northern Affairs officials had little to do with the purchase of water systems by First Nations communities. Therefore, Carson's extensive political connections mattered negligibly. CBC News, "Carson Not Guilty."

69   David Keith, "The Real Bruce Carson Scandal," *Toronto Star*, September 22, 2015, http://www.thestar.com/opinion/commentary/2015/09/22/the-real-bruce-carson-scandal.html.

70   Canada School of Energy and Environment, *Annual Report 2009–10*, 6.

71   The CAPP representatives on this working group are redacted from the document obtained through the federal *Access to Information Act*. See ATIP-Carson-O&G_WkgGp2009, https://drive.google.com/a/ualberta.ca/file/d/0B_0MqnZ4wmcMamwwTXRQNjdrYlU/view.

72   ATIP-Carson-O&G_WkgGp2009. Environment Canada's Deputy Minister, Ian Shugart, described Mike Beale as being "heavily involved in our climate change policy." See Canada, House of Commons, Standing Committee on Environment and Sustainable Development, *Evidence—Minutes of Proceedings*, April 2, 2009, Meeting No. 13, 2nd Session, 40th Parliament.

73   Canada School of Energy and Environment, *Annual Report 2009–10*, 7; Bruce Carson, "Notes for a Speech on 'Banff Dialogue' and Canada's

Plan to Reduce Carbon," June 19, 2009, https://drive.google.com/file/d/0B_0MqnZ4wmcMNTkxMU1jZkpoNDA/view?pli=1.

74   Energy Policy Institute of Canada, *A Canadian Energy Strategy Framework: A Guide to Building Canada's Future as a Global Energy Leader* (August 2012), 7; Royal Canadian Mounted Police, *Information to Obtain a Production Order.*

75   RCMP, *Information to Obtain a Production Order*, 7; the Business Council on National Issues/Canadian Council of Chief Executives was an organization representing 150 of the leading corporations and entrepreneurs in Canada.

76   Protti's petroleum industry experience included being the founding president of CAPP. See Alberta Energy Regulator, "Alberta Energy Regulator, Chair of the Transition Committee and Board Chair," http://www.energy.alberta.ca/Org/pdfs/REDAchairGerryProttiBIO.pdf.

77   RCMP, *Information to Obtain a Production Order.*

78   RCMP, *Information to Obtain a Production Order*, 31.

79   Doug Black called Carson EPIC's "secret sauce" in a November 19, 2010, e-mail to Carson. See RCMP, *Information to Obtain a Production Order*, 33.

80   Reading EPIC's report you wouldn't know that its disgraced co-chair had ever been associated with the Institute. In describing the two years of work done by the policy work group that Carson was a key member of, the Institute writes: "The entire process was managed by our Vice Chairs Gerry Protti and Daniel Gagnier." See Energy Policy Institute of Canada, *A Canadian Energy Strategy Framework*, 9.

81   Erin Flanagan and Jennifer Grant, "Losing Ground: Why the Problem of Oilsands Tailing Waste Keeps Growing" (Pembina Institute: July 2013), 1, https://www.pembina.org/reports/losing-ground-oilsands-tailings-fs.pdf.

82   Alberta Energy Regulator, *Directive 074: Tailings Performance Criteria and Requirements for Oil Sands Mining Schemes* (Calgary: Energy Resources Conservation Board, February 2009), 2.

83   This area is equivalent to 896 square kilometres or 346 square miles.

84   Alberta, *Oil Sands Mine Reclamation and Disturbance Tracking by Year*, http://osip.alberta.ca/library/Dataset/Details/27.

85   Lee Foote, "Threshold Considerations and Wetland Reclamation in Alberta's Mineable Oil Sands," *Ecology and Society* 17, No. 1 (2012).

86   Alberta Energy Regulator, *Directive 074: Tailings Performance Criteria and Requirements for Oil Sands Mining Schemes* (Calgary: Energy Resources Conservation Board, February 2009), 2; Kelly Cryderman, "Obama and the Oilsands; 'Dirty Oil' Debate Back in Spotlight," *Calgary Herald*, February 22, 2009, A1.

87   Elsie Ross, "Regulator Demonstrate[s] Its Independence Through Its Actions, Says ERCB Head," *Daily Oil Bulletin*, December 22, 2008.

88   Norval Scott, "Alberta Set to Unveil New Rules for Oil Sands Waste," *Globe and Mail*, November 26, 2008, B3.

89   Alberta Energy Regulator, *Directive 074*, 4.

90   Jim Macdonald, "Alberta's Energy Regulator Issues Tough New Directive for Oilsands Tailings Ponds," Canadian Press, February 3, 2009.

91   Pembina Institute, "Implementation and Enforcement Critical to Success of First Attempt at Tailings Regulation," media release, February 3, 2009, www.pembina.org/media-release/1776.

92 Macdonald, "Alberta's Energy Regulator Issues Tough New Directive"; Dan Healing, "Reactions Cool to New Tailings Pond Rules; Implementation Is 'Going to Be a Challenge'," *Calgary Herald*, February 4, 2009, D4.

93 Darcy Henton and Dan Healing, "Tailings Rules Given 'Teeth'; New Oilsand Regulations Designed to Clean Up Province's Image After 500 Ducks Killed in Syncrude Pond," *Edmonton Journal*, February 4, 2009, A1.

94 In 2009, the Fort Hills mine, the second complying submission, wasn't planned to begin generating fine tailings until 2014. Although the company says the project is proceeding, it hasn't produced any crude or tailings yet. It is now expected to begin mining and processing bitumen in 2017.

95 Imperial Oil, *Kearl Oil Sands Project: 2009 Annual Tailings Plan Submission, September 30, 2009*, https://www.aer.ca/documents/oilsands/tailings-plans/Imperial_2009_Kearl_TailingsPlans.pdf, 8.

96 Imperial Oil, *Kearl Oil Sands Project*.

97 Canadian Natural Resources Ltd., *2009 Horizon Tailings Management Plan*, 7, https://www.aer.ca/documents/oilsands/tailings-plans/CNRL_2009_Horizon_TailingsPlans.pdf.

98 Canadian Natural Resources Ltd., *2009 Horizon Tailings Management Plan*, i.

99 Alberta Energy Regulator, *Directive 074*, 3.

100 When the ERCB approved the last of the tailings management plans in December 2010, it claimed the miners had committed more than $4 billion to address the tailings issue, a staggering $2 billion more than it reported only two months earlier. See Alberta Energy Regulator, "ERCB Conditionally Approves Tailings Plan for Shell Muskeg River Project," news release, September 20, 2010, http://www.aer.ca/about-aer/media-centre/news-releases/news-release-2010-09-20-nr2010-13; Alberta Energy Regulator, "ERCB Conditional Approval of Final Two Tailings Plans Ends Initial Phase of Directive 074," news release, December 17, 2010, http://www.aer.ca/about-aer/media-centre/news-releases/news-release-2010-12-17-nr2010-20.

101 Jesse Snyder, "A Fine Mess: The AER's Directive 074," *Alberta Oil: The Business of Energy*, July 28, 2015, http://www.albertaoilmagazine.com/2015/07/alberta-energy-regulator-directive-074/.

102 Alberta Energy Resources Conservation Board, *2012 Tailings Management Assessment Report, Oil Sands Mining Industry* (June 2013), 11.

103 Alberta, *Lower Athabasca Region—Tailings Management Framework for the Mineable Athabasca Oil Sands* (March 2015), 12.

104 Alberta, *Lower Athabasca Region*, 14 [emphasis added].

105 As noted, Directive 074 was suspended in March 2015. In July 2017, the Alberta government continued to misinform visitors to its Oil Sands Facts and Statistics website about the status of tailings regulation in the province. It said: "In February 2009, the Alberta Energy Resources Conservation Board issued Directive 074 with aggressive criteria for managing tailings." Visitors were not told the Directive had been suspended and that a less "aggressive" draft had been circulated by the Alberta Energy Regulator. See Alberta, "About Oil Sands: Facts and Statistics," http://www.energy.alberta.ca/OilSands/791.asp.

106 These volumes respectively are 193.4 and 257.7 billion US gallons. Alberta, Environment and Parks, "Total Volume of the Oil Sands Tailings Ponds over Time," (March 4, 2015), http://osip.alberta.ca/library/Dataset/Details/545;

Alberta, Environment and Parks, "Total Area of the Oil Sands Tailings Ponds over Time," http://osip.alberta.ca/library/Dataset/Details/542.

107 Brookings Institution, *U.S.-Alberta Energy Relations: A Conversation with Premier Alison Redford.*

108 Alberta, *Water Act*, Section 109 and 115, Revised Statutes of Alberta, 2000, Chapter W-3; Alberta, *Environmental Protection and Enhancement Act*, Section 44(6), 73(1), and 91, Revised Statutes of Alberta 2000, Chapter E-12.

109 The briefing note is reprinted in its entirety in *Pembina Institute v. Alberta (Environment and Sustainable Resource Development)*, 2013 ABQB 567. See also Cindy Chiasson, "Pembina Ruling Shines Spotlight on Need for Reform," October 4, 2013, http://elc.ab.ca/pub-archives/pembina-ruling-shines-spotlight-on-need-for-reform/; Shaun Fluker, "The Smoking Gun Revealed: Alberta Environment Denies Environmental Groups Who Oppose Oil Sands Projects the Right to Participate in the Decision-Making Process," October 3, 2013, http://ablawg.ca/2013/10/03/the-smoking-gun-revealed-alberta-environment-denies-environmental-groups-who-oppose-oil-sands-projects-the-right-to-participate-in-the-decision-making-process/; Ian Urquhart, "Blacklisted: Pembina Institute v. Alberta," *Wild Lands Advocate* 21, no. 4/5 (October 2013).

110 *Pembina Institute v. Alberta (Environment and Sustainable Resource Development)*, 12.

111 "Still Alberta's Prerogative to Say Who Speaks at Oilsands Reviews," Canadian Press, October 4, 2013; Nigel Bankes, "Separation of Powers and the Government's Response to the Judgment in *Pembina Institute v Alberta (Environment and Sustainable Resources Development)*, 2013 ABQB 567," October 11, 2013, http://ablawg.ca/2013/10/11/separation-of-powers-and-the-governments-response-to-the-judgment-in-pembina-institute-v-alberta-environment-and-sustainable-resources-development-2013-abqb-567/.

112 For examples of the provincial government's rhetorical commitment to the environment, see Alberta, "Albertans to Benefit from a More Efficient, Effective Regulatory System," news release, October 24, 2012, http://alberta.ca/release.cfm?xID=3316894717280-EB7E-BBC2-D83D1C8E1B1F8C34.

113 Shaun Fluker, "Bill 2 *Responsible Energy Development Act*: Setting the Stage for the Next 50 Years of Effective and Efficient Energy Resource Regulation and Development in Alberta," November 8, 2012, http://ablawg.ca/2012/11/08/bill-2-responsible-energy-development-act-setting-the-stage-for-the-next-50-years-of-effective-and-efficient-energy-resource-regulation-and-development-in-alberta/.

114 Cindy Chiasson, "Single Energy Regulator Bill a Poor Deal for Alberta's Environment," November 1, 2014, http://elc.ab.ca/?s=Single+energy+regulator+a+poor.

115 Shaun Fluker, "Amended Rules of Practice for the Alberta Energy Regulator: More Bad News for Landowners and Environmental Groups," December 11, 2013, http://ablawg.ca/2013/12/11/amended-rules-of-practice-for-the-alberta-energy-regulator-more-bad-news-for-landowners-and-environmental-groups/.

116 Fluker, "Amended Rules of Practice."

117 Natural Resources Canada, "An Open Letter from the Honourable Joe Oliver, Minister of Natural Resources, on Canada's Commitment to Diversify Our

Energy Markets and the Need to Further Streamline the Regulatory Process in Order to Advance Canada's National Economic Interest," January 9, 2012, http://www.nrcan.gc.ca/media-room/news-release/2012/1/1909.

118 Canada, *National Energy Board Act*, Section 53, R.S.C., 1985, c. N-7 (version of Act in effect from July 12, 2010 to July 5, 2012).

119 Canada, *National Energy Board Act*, Section 55.2, R.S.C., 1985, c. N-7 (version of Act current to November 13, 2013) [emphasis added].

120 Canada, "Regulations Designating Physical Activities," SOR/2012–147.

121 Block, "Polanyi's Double Movement," 2.

8

The Tar Sands and the Politics of Climate Change

"Our greenhouse gas emissions profile is strongly linked to the production and use of fossil fuels. Our policy approach to climate change is mindful of this reality and in fact helps strengthen our current economic structure."

—Government of Alberta, 2008

"America is now a global leader when it comes to taking serious action to fight climate change. And frankly, approving this project would have undercut that global leadership."

—President Obama on rejecting the Keystone XL pipeline, November 2015

Introduction

Climate change, the most important environmental challenge facing modern civilization, figured importantly in the emerging global environmental critique of the tar sands. Would this issue, unlike the international focus on toxic tailings ponds, stimulate Canadian governments to slow tar sands production growth or to demand a much-improved greenhouse gas (GHG) emissions performance? Alternatively, would transnational and foreign environmental groups be able to convince US politicians and consumers to restrict tar sands imports into American markets?

Throughout this book we have placed much importance on the structural power of the tar sands industry in the Alberta political economy. Climate change, given its prominence on the global agenda, couldn't be ignored. However, in this chapter we stress that the structural power of the industry and the ideological appeal of free markets shaped the provincial government's response. These factors were behind the government's choice to address climate change through a program designed to reduce GHG emissions intensity. At its climate change worst, but arguably its political best, provincial policy created the illusion that Alberta was seriously interested in reducing the total amount of greenhouse gases emitted into the atmosphere.

One recurring theme in this book is the institutional support offered to the version of market fundamentalism that took root in Alberta's tar sands. This theme lives in details about the place of the tar sands' advocates and critics in the advisory and decision-making bodies that shaped the state's role in development. It appears in this chapter with respect to the Climate Change and Emissions Management Corporation (CCEMC), a nonprofit corporation established to help Alberta reduce GHG emissions and adapt to climate change. This chapter will show how this corporation's board of directors, a board with significant representation from Alberta's largest GHG-producing sectors, interpreted and implemented its mandate. We will see that the ideas of the CCEMC didn't offer much of a challenge to the fossil fuel industry. The examination of the CCEMC repeats the point made in the previous chapter—key state institutions remained resolutely in the corner of the tar sands industry despite intensifying environmental criticism.

"Rules affect behaviour" is another important thread of this book's institutional theme. Defining who could participate in a regulatory hearing or what constituted a legitimate interest or argument therein helped delay and weaken opposition to the tar sands. In addition, following the argument of Peter Hall and Rosemary Taylor, political institutions or rules affect an actor's strategic calculations.[1] Actors should look to pursue their goals in favourable institutional settings, those offering the greatest likelihood of success. They should try to avoid settings hard to access or those that over time have proven inhospitable to their ambitions. These political calculations contributed to why opposition to the tar sands shifted to foreign arenas after Canadian institutions had blessed market fundamentalism in the tar sands and facilitated a decade of frenzied growth.

Since the contribution of institutional settings depends on the ideas and interests of actors, the ideological outlook of the US President and Congress helped influence the receptiveness of American political settings to anti-tar sands campaigners. During the Bush administration, both the Executive branch and sizeable blocs in Congress were cool to the reality of global warming and to suggestions that the US military shouldn't rely on fuels derived from sources such as the tar sands. The link those state actors made between the tar sands and US energy security trumped climate change. In this chapter we see that dynamic unfold with respect to what passage of the *Energy Independence and Security Act* (EISA) would mean for the future of tar sands crude in American markets.

Environmentalists had more success during the Obama administration when they could make their anti-tar sands demands ones the president alone could satisfy. Here they relied on a rule, the requirement that any pipeline crossing an international border needs presidential permission. The transnational environmental group 350.org, founded by Bill McKibben, used the presidential permit condition to make the climate change/tar sands relationship an issue in the 2012 presidential election. President Obama had committed to act on climate change during his 2008 election campaign.

In June 2008, Obama vowed that, if elected president, he would pursue the "limitless" possibilities of renewable energy. He wanted to reverse America's increasing addiction to oil, a "dirty, dwindling, and dangerously expensive" fossil fuel.[2] His senior energy advisor pointedly refused to confirm that, during an Obama presidency, tar sands crude would continue to enjoy its growing place in American petroleum consumption. If oil sands production delivered "a significant penalty to climate change," Jason Grumet said, "then we don't believe that those resources are going to be part of the long-term, are going to play a growing role in the long-term future."[3]

TransCanada Corporation's 830,000 barrel-per-day Keystone XL pipeline proposal, a pipeline the famous US climate scientist James Hansen called in 2011 the "fuse to the biggest carbon bomb on the planet,"[4] figured prominently in 350.org's climate change campaign. A Canada–United States tar sands pipeline was a nearly perfect issue for this campaign. The hostility of Congress and the Canadian regulatory process to acting on climate change was not part of the equation. Environmentalists might be able to deliver a body blow to the tar sands if they could convince the president that turning down Keystone XL was important both to his re-election chances and to his administration's efforts to address climate change. The anti-Keystone XL focus and campaign might not prompt Canadian and Albertan regulators to change their perspectives on the tar sands, but it might slow down expansion if a sympathetic president could be persuaded not to issue the required permit.

Dirty Oil, Climate Change, and the Transnational Environmental Critique

Hansen's representation of Keystone XL may have been the most dramatic link between the tar sands and climate change in the global critique. But it certainly wasn't the first. GHG emissions were central to NRDC's objections to Alberta's participation in the Smithsonian Folklife Festival. NRDC claimed that tar sands production sent two-and-one-half to three times (150 to 200 percent) more GHG emissions into the atmosphere than less-dirty conventional oil production.[5] These claims were reiterated in a 2007 joint NRDC/Western Resource Advocates/Pembina Institute report and were front and centre in a 2008 letter to the Western Governors' Association.[6] NRDC then joined 10 other environmental organizations to urge the governors to appreciate the greenhouse gas and wildlife impacts of tar sands production. NRDC also had joined other environmental organizations in advertising their opposition to the tar sands in Capitol Hill's *Roll Call* newspaper on the eve of the news about the duck deaths on Syncrude's Aurora tailings pond. The ad responded to Deputy Premier Stevens's mission "to promote the importation of dirty tar sands oil" to members of Congress and the Bush administration. The tar sands' "enormous amounts of global warming and toxic pollution" figured prominently there.[7]

The Factiva database suggests that 2008 was the year when the phrase "dirty oil" became commonplace in critiques. Candidate Obama's use of the phrase and the publication of Andrew Nikiforuk's best-selling book *Tar Sands: Dirty Oil and the Future of a Continent* may have contributed to this.[8] Greenpeace made Nikiforuk's work central to its critique. It commissioned him to write a "report to provide an analysis of the significant role dirty oil from the Alberta tar sands plays in the global climate crisis."[9] The tar sands' carbon dioxide emissions claimed by Nikiforuk, two to three times those of normal crude oil, became a foundation of Greenpeace's campaign and climate change–based international criticisms.[10]

Whether or not GHG emissions from the tar sands actually are "enormous" relative to conventional oil production is hotly contested. Assertions that tar sands production emits two, three, or perhaps five times as much greenhouse gases are commonly made by environmentalists.[11] These assertions clash loudly with industry's claims. CAPP, for example, states that oil sands petroleum is on average around 6 percent more GHG-intensive than the average barrel of crude oil in the United States. Other important sources of American petroleum supplies, such as Venezuelan crude, are responsible for more GHG emissions than the tar sands on a life-cycle or well-to-wheels basis, according to CAPP.[12] The ultimate persuasiveness of the climate change strand of the environmental critique hinged importantly on the seriousness with which actors regarded climate change and the legitimacy given to these two sharply clashing GHG emissions narratives.

In the United States, there was an early sign that the link between the tar sands' "dirty oil" and climate change would bear fruit for environmentalists. As ducks died and environmental groups made their climate change arguments, the US Conference of Mayors embraced the type of action tar sands activists hoped for. The 2008 conference saw the mayors express their concerns about global warming. Their proposed actions targeted, in part, the tar sands. The mayor of Eugene, Oregon, Kitty Piercy, sponsored the resolution targeting the tar sands because "We don't want to spend taxpayer dollars on fuels that make global warming worse … Our cities are asking for environmentally sustainable energy and not fuels from dirty sources such as tarsands."[13] The conference passed her resolution on high-carbon fuels. It read as if the NRDC was its author:

> the production of tar sands oil from Canada emits approximately three times the carbon dioxide pollution per barrel as does conventional oil production

and significantly damages Canada's Boreal forest ecosystem—the world's largest carbon storehouse...

Later that same resolution encouraged

the use of life cycle analyses that evaluate the greenhouse gas emissions from the production—including extraction, refining, and transportation—of fuels, including unconventional and synthetic fuels.

Finally, the resolution also encouraged American municipalities

to track and reduce the lifecycle carbon dioxide emissions from their municipal vehicles by preventing or discontinuing the purchase of higher-carbon unconventional or synthetic fuels for these vehicles.[14]

This was the first time an effort to restrict tar sands' access to American markets had any success. Whether the environmentalist narrative would have similar success in US national politics is considered now.

Congress, the Bush Administration, and the Security of Tar Sands Access to US Markets

The *Energy Independence and Security Act,* passed by a Democratic Congress and signed by President Bush in 2007, was the most ambitious American energy law since the OPEC crises of the 1970s. At more than 300 pages, the law proposed a wide suite of actions. Likely most known for its increase in vehicle fuel economy standards, the law surprised and caught the attention of the Alberta and Canadian governments for another reason. Section 526 of EISA specifically listed "nonconventional petroleum sources"—like the tar sands—as fuel federal agencies could not purchase unless the lifecycle greenhouse gas emissions of the nonconventional oil were equal to or less than those from a barrel of conventional oil.[15] No one in Edmonton, Calgary, or Ottawa caught this last-minute addition to the legislation and the threat it might pose to Alberta's interests, especially if it became a precedent for broader market access attacks.[16]

Once President Bush signed EISA, Canadian officials and the petroleum industry immediately started to work to ensure Section 526 wouldn't be interpreted liberally. Representative Henry Waxman (D–California), one of the greenest members of Congress, authored Section 526. It appeared originally in H.R. 2635, the *Carbon-Neutral Government Act of 2007* that Waxman sponsored in June 2007—a bill that never came to a vote in Congress.[17] According to Canadian embassy staff, the NRDC urged Waxman to add Section 526 to EISA. Canadian officials believed Waxman "pitched the provision to his Democratic colleagues as an anti–coals-to-liquid measure, without mentioning oil sands."[18] A coals-to-liquids program was part of the US Air Force's search for a synthetic fuel that would reduce its dependence on conventional oil.[19] Soon after EISA was signed, Waxman, echoing the NRDC's concerns, wrote to Secretary of Defense Gates to ask how Defense intended to comply with Section 526 when it came to fuel derived from the oil sands.[20] To Canadian embassy staff, Waxman was "endeavouring to have Section 526 apply to commercially available fuels made in part from oil sands."[21] The Canadian embassy mobilized to do its best to ensure this interpretation would never guide American decision-making.

Canada enlisted the petroleum industry in its fight against Section 526. The Canadian Embassy wrote to ExxonMobil's senior director of federal relations to alert her to the likelihood the NRDC would use a broad reading of Section 526 to oppose exploiting the oil sands. A narrow reading of this provision wouldn't pose a danger to tar sands access to this American market. "I would encourage your firm," he wrote, "to make its views known to DOE and the Hill."[22] The embassy delivered a similar message to the other majors importing bitumen from Canada (BP, Chevron, ConocoPhillips, Encana, Marathon, and Devon) as well as the American Petroleum Institute, the Alberta office in Washington, and CAPP.

The Bush administration, "at the highest level," shared the Canadian position and also sought to neuter Section 526's impact on the tar sands. The Bush administration went so far as to encourage Canadian diplomats to suggest that Section 526 might violate NAFTA; if Canada played the NAFTA card, this would help the Bush administration insist on a narrow interpretation of the section.[23] The NAFTA angle appealed to Canadian embassy officials; Paul Connors, one of the embassy staffers working on the fight against Section 526, suggested the section likely violated NAFTA's government procurement chapter. But the NAFTA argument never made it into the letter Canada's ambassador to the United States sent to Defense Secretary Gates. Instead Ambassador Wilson argued that Section 526 was impractical. All fuels refined in the United States were blends of light and heavy oil because refineries mix feedstocks. Blending feedstocks meant that little of the commercial fuel supplies available to American consumers were derived exclusively from conventional oil. "Oil sands–derived petroleum," the ambassador asserted, "represents approximately 5% of US supply and is not segregated from other petroleum." Ambassador Wilson also asked the Defense Secretary to consider the energy security/oil sands relationship. A liberal interpretation of Section 526's reach would clash with the energy policy positions of President Bush and Energy Secretary Bodman. They had both "publicly welcomed expanded oil sands production, given the increased contribution to US energy security."[24]

The Canadian embassy believed they could count on at least two Congressional camps to oppose the environmentalists' preferred interpretation of Section 526. Members who supported biofuel development such as corn-based ethanol were concerned the provision could damage the future of biofuels.[25] It may go without saying that what embassy staff called the "Security-comes-first Members" were very strong in Congress. In their world "olive trumps green," and they didn't want any interpretation that would impair the mobility of the US military.[26]

Waxman himself began to back away from pushing for the expansive interpretation the NRDC and more than two dozen North American environmental and social justice groups sought.[27] When he first wrote Secretary Gates to ask how the Department of Defense regarded fuel from the tar sands, Waxman asked the secretary to "describe how the Department will ensure that fuel supply contracts are drafted so as to exclude the provision of such fuels if they have higher greenhouse gas emissions than conventional fuel."[28] This tough stand mellowed by March 2008 when he wrote to Senator Jeff Bingaman, chairman of the Senate Committee on Energy and Natural Resources. Waxman told Bingaman that, as Section 526's author, he wrote it with two concerns in mind. First, he was concerned about the interest in developing a coal-to-liquid fuels program, since these fuels would emit nearly twice the greenhouse gases as conventional fuel. Second, he was concerned about the tar sands. But Waxman said his concerns should be pursued "in a manner that makes sense" according to federal contracting norms. While he was opposed to taxpayer support for developing synthetic fuels from non-conventional feedstocks, he didn't mean to stop federal purchases of generally available fuels that might contain "incidental" amounts of nonconventional petroleum. Section 526 then should not be applied to purchases of generally available fuels that were not *predominantly* produced from an unconventional fuel source."[29] Rep. Waxman wrote a similar letter to the chairman and ranking member of the Senate Armed Services Committee in May. There he said he wasn't aware of any federal agency that was negotiating fuel purchase contracts to promote or expand the use of the tar sands.[30]

By March 2008, the Canadian embassy was confident Section 526 wouldn't apply to the tar sands. Inconsequential as federal government purchases as a percentage of the total US market were, this was an important victory for Canadian governments and the tar sands industry.[31] It reduced the likelihood that Section 526 could be used as a springboard for more sweeping restrictions on tar sands access to the US market. Senior Bush administration officials had assured their Canadian counterparts that "they will take action to ensure that section 526 does not apply to commercial fuel made in part from oil sands."[32]

Events since 2008 pertaining to Section 526 cemented this victory for Canadian governments and the tar sands industry. In 2011, the US District Court for the Eastern District of Virginia rejected the Sierra Club's efforts to win a declaratory judgement and injunctive relief against the Defense Department for purchasing fuel derived in part from the tar sands. Judge Hilton found the Sierra Club didn't have standing to bring its lawsuit against the federal government.[33] But the case prompted the Department of Defense to submit an environmental assessment of its fuel purchasing programs. The department, following the *National Environmental Protection Act*, submitted an environmental assessment of those programs in 2013. That assessment led Defense to propose that its fuel purchases wouldn't have a significant environmental impact. This environmental assessment only attracted two submissions during the comment period. Neither submission came from any of the more than one dozen environmental and social justice groups who wrote to members of the House and the Senate in May 2008 to support the expansive interpretation of Section 526. The only comments received were from Gary Doer, Canada's ambassador to the United States, and the American Petroleum Institute. The American Petroleum Institute said in part that, in the real world, it simply wasn't feasible to restrict the use of heavy oil feedstocks in refineries.[34] Ambassador Doer concluded that "Canada's oil sands represent a safe, secure and environmentally responsible source of energy for North America."[35] He applauded Canadian efforts to tackle GHG emissions. Here he praised Alberta's climate change initiatives:

> At the provincial level, Alberta was the first jurisdiction in North America to require large industrial facilities, including oil producers, to improve their GHG emissions performance against set targets. For every tonne of emissions that they fall short, emitters must pay into a clean energy technology fund.[36]

Whether this praise was warranted is looked at next. If the "tar sands monster," in James Hansen's words, was coming under increasing criticism for fuelling climate change, what was Alberta doing to show it took this branch of the global critique seriously?

What to Reduce in Alberta? Emissions and/or Emissions Intensity?

Alberta's 2003 *Climate Change and Emissions Management Act* inspired Doer's praise. This law was the foundation for Alberta's climate change policy between 2003 and 2015. One aspect of that policy is considered in this section: the type of GHG emissions reductions promised. Alberta's choice didn't respond generously to environmentalists' climate change criticisms. Instead it confirmed Alberta's refusal to challenge the market/business-friendly pattern of development in the tar sands. Government would not cap, let alone demand reductions in, the tonnes of greenhouse gases tar sands operations sent skyward. This choice was made before the international criticisms of the tar sands gathered steam and was not changed in the face of that subsequent criticism.

Simply put, the political advantages and the environmental shortcomings of Alberta's approach rested in the same place: the use of emissions intensity as the measure of success in reducing GHG emissions. This measure let Alberta promise quite staggering percentage reductions in emissions, without actually requiring industry to emit fewer tons of greenhouse gases. It was a brilliant obfuscating strategy. As noted in the previous chapter, the emissions intensity approach measures greenhouse gas emissions relative to some yardstick of output or production. Alberta selected provincial GDP as the yardstick for its climate change plan. It promised that, in 2020, emissions intensity would be 50 percent below the province's 1990 emissions intensity level. By 2010, its action plan would reduce Alberta's emissions intensity to 22 percent below 1990 levels.[37] But this plan also didn't call for Alberta to reduce its absolute GHG emissions to below 1990 levels, as the Kyoto Protocol stipulated Canada must do. Alberta's 2010 emissions intensity target, translated into absolute emissions, called for Alberta to emit 238 million tonnes of greenhouse gases. That level was 36 percent higher than the 175 million tonnes Alberta emitted in 1990.[38]

Alberta adopted the emissions intensity approach because the provincial government regarded it as a "more realistic" approach than Kyoto. Capital would flee from Canada and Alberta if the state acquiesced to Kyoto's demand for a 6 percent cut in absolute emissions from 1990 levels. Alberta and Canada would "bear the costs of emission reductions while displacing investment, jobs and emissions to nations without greenhouse gas emission reduction targets."[39] It was as if the corporations lining up for regulatory permission to exploit the tar sands could take that bitumen with them to sunnier locales for greenhouse gas emitters.

In 2002, there wasn't much political urgency in Alberta or Canada to be more ambitious. Premier Klein's Progressive Conservatives decimated the opposition parties in the 2001 provincial election, taking 74 of the legislature's 83 seats. Alberta's economy, riding on the crest of the tar sands boom, grew more than in any other province; personal income per capita was the highest in the country; Alberta's population grew faster than anywhere else in Canada; nonrenewable resources contributed more than

$10 billion to the provincial treasury, due mostly to high natural gas prices. The federal government did little more than talk about the need to address climate change.[40] OSEC and First Nations still were content to accommodate industry and government regulators. Times were good for the tar sands.

The vagueness of key provisions of the *Climate Change Act* and the unhurried approach to fleshing out those provisions reflected this lack of urgency. GHG emissions targets, for example, would be set for sectors of the economy. They weren't specified. It wasn't until four years after the law was passed that the provincial government finally introduced the climate plan's key implementation measure, the *Specified Gas Emitters Regulation* (SGER). The regulation abandoned the commitment to negotiate different sectoral agreements. Instead large emitters, all facilities emitting more than 100,000 tons of carbon dioxide equivalent gases, would have to reduce their emissions intensity. The regulation would apply to approximately 100 facilities that collectively emitted nearly 70 percent of Alberta's industrial emissions. A more detailed evaluation of the SGER follows in the next section of this chapter.

Did Alberta choose wisely? The reductions in GHG emissions intensity recorded in Table 8 might suggest so. Relative to the size of the economy, Alberta's 2010 emissions were 27 percent lower in 2010 than they were in 1990; the province met the first milestone of its plan. The problem, however, is that Alberta actually emitted many more tonnes of greenhouse gases in 2010 than it had in 1990, 38 percent more than the 175 million tonnes it emitted in 1990. Matthew Bramley pointedly noted how Alberta's economic growth enabled emissions intensity to fall over the course of the 1990s despite significant increases in absolute emissions. Alberta's plan was "a plan to increase emissions."[41]

Alberta's auditor general had a different criticism of Alberta's climate change plans. Fred Dunn didn't quarrel with using the emissions intensity yardstick. But his 2008 audit showed that Alberta Environment's climate

Table 8 Alberta's GHG Emissions and Emissions Intensity, Selected Years

	1990	2000	2010	2014
Total GHG emissions (millions of tonnes)	175	232	242	274
Emissions intensity (millions of tonnes of GHG emitted/GDP in millions at market prices in chained 2007 dollars)	1.26	1.14	0.92	0.85

Sources: Environment and Climate Change Canada, *National Inventory Report 1990–2014: Greenhouse Gas Sources and Sinks in Canada, Part 3* (Ottawa: Environment and Climate Change Canada, 2016), 61; Statistics Canada, CANSIM, v62788314 "Alberta, Chained (2007) Dollars, Gross Domestic Product at Market Price."

change management systems needed significant improvements. The government hadn't identified and tracked the key elements of its action plan; it hadn't evaluated if its actions were successful or not.[42] His assessment doesn't suggest there was much political will to ensure the plan's success.

When the international spotlight began to focus more intensely on the tar sands, Alberta revisited and revised its climate change plan. First, the strategy reaffirmed the commitment to emissions intensity reductions from industry. Firms covered by the SGER would have to reduce the GHG emissions intensity of their operations by 12 percent. But second, the 2008 plan promised real emissions reductions as well. Alberta promised that 2050 would see a staggering 200-million-tonne reduction in GHG emissions from what it called the "business as usual" level. Alberta had the most ambitious GHG reduction target in Canada. For those who had trouble appreciating what a 200-million-tonne reduction would look like, Alberta said it was like taking 40 million cars off the road—more than 2.5 times the number of automobiles in Canada in 2008.[43] By 2050, Alberta would reduce its GHG emissions to 14 percent below 2005 levels.[44] Seventy percent of the promised 200 million tonnes in reductions would come from carbon capture and storage technology—a technology that hadn't been used commercially anywhere in Alberta. Nonetheless, Premier Stelmach pledged his administration's targets were "practical and achievable" and were the product of "sound research, not wishful thinking."[45] Perhaps Alberta really had warmed to the need to make real reductions in GHG emissions.

Alberta's auditor general wasn't convinced. His analysis of the renewed and updated plan raised questions about the seriousness of the provincial government's commitment to real reductions. Alberta Environment used computer modelling to predict Alberta's future greenhouse gas emissions trajectory and to identify policies and actions that could achieve the new GHG emissions reduction goals. The model identified actions that could produce the 200-megatonne/million tonnes emissions reduction goal set by the Stelmach government.[46] But those actions were never incorporated into the strategy. Why? They were discarded likely because they promised heavy political costs, not least because of how they would disrupt the petroleum industry's bottom line. The 200-million-tonne reduction could be reached if Alberta insisted that all new large industrial emitters adopted carbon capture and storage technologies by 2015 wherever possible. The 200-megatonne reduction could be reached if Alberta made its $15/tonne carbon charge economy-wide and increased it substantially over time. The model proposed doubling this tax to $30/tonne in 2020 and to double it again to $60/tonne in 2030. In 2050, this economy-wide carbon tax would increase to $100/tonne.

Rather than adopting these politically risky measures, Alberta's 2008 strategy instead chose a suite of actions that hadn't been modelled. Alberta Environment didn't know what their impact would be. Technology subsidies, capacity building, removing barriers to deploying greener technologies, and the always popular tactic of "raising awareness" were included in the strategy despite their absence from the department's model. The auditor general concluded, "The 14% reduction target in the Strategy is based on actions that are more stringent than the actions the Strategy chose." Given this conclusion, one might doubt the seriousness of the province's commitment to real reductions by 2050; it's plausible that, given its longstanding refusal to slow tar sands growth, the government knowingly fed the public disinformation about its intentions. If Alberta was going to reach its modest 2050 target, it would be up to a future generation to design and implement the laws and regulations to do so.

It's not cavalier to suspect the Progressive Conservative government misled the public when, in the government's words, it came to "addressing the serious and world-wide challenge of climate change" or taking "decisive action to reduce greenhouse gas emissions."[47] The auditor general's 2008 report, as the *Edmonton Journal* editorial board concluded, showed that Alberta was doing "little more than blowing smoke" when it came to fulfilling its 2050 ambitions.[48] In 2008, the auditor general recommended the Ministry of Environment improve its public reporting of Alberta's efforts to meet its climate change targets and of the costs incurred in pursuing those targets.[49] Government ignored this recommendation. Four years later, the auditor general revisited the Ministry's progress on implementing that recommmendation. The auditor general's 2012 report offered three key findings. First, the department had not issued any public reports on Alberta's progress in meeting the emissions intensity objective set in the *Climate Change and Emissions Management Act*. Second, the department's public reporting about the 2008 strategy presented interim targets that could not be compared with the reported results. Finally, public reporting on emissions reductions achieved through the province's climate change actions and the costs of those actions was completely absent. The auditor general repeated his 2008 recommendation: government should "improve the reliability, comparability and relevance of its public reporting on Alberta's results and costs incurred in meeting climate change targets."[50] The department continued to stonewall. The auditor general repeated the recommendation in his October 2013, October 2014, July 2015, and October 2015 reports. Seven years after the auditor general first called for action, the government still hadn't moved to address these concerns about the quality and accuracy of the information Alberta dispensed to the public.

The Specified Gas Emitters Regulation: Alberta's 12 Percent Solution

Government touted the *Specified Gas Emitters Regulation* as a "major factor" in implementing Alberta's action plan; the regulation's rules represented "significant and important steps in the right direction."[51] This regulation, when it was released finally in March 2007, targeted large emitters and required them to reduce their emissions intensity by 12 percent.[52] If a company's emissions intensity baseline was 1.0, that meant the firm emitted one tonne of greenhouse gases per barrel of production. The SGER required the company to reduce that one-to-one baseline ratio to 0.88 tonnes per barrel of production. To reiterate a point made earlier, this approach didn't require Alberta or large emitters to put an absolute cap on or reduce the amount of GHG emissions sent skyward. As we see here, firms in the tar sands could meet the regulation's 12 percent emissions intensity reduction *and* maintain or increase their actual emissions.

Large emitters could use four options, singly or in combination, to meet the required reductions. First, the company could improve efficiencies, produce the same amount of or even more crude while reducing the amount of fossil fuels used to produce it. Second, firms could use emission performance credits (EPCs). These credits are created when a company more than met its 12 percent reduction goal in any given year. Large emitters creating EPCs could bank them for possible future use or sell them to one of their peers. Third, a large emitter could purchase offset credits from companies not subject to the regulation. For example, Alberta's Carbon Farmer is a company specializing in growing trees to pull carbon dioxide from the atmosphere. It generates tonnes of carbon credits that large emitters can purchase to count against the emissions they otherwise would have to record on their ledgers. Fourth, a gap between a large emitter's emissions intensity obligation and performance could be addressed by paying into the Climate Change and Emissions Management Fund (the Fund). The Fund would finance initiatives with the potential to reduce GHG emissions. Each $15 payment bought large emitters a credit for one tonne of GHG emissions. For example, in 2011 government credited Syncrude with the equivalent of reducing emissions by more than 1.4 million tonnes in return for the more than $21.1 million Syncrude contributed to the Fund.[53] Large emitters that selected the third and/or fourth paths effectively practised "chequebook environmentalism." Writing cheques to purchase GHG emission credits would let them comply with the SGER without necessarily reducing their actual emissions intensity, let alone their actual aggregate emissions.

The second option, if EPCs were purchased from a fellow large emitter, also enabled tar sands firms to pay their way out of their obligation. The government's regulatory options didn't demand the tar sands make real reductions in the total amount of greenhouse gases they emitted.

Did this regulation deliver the results the international critics of the tar sands wanted?

No. Chart 1 speaks well to how success in reducing emissions intensity may fail miserably in delivering the only outcome that would satisfy international critics—lower absolute emissions. Between 2010 and 2014, tar sands GHG emissions grew impressively. Direct emissions grew by 29 percent from their 2010 level, to 65.6 million tonnes in 2014. Large emitters complied with the 12 percent emissions intensity reduction demanded by the SGER throughout these years. This starkly confirms the skeptics' assertion that an emissions intensity policy very likely wouldn't produce any real reduction in the absolute emissions of tar sands greenhouse gases.

Within this general picture of dramatic absolute GHG emissions growth, another sketch details the options tar sands companies used to meet the 12 percent reduction requirement. Chart 2 presents this picture. Facilities reductions, reducing emissions by improving a facility's efficiencies, only

Chart 1 Oil Sands Sector GHG Emissions in Megatonnes (Mt), Selected Years

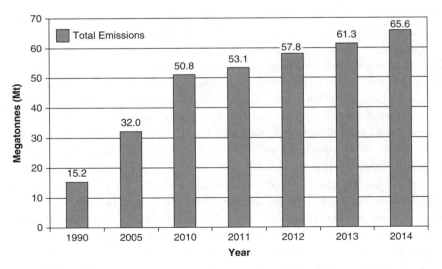

Source: Environment and Climate Change Canada, *National Inventory Report 1990-2014: Greenhouse Gas Sources and Sinks in Canada* (Canada's Submission to the United Nations Framework Convention on Climate Change, 2016), 81.

Chart 2 Oil Sands Sector, Options Used to Meet 12 Percent Reduction in GHG Emissions Intensity, in Tons, 2009–2014

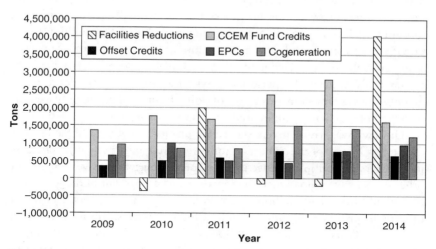

Source: Alberta Environment and Parks, *Specified Gas Emitters Regulation Compliance Reporting Summary, 2009–2014*.

contributed positively to meeting the sector's emissions intensity in 2011 and 2014. The negative values for all the other years indicate GHG additions, not reductions.[54] In four of the six years detailed here, tar sands companies most often turned to buying credits from the Fund. As noted above, the emissions reductions credited this way are fictitious. For example, the 2,793,745 ton credits purchased in 2013 didn't reduce GHG emissions by a single ton in that year. The $41.9 million these credits added to the Fund may or may not produce, through the programs/projects the CCEMC funds, future emissions reductions. Whatever its future promise might have been, the Fund allowed tar sands companies to buy their way out of making real reductions or pursuing efficiency improvements.

Sector-wide data obscure the choices individual companies made with respect to complying with the regulation. Syncrude and Suncor, the two largest tar sands companies, took very different approaches to meeting their emissions intensity reduction requirements. Suncor committed to meeting the SGER's demands largely by improving the efficiency of its energy use in its operations. In every year except 2012, Suncor secured intensity reductions from its operations. SGER compliance data also show that when Suncor owed tons after making operational improvements, it preferred to cover its deficits by submitting offset and emission performance credits. It only contributed to the Climate Change and Emissions Management Fund three times between 2009 and 2014.[55]

Syncrude didn't share Suncor's commitment to reducing greenhouse gas emissions from its operations. Syncrude made facilities reductions only in 2009. All of the tons in emissions reductions that Syncrude owed regulators from 2009 to 2014 were the imaginary tons paid for through contributing to the Fund. From 2009 to 2014, Syncrude contributed $102 million to the province's emissions fund. This rather stunning figure meant that Syncrude alone contributed 53 percent of all the CCEM Fund purchases made by the tar sands sector in this period. For Syncrude, the fee of $15 per tonne of greenhouse gas emissions was a cost of doing business that the joint venture preferred over making genuine reductions to its emissions.

This levy was trivial, given Syncrude's profits. Canadian Oil Sands, then the largest owner of the Syncrude joint venture (36.74 percent), generated just over $5 billion in total net income (profit) over these five years.[56] The other six partners who owned the remaining 63.26 percent of the joint venture would have made billions more from this partnership. Set against the billions in profits Syncrude generated for its owners, the project's $102 million in SGER compliance costs looks minuscule.[57] While Canadian governments and industry were uneasy about the growing international criticism of the tar sands, this unease didn't nudge Alberta closer to demanding real GHG emissions reductions. The state stayed the course in a manner that, to uncritical eyes, would look as if government regulations demanded and secured real reductions.

The Climate Change and Emissions Management Corporation (CCEMC)

A key characteristic of market fundamentalism in the tar sands appears as the state ensuring its decisions defer to the immediate demands of tar sands interests. That's reflected well in the previous section. Another characteristic is to delegate state authority to those same interests. The National Oil Sands Task Force reflected this characteristic, the Cumulative Enviromental Management Association reflected this characteristic, and so did the creation and operation of the Climate Change and Emissions Management Corporation.

The CCEMC was established in 2009 to pursue the two objectives of the Climate Change Emissions and Management Fund: to help sectors of the economy reduce greenhouse gas emissions and to "invest in Alberta energy conservation, energy efficiency and technology."[58] Large emitters contributed $740.1 million to the Fund between 2007 and 2015.[59] Only petroleum industry media publicized the government's May 6, 2009, press release announcing the birth of the CCEMC and the appointment of Eric Newell, the tar sands industry veteran, as its chair.[60] The Corporation flew well below the radar of the Canadian media and Alberta opposition parties. Announcing the CCEMC's creation in the legislature was the only occasion the Corporation was mentioned there during the 2009–10 legislative session. Created by regulation, not by legislation, the CCEMC was essentially neither noticed nor debated. Only one Canadian metropolitan newspaper, the *Edmonton Journal*, appears to have covered any aspect of the CCEMC's appearance on Alberta's climate change stage in 2009.[61] Between its creation and 2015, the Corporation was never the focus of a question in the legislature, never the subject—other than in a tangential way—of debate in the legislature.

The CCEMC testified to the Progressive Conservative faith in delegating government authority, with loose accountability provisions, to private interests. The nonprofit corporation's first board of directors resembled a who's who of big business in Alberta. Five members of the 15-member board, including board chair Newell, came from firms or associations involved in the tar sands.[62] That number became six if you counted Dr. David Lynch, the University of Alberta dean of engineering whose enthusiasm for exploiting the tar sands was noted in the previous chapter. Dean Lynch was the first representative on the board from academia; Dr. Joseph Doucet, current dean of the University of Alberta School of Business and the School's Enbridge Professor of Energy Policy from 2005 until 2013, replaced Lynch on the CCEMC board in the 2014–15 reporting period. Two other original board members came from principals in Alberta's largely coal-fired electricity sector (ENMAX and Epcor/Capital Power). Individuals whose careers had propelled them into senior positions in Nova Chemicals, Agrium, and Weyerhaeuser also were on CCEMC's first board. In more than a few cases, the "public at large" label worn by some board members masked impressive corporate credentials. Gary Holden, the CEO and president of ENMAX, was on the original board as a public member; Patrice Merrin, the former CEO and president of the coal mining firm Luscar, also sat on the board as a public member. At the beginning of 2016 the four public at large members included a former Alberta minister of finance, a vice-president from Scotiabank, and a former president and CEO of TransAlta Corporation whom *Alberta Oil* recognized as Alberta's CEO of the year in 2011.[63] Large GHG emitters certainly were very well represented on the board that decided how to spend the hundreds of millions those emitters paid in order to obey the letter of Alberta's key climate change regulation.

The provincial government never offered the Corporation much guidance or subjected it to much oversight. During the 2011 debate on Environment's Main Estimates, the New Democratic Party's Rachel Notley asked Minister Renner what performance measures his department had established to ensure the hundreds of millions of dollars collected from large GHG emitters through the $15 per tonne GHG emissions levy were well spent. The minister referred Notley to the Corporation's website; neither his department nor cabinet had set performance measures for the CCEMC. The Progressive Conservative government left it to the Corporation to develop its own performance measures since the CCEMC was "an arm's length corporation." As such, Renner said his department had "to be careful that we do not try and exert too much direction over that board."[64] The CCEMC's performance measures published for its first two years of operations were commonsensical, yet vague. They were GHG emissions reductions (which were hypothetical since the Corporation couldn't report them until funded projects were completed and operating), allocating funds to the sectors and areas outlined in Alberta's climate change plan (with no indication of what the relative shares should be), monitoring project success including how projects progressed "along the innnovation spectrum" (whatever that means), and CCEMC's ability to operate "as efficiently as possible" (corporate efficiency).

Minister Renner couldn't have pointed Notley to the CCEMC's website a year later. The CCEMC stopped publishing performance measures after its 2010–11 annual report. A search for performance measures on the CCEMC's website in late 2015 came up empty. The post-2011 disappearance of these performance measures was never raised, never questioned in the legislature.

Minister Renner also likened his department to a conduit, really an Automated Teller Machine, when it came to the Fund; the fees collected by government and deposited there were "funds that flow through our department from compliance costs associated with CO_2 mitigation."[65] The CCEMC had the only client card and would spend its withdrawals according to its assessments of how best to address climate change.

The government's intent to give the CCEMC free rein was also reflected in the decision to establish the CCEMC as a nonprofit corporation. This choice weakened the CCEMC's accountability to the legislature. Section 9(1) of the *Government Organization Act* gave ministers sweeping powers to delegate authority.[66] Any power, duty, or function the minister of the environment possessed pursuant to the *Climate Change and Emissions Management Act* or any other law could be handed over to any person. Corporations and a wide range of organizations were "persons" according to the Alberta legislation.

Bill 41, the *Government Organization Act*, was a signature law passed by Premier Ralph Klein's administration in 1994. During the legislative debates over Bill 41, speaker after speaker from the opposition Liberals claimed the bill was another government measure intended to privatize public responsibilities. Minister of Economic Development and Tourism Murray Smith opened second reading debate on this bill in October 1994. He noted the bill expanded the powers of delegation, a move inspired by the government's wish to turn more matters over to the private sector. In Smith's words, the legislation was "consistent with the government's business plan of being able to reflect the move into the private sector."[67] In a related vein, the Liberals raised concerns about how the bill would corrode government accountability. Perhaps the most pointed remarks on this subject came from Liberal MLA Dr. Michael Percy:

> There are no mechanisms of accountability in this Bill. There are mechanisms of subterfuge. There are mechanisms by which accountability can be off-loaded onto others. There are mechanisms by which responsibility could be delegated to others, but certainly no mechanism by which accountability is held to the minister that delegates.[68]

The Klein government's version of delegation exempted delegated administrative organizations from normal accountability expectations. For example, the auditor general's authority extends only to "every ministry, department, regulated fund and Provincial agency."[69] It doesn't extend to the actions of nonprofit societies or corporations such as the CCEMC. Furthermore, the *Climate Change and Emissions Management Administration Regulation* exempted the CCEMC from the controls and strictures imposed on government agencies by the *Financial Administration Act*. The minister wasn't required to table the CCEMC's business plans or annual reports in the legislature. In fact, the minister wasn't required to report to the legislature about the CCEMC in any fashion at all. Without regular reporting requirements, it might not have been surprising that no one noticed some troubling CCEMC decisions—such as abandoning a public statement about its performance measures.

Government appointments to boards of directors may be another accountability measure. Government appointees could use their positions to evaluate and monitor the performance of the CCEMC. Alberta Environment saw appointments in this light.[70] It appointed senior officials to the boards of delegated administrative organizations such as the Alberta Recycling Management Authority, the Alberta Used Oil Management Association, and the Beverage Container Management Board. This practice wasn't followed when the first CCEMC board was appointed. In fact, a departmental representative wasn't appointed to the CCEMC's board until sometime in 2014–15. Not to make light of what the Beverage Container Management

Board does for Albertans and a healthier environment, but I suspect the responsibilities of the CCEMC were at least as significant. You might expect that, if the provincial government took its evaluation and monitoring duties seriously, the minister would have put a senior official on the CCEMC's board before 2014–15. After all, by the end of CCEMC's 2013–14 year the Corporation had committed more than $222.4 million to 87 GHG emissions reductions projects.[71]

By 2015, the CCEMC speculated that its project commitments would reduce GHG emissions by 11.1 million tonnes by 2020.[72] Table 9 details how that funding was allocated between seven different types of projects. It portrays the extent to which the tar sands/petroleum sector benefited from the Fund. The Renewable Energy category received the most support from the Fund. Thirty-five percent of the funds committed by the CCEMC were channelled into wind, solar, and other renewable projects that promised to reduce greenhouse gas emissions by 6.45 million tons by 2020. The CCEMC data suggest that tar sands interests did not benefit from any of the renewable energy project funding.

The tar sands sector fared much more favourably when it came to how the CCEMC allocated funds to carbon capture and sequestration, cleaner energy production, and energy efficiency projects. By 2015, the Corporation had allocated an aggregate total of just over $114 million to projects in these categories, projects estimated to reduce GHG emissions by 3.57 million tonnes. This projected contribution to reducing emissions is 45 percent less than what CCEMC-supported renewable energy projects are expected to deliver by the 2020 target date. Virtually all—nearly 94 percent—of the dollars devoted to these three types of projects went to oil and gas interests. China National Offshore Oil Corporation, Cenovus, ConocoPhillips, Devon, Encana, Husky, Imperial Oil, MEG Energy, and Suncor—all companies with tar sands interests—were among the oil and gas companies receiving some of the more than $106 million the CCEMC channelled into these types of projects. As of 2015, the petroleum sector had received just over 50 percent of all the financial support GHG emissions reduction projects received from the Fund.

The Fund subsidized petroleum companies in some cases. Some beneficiaries of CCEMC decisions recognize the Fund's dollars are implementing technologies the companies already knew would improve the energy efficiency of their operations. The nearly $20 million the Fund contributed to energy efficiency projects involving Suncor, Encana, Cenovus, NR Green Power/Alliance Pipeline, and ConocoPhillips were essentially dollars that lowered the costs of implementing proven technologies.

Some deflect or counter the subsidization argument by emphasizing the leveraging impact of the Fund. The availability of CCEMC dollars prompts

Table 9 CCEMC Projects, by Sector, as of 2015

	Total No. of projects	Total project $	No. of oil/gas projects	Oil/gas projects	Oil/gas $ as a percentage of total
Carbon capture & sequestration	8	11,442,331	7	10,942,332	95.6
Renewable energy	13	74,321,788	0	0	0.0
Cleaner energy production	12	67,101,984	11	66,596,190	99.2
Energy efficiency	13	35,501,957	10	29,302,757	82.5
Adaptation	3	7,000,000	0	0	0.0
Carbon uses	24	11,976,215	0	0	0.0
Biological	15	4,989,784	0	0	0.0
Totals	**88**	**212,334,059**	**28**	**106,841,279**	**50.3**

Source: Climate Change and Emissions Management Corporation, *Annual Reports*, various years.

or stimulates corporate investments that otherwise wouldn't be made. Minister Renner drew on this relationship when he answered a question in the legislature from a fellow Progressive Conservative in 2011:

> I think it's interesting to note that the rate at which the leveraging occurs on these programs is about 5 to 1, so to date approximately a hundred million dollars have been expended by this board, and that has resulted in about a $500 million investment.[73]

The CCEMC 2013–14 annual report claimed an average leverage ratio of 6.3:1; on average, other investors will contribute $6.30 to a project for every $1 the CCEMC invests.[74] Some of the comments on the Corporation's website acknowledged that the Fund supported investments that weren't first priorities on corporate drawing boards. Cenovus, for example, was pleased by the CCEMC's decision to contribute 35 percent of the $7.7 million cost of an energy efficiency project. That support enhanced the financial attractiveness to the company of becoming more efficient.[75] This logic appears, too, in Encana's reaction to the Fund's 41 percent contribution to the company's $5.9 million vent gas project:

> This project has to compete with a number of other projects in the rest of the corporation. Often energy efficiency projects aren't as competitive, so funding such as this enables the project to move ahead.[76]

The leveraging impact of the Fund is clear. But increasing investment or leveraging more investment isn't the objective of the Fund; reducing greenhouse gas emissions and improving adaptability to climate change are. The Fund's goal is to reduce greenhouse gas emissions by 2020. This should privilege projects with real promise to deliver on that reduction commitment. As noted above, the renewable energy projects, not the oil and gas projects, are estimated to make the most serious contribution to that 2020 objective.[77] That renewable energy projects didn't see more support suggests the CCEMC complemented a climate change policy that catered to large emitters of greenhouse gases such as the tar sands.[78]

The Keystone XL Pipeline

The climate-change thrust of the nascent international critique of the tar sands realized, at most, modest gains by the end of 2009. Transnational or foreign ENGOs enjoyed some success in getting their message into the media. But this success at awareness-raising didn't inspire Canadian policy makers to change their perspective or policies on the tar sands and climate change. They responded to media criticisms in kind with their own efforts to advertise the good things they claimed to already be doing in the tar sands. Their primary response was public relations: "We care, we are working hard, trust us."

In the United States the resolution from the 2008 Conference of Mayors might be the only notable victory for US anti-tar sands activists in the first decade of the twenty-first century. At the national level, Congress and the Executive Branch refused to limit the federal government's purchase of fuels derived in part from tar sands crude; this suggested that initiatives to restrict generally the supply of tar sands crude into American markets would be dead on arrival.

In 2011, a freshly minted transnational environmental group, 350.org, chose the tar sands as one focal point for its climate change campaign.[79] Founded by environmental writer Bill McKibben in 2008, the organization's ambitions were as sweeping as climate change itself—nothing less than creating a global climate movement.[80] 350.org's tar sands target was the Keystone XL pipeline project. TransCanada Corporation's Keystone XL project proposed to nearly double the capacity of the Keystone pipeline. It proposed to transport 830,000 barrels per day of petroleum, mostly from the tar sands, to the US Gulf Coast. Secretary of State Condoleezza Rice issued a presidential permit for the original Keystone pipeline in March 2008. Then the Bush administration welcomed the project because Keystone increased "US market access to crude oil supplies from a stable and reliable trading partner, Canada, that is in close proximity to the United States."[81] If 350.org could build a movement to stop Keystone XL, it would give the transnational environmental opposition its most important success in its climate change campaign against the tar sands.

Keystone XL speaks importantly to this book's themes. For those interested in the potential vitality of a transnational countermovement to market fundamentalism, Keystone XL highlights how important national political openings and institutions remain to the possibilities of such oppositional success. Bill McKibben realized that, by crossing the Canada–United States border, the Keystone XL pipeline was a different beast from domestic interstate pipelines. Keystone XL required a presidential permit to cross that border.[82] This requirement gave 350.org an opening to try to make Keystone XL an issue in the 2012 presidential election. It didn't have to concern itself with climate-change deniers in Congress. Instead this project had a regulatory focal point in the office of a president who took climate change seriously and had pledged to take action. McKibben wrote the following about what this institutional context meant for opposing Keystone XL:

> But this decision would be made by Barack Obama, and Barack Obama was fifteen months away from an election. Maybe we had an opening to apply some pressure—an opening to see if we'd nurtured a climate movement strong enough to make a difference.[83]

When McKibben and 350.org selected Keystone XL as a target, it looked like they might be too late. In October 2010, Secretary of State Hillary Clinton signalled that the United States likely was going to grant a presidential permit to Keystone XL. She told a San Francisco audience that, after her department had approved the Alberta Clipper tar sands pipeline in 2009, her office hadn't approved Keystone XL yet but she "was inclined to do so." National security figured importantly in her position because the United States was "either going to be dependent on dirty oil from the Gulf or dirty oil from Canada."[84]

Nonetheless 350.org and its allies pressed ahead. They made President Obama respond to their concerns about Keystone XL as he headed into the 2012 presidential election. They accomplished this first through impressive demonstrations at the White House in August, September, and November 2011. Here they departed from the "conventional political means" that most of their peers in the foreign and transnational anti-tar sands movement had used—information and lobbying. "We don't have the money to compete," McKibben wrote in an open letter to fellow environmentalists, "but we do have our bodies."[85] By the time the summer 2011 nonviolent mass protests ended, a total of 1,253 protesters had been arrested. More people had experienced the hospitality found in the cells of the Washington, DC, police department over those two weeks of anti-Keystone XL protests than had been arrested at any civil disobedience action in the United States since the nuclear protests of the 1980s.[86] As the last of the protesters was arrested, McKibben met with a senior White House official and promised that this climate action hadn't ended. Anti-Keystone XL activists would dog Obama as he toured the United States and demand that, if he wanted their support in 2012, he needed to reject the pipeline. Here they were joined by groups such as the NRDC, the Sierra Club, and Friends of the Earth.[87] While the environmentalists and landowners opposed to Keystone XL didn't secure their ultimate goal—presidential rejection of TransCanada's permit application—they succeeded in convincing President Obama to delay his decision until after the 2012 election.[88] In November 2011, the Department of State announced it needed to obtain additional information about issues such as alternatives to the proposed route through Nebraska's Sand Hills. Climate change concerns also were mentioned.[89] The announcement came three days after more than 10,000 protesters surrounded the White House and—exactly one year before the 2012 election—demanded that Obama reject Keystone XL.[90] The American Petroleum Institute's president saw the delay as being motivated by nothing more than electoral politics: "This is all about politics and keeping a radical constituency, opposed to any and all oil and gas development, in the president's camp in 2012."[91]

The Republican-controlled House of Representatives tried to force Obama's hand to decide the issue by February 21, 2012. Obama wouldn't rush to judgement. He responded to what a New York Times editorial called this "foolish requirement" by rejecting the permit until the Department of State had sufficient time to conduct a comprehensive environmental assessment.[92] Republican candidates for their party's presidential nomination relished the opportunity to make the pipeline an election issue; they supported its construction on national security and employment grounds. Mitt Romney, the party's eventual nominee, slammed Obama for demonstrating "a lack of seriousness about bringing down unemployment, restoring economic growth and achieving energy independence."[93] Several weeks after this interim decision from the president, 350.org spearheaded efforts by the environmental movement to flood the US Senate with messages opposing Keystone XL. In a 24-hour period, more than 800,000 anti-Keystone XL messages were delivered to US senators.[94]

350.org and a growing coalition of groups maintained, if not increased, this anti-Keystone XL campaign after the 2012 elections. Even the leaders of polite, mainstream environmental groups now were prepared to be arrested in anti-Keystone XL protests. In February 2013, Michael Brune, the Sierra

Club's executive director, was arrested in front of the White House. That arrest ended the Sierra Club's 120-year policy against civil disobedience. To read Brune's words you might think Keystone XL was the Antichrist. Brune said the pipeline "is so horrendous, it's so wrong, and it's being proposed at such an important time that we don't want to leave any tool on the table"; approving it would be apocalyptic, a "guarantee that we're locked into the most carbon-intensive fuel source on the planet for the next half-century."[95]

Days later, more than 35,000 rallied on the National Mall in Washington, DC, a rally organized by 350.org, Sierra Club, and the Hip Hop Caucus. Their point was a simple one—to show the president that they still expected him to reject the pipeline once and for all. The pressure from this movement didn't relent. Its resonance in the White House rested importantly in President Obama's wish for climate change action to be part of his legacy. 350.org finally got the decision they wanted from President Obama in November 2015. It was no coincidence that the president's decision to refuse to issue a permit because Keystone XL wasn't in the national interest came on the eve of the UN Paris Climate Change Conference. Rejecting Keystone XL reinforced the position President Obama wanted to portray in Paris. He wanted the world to believe that during his presidency the United States had become a leader in the global campaign to limit increases of greenhouse gases into the atmosphere. It would be hypocritical, a blow to Obama's credibility, to approve Keystone XL while sitting for his climate change portrait.[96]

Before leaving the Keystone XL issue, two other points should be made. The unexpected and explosive increases in US oil production courtesy of exploiting the shale oil resources in fields such as North Dakota's Bakken and Texas's Eagle Ford diminished the importance of national security concerns in the second term of Obama's presidency. The dramatic increases in US shale oil and gas production led the International Energy Agency to a stunning conclusion in its 2013 edition: the United States could meet all of its energy needs from domestic sources by 2035.[97] That diminished the need to evaluate Keystone XL according to the petroleum security perspective.

Also, Keystone XL wasn't the first opportunity environmentalists had during the Obama administration to play the presidential permit card. In August 2009, Secretary of State Hillary Clinton granted a permit to Enbridge's Alberta Clipper, a 450,000 barrels-per-day project that now delivers tar sands crude to Midwest refineries. This project received little to no attention during the 2008 electoral season. A cursory search of the Factiva database from May 2007 to November 2008 didn't uncover any stories suggesting any group was attempting to develop the type of national campaign Keystone XL faced. Plenty of weather stories about "Alberta Clippers" sweeping into the Dakotas, Minnesota, and the northeastern US were found; the only US story featuring environmental arguments against the pipeline version appeared in the Minneapolis *Star Tribune* on November 26, 2008, after the elections.[98] Minnesota's Public Utilities Commission gave its unanimous approval to the pipeline; the Minnesota Center for Environmental Advocacy first opposed the Alberta Clipper on greenhouse gas emission grounds. It also contended that American consumption and conservation trends suggested additional Canadian petroleum wasn't needed.[99] A coalition of environmental groups subsequently argued unsuccessfully that the Department of State's approval of the Enbridge pipeline violated the *National Environmental Policy Act*.[100] The absence of attention to the Alberta Clipper project compared to Keystone XL highlights that groups may not grasp the oppositional opportunities institutional openings afford them. Awareness and capacity are vital to seizing those opportunities. In the case of 350.org, the group was still in swaddling clothes. "We were in the process of organizing our first big day of action and had no capacity for fights like that," wrote Bill McKibben, "even if we'd known they were going on." Furthermore, a paper on Keystone XL that James Hansen published in June 2011 was very important in helping McKibben to understand the scale of what Hansen called the "tar sands monster." Hansen's work helped prompt 350.org to join Native Americans and landowners fight against Keystone XL.[101]

Conclusion

Alberta's environment department, the Climate Change and Emissions Management Corporation, and the Alberta Energy Regulator all used various forms of the word "transform" to describe the policy paths they followed after a more global environmental critique of the tar sands emerged. Alberta Environment claimed in 2011 to be transforming itself; it was moving away from focusing on specific projects toward taking a holistic, cumulative effects approach to evaluating environmental impacts. Year after year the department's annual reports highlighted the transformative nature of the CCEMC. The Corporation invested in projects with "transformative technologies";[102] it was "stimulating transformative change."[103] CCEMC Board Chair Eric Newell was confident his corporation would produce "transformative change."[104] The Alberta Energy Regulator also declared its loyalty to transformation. Transforming how the AER did its business was part of the Regulator's mission to be a "best-in-class regulator." This ambition included "becoming more effective in ensuring the safe, environmentally responsible development of Alberta's energy resources."[105]

As easy as it is to see claims about environmental transformation in government documents, it's very difficult to see the provincial policy changes required to lend credence to those claims. The transnational focus on climate change, with its demands for GHG emissions reductions from the tar sands, didn't budge successive Progressive Conservative administrations off the path of market fundamentalism the Klein administration had placed Alberta on. It was a heresy to suggest that the tar sands should be either taxed or regulated in ways that would force the sector to cap or reduce its aggregate emissions, or even to slow the rate of emissions growth. Rhetorically the government claimed great things would follow from its action on climate change. If Earth still was habitable in 2050, Alberta's GHG emissions reduction ambitions could claim credit for reducing the number of automobiles on the road by 40 million! Of course, realizing such heady ambitions assumed government would implement the suite of policies needed to realize them. Alberta's auditor general concluded plainly and categorically that such a commitment was nowhere to be found.

The emissions reduction intensity targets set through the *Specified Gas Emitters Regulation* were not very demanding on the tar sands sector. Their inconsequential impact was illustrated well by Syncrude's compliance history. Why reduce your emissions if it made more financial sense to pay a tax? Pay the state its $15 per ton carbon tax, continue business as usual, and generate exponential profits relative to the amount surrendered through this tax.[106]

The creation of the Climate Change Emissions Management Corporation continued Alberta's habit of delegating significant policy-making authority to corporate-dominated institutions with little or no accountability to government. The CCEMC's members were drawn overwhelmingly from the very sectors that were responsible for the explosive growth of industrial GHG emissions in Alberta. The healthy presence of petroleum sector capital on the CCEMC sometimes coincided with funding decisions that subsidized the very sectors whose members used the Fund to pay for, rather than reduce, emissions at their facilities.

If the state remained stubbornly unsympathetic to calls from ENGOs for more stringent policy, did the transnational climate change critique enjoy more success abroad? In the United States this critique's success varied from one institutional setting and one presidency to another. When the access of tar sands crude to American markets was raised as part of the legislative process, as it was with respect to the *Energy Independence and Security Act*, Congressional politics helped neuter the concerns about the tar sands' contribution to climate change. President Bush's support for expanding tar sands production and his lack of interest in being a global leader on the climate change file were also important obstacles to the environmentalist critique.

In the case of Keystone XL, the success of the opposition led by 350.org was owed in part to institutions—the presidential permit requirement.

Unlike in EISA, the executive branch was the only branch that needed to be convinced of the harm Keystone XL would contribute to. That permit requirement plus Obama's more sympathetic position to climate change concerns gave the opponents of the pipeline project genuine hope of success. Finally, there was the president's re-election prospects to consider. The ability of 350.org and other organizations to mobilize thousands to protest against Keystone XL certainly suggested that, if President Obama wanted their support in the 2012 election, he was wise to avoid approving the project.

Notes

1   Peter A. Hall and Rosemary C. R. Taylor, "Political Science and the Three New Institutionalisms," *Political Studies* 44 (1996).

2   Barack Obama, "Remarks in Las Vegas, Nevada," June 24, 2008, online at *The American Presidency Project*, Gerhard Peters and John T. Woolley, http://www.presidency.ucsb.edu/ws/?pid=77554.

3   Sheldon Alberts, "Obama Has Oilsands in His Sights; Pledge to Reduce Dependence on 'Dirty' Oil a Warning to Alberta Producers," *Vancouver Sun*, June 25, 2008, A12.

4   McGowan, "NASA's Hansen Explains Decision."

5   Natural Resources Defense Council, "Strip Mining for Oil in Endangered Forests," June 1, 2006, https://www.nrdc.org/resources/strip-mining-oil-endangered-forests; Natural Resources Defense Council, "Alberta Tar Sands Feed US Addiction to Oil," press release, June 30, 2006, https://www.nrdc.org/media/2006/060630.

6   Natural Resources Defense Council, Western Resource Advocates, and Pembina Institute, *Driving It Home: Choosing the Right Path for Fueling North America's Transportation Future* (June 2007), https://www.nrdc.org/sites/default/files/drivingithome.pdf; Natural Resources Defense Council, "Letter to the Governors of the Western Governors' Association on Tar Sands," June 26, 2008, https://www.nrdc.org/resources/letter-governors-western-governors-association-tar-sands.

7   Natural Resources Defense Council, "Don't Buy It; Tar Sands Oil Is Still Dirty," press release, April 29, 2008, https://www.nrdc.org/media/2008/080429-1.

8   Nikiforuk, *Tar Sands*.

9   Andrew Nikiforuk, *Dirty Oil: How the Tar Sands Are Fueling the Global Climate Crisis* (Greenpeace Canada: September 2009), http://www.greenpeace.org/canada/en/campaigns/Energy/tarsands/Resources/Reports/tar_sands_report/.

10   Nikiforuk, *Tar Sands*, 119; Nikiforuk, *Dirty Oil*, 5.

11   For examples, see Greenpeace Canada, "Tar Sands and Climate Change," fact sheet, 2010, http://www.greenpeace.org/canada/Global/canada/report/2010/4/ClimateChange_FS_Footnotes_rev_4.pdf and Polaris Institute, "Tar Sands Showdown—Climate Change", https://d3n8a8pro7vhmx.cloudfront.net/polarisinstitute/pages/78/attachments/original/1418934644/Factsheet_-_Climate_Change.pdf?1418934644.

12   Canadian Association of Petroleum Producers, "Greenhouse Gas Emissions," http://www.capp.ca/responsible-development/air-and-climate/greenhouse-

gas-emissions; Canadian Association of Petroleum Producers, "Canada's Oil Sands: GHG Emissions," http://www.canadasoilsands.ca/en/explore-topics/ghg-emissions.

13 Jon Harding, "Oilsands Hit Back at 'Dirty' Tag: Industry Launches Website as US Mayors Threaten to Stop Buying 'Tarsands' Fuel," *Calgary Herald*, June 24, 2008, A1.

14 United States Conference of Mayors, 76th Annual Meeting, Miami, 20–24 June 2008, "2008 Adopted Resolutions—High-Carbon Fuels," http://www.usmayors.org/resolutions/76th_conference/energy_05.asp, accessed September 27, 2015.

15 Section 526, entitled "Procurement and Acquisition of Alternative Fuels," read: "No Federal agency shall enter into a contract for procurement of an alternative or synthetic fuel, including a fuel produced from nonconventional petroleum sources, for any mobility-related use, other than for research or testing, unless the contract specifies that the lifecycle greenhouse gas emissions associated with the production and combustion of the fuel supplied under the contract must, on an ongoing basis, be less than or equal to such emissions from the equivalent conventional fuel produced from conventional petroleum sources." United States, Government Printing Office, *Energy Independence and Security Act of 2007*, Public Law 110–140-Dec. 19, 2007.

16 Paula Simons, "Alberta Blindsided by US Fuel Law; Ottawa, Province Must Work Together to Protect Our Interests on Capitol Hill," *Edmonton Journal*, September 16, 2008, A12.

17 *Carbon-Neutral Government Act of 2007*, H.R. 2635, 110th Cong. (2007–2008).

18 Pembina Institute, "Foreign Affairs Access to Information on Section 526," November 29, 2010, http://www.pembina.org/reports/foi-foreign-affairs.pdf, 26, 4.

19 Michael E. Canes and Rachael G. Jonassen, *EISA Section 526: Impacts on DESC Supply, Report DES86T1* (LMI Government Consulting, March 2009), A-9, www.dtic.mil/get-tr-doc/pdf?AD=ADA502264.

20 Canes and Jonassen, *EISA Section 526: Impacts on DESC Supply*, 2–1.

21 Pembina Institute, "Foreign Affairs Access," 3.

22 Pembina Institute, "Foreign Affairs Access," 6.

23 Pembina Institute, "Foreign Affairs Access," 15.

24 Ben Geman, "Canada Warns US Against Using Energy Law to Bar Fuel from Oil Sands," *Greenwire*, February 28, 2008.

25 These members of Congress were concerned despite Rep. Waxman's desire to exempt biomass fuels from Section 526.

26 Pembina Institute, "Foreign Affairs Access," 21, 22.

27 In May, the NRDC joined 26 other American and Canadian environmental groups in writing a letter to Members of the House and the Senate to express their opposition to repealing Section 526. Natural Resources Defense Council, "Environmental Groups Fight Attempt to Repeal Crucial Climate Provision from 2007 U.S. Energy Bill," press release, May 8, 2008, http://www.nrdc.org/media/2008/080507a.asp.

28 Canes and Jonassen, *EISA Section 526: Impacts on DESC Supply*, 2–1.

29 Representative Henry Waxman, "Letter to the Honorable Jeff Bingaman, Chairman, Senate Committee on Energy and Natural Resources," March 17, 2008 [emphasis added], http://www.alston.com/files/docs/Waxman-Bingaman%20Letter%20(2).pdf.

30   Canes and Jonassen, *EISA Section 526: Impacts on DESC Supply,* 2–1, 2–2.

31   In the 2010 fiscal year, US federal government fuel purchases represented about 2 percent of total American consumption of finished petroleum products. Harry M. Ng, American Petroleum Institute, "Letter to Donald Martin, Project Manager for NEPA, DLA Installation Support for Energy," Comment on DOD-2013-OS-0055–0001, April 22, 2013, http://www.regulations. gov/#!documentDetail;D=DOD-2013-OS-0055-0002.

32   Pembina Institute, "Foreign Affairs Access," 27.

33   *Sierra Club v. U.S. Defense Energy Support Center,* 41 ELR 20253.

34   Ng, "Letter to Donald Martin."

35   Gary Doer, Ambassador to the United States, "Letter to the Honorable Chuck Hagel, Secretary, U.S. Department of Defense," Public Comment on Department of Defense (DOD) Notice: Environmental Assessments; Availability, etc.: DLA Energy Mobility Fuel Purchasing Programs, April 18, 2013, http://www. regulations.gov/#!documentDetail;D=DOD-2013-OS-0055-0003.

36   Doer, "Letter to the Honorable Chuck Hagel."

37   Alberta, *Albertans & Climate Change: Taking Action* (October 2002), 11.

38   Alberta, *Albertans & Climate Change.* Alberta's emissions in 1990 actually were 175 million tonnes, not 171 million tonnes.

39   Alberta, *Albertans and Climate Change,* 12. See also the remarks by Dave Broda, the Progressive Conservative member for Redwater, in the Alberta legislature during the second reading debate on Bill 37. Alberta, *Alberta Hansard 25th Legislature, 3rd Session,* November 18, 2003, 1707 –1708.

40   Ian Urquhart, "The Devil Is in the Details: Implementing the Kyoto Protocol," in *Braving the New World: Readings in Contemporary Politics* (3rd ed.), edited by Roger Epp and Thomas Bateman (Scarborough, ON: Nelson Thomson Learning, 2004).

41   Bramley, *An Assessment of Alberta's Climate Change Action Plan,* 3.

42   Alberta, Auditor General of Alberta, *Report of the Auditor General of Alberta* (October 2008), 99.

43   Alberta, Alberta Environment, *Alberta's 2008 Climate Change Strategy: Responsibility/Leadership/Action* (January 2008), 24.

44   Alberta, like other major emitters of GHG emissions, changed the baseline for evaluating reductions from 1990 to 2005. A 14 percent reduction from the 233 million tonnes Alberta emitted in 2005 would have put Alberta's 2050 emissions at 200.4 million tonnes or 14.5 percent higher than the province's 1990 emissions. Alberta's 2008 strategy mistakenly reported that Alberta's emissions in 2005 were 205 million tonnes; in fact, according to the national inventory of greenhouse gases published by Environment Canada in 2007 the province's emissions were 231 million tonnes. Environment Canada, *National Inventory Report 1990–2005: Greenhouse Gas Sources and Sinks* (April 2007), 546.

45   Alberta Environment, *Alberta's 2008 Climate Change Strategy,* 4.

46   A megatonne is one million tonnes.

47   Alberta Environment, *Alberta's 2008 Climate Change Strategy,* 9.

48   "We're Lucky to Have an AG with Chutzpah," *Edmonton Journal,* October 4, 2008, A18.

49   The recommendation read in part: "We recommend that the Ministry of Environment improve the reliability, comparability and relevance of its public reporting on Alberta's success and costs incurred in meeting climate-change

targets." Auditor General of Alberta, *Report of the Auditor General of Alberta* (October 2008), 101.

50   Alberta, Auditor General of Alberta, *Report of the Auditor General of Alberta* (October 2012), 38.

51   Alberta Environment, *Alberta's 2008 Climate Change Strategy*, 23, 29.

52   Established facilities would have to satisfy this reduction immediately, beginning in 2008. New facilities wouldn't be allowed to exceed 98 percent of their baseline emissions intensity in their fourth year of operation. Their allowances in the fifth, sixth, seventh, and eighth years of operations would be 96, 94, 92, and 90 percent of their baseline emission intensity.

53   Alberta, Alberta Environment and Parks, "Specified Gas Emitters Regulation Compliance Reporting Summary, 2009–2014," data set.

54   The negative value for GHG emissions from facilities in 2009 was so slight (−5,461 tons) that it is difficult to see on Chart 2.

55   Suncor used 2,314,861 EPCs and offset credits between 2009 and 2014; it used 1,054,258 credits from the Climate Change Emissions and Management Fund. In the first three years of this period. Suncor generated 198,136 emission performance credits from its in situ operations. These could have been submitted as part of the 1,604,515 EPCs Suncor used in these years.

56   In January 2016, Canadian Oil Sands and Suncor agreed on a merger. Canadian Oil Sands shareholders received 0.28 of a share in Suncor for each share they held of Canadian Oil Sands. Jeff Lewis, "Suncor Reaches $4.2-Billion Deal with Canadian Oil Sands," *Globe and Mail*, January 18, 2016.

57   In 2009, the other six partners of Canadian Oil Sands in the Syncrude project were Imperial Oil (25%), Suncor (12%), ConocoPhillips Oilsands (9.03%), Nexen Oil Sands (7.23%), Murphy Oil (5%), and Mocal Energy (5%). In 2010, Sinopec Oil Sands purchased ConocoPhillips' share of the joint venture. In February 2013, CNOOC (China National Offshore Oil Corporation) completed its purchase of Nexen and assumed Nexen's share in Syncrude.

58   Alberta, "Legislation Backs Alberta's Plan to Reduce Emissions," news release, April 7, 2003, http://alberta.ca/release.cfm?xID=14168.

59   Alberta, Alberta Environment, "Industrial Emissions Management," http://aep.alberta.ca/climate-change/programs-and-services/industrial-emissions-management.aspx.

60   Alberta, "Chair Named to Manage Provincial Climate Change Fund," news release, May 6, 2009, http://www.alberta.ca/release.cfm?xID=2588916EB7350-94B1-016E-779CDCE024F9CDBE.

61   This conclusion is based on a search in the Factiva database for the phrase "Climate Change and Emissions Management Corporation" from May 1, 2009, to December 31, 2009. Only nine stories were discovered; two of them appeared in the *Edmonton Journal*, one in July and the other in November.

62   The other four members from businesses/sectors with interests in the tar sands were Jim Carter, O.C. (Syncrude), Charles Fischer (Nexen), Paul Galachiuk (Suncor), and Dr. Brenda Kenny (Canadian Energy Pipeline Association). Climate Change and Emissions Management Corporation, *2010 Annual Report*, 3.

63   In December 2015, the CCEMC board members were Kathleen Sendall, O.C. (chair), Doug Beever (fertilizer industry), Rick Blackwood (Government of Alberta), Jim Carter, O.C. (mineral manufacturing), Paul Clark (chemical

producers), Dr. Joseph Doucet (academia), Iris Evans (public at large),
Dr. Brenda Kenny (pipeline industry), Dr. Robert Mansell (public at large),
Patricia Mohr (public at large), Stephen Snyder (public at large), Aleasa Tasker
(forestry industry), Dr. Dan Wicklum (oil sands). The NDP government's
Climate Leadership Plan changed CCEMC's name to Emissions Reduction
Alberta in 2015. Sendall remained as board chair, and Kenny, Mansell, Carter,
Mohr, and Doucet remained as board members. Clive Mather, a former
Shell Canada CEO, joined the board, as did Sandra Locke (a Government
of Alberta representative) and Céline Bak, a senior Fellow of the Centre for
International Governance Innovation. The board now also contains its first
genuine representative from the ENGO sector, Sara Hastings-Simon from the
Pembina Institute.

64   Alberta, *Alberta Hansard, 27th Legislature, 4th Session*, Issue 17, March 22, 2011, 502.
65   *Alberta Hansard, 27th Legislature, 4th Session*, Issue 17, March 22, 2011, 496.
66   Alberta, *Government Organization Act*, Revised Statutes of Alberta 2000, Chapter
     G-10, Section 9(1).
67   Alberta, *Alberta Hansard, 23rd Legislature, 2nd Session* (1994–1995), October 24,
     1994, 2506.
68   Alberta, *Alberta Hansard, 23rd Legislature, 2nd Session* (1994–1995), October 26,
     1994, 2628.
69   Alberta, *Auditor General Act*, Revised Statutes of Alberta 2000 Chapter A-46,
     Section 11 (a). Sue Olsen, an Edmonton MLA, wrote a critical assessment of
     the emergence of delegated administration organizations in Alberta. See Sue
     Olsen, "The 'Delegated Administrative Organization' in Alberta," *Canadian
     Parliamentary Review* 20, no. 3 (Autumn 1997), 5–7.
70   Alberta, Alberta Environment, *Delegated Administrative Organizations: Monitoring
     and Evaluation Workbook* (December 2006), http://environment.gov.ab.ca/info/
     library/8271.pdf, accessed December 12, 2015.
71   Climate Change and Emissions Management Corporation (CCEMC),
     2013/2014 Annual Report, 13.
72   Climate Change and Emissions Management Corporation, "Projects," http://
     ccemc.ca/projects/.
73   Alberta, *Alberta Hansard, 27th Legislature, 4th Session*, Issue 5a, March 1, 2011,
     116–117.
74   Climate Change and Emissions Management Corporation, *2013/2014 Annual
     Report*, 10, 23.
75   Climate Change and Emissions Management Corporation, "Remvue/
     Slipstream Air/Fuel Ration Control and Vent Capture Project," http://ccemc.
     ca/project/remvueslipstream-airfuel-ratio-control-and-vent-capture-project/,
     accessed December 14, 2015.
76   Climate Change and Emissions Management Corporation, "Vent Gas Capture
     for Engine Fuel Use," http://ccemc.ca/project/vent-gas-capture-for-engine-
     fuel-use/, accessed December 14, 2015.
77   The lion's share of the 6.453653 million tonnes of greenhouse gas reductions
     promised by CCEM Fund-supported renewable energy projects came from
     one project, the 300 megawatt Blackspring Ridge Wind Project (4.2 million
     tonnes). CCEMC contributed $10,000,000 to this $600,000,000 project. The
     leverage ratio for this investment was a staggering 60:1.

78   The favourable treatment of large emitters by the CCEMC in the Corporation's awarding of renewable energy project funding has already been noted. Further confirmation of this predisposition to favour large emitters came from an interview with an owner of a renewable energy company. I was pointed to the eligibility criteria for the Corporation's September 2010 Renewable Energy Call for Proposals. Section 2.3 reads in part: "Engagement with an industry partner(s) responsible for GHG reductions is considered an asset." Climate Change and Emissions Management Corporation, *2010 Call for Proposals Guide and Instructions* (September 2010), 5.

79   350.org takes its name from Dr. James Hansen's conclusion that we must reduce carbon dioxide levels in the atmosphere to no more than 350 ppm (parts per million) in order to keep Earth in roughly the same climatological conditions we find her in today. In 2014, the global annual average of carbon dioxide in the atmosphere was 400 ppm. See World Meteorological Organization, "Globally Averaged CO_2 Levels Reach 400 Parts per Million in 2015" (press release), October 24, 2016, http://public.wmo.int/en/media/press-release/globally-averaged-co2-levels-reach-400-parts-million-2015.

80   350.org claimed to have members, friends, and allies in 188 countries in 2016.

81   United States, Department of State, "Keystone Pipeline Presidential Permit," media note, March 14, 2008, https://2001-2009.state.gov/r/pa/prs/ps/2008/mar/102254.htm.

82   The Department of State evaluates cross-border pipeline applications and recommends to the President whether the application should be approved or rejected. For a fuller discussion of the presidential permit requirement, see Ian Urquhart, "Institutions and Environmental Politics: The Keystone XL Pipeline Controversy," Paper presented at the Annual Meeting of the Midwest Political Science Association, Chicago, IL, April 2015.

83   Bill McKibben, *Oil and Honey: The Education of an Unlikely Activist* (New York: Henry Holt and Company, 2013), 16. Also see McKibben's account in *Ibid.*, 45–48.

84   Hillary Rodham Clinton, "Remarks on Innovation and American Leadership to the Commonwealth Club," excerpts, Global Washington, October 15, 2010, http://globalwa.org/2010/10/secretary-clintons-remarks-on-innovation-and-american-leadership-to-the-commonwealth-club/, accessed July 30, 2017. The official State Department text of Secretary Clinton's remarks was removed from the State Department website after the 2016 presidential election; Clinton's comments on Keystone XL are also reported in Lee-Anne Goodman, "US Set to Approve Keystone XL Pipeline," *Globe and Mail*, October 20, 2010.

85   Jane Mayer, "Taking It to the Streets," *New Yorker* 87, no. 38 (November 28, 2011), 19.

86   McKibben, *Oil and Honey*, 43.

87   Mayer, "Taking It to the Streets," 20.

88   Landowners, represented by the group Bold Nebraska, were part of the coalition that formed to oppose Keystone XL.

89   US Department of State, "Keystone XL Pipeline Project Review Process: Decision to Seek Additional Information," press release, November 10, 2011. http://www.state.gov/r/pa/prs/ps/2011/11/176964.htm, accessed April 11, 2015. This press release is no longer on the US Department of State website.

90   Democracy Now, "10,000 Surround White House to Protest Keystone XL Tar Sands Oil Pipeline," November 7, 2011, http://www.democracynow.org/2011/11/7/10_000_surround_white_house_to.

91   John M. Broder and Dan Frosch, "US Delays Decision on Pipeline Until After Election," *New York Times*, November 10, 2011. http://www.nytimes.com/2011/11/11/us/politics/administration-to-delay-pipeline-decision-past-12-election.html?_r=0.

92   "A Good Call on the Pipeline," *New York Times*, January 18, 2012.

93   John M. Broder and Dan Frosch, "Rejecting Pipeline Proposal, Obama Blames Congress," *New York Times*, January 18, 2012.

94   McKibben, *Oil and Honey*, 83–85; 350.org, "Over 800,000 Americans Tell the Senate: Stop Keystone XL," February 14, 2012, https://350.org/over-800000-americans-tell-senate-stop-keystone-xl/.

95   Lauren Feeney, "Why the Sierra Club Broke Tradition to Protest the Keystone Pipeline," *Moyers & Company*, February 13, 2013, http://billmoyers.com/2013/02/14/sierra-club-lifts-120-year-ban-on-civil-disobedience-to-protest-keystone-xl-pipeline/.

96   The White House, "Statement by the President on the Keystone XL Pipeline," November 6, 2015, https://www.whitehouse.gov/the-press-office/2015/11/06/statement-president-keystone-xl-pipeline; Sarah Wheaton, "Obama's Fragile Climate Legacy," *Politico*, December 13, 2015, http://www.politico.com/story/2015/12/climate-change-obama-paris-216716.

97   International Energy Agency, *World Energy Outlook 2013 (Executive Summary)* (Paris: International Energy Agency, 2013), 1.

98   An Alberta clipper is a winter low-pressure weather system, originating in Alberta, that moves very rapidly in a southeasterly direction.

99   H. J. Cummins, "New Oil Pipeline Across State Approved; It Would Be a Boon to the North Central US, Supporters Argued. Foes Cited Extracting Methods Used for the Oil," *Star Tribune*, November 26, 2008, 2D.

100 *Sierra Club v. Clinton*, 689 F. Supp. 2d 1147 (2010).

101 Bill McKibben, e-mail message to author, November 2, 2016; James Hansen, "Silence Is Deadly," June 3, 2011, http://www.columbia.edu/~jeh1/mailings/2011/20110603_SilenceIsDeadly.pdf.

102 Alberta Environment, *Annual Report 2010–2011*, 50.

103 Alberta Environment and Sustainable Resource Development, *Annual Report 2014–2015*, 15.

104 Climate Change and Emissions Management Corporation, *2010 Annual Report: Charting a Path for Change*, 1. This mission is reiterated in the Corporation's *2013–14 Annual Report*. Other phrases used by the Corporation since its inception in its annual reports are: "transformative technology," "transformational discoveries and ways of doing business," "potentially transforming our economy," and "transforming carbon from a liability into an asset."

105 Alberta Energy Regulator, "AER Bulletin 2014-31: Changes to the Guidelines for Submission of a Predisturbance Assessment and Conservation and Reclamation Plan," October 9, 2014, http://www.aer.ca/documents/bulletins/AER-Bulletin-2014-31.pdf. The transformation theme also animates the AER's update to its strategic plan. See Alberta Energy Regulator, "AER Strategic Plan," https://www.aer.ca/aer-strategic-plan.

106 Before the end of the Chrétien Liberal government, Ottawa proposed to levy a carbon tax of no more than $15 per ton on oil sands producers as part of a proposed plan to meet Canada's Kyoto Protocol obligations. Canadian Oil Sands Ltd. estimated in January 2003 that such a tax would increase Syncrude's operating costs by 22 to 30 cents per barrel; "Trust Puts Kyoto Cost at Up to 30 Cents a Barrel," *Globe and Mail*, January 25, 2003, B2; Urquhart, "The Devil Is in the Details."

9

An Inconvenient Truth: New Government, Same Approach

"Do nothing by halves
Which can be done by quarters."
–F. R. Scott, "W.L.M.K." 1957

Introduction

Progressive Conservative Premier Jim Prentice was joyful. He smiled at his audience, hands upraised in V for victory signs. The accompanying text to this cover photo on the March 2015 issue of *Alberta Views* explained why. He had "RESCUED THE PCs, SWALLOWED THE OPPOSITION AND TOOK TOTAL CONTROL OF ALBERTA." Two months later, that photo and text were as mistaken as the famous *Chicago Daily Tribune* headline the day after the 1948 American presidential election: "DEWEY DEFEATS TRUMAN." Jim Prentice's "total control" in Alberta vanished in May 2015 when Rachel Notley and the New Democratic Party stunned Prentice and the Progressive Conservative dynasty. The NDP routed the party that had ruled Alberta continuously since 1971. Prentice had called an early election, ostensibly to secure a mandate from Albertans to implement his April 2015 budget. The election decimated and humiliated the PCs. They lost 60 of the 70 seats they had held previously in the 84-seat legislature. Notley, the bright, charismatic, and pragmatic NDP leader, was swept into power with 54 seats, 50 more than the New Democrats held after the 2012 general election.

This seismic event in Alberta politics tossed out the political architects of the market/business-led tar sands boom in Alberta. A centre-left party replaced the disciples of market fundamentalism. The New Democrats had consistently criticized Progressive Conservative governments for privileging business at the expense of the public and the environment. The Progressive Conservatives hadn't secured enough economic rent for Albertans; they hadn't sufficiently protected Alberta's air, water, and land. Environmentalists from all points on the activist continuum welcomed the NDP's victory as a signal that Albertans wanted change. Pembina Institute Executive Director Ed Whittingham applauded the NDP for aspiring to be a climate change leader, for wanting to craft "a credible plan to manage the growth in greenhouse gas pollution from the oilsands, and meet Alberta's 2020 climate target."[1] Greenpeace's Mike Hudema looked forward to working with the NDP government "to create a prosperous province that not only does its fair share to fight climate change, but leads the country in creating the diverse, green energy economy our world so desperately needs."[2]

Did a new, centre-left government in Alberta challenge the importance of market fundamentalism to tar sands policy-making? That's the question we consider here with respect to royalties, tailings ponds regulations, and climate change. The enthusiasm of environmentalists for the NDP is understandable, since centre-left or left-wing political parties would be more likely than parties to their right to challenge market fundamentalism. Yet, to the extent that market fundamentalism is embedded in society and is considered vital to electoral success, centre-left parties may need to temper their criticism or policy challenges to market fundamentalism in order to secure needed political support.

The Bill Clinton administration in the US offers one example of this. One of Clinton's 1992 campaign promises was to "end welfare as we know it." Two years—that was the maximum amount of time he proposed to allow welfare recipients to receive that state benefit. Clinton's oversimplified rhetoric— "bumper-sticker politics"—paid dividends; it helped the Democrats win the White House in the 1992 election.[3] This plank of his platform appealed to elites and the public alike. Both viewed the welfare system as the problem, not the solution, when it came to reducing poverty. Welfare rewarded laziness and broke up the nuclear family.[4] On the eve of the 1996 presidential election, Clinton approved a stricter reinterpretation of his position presented in Republican-sponsored legislation as he signed their welfare reform legislation.[5] The *Personal Responsibility and Work Opportunities Reconciliation Act* was an ode to market fundamentalism and pulled the safety net out from under many of America's poor.[6] Block and Somers attribute greater Democratic success in presidential elections beginning with Clinton in part to the fact that, by bowing to market fundamentalism in welfare policy, the Democrats immunized themselves from Republican attacks on this issue.[7]

Great Britain's Tony Blair government is an even more pertinent example for this book of how centre-left parties may stay, at least in part, on the path of market fundamentalism. The assessment of Anthony Giddens, one architect of the "Third Way" ideological positioning of Blair's New Labour, speaks to this British political reality. It is a mistake to view Blair's efforts on the social justice front during his years in power as simply a continuation of Thatcherism, according to Giddens. But Blair's courting of business and the financial sector went too far; that political necessity evolved "into fawning dependence" and turned Britain "into a kind of gigantic tax haven":[8]

> Yet Blair and Brown should have made it much clearer than they did that recognizing the virtues of markets is quite different from prostrating oneself before them. Market fundamentalism should have been more explicitly criticised and its limitations exposed.[9]

This loyalty to market fundamentalism was particularly pronounced in the energy sector. Chapter Three noted Britain's place in the liberal renaissance in petroleum of the early 1990s. Rather than pull back from that embrace, this orientation became more powerful during the Blair years. Rather than being challenged, market fundamentalism in British energy policy "reached its apogee" under Tony Blair.[10]

The policy history of Canada's Chrétien Liberals also did not challenge the dominance of market fundamentalism in tar sands policy-making. Their taxation and climate change policies between 1995 and 2006 helped facilitate the tar sands boom. All of these political records suggest we shouldn't expect that a change in Alberta's governing party, in and of itself, would necessarily deflate the importance of market ideology and business interests in provincial policy-making toward the tar sands.

Let's Talk Royalties[11] (Again)

Both the Liberal and the New Democrat opposition parties scorned the royalty changes Premier Stelmach's Progressive Conservative government made in October 2007. Brian Mason, the NDP leader in 2007, asserted that the changes meant Alberta would collect "less royalties than almost every other country in the world"; the changes subsidized tar sands projects; and Alberta needed to follow in the footsteps of Republican Governor Sarah Palin of Alaska or Progressive Conservative Premier Danny Williams of Newfoundland and Labrador and raise royalties.[12] In her first session as an MLA, Rachel Notley echoed her leader's charges. Premier Stelmach had delivered "a trivial royalty increase."[13] Nearly seven years later, the NDP were still calling for increases in petroleum royalties; Notley asserted that Alberta's royalty regime collected less than what the province's peers received:

> I will say simply that the measures of what we collect relative to other jurisdictions in a similar situation to ours show that we collect the lowest amount. That says to me that there is room for us to capitalize on our natural resources for the benefit of the people who elected us as opposed to for the benefit of the multinational companies who are extracting that oil.[14]

On the eve of the 2015 provincial election, Rachel Notley sponsored a private member's bill in the legislature. Bill 209, the *Commission to Safeguard*

Albertans' Interests in Natural Resources Act, would constitute the NDP's open-ing position in the election campaign on the issue of royalties. The pro-posed Commission would recommend targets and indicators that should be used in order for Albertans to receive fair returns from their nonrenewable resources. It would hold public hearings and report annually to the legisla-ture. First Nations, industry, labour, energy economics experts, and sustain-able development experts all would be guaranteed representation on the Commission. Royalties joined value-added processing of resources such as upgrading bitumen and long-term, sustainable management of nonrenew-able resources as a target and indicator the Commission would have to take into consideration. Increasing the amount of bitumen upgraded into syn-thetic crude oil or other products in Alberta had been a longstanding policy of the New Democrats, not least because it was central to the oil sands policy perspective of a key political supporter—the Alberta Federation of Labour.[15]

The importance of this institutional innovation to governing the petro-leum sector faded throughout the campaign, although it featured promi-nently at the outset. Notley promised the NDP would create a Resource Owner's Rights Commission (ROR Commission) that would make recom-mendations within six months of the NDP forming a government; a Not-ley administration would act on these recommendations within a year. The Commission was the NDP's response to Progressive Conservative govern-ments that had "blindly refused" to promote upgrading resources in Alberta. She said the Progressive Conservatives had "squandered our wealth with the fire sale of our resources and with royalties that have not earned fair and full value of those resources for the people of Alberta."[16]

As the unthinkable seemed increasingly likely—that the New Democrats would form a government—industry joined the PCs and Wildrose Party in attacking the NDP's proposal to establish a commission to review royalties. Cenovus CEO Brian Ferguson reprised the response his company had made to the proposals of the 2007 Royalty Review Panel. There wasn't any room to increase royalties, and if future changes made Alberta's regime uncompetitive then investment in the province would suffer, he said.[17] Notley responded by shifting course. She wouldn't threaten oil and gas, the strengths of Alberta's economy; she agreed with Ferguson about the importance of competitive-ness and pledged to work closely with Ferguson and his industry on any royalty review her government went ahead with. Her position on increasing royalties now was more ambiguous than what she had told NDP supporters at the start of the campaign: "We can't predetermine the outcome of that review—it may or may not determine an increase is necessary."[18] The "fire sale" metaphor had vanished. To Don Braid, the *Calgary Herald* columnist, Notley sounded "far less zealous than Stelmach did about raising royalties."[19]

The course of events after the election confirmed Braid's suspicions. The Resource Owner's Rights Commission vanished from the policy option landscape. Instead, Premier Notley opted to create an ad hoc, "one-time only" royalty review panel. It was a pale reflection of what the ROR Commission promised. Bill 209's imperative to include representatives from First Nations and labour on a royalty review panel was dismissed. So too was the idea that Albertans needed an independent commission to monitor and report annually to the legislature about whether they were getting a fair return from exploiting their nonrenewable resources.

The NDP government's timidity certainly responded to the dramatic post-June 2014 fall in the price of oil. West Texas Intermediate fetched US$105.15 per barrel in June 2014; that same barrel could be bought for $59.83 in June 2015. Western Canadian Select, the heavy oil blend that approximates the product used to calculate oil sands royalties in Alberta, fell in lockstep with WTI. In June 2015, the per-barrel price of WCS had fallen to US$51.29 from $86.56 the previous year. The crude oil price collapse continued into 2016 and seemed to have reached a bottom in February when the prices for WTI and WCS were US$30.62 and $16.30 respectively.[20] With the oil price collapse responsible for the loss of tens of thousands of direct and indirect jobs, the notion of increasing government's share of industry revenues was politically nonsensical.[21] This didn't mean, though, that the institutional changes to governing the petroleum sector outlined by the New Democrats needed to be discarded. The ROR Commission's promised changes—broader representation of Albertans and regular monitoring and reporting to elected representatives—were not tied to any specific royalty rate. Those governance modifications didn't depend on whether royalties were increased, decreased, or left unchanged.

Premier Notley's Royalty Review Advisory Panel was a pale reflection of the review panel Premier Stelmach established in 2007. The Stelmach panel was larger (six members as opposed to four) and, in one important sense, more transparent than the Notley government's advisory panel. In the case of the first panel's work, transcripts from 14 days of public hearings were published. No transcripts were published of the meetings held by the 2015 review panel.

As well, there was a vital difference between the two panels with respect to the depth of their economic expertise. With three economists—Judith Dwarkin, Kenneth McKenzie, and André Plourde—the first review panel exhibited a wealth and breadth of academic and private sector economic expertise. Peter Tertzakian, the chief energy economist and managing director of ARC Financial Corporation, was the only economist the Notley government appointed to its four-member advisory panel. He was appointed "for his passion for energy issues, his unique financial and operational expertise in the industry, and for his understanding of domestic and global economies."[22] At ARC Financial since 2002, Tertzakian was undoubtedly well-qualified to further the company's mission "to be Canada's leading energy focused private equity investor."[23] In 2007, the company was indeed Canada's largest energy-focused private equity firm, managing $1.9 billion of equity capital; in 2016, ARC retained that distinction—only the capital it was managing had nearly tripled to $5.3 billion.

Appointing Tertzakian as the only economist on the panel made perfect sense if the government wanted to reassure CEOs like Brian Ferguson that its advisory panel was acutely sensitive to a pro-investment perspective. Here it's important to appreciate that the officials who would have recommended and vetted Tertzakian's appointment came from the "old guard," a cadre of senior public servants who had served Alberta Energy under the Progressive Conservatives. Premier Notley didn't make any changes at the most senior administrative levels—assistant deputy minister and deputy minister—of Alberta Energy when her administration took power. Long-serving assistant deputy ministers such as Mike Ekelund (Strategic Initiatives/Resource Revenue and Operations) and Steve Tkalcic (Oil Sands) would have been well aware of Tertzakian's previous experience with an Alberta government royalty review panel. In 2007, he presented ARC Financial's submission to Premier Stelmach's panel. At a time when WTI was trading at US$67.53 ($77.19 in 2015 dollars), the ARC Financial submission asserted that Alberta's prosperity was at risk; there was no evidence that long-term excess resource rent existed; actors outside Alberta were concerned about the province's fiscal stability; many junior companies were struggling; Canada was "one of the highest cost sources of oil and gas in the world"; natural gas investment capital was going elsewhere because of Canada's high costs. Accordingly, ARC Financial urged the government to avoid putting the "burden" of additional royalties on the oil and gas industry. "We suggest maintaining the current royalty structure," the submission read, "until Alberta's citizens can be assured that risks and vulnerabilities are mitigated, and that a sustainable level of excess rent is available."[24]

Less than a month before the May 2015 election, ARC Financial released a report written by Tertzakian and Kara Jakeman. The report detailed the sad state of the Canadian oil and gas industry. Cash flow, so crucial to the ability of operating firms to reinvest, was at a 15-year low. The industry's pulse was weak and, even if prices rose by 10 to 15 percent in 2016, the industry wouldn't be in "full health."[25] Even if WTI wasn't trading at only US$45.47 in September 2015, it's not unreasonable to suggest that Tertzakian's policy analyses and recommendations from 2007 and 2015 didn't make him a panelist likely to recommend increasing the "burden" of royalties on the Alberta oil and gas industry.

There is a striking symmetry between Tertzakian's comments to the Stelmach review panel and one of the significant planks of the advisory panel report he helped to craft in 2015. Investment was a central theme of his presentation in 2007. When Tertzakian appeared before the 2007 royalty review panel, he declared himself to be "a representative of the financial community." In that role he noted that ARC Financial had embarked on a global strategy and that his company may or may not invest in Alberta or in other jurisdictions based on "where the most favourable rates of return are for the types of risks that we take." Alberta depended heavily on investment "from financial institutions and sources of capital from all around the world." The province's prosperity, its energy security, and its energy affordability all depended "on a healthy climate for investment and reinvestment."[26] The 2015 panel report echoed this sentiment:

> *Alberta companies compete for capital investment.* As a relatively small jurisdiction, we depend on outside investment to produce and sell our resources. Today's interconnected world offers investors many different options in many different sectors and countries.[27]

The 2015 panel decided to add "competitive" and "economic standpoint" overlays to its approach to royalties, which coincided well with the perspective that Tertzakian and ARC Financial presented to the 2007 review panel.[28] So too did the 2015 panel's point that the smaller size of Alberta's resident workforce allegedly drove up labour costs in the petroleum sector.[29]

The appointment of Doug Mowat, the President and CEO of ATB Financial, to chair the Notley royalty review panel also signalled the NDP panel would be unlikely to recommend increasing petroleum royalties. Unlike Bill Hunter, the chair of the 2007 Royalty Review Panel, Mowat had a direct corporate interest in Alberta's oil and gas sector through his leadership position in ATB Financial. ATB Financial's 2015 *Annual Report* stated that the Corporate Financial Services group (CFS)—the group responsible for lending to the energy sector—generated 23 percent of the company's revenue; the CFS syndication group was second-ranked among banks in terms of the number of energy deals led.[30] ATB Financial's website describes the energy group within CFS as "one of the largest units in Canada that specializes in energy lending."[31] The importance of lending to energy firms had a sadder face as oil prices collapsed after August 2014; ATB Financial increased its provision for credit losses by 71 percent in 2015, to $72.6 million. Not surprisingly, the health of the Alberta petroleum sector figured prominently in ATB Financial's discussion of risk management:

> The effects of the recent plunge in oil prices have shown that the volatility of energy prices, particularly oil prices, is a profound risk to both the Alberta economy and ATB. Alberta is Canada's largest oil-producing province, and ATB is geographically bound by its mandate to operate predominantly in this province.[32]

As was the case for Peter Tertzakian, it's difficult to see Doug Mowat as a potential champion of increasing the public treasury's share of petroleum rents, not least because of the "profound risk" oil price volatility presented to his company.

Unlike Premier Stelmach in 2007, Premier Notley responded immediately to the advisory panel's recommendations—simultaneously, in fact, with the release of the panel's report. Her government accepted all of the panel's recommendations. With respect to the tar sands, the report was, on the royalty rate front, a non-event. No changes were recommended to oil sands royalties; no changes would be made to the rates on the product that would deliver most of Alberta's future nonrenewable resource revenues. The panel concluded the place where improvements could be made in the tar sands was with respect to the royalty calculation/collection process, not rates. Government should increase its diligence in ensuring that tar sands companies followed the letter of the law with respect to the costs they deducted from their revenues for royalty purposes. Government should also improve the disclosure of information to the public about tar sands operations.[33] Premier Notley promised "an unprecedented level of transparency."[34] When it came to upgrading bitumen, the panel would not go any further than recommending government should examine what opportunities there might be for accelerating the partial upgrading of bitumen—this was a far cry from what the NDP had said in opposition and during the early days of the 2015 campaign. Furthermore, the recommendation, and Notley's acceptance of it, refuted the research the Alberta Federation of Labour had commissioned on building bitumen upgraders in Alberta.[35]

Industry was pleased. CAPP complimented the advisory committee for its "balanced" report; the report and the premier's reaction to it had "been the result of a fair and credible process, one Albertans can trust"; the new royalty structure was "principle-based" and gave industry the predictability it needed to make future investments.[36] The Alberta Federation of Labour, on the other hand, was far from happy. The AFL released its own position paper on royalties—one that contradicted the direction the government followed when it accepted the advisory panel's recommendations.[37] Gil McGowan, the Federation's president, sharply criticized the premier's refusal to increase royalty rates at higher prices, were those prices to return. "To say that we are disappointed," he said, "would be an understatement. Virtually none of the evidence that the NDP itself has relied upon over the years was considered by the panel."[38] Neither the report, the premier's endorsement, nor subsequent policy announcements endorsed the AFL's call to build bitumen upgraders in Alberta.[39] At the end of the day the only difference between the Notley government's handling of the tar sands royalty framework and that of Premiers Prentice and Redford was that those Progressive Conservative premiers didn't spend $3 million on a review panel before standing pat.

Directive 085: Letting the Fox Guard the Henhouse?

That was the rhetorical question NDP leader Brian Mason posed in 2008 as dead birds were being fished out of the Aurora tailings reservoir. Syncrude, Mason charged, failed to follow regulations, behaviour he equated with the government letting industry monitor itself and letting the fox guard the henhouse.[40] Mason questioned whether the Progressive Conservative government had the political will to act. He asked Minister Renner when the government was "going to take action and bring forward a plan for the systematic reduction and elimination of these tailings ponds."[41] Nearly a year later he urged the government to bring in a plan to clean up tailings reservoirs in no more than 10 to 20 years and to insist on new projects using dry tailings technology.[42]

With a majority in the legislature, Notley's New Democrats had an excellent opportunity to blaze a new trail and implement the type of plan the former leader of the NDP had called for. It didn't seize that opportunity. Instead the NDP followed its predecessor's script for addressing the environmental blight caused by tailings reservoirs. By the fall of 2016, nothing significant distinguished the NDP approach from the Progressive Conservative one. When the Alberta Energy Regulator suspended Directive 074 in March 2015, the government simultaneously released *Lower Athabasca Region—Tailings Management Framework for the Mineable Athabasca Oil Sands*.[43] The framework surrendered to industry's criticisms of Directive 074. As noted in Chapter Seven, the PC government abandoned the regulator's increasingly stringent targets for industry; it discarded an industry-wide goal for tailings management and reclamation—instead the "unique features of every project" must be considered; operational success demanded that cost-effectiveness join environmental and social considerations in managing tailings.

This new framework ironically identified Directive 074 as an important contributor to making Alberta's regulatory regime for tailings management "stringent." The failure to implement Directive 074 casts doubt on that characterization. But if the framework's claim lacked accuracy, it more than made up for that with chutzpah—the AER suspended the directive on the very same day the new framework, noting Directive 074's important contribution to the regulatory system, was released.[44] To read the *Tailings Management Framework* you wouldn't suspect that Directive 074 had been suspended.

The new NDP government neither abandoned nor tightened this more relaxed framework. It guided the AER as the Regulator prepared a new tailings management regulation. Not surprisingly, this new regulation—Directive 085—institutionalized the more flexible and industry-friendly regulatory approach. It affirmed that all fluid tailings would have to be ready to reclaim within 10 years of the end of a tar sands mine's life. The "ready to reclaim" condition is noteworthy, since meeting it signalled only that the actual reclamation of a mine could commence. Mine operators were left to identify the optimum solutions for managing the tailings produced by their projects without an assigned universal, industry-wide standard or requirement to strive for. Although operators will report annually to the AER about how their optimal solutions are progressing, Directive 085 strikes a lenient and accommodating posture when it comes to the consequences of noncompliance. The specific requirements that would be incorporated into the Directive's surveillance and compliance processes weren't finalized. Initially the AER would be relying on its existing compliance and enforcement tools as well as the suite of "potential management actions" listed in the tailings management framework document. "Potential" is a telling adjective. Even if, years from now, a mine's tailings volume was 140 percent of the end-of-mine-life target, the Regulator wouldn't necessarily impose the "highest consequence regulatory instruments" on the company. It wouldn't necessarily curtail production or impose penalties or reject new approvals.[45] These "most critical pieces," in the words of the Pembina Institute's Chris Severson-Baker, still needed to be developed.[46]

Chris Varcoe, a *Calgary Herald* business columnist, astutely used the term "guidelines" to describe the substance of Directive 085.[47] The CAPP endorsed the new directive as "a positive outcome that establishes a clear and achievable regulatory environment for industry—one that ensures full reclamation of oil sands tailings over a reasonable timeframe."[48] If the Notley government was going to demand and enforce a better, more immediate, environmental performance from the tar sands industry, it wasn't going to happen in the area of tailings reservoir reclamation.

Alberta's Climate Leadership Plan

Expectations were high that, if given the opportunity, the New Democrats would make significant changes to Alberta climate change policy. Premier Notley criticized the Progressive Conservatives' emissions intensity approach to tackling climate change on several occasions in 2008 and 2009. She pinned unflattering labels such as "fundamentally flawed," "completely ineffective," and "laughable" on that approach.[49] The Progressive Conservatives were chastised for not promising any real reductions in emissions until 2050 and for not doing anything to change that.[50] Notley charged that Environment Minister Renner's "stubborn reliance on intensity targets" threatened Alberta's access to US markets.[51]

She suggested that, if Alberta exhibited some political will, it could start to transition to a green economy. NDP leader Brian Mason proposed to create a $20 billion fund that a future NDP government would use to remove fossil fuels as an economic foundation in Alberta, develop renewable energy on a major scale, and become a world leader in green energy production.[52] For both MLAs, Alberta's resource wealth and royalties would finance this fund. "We can use our resource wealth," Notley argued, "to develop a strong green energy system and diversify our economy."[53]

As the criticisms above underlined, Notley's government inherited what charitably should be called an unambitious climate policy legacy. Alberta's legacy was that of a laggard; Alberta's contribution to Canada's GHG emissions, thanks largely to the tar sands boom, had grown spectacularly. At 274 megatons in 2014, Alberta's emissions were 57 percent higher than they were in 1990 (175 megatonnes). Alberta's 2014 emissions were only 14 megatonnes shy of the sum of emissions for *all* the other provinces and territories minus Ontario.[54] The climate change cards Premier Notley had to play were terrible.

Rather than fold, the premier committed to reversing that legacy and to becoming a climate change leader. Her minister responsible for the environment promised an effective plan that would help Alberta "achieve real, demonstrable reductions in greenhouse gas emissions."[55] The most important step on this quest was establishing a climate change policy review panel. Andrew Leach, an expert on the economics of climate change, would chair the panel. Five months later, after a wide-ranging consultation with the public, government, and industry, Premier Notley released and endorsed the panel's report. Four tar sands company CEOs and the Executive Directors of the Pembina Institute and Environmental Defence Canada were among those who shared the stage with the premier when she unveiled Alberta's climate leadership plan. Her remarks highlighted that Alberta, in repudiating past policies and providing climate change leadership, would implement the following recommendations from the Panel: phase out all coal-fired electricity generation by 2030 and source two-thirds of that electricity from renewables; introduce an economy-wide carbon tax; invest some of the carbon tax revenues in the transition to a greener energy grid and economy; devote some of those revenues to help lower-income Albertans, workers and affected communities adjust to the new carbon tax and the retirement of coal-fired generation.[56]

With respect to the tar sands, Premier Notley seemed to make one significant addition to the Panel's suite of recommendations. The leaders of CNRL, Cenovus, Shell Canada, and Suncor, who Peter Foster disparagingly called "The Gang of Four," met with the leaders of Pembina, Environmental Defence Canada, and two other environmental organizations to discuss issues such as a cap on tar sands emissions and export pipelines.[57] Between themselves they decided to recommend the government establish a 100-million-tonne cap on tar sands emissions. In exchange for agreeing to this cap on emissions, the four tar sands CEOs expected the four ENGOs to withdraw their opposition to tar sands export pipeline proposals.[58] The premier, who reportedly received this recommendation just days before announcing Alberta's plan, took this informal policy advisory group's advice.[59] Alberta would establish a 100-million-tonne ceiling on tar sands emissions, with provisions or exceptions for cogeneration and for additional emissions to be allocated for new upgrading.[60] The agreement served Notley's immediate political interests in two ways. It suggested government, not markets, would limit tar sands emissions, and it apparently secured the agreement of some export pipeline opponents to stand aside.

The premier was effusive in praising the panel, the handful of tar sands companies, and the ENGOs for their work and advice. Notley's praise foreshadowed well the general tenor of the reaction from governments, the media, industry, and environmentalists to her initiative. Those responses didn't detect any hyperbole in Notley's stance or in the title of the review panel's report: *Climate Leadership: Report to Minister.*[61] The federal and Ontario governments congratulated Alberta for taking a leadership role.[62] No one fancied the government's intentions more than the Broadbent Institute. "On a public policy Richter scale," Rick Smith, the Institute's executive director said, "Alberta's new Climate Leadership Plan is an 11."[63] The Union of Concerned Scientists called it "impressive in its scope and ambition"; Environmental Defence Canada, one of the negotiators of the 100-million-tonne tar sands emissions ceiling, not surprisingly said the plan made Alberta "a climate leader"; World Resources Institute urged countries gathering for the forthcoming Paris Climate Change conference to learn from Alberta's "historic announcement"—they "should aim for an equally inspired vision to deliver a truly transformative agreement"; NRDC congratulated Alberta for taking "a strong first step in transitioning the province from tar sands toward a sustainable economy based on clean energy";[64] Pembina, another negotiator of the tar sands ceiling, complimented the government, the tar sands CEOs, and itself when it said "the world needs more of this kind of leadership" and that the tar sands limit was "a game changer and will change the debate about the oil sands industry doing its part to address climate change";[65] even Greenpeace granted that these policies, by starting to slow emissions, were "important first steps."[66]

For the tar sands, the Greenpeace reference to starting to slow emissions inferred there was an inconvenient truth about Alberta's climate plan that none of those who applauded the government, including Al Gore himself, either recognized or saw fit to mention.[67] That truth was that the plan didn't demand any reductions in GHG emissions from the tar sands. In fact, the NDP government's vision of climate leadership would allow tar sands GHG emissions to increase by a stunning 52 percent from the 65.6 mega-tonnes of greenhouse gases Environment Canada reported were emitted by tar sands mining, in situ, and upgrading operations in Alberta in 2014.[68] The plan's ceiling for tar sands wouldn't be hit until the sector emitted 100 million tonnes (plus a then-unspecified additional amount of emissions to be allowed for new upgrading facilities and cogeneration). The government added another 10 million tonnes for new upgrading facilities through the terms of Bill 25, the *Oil Sands Emissions Limit Act*.[69] Alberta's climate leadership vision will allow tar sands emissions to increase by up to 68 percent over 2014 levels.[70] This remarkable increase may be even higher since it doesn't include the greenhouse gases emitted as part of the electricity generated by cogeneration plants. Those emissions don't count when it comes to setting the tar sands ceiling despite their contribution to greenhouse gas concentrations in the atmosphere.[71]

This inconvenient truth led to others. The most significant of these might be that, ministerial claims and media reports to the contrary, NDP leadership on climate change likely will deliver, at best, a rather emaciated version of the "real, demonstrable reductions in greenhouse gas emissions" Environment and Parks Minister Phillips promised in June 2015—not in terms of total provincial emissions anyways. The Leach panel's proposed policies "would roughly stabilize emissions, by 2030, at just above current levels, at approximately 270Mt."[72] The NDP plan will not realize the long-term targets set by the Progressive Conservatives in their 2008 strategy—not that the PCs ever showed any commitment to realizing those targets. The Leach panel concluded that achieving the targets set by previous governments "would require policies outside the scope of stringency that we are prepared to recommend."[73]

Or the most significant other inconvenient truth might be that the Alberta plan, welcomed as it was by federal Environment and Climate Change Minister Catherine McKenna and Ontario Premier Katherine Wynne, may well make it very difficult to realize the Trudeau government's 2030 GHG emissions reduction target. This target, 30 percent below 2005 levels by 2030, was set by the Harper Conservatives as Canada's commitment after the conclusion of the Copenhagen Climate Change Conference in 2009. The Trudeau Liberals, who pilloried the Harper commitment when they were in opposition for its insufficiency, ultimately accepted it.[74] Before Prime Minister Trudeau announced he would introduce a $10 per tonne national carbon tax in 2018 that would rise to $50 per tonne in 2022, Paul Boothe suggested that Alberta's decision to allow tar sands emissions to grow likely meant Canada would miss its 2030 obligation by approximately 100 million tonnes.[75] The Pembina Institute's Simon Dyer disputes the suggestion that the 100+million tonne limit on tar sands emissions won't further reduce Alberta's emissions from the 270Mt total suggested by the Leach panel and thereby make something of a positive contribution to Canada's 2030 commitment.[76] He's quite correct to point out that the Leach panel's 270Mt GHG target didn't include a 100+million tonne tar sands emissions limit. However, Leach himself reportedly suggested that, according to the National Energy Board low-oil-price scenario, the cap on tar sands emissions will not have any impact on tar sands companies before 2030.[77] The 100+million tonne cap *may* be a constraint, possibly a "severe constraint," if oil prices follow the NEB's early 2016 reference scenario.[78] This calls for WTI to rise steadily to US$80 per barrel in 2020 and $100 in 2040 (in 2010 US$).[79]

To Boothe, a former federal deputy minister of Environment Canada, Alberta's plan will allow for a "staggering" increase in emissions from the tar sands. Such an increase certainly helps explain why the CEOs of CNRL, Cenovus, Shell Canada, and Suncor supported the NDP's vision of climate leadership. So too does the expectation that this cap would lead Environmental Defence Canada, Équiterre, Forest Ethics Canada, and the Pembina Institute to set aside whatever plans they may have had or developed to oppose export pipelines. The CEOs also would have been attracted by what Boothe called a "new subsidy" that their companies and other large emitters will receive under this plan. Economist Trevor Tombe, analyzing the plan the day of its release, suggested this subsidy might be the largest cost of the plan, larger than the promised rebates to low- and middle-income households. Under Alberta's first centre-left government, wealthy Canadian companies will join low- and middle-income residents in receiving a state subsidy to defray the costs of paying Alberta's carbon tax.[80]

The Leach panel used competitiveness concerns, the trade exposure of Alberta's large emitters, to justify recommending they receive a subsidy based on their output.[81] Taxing greenhouse gas emissions in a fashion that increases industry production costs in Alberta could lead firms to shift their activities to other jurisdictions. This would depress economic activity in Alberta and perhaps have a negligible impact on global emissions. For large emitters in the tar sands, raising production costs by imposing a carbon tax may constrain future investments.[82] This constraint on future investment would arise because tar sands capital has not yet discovered a way to pack the tar sands and processing facilities in its bags if it wants to flee from undesirable government policies. Tombe estimated this subsidy per unit of production would initially amount to $1.50 per barrel and that oil and gas companies would receive $1.5 billion of the $2.5 to $3 billion the government will spend on this subsidy.[83] Subsequently, he inferred that in Alberta roughly 75 percent of the carbon taxes large emitters will pay will be returned to them through output-based allocation payments.[84] Some low carbon intensity large emitters, according to economist Kenneth McKenzie, "may actually receive more in subsidy than they pay in carbon levy."[85] This approach also leaves open the possibility that firms that improve the GHG intensity of their operations not only will receive more than they pay in carbon taxes but may increase their greenhouse gas footprint as well. Improving their GHG emissions intensity may be accompanied by emitting more greenhouse gases into the atmosphere.[86] This possibility was one reason why the Pembina Institute and other environmentalists criticized GHG emissions intensity approaches to tackling climate change.[87] Operations owned by Cenovus, whose CEO joined the premier in announcing Alberta's plan, are low carbon intensity large emitters. This subsidy provided another reason for them to support Alberta's initiative; it may have helped Suncor CEO Steve Williams conclude that Alberta's Climate Leadership Plan constituted a "sensible, reasonable balance."[88]

The support of the Pembina Institute for how Premier Notley would treat the tar sands in its climate change plan reaffirms the Institute's fundamental faith in collaborating with and accommodating the business interests of tar sands companies. Many of those companies still could be counted among Pembina's clients and supporters in 2011 and 2012, the last two years Pembina included some client/supporter information in its annual financial report.[89] As noted in the previous chapter, after a decade of failure to slow tar sands development through the regulatory process Pembina became more assertive and collaborated with American ENGOs in campaigns against the tar sands. In 2005, Marlo Raynolds, then Pembina's executive director, called the oil sands the "elephant in Canada's climate change room." Citing climate change science, he called for oil sands producers to be leaders in "a deep reduction scenario." The oil sands needed to become carbon neutral.[90] This was the year the Pembina Institute joined the David Suzuki Foundation in proposing that Canada's greenhouse gas emissions in 2020 should be 25 percent below 1990 levels. By 2050, Canada's emissions should be 80 percent below 1990 levels.[91] This Canadian contribution to the global effort to address climate change was strengthened in the OSEC's 2006 submission regarding Imperial Oil's Kearl tar sands mine. Then OSEC said that Canadian emissions "must be reduced" by these percentages.[92] In 2009, Pembina joined other Canadian and American environmental/conservation organizations in demanding "a moratorium on expansion of tar sands development."[93] At that time Pembina joined a coalition that called for a very different type and direction of leadership than what Pembina Executive Director Ed Whittingham applauded after Premier Notley unveiled her climate change strategy. Now, as the direction and pace of climate change has arguably become even more worrisome, Pembina's more collaborative demeanour is being emphasized again. It seems to have stopped flirting with more aggressive positions.

When asked to explain Pembina's move away from calling for a moratorium on tar sands development, Pembina's Alberta director replied that Alberta's new plan represented "a significant step forward in climate policy in Alberta," a step he believed was farther than that taken by any other jurisdiction. Legislating a tar sands emissions limit was "precedent setting" and would propel the industry to make much needed emissions reductions.[94] On the anniversary of Alberta's climate leadership plan, Whittingham and Shell Canada's President Michael Crothers coauthored a column that largely celebrated that plan and expressed their continued support of the plan and its principles. They wrote:

> The legislated cap on oil sands emissions in Alberta's climate plan is unprecedented globally. It gives the world certainty on oil sands CO_2 emissions growth. And for us, it deflates arguments over how big it could be. It also creates a significant incentive to achieve an oil sands carbon intensity that compares favourably with other global sources of crude oil, something that industry has aspired to for some time.[95]

It's understandable why a tar sands CEO would write this. Alberta's unprecedented cap likely doesn't force the tar sands sector to pursue a lower emissions trajectory until at least 2030. The cap, and how it was reported, disguised from the public the staggering increase in tar sands emissions from 2014 levels that the Notley government is willing to concede. The mere existence of a cap apparently trumps concerns about its generosity (and the precedent Alberta's generosity sets for how other oil-producing jurisdictions should view the GHG emissions increases they might consider allowing for their oil producers). This plan's new subsidy for reducing the carbon intensity of tar sands production reinforces a focus on emissions intensity—the hallmark of the Progressive Conservative approach to the GHG emissions issue. The enthusiasm of ENGOs such as Pembina and Environmental Defence Canada for this treatment of the tar sands is more counterintuitive, given their express concern to see the world meet the Paris Accord's 2° C target. It is light years away from the demands Pembina made in 2005 and 2006.[96]

Climate change is a collective action problem. Rational choice theory argues that since GHG emissions reductions are a public good, individual countries and other actors are tempted to be free riders when it comes to reducing GHG emissions. Climate change free riders will look to other parties to cut their GHG emissions, and bear the costs such cuts will entail, while refusing to make similar commitments of their own. They free ride on the efforts of others. This leads to what Anthony Giddens called the "I won't until you do" syndrome: My western, industrialized country shouldn't reduce our GHG emissions until developing countries that are among the world's largest GHG emitters reduce theirs.[97] By that logic, Canada shouldn't be forced to reduce its emissions until China and India, the world's first and fourth largest GHG emitters, do as well.[98] David Montgomery, who consulted for CAPP about GHG emissions credits, captured the political appeal of climate change free riding when he said: "Everyone wants to appear green without doing anything."[99]

Canada and Alberta have been climate change free riders for a generation now. Government after government has attested to the seriousness of climate change only to steadfastly refuse to take any of the actions needed to reduce GHG emissions.[100] The Leach panel's recommendations and Alberta's subsequent actions only marginally alter this pattern. Phasing out coal-fired electricity stands out here as a very positive action.[101] It's the commitment to eliminate Alberta's exceptional dependence on coal-fired electricity by 2030 that has allowed Alberta to propose to hold overall emissions in 2030 steady while increasing tar sands emissions dramatically.[102] The commitment to replace much of the province's coal-fired generation with renewables is also a welcome climate-friendly initiative. But when it comes to the tar sands the approach reads much like what one would expect from those with the "I won't until you do" syndrome. The Leach panel concluded that more stringent policies simply were not reasonable or justifiable "until our peer and competitor jurisdictions adopt policies that would have a comparable impact on their industrial sectors."[103] If others act, Alberta would act too. This is the same climate change play the Canadian and Alberta governments have directed over and over again for decades now. In Alberta's case, it now presents a policy package that aims for the province's GHG emissions in 2030 to be essentially where they are today. The 110+million tonnes tar sands limit may or may not change that. The panel suggested that "in some sense" it would be true to claim that the report's recommendations didn't put Alberta on a path consistent with the 2° C global temperature increase target. This should be attributed to the liberal, state-subsidized treatment of tar sands emissions and Premier Notley's reluctance or inability to repudiate the free rider legacy she inherited.

Conclusion

May 2015 saw Albertans elect the first centre-left government in the province's history. In this chapter we have explored the extent to which the Notley government challenged the vision of market fundamentalism that animated tar sands exploitation for the past generation. While it may be too early in the government's life to draw firm conclusions, the government's approaches to the economic and environmental dimensions of the tar sands don't appear to constitute much of a departure from the policy pattern established by the Progressive Conservatives. In the tar sands the New Democrats' challenge to market fundamentalism is as muted as New Labour's was to energy policy in Great Britain.

Perhaps this refusal to challenge tar sands capital now or in the future means it is politically suspect, or suicidal, to mount that challenge. If so, that would be an emphatic confirmation of the belief that markets and the tar sands sector enjoy a privileged position in a society where parties compete for office. Seriously questioning the place of oil and gas in Alberta's political economy is deadly to one's chances of political success.

The low oil prices that greeted Premier Notley's government certainly didn't make the prospects of increasing royalty rates, even at hypothetically higher prices, very bright. That she rushed ahead with a royalty review in such an inhospitable price environment and discarded her Resources Owners' Rights Commission reflects the power of Alberta's oilpatch and its view of the proper relationship between state, society, and industry. They demanded certainty, not for their industry in the spring of 2016, but for their sector in the springs of Alberta's medium- to long-term future. The premier obliged.

The first 18 months of the Notley government may testify well to the continued importance of an observation Seymour Martin Lipset made nearly 70 years ago. In *Agrarian Socialism*, Lipset studied the rise to power of North America's first social democratic government. In the 1944 provincial election the Co-operative Commonwealth Federation (CCF) defeated the Liberals, the party that had governed Saskatchewan for all but five years between 1905 and 1944. The bureaucracy the CCF inherited wasn't sympathetic to the party's reform agenda. "The goals and values of the civil service," he wrote, "are often as important a part of the total complex of forces responsible for state policy as those of the ruling political party."[104]

Alberta's ministries of energy and environment as well as the Alberta Energy Regulator could be seen in a similar light after the New Democrats ended the Progressive Conservative dynasty. These agencies had promoted the unconstrained development of the tar sands for decades. They were necessary institutional supports for the market-led blueprint for exploiting the tar sands. The officials responsible for the energy and environmental policies of the Progressive Conservative government were still in their offices when the new NDP ministers moved into theirs. Those officials helped their new bosses decide if a royalty review should take place, when a royalty review should take place, and finally who should be appointed to the review panel. Long-serving officials in Energy, for example, would have been very familiar with Peter Tertzakian's views on royalties. His views fit well with Energy's ideological outlook and the tenets of market fundamentalism in the petroleum sector. The same should be said of the Alberta Energy Regulator. AER's history is one of consistent support for tar sands expansion. With no changes at the senior levels of AER after the New Democrats took power, the Regulator arguably was predisposed to perpetuate the lenient regulatory approach to the tailings ponds it had taken during the brief, troubled life of Directive 074. The arrival and substance of Directive 085 confirms that.

Climate change, as inferred earlier, is one policy area where some distance separates the New Democrats from the Progressive Conservatives. One example of that is the NDP decision to eliminate all coal-fired electricity generators in Alberta by 2030. This decision, if respected by future governments, will close the six coal-fired electricity units that wouldn't be shut down by 2030 according to the Harper government's 2012 coal regulations. Another example is the accompanying commitment to replace two-thirds of Alberta's coal-fired electricity with renewables.

But even here the imperatives of market fundamentalism and currying investor confidence animate state action. The government will pay $1.1 billion (in 2016 dollars) over 14 years to the owners who had planned to run these six generating units past 2030. Terry Boston, the former president and CEO of a US electricity system operator, recommended the government make this "voluntary payment" to these electricity generators. The premier accepted. Boston's letter to the premier talks about the need to "maintain investors' confidence in Alberta." The cheques he recommended she write "will go a long way to securing a positive investment climate in the province." Looking ahead to Alberta's electricity future, his experience recommended "employing market forces as the best way" to secure the $20–30 billion he believes Alberta's electricity shift would require. He made it perfectly clear that he believed Alberta must buy out the owners of these facilities if it wanted future electricity investments; buying out coal facilities and maintaining a competitive electricity market were "essential elements" Alberta had to put in place to attract the private capital needed to build Alberta's new electricity infrastructure.[105]

But when it comes to the tar sands, the difference between the two governments is more a difference in degree than in kind. The legislated cap on tar sands emissions, what Pembina's Ed Whittingham described as a "game-changer," is set very high relative to emissions in 2014 and may not even be reached by 2030. By sanctioning a 68 percent increase in emissions from the tar sands through the *Oil Sands Emissions Limit Act*, the Notley government seems quite satisfied with the results of the original game.

This observation applies equally to the environmental groups that negotiated the 110+million tonnes cap and applauded the other tar sands–related aspects of the Climate Leadership Plan. It's hard to believe their accommodation to future tar sands growth puts them in the vanguard of any environmental countermovement that might emerge from society to challenge exploiting the tar sands. The demands that even a moderate group like the Pembina Institute made between 2006 and 2009 for moratoriums on all new tar sands projects—for climate change and tailings reservoir reasons—now will sit and gather dust in the Institute's archives.

The emissions intensity approach to the GHG emissions issue, called "laughable" by the premier when she was in opposition, survives in the NDP plan. Reductions in emissions intensity will be encouraged as a means to ensure tar sands emissions don't increase by more than 68 percent from today's levels. Under the Progressive Conservatives, tar sands companies received funding from the Climate Change and Emissions Management Fund in order to help them defray the costs of projects to reduce GHG emissions. This subsidization of good behaviour is reinforced in the NDP Climate Leadership Plan through the new subsidy represented in output-based allocations. It will be interesting to see if, when implemented, this subsidy will allow some tar sands companies, as McKenzie's earlier observation might suggest, to receive more dollars through the subsidy than they actually pay in carbon taxes.

With respect to both economy and environment then, the protected, privileged position the tar sands have enjoyed for the last generation isn't under any threat so far from a centre-left government. With respect to energy policy, as a friend and colleague suggested, in the 2015 election Albertans replaced the Progressive Conservatives with the conservative progressives.[106]

Notes

1   Pembina Institute, "Pembina Reacts to the Results of the Alberta Election," media release, May 5, 2015, https://www.pembina.org/media-release/pembina-reacts-to-the-results-of-the-alberta-election.

2   Greenpeace Canada, "Statement: NDP Win Opens Door to Greener Economy in Alberta," May 6, 2015, http://www.greenpeace.org/canada/Global/canada/pr/2015/05/AlbertaElection.pdf.

3   Peter Edelman, "The Worst Thing Bill Clinton Has Done," *Atlantic*, March 1997.

4   Block and Somers, *The Power of Market Fundamentalism*, 180–81.

5   Edelman, "The Worst Thing Bill Clinton Has Done."

6   Alana Samuels, "America's Once-Robust Safety Net Is No More," *Atlantic*, April 1, 2016.

7   Block and Somers, *The Power of Market Fundamentalism*, 187.

8   Anthony Giddens, "The Rise and Fall of New Labour," *New Statesman*, May 17, 2010.

9   Giddens, "The Rise and Fall of New Labour."

10 Ian Rutledge, "UK Energy Policy and Market Fundamentalism: A Historical Overview," in *UK Energy Policy and the End of Market Fundamentalism*, edited by Ian Rutledge and Philip Wright (Oxford: Oxford University Press, 2010), 3.

11 "Let's Talk Royalties" was the phrase the Notley government coined for its royalty review process. See Alberta, "Let's Talk Royalties," https://letstalkroyalties.ca/.

12 Alberta, Legislative Assembly, *Alberta Hansard, 26th Legislature, 3rd Session (2007–2008)*, November 6, 2007, 1820; *Alberta Hansard, 26th Legislature, 3rd Session (2007–2008)*, November 7, 2007, 1854; *Alberta Hansard, 26th Legislature, 3rd Session (2007–2008)*, November 13, 2007, 1924; *Alberta Hansard, 26th Legislature, 3rd Session (2007–2008)*, November 26, 2007, 2174.

13 Alberta, Legislative Assembly, *Alberta Hansard, 27th Legislature, 1st Session (2008–2009)*, November 20, 2008, 1954.

14 Alberta, Legislative Assembly, *Alberta Hansard, 28th Legislature, 2nd Session (2014)*, April 22, 2014, 563.

15 Alberta Federation of Labour, "The Bitumen Glut Has a Silver Lining," January 30, 2013, http://www.afl.org/bitumen_glut_has_silver_lining_6xph6dfam m9y4lliy8jvoz1ulo4; Salman Nissan and Ed Osterwald, *In-Province Upgrading: Economics of a Green-field Oil Sands Refinery* (Prepared for Alberta Federation of Labour) (CEG, April 7, 2014), http://www.unifor.org/sites/default/files/documents/document/ceg_economics_of_in-province_upgrading_in_alberta_final_07_april_2014.pdf.

16 Matt Dykstra, "NDP Proposes to Rejig Alberta's Royalty Structure," *Edmonton Sun*, April 10, 2015; Alberta NDP, "Notley Promotes Value-Added, Fair Resource Royalties—Alberta NDP," http://www.albertandp.ca/notley_promotes_value_added_fair_resource_royaltiesold.

17 In 2007, Cenovus was part of Encana Corporation. In 2009, Encana split into two corporations and the conventional oil and oil sands assets of Encana were transferred to Cenovus. For Ferguson's statement, see Geoffrey Morgan, "Cenovus Energy Inc. Warns of 'Negative' Fallout If NDP Changes Royalty Structure," *Financial Post*, April 29, 2015.

18 James Wood, "NDP's Call for Royalty Review Heats Up as Alberta Election Issues," *Calgary Herald*, April 29, 2015.

19 Don Braid, "Really, Just How Scary Is Notley?," *Calgary Herald*, April 30, 2015, A4.

20 Alberta, "Economic Dashboard: Oil Prices," http://economicdashboard.alberta. ca/OilPrice.

21 CAPP claimed that 110,000 indirect and direct jobs had been lost by early 2016. CAPP, "Capital Investment in Canada's Oil and Gas Industry Down 62% in Two Years," news release, April 7, 2016, http://www.capp.ca/media/news-releases/ capital-investment-in-canada-oil-and-gas-industry-down-62-per-cent-in-2-years.

22 Alberta, "The Panel: Peter Tertzakian," https://letstalkroyalties.ca/panel/ peter-tertzakian/.

23 ARC Financial Corp., "About ARC: Mission," http://arcfinancial.com/about/ mission/.

24 ARC Financial Corp., "The Alberta Royalty Review Submission by ARC Financial Corp." presented by Peter Tertzakian, Chief Energy Economist, May 23, 2007, 4. The conversion of 2007 US dollars to 2015 US dollars was made with the United States Department of Labor's Consumer Price Index inflation calculator. United States, Department of Labor, "CPI Inflation Calculator," https://www.bls.gov/data/inflation_calculator.htm.

25 Peter Tertzakian and Kara Jakeman, "The Fiscal Pulse of Canada's Oil and Gas Industry, First Quarter 2015" (Calgary: ARC Financial Corp., April 2015), 6–7.

26 Alberta Royalty Review Panel, *Hearings: Radisson Calgary Airport Hotel, Calgary Alberta (transcripts)*, Vol. 7, May 23, 2007, 183–184, 188, 192.

27 Alberta Royalty Review Advisory Panel, *Alberta at a Crossroads: Royalty Review Advisory Panel Report* (2016), 6 [emphasis in original].

28 Alberta Royalty Review Advisory Panel, *Alberta at a Crossroads*, 17.

29 Alberta Royalty Review Advisory Panel, *Alberta at a Crossroads*, 6; Alberta Royalty Review Panel, *Hearings: Radisson Calgary*, 188.

30 ATB Financial, *ATB 2015 Annual Report*, 6–7, 92. http://www.atb.com/ SiteCollectionDocuments/About/annual_reports/atb_2015_annual_report.pdf.

31 ATB Financial, "Corporate Financial Services: Energy Expertise," http://www. atb.com/business/cfs/expertise/Pages/energy-expertise.aspx.

32 ATB Financial, *ATB 2015 Annual Report*, 116.

33 Alberta Royalty Review Advisory Panel, *Alberta at a Crossroads*, 66–67.

34 Alberta, "Alberta's New Royalty Framework Speech," January 29, 2016, https://www.alberta.ca/release.cfm?xID=401538F1E58AB-B873-40B1-E9C9A284B7AF4D22.

35 Alberta Royalty Review Advisory Panel, *Alberta at a Crossroads*, 12–13.

36 CAPP, "Royalty Report Sets Stage to Review Alberta's Competitiveness: CAPP," news release, January 29, 2016, http://www.capp.ca/media/news-releases/royalty-report-sets-stage-to-review-albertas-competitiveness-capp.

37   Alberta Federation of Labour, "Royalty Policy Is the Biggest Decision Any Alberta Government Has to Make: Advice to Government on Energy and Royalty Policy," January 2016, https://d3n8a8pro7vhmx.cloudfront.net/afl/pages/2770/attachments/original/1454352012/AFL_Advice_on_AB_energy_and_royalty_policy_26Jan201r2FINAL.pdf?1454352012.

38   Mariam Ibrahim, "Alberta NDP 'Got It Wrong on Royalties,' Labour Leader Gil McGowan Says," *Edmonton Journal*, February 1, 2016.

39   Bill 25, the *Oil Sands Emissions Limit Act*, introduced in the fall of 2016 allocates a specific amount of new GHG emissions—10 megatonnes—to any upgraders started after December 2015.

40   Alberta, Legislative Assembly, *Alberta Hansard, 27th Legislature, 1st Session (2008)*, April 30, 2008, 341.

41   Alberta, Legislative Assembly, *Alberta Hansard, 27th Legislature, 1st Session (2008)*, May 6, 2008, 471.

42   Alberta, Legislative Assembly, *Alberta Hansard, 27th Legislature, 2nd Session (2009–2010)*, March 17, 2009, 445.

43   Alberta, *Lower Athabasca Region—Tailings Management Framework for the Mineable Athabasca Oil Sands* (March 2015).

44   Alberta Energy Regulator, "AER Suspends Directive 074: Tailings Performance Criteria and Requirements for Oil Sands Mining Schemes," news release, March 13, 2015, https://www.aer.ca/about-aer/media-centre/news-releases/news-release-2015-03-13.

45   Alberta Energy Regulator, "Directive 085," 30–31.

46   Chris Varcoe, "Tailings Ponds, Pipeline Leaks Keep Heat on AER," *Calgary Herald*, July 16, 2016, B1.

47   Varcoe, "Tailing Ponds, Pipeline Leaks."

48   Canadian Association of Petroleum Producers, "New Tailings Regulations: Directive 085," in *Context: Energy Examined (CAPP's member magazine)* 4, no. 3 (August 2016): 6.

49   Alberta, Legislative Assembly, *Alberta Hansard, 27th Legislature, 1st Session (2008–2009)*, October 21, 2008, 1453; *Alberta Hansard, 27th Legislature, 2nd Session (2009–2010)*, April 20, 2009, 698; *Alberta Hansard, 27th Legislature, 2nd Session (2009–2010)*, November 26, 2009, 2074.

50   Alberta, Legislative Assembly, *Alberta Hansard, 27th Legislature, 2nd Session (2009–2010)*, April 16, 2009, 679.

51   *Alberta Hansard*, April 20, 2009, 698.

52   Alberta, Legislative Assembly, *Alberta Hansard, 27th Legislature, 1st Session (2008–2009)*, June 2, 2008, 1138.

53   Alberta, Legislative Assembly, *Alberta Hansard, 27th Legislature, 2nd Session (2009–2010)*, February 19, 2009, 138.

54   Paul Boothe, Félix-A. Boudreault, and Christopher Frankel, "Getting to 2030: Comparing and Coordinating Provincial Climate Policies" (Toronto: Institute for Competitiveness & Prosperity, October 2016), 7.

55   Alberta, "Province Takes Meaningful Steps Toward Climate Change Strategy," media release, June 25, 2015, https://www.alberta.ca/release.cfm?xID=38232B11A8C17-0B34-BB8E-6B03088D90D1C786.

56   Alberta, "Climate Leadership Plan Speech" media release, November 22, 2015, https://www.alberta.ca/release.cfm?xID=38886E9269850-A787-1C1E-A5C90ACF52A4DAE4.

57   The ENGOs were Environmental Defence Canada, Equitérre, Forest Ethics Canada, and the Pembina Institute. Foster was apoplectic that these four corporate "appeasers" were willing to "do a deal" with "radical groups" in order to try to buy off their "rabid opposition." See Peter Foster, "The Gang of Four's Oil Cap Blunder," *Financial Post*, December 4, 2015.

58   Claudia Cattaneo, "Secret Oilsands Deal Spurred by Alberta NDP's Concern over Project Cancellations, Green Group Says," *Financial Post*, December 3, 2015.

59   Claudia Cattaneo, "Secret Deal on Alberta's Oilsands Emissions Limits Divides Patch," *Financial Post*, December 1, 2015.

60   Co-generation refers to a process where heat and electricity are produced simultaneously. Any electricity produced that is surplus to a facility's demands may be sold in the market. For example, ATCO Power built a 170-megawatt (170 million watts) cogeneration plant to supply the Athabasca Oilsands Upgrader with power and heat. The upgrader uses two-thirds of the electricity produced by the ATCO cogeneration plant; energy from the gas turbines is recovered and supplies steam to the upgrader and steam turbine. See ATCO Power, "Scotford Cogeneration Plant," http://www.atcopower.com/Our-Facilities/Our-Power-Technologies/Cogeneration/Scotford.

61   Andrew Leach et al., *Climate Leadership: Report to Minister* (Edmonton: Government of Alberta, 2015).

62   James Wood, "Notley's Carbon Plan Wins Praise from Ontario, Federal Leaders," *Calgary Herald*, November 23, 2015.

63   Kaur Communications, "Reactions from Around the World to Government of Alberta's New Climate Change Strategy," *Canada NewsWire*, November 22, 2015.

64   Kaur Communications, "Reactions from Around the World."

65   Bob Weber, "Alberta to Implement Carbon Tax in Climate Change Policy," *Canadian Press*, November 22, 2015; Justin Giovannetti and Jeffrey Jones, "Alberta Carbon Plan a Major Pivot in Environmental Policy," *Globe and Mail*, November 22, 2015.

66   Greenpeace, "Alberta Climate Plan an Historic First Step But More Needs to Be Done," news release, November 22, 2015, http://www.greenpeace.org/canada/Global/canada/pr/2015/11/AB-climate-statement.pdf.

67   Al Gore's enthusiasm for Alberta's climate leadership plan is found in Giovannetti and Jones, "Alberta Carbon Plan a Major Pivot in Environmental Policy."

68   The figure of 52 percent is based on the GHG emissions from Alberta's oil sands in 2014 as reported in Environment and Climate Change Canada, *National Inventory Report 1990–2014, Part 3*, 81. Premier Notley claimed in her speech that Alberta's oil sands emitted "approximately 70 megatons of carbon" annually. Accepting this approximation as Alberta's actual emissions likely led a number of commentators to conclude that the legislated limit would allow oil sands emissions to increase by 43 percent. See Paul Boothe, "Alberta's Greenhouse Gas Plan: A Glass Half Full or Half Empty?," *Maclean's*, November 24, 2015, http://www.macleans.ca/economy/economicanalysis/albertas-greenhouse-gas-plan-a-glass-half-full-or-half-empty; Gordon Laxer, "Alberta's Plan Guts Efforts to Cut Greenhouse Gases," *Winnipeg Free Press*, December 10, 2015, A11; Kevin Washbrook, "Why Are People Cheering Alberta's Climate Plan?," *The Tyee*, December 16, 2015, https://thetyee.ca/Opinion/2015/12/16/Cheering-Alberta-Climate-Plan/. Still other reports said that additional emissions

granted to oil sands amounted to a 40 percent increase. See Jeff Lewis, "Oil Sands Growth Plans at Risk under Alberta's New Climate Rules," *Globe and Mail*, November 23, 2015; Mike De Souza, "Update 1—Canada's Alberta to Introduce Economy-Wide Carbon Tax in 2017," *Reuters News*, November 22, 2015. According to the Environment Canada data, all of those percentages are inaccurate; they significantly underestimate the increase in oil sands emissions the Notley government sanctioned.

69   Nigel Bankes points out that Bill 25 is silent about some very significant aspects of the emissions limit. For example, there's no mention in the legislation of how the emissions limit will be shared between current and future emitters. Will projects be able to secure entitlements to part of the total emissions allowed? If so, will firms be able to trade entitlements? Nigel Bankes, "Oil Sands Emission Limit Legislation: A Real Commitment or Kicking It Down the Road?," *Ablawg.ca* (blog), November 3, 2016, http://ablawg.ca/2016/11/03/oil-sands-emission-limit-legislation-a-real-commitment-or-kicking-it-down-the-road/.

70   This percentage doesn't include the greenhouse gas emissions that cogeneration will produce, since cogeneration is excluded from the 110-million-tonne cap.

71   Alberta, *Bill 25—Oil Sands Emissions Limit Act*, section 2(2)a.

72   Leach et al., *Climate Leadership: Report to Minister*, 40. If the reference point for this conclusion was Alberta's level of greenhouse gas emissions in 2014, then, according to Environment Canada data, the 270 Mt level would be slightly below the 273.8 Mt emitted in Alberta in 2014. Environment and Climate Change Canada, *National Inventory Report 1990–2014, Part 3*, 81.

73   Leach et al., *Climate Leadership: Report to Minister*, 25. As pointed out previously, Alberta's auditor general cast serious doubt on whether the Progressive Conservatives were prepared to adopt the policies needed to reach those long-term targets.

74   Lorrie Goldstein, "Trudeau Adopts Harper's Climate Targets," *Toronto Sun*, September 19, 2016.

75   Boothe, "Alberta's Greenhouse Gas Plan"; see also Boothe et al., "Getting to 2030." After the federal carbon tax announcement, Boothe and two other members of the Ecofiscal Commission wrote that meeting the 2030 emissions target required a carbon tax in the vicinity of $125 per ton or higher. They credited the Liberals for their ultimatum that there had to be a national price placed on carbon, but they didn't see any indication that the tax would increase to the levels needed to keep Canada's climate change commitment to the United Nations. See Paul Boothe, Mel Cappe, and Christopher Ragan, "A Federal Carbon Price Demonstrates Policy Progress, Perils," *Globe and Mail*, October 16, 2016.

76   Simon Dyer, e-mail message to author, November 24, 2016.

77   Shawn McCarthy, "Canada's Carbon Challenge: Turning Promises into Reality," *Globe and Mail*, January 22, 2016.

78   Marc Jaccard, Mikela Hein, and Tiffany Vass, "Is Win-Win Possible?: Can Canada's Government Achieve Its Paris Commitment… and Get Re-Elected?" (Burnaby, BC: Simon Fraser University School of Resource and Environmental Management, September 20, 2016), 25.

79   Jaccard, Hein, and Vass, "Is Win-Win Possible?," 10–11.

80   Trevor Tombe, "Here's What We Know—and Don't Know—about Alberta's Carbon Tax," *Maclean's*, November 23, 2015, http://www.macleans.ca/economy/economicanalysis/heres-what-we-know-and-dont-know-about-albertas-carbon-tax/.

81   As noted in Chapter Eight, the large emitter category includes, but isn't limited to, oil sands companies. It refers to any industrial facility emitting more than 100,000 tonnes of greenhouse gases per year.

82   Leach et al., *Climate Leadership: Report to Minister*, 34–35.

83   Tombe, "Here's What We Know—and Don't Know."

84   Trevor Tombe, "Here's How Much Carbon Pricing Will Likely Cost Households," *Maclean's*, October 11, 2016, http://www.macleans.ca/economy/economicanalysis/heres-how-much-carbon-pricing-will-likely-cost-households/.

85   Kenneth J. McKenzie, "Make the Alberta Carbon Levy Revenue Neutral," *SPP Briefing Paper* (University of Calgary School of Public Policy) 9, no. 15 (April 2016), 2, https://www.policyschool.ca/wp-content/uploads/2016/05/carbon-levy-revenue-neutral-mckenzie.pdf.

86   For example, Shell Canada's in situ operations, Muskeg River Mine, Jackpine Mine, and Scotford Upgrader increased their total GHG emissions by 10 percent between 2011 and 2014 while the GHG emissions intensity of these facilities fell by 9 percent. See Shell Canada Ltd., *Oil Sands Performance Report 2015* (April 22, 2016), 6, http://www.shell.ca/en_ca/promos/energy-and-innovation/oil-sands-performance-report-2015/_jcr_content.stream/1463441702776/00cfc57a8625b41538ec24a2fc9d2e7160147b85367300b8dd8b9cb735aa1736/she-2055-oil-sands-performance-report-2015-final1.pdf.

87   Bramley, *An Assessment of Alberta's Climate Change Action Plan*. What differentiates the NDP's emissions intensity approach to tar sands emissions from the situation that Bramley critiqued is the establishment of an absolute tar sands emissions ceiling of 110+million tonnes. Whether that ceiling is reached and whether increased tar sands emissions represent a positive contribution to tackling climate change are separate issues.

88   Geoffrey Morgan, "Anyone Who Emits Carbon Will Pay, Alberta Says as It Releases Tough Climate Change Policies," *Financial Post*, November 22, 2015.

89   In 2011, Pembina's clients included Alberta Oilsands Inc., Encana Corporation, Shell Canada Ltd., Suncor Energy, Total E&P Canada, and TransCanada Pipelines. In 2012, those clients included Cenovus Energy, Shell Canada, and Statoil. Supporters giving Pembina $5,000 or more in 2012 included Shell Canada, Statoil, Imperial Oil, Encana Corporation, and Suncor Energy. Talisman Energy Inc., Suncor Energy, Cenovus Energy, and Shell Canada were found on that same list in 2011. Governments, financial corporations, and a handful of renewable energy businesses/associations and environmental organizations also appear on those lists. Pembina Institute, *Annual Financial Report 2011*; Pembina Institute, *Annual Financial Report 2012*.

90   Pembina Institute, "Oilsands Responsible for Up to Half of Canada's Emissions Growth," media release, November 29, 2005, http://www.pembina.org/media-release/1164. Raynolds, a candidate for the federal Liberal Party in the October 2015 election, subsequently became chief of staff for Environment and Climate Change Minister Catherine McKenna.

91   Matthew Bramley, *The Case for Deep Reductions: Canada's Role in Preventing Dangerous Climate Change* (Vancouver: David Suzuki Foundation and Pembina Institute, 2005), 5, https://www.pembina.org/pub/536.

92   Oil Sands Environmental Coalition, *Submission in the Matter of the Kearl Oil Sands Project.*

93   "Declaration of US and Canadian Environmental and Conservation Leaders on US-Canada Cooperation on Climate, Energy, and Natural Areas Conservation," June 4, 2009, https://www.pembina.org/reports/us-can-ceo-declaration.pdf.

94   Simon Dyer, e-mail message to author, November 24, 2016.

95   Michael Crothers and Ed Whittingham, "On the First Anniversary, Much to Celebrate, and Even More to Do," *Globe and Mail*, November 22, 2016, B4.

96   For its part, the David Suzuki Foundation urged Alberta in September 2015 to consider the following GHG emissions reduction targets: at least a 35 percent cut in GHG emissions from 2005 levels by 2030 and an 80 percent cut from 2005 levels by 2050. See David Suzuki Foundation, *Seizing Alberta's Climate Leadership Opportunity* (Vancouver: David Suzuki Foundation, September 2015), 3, http://www.davidsuzuki.org/publications/downloads/2015/Addressing%20Climate%20Change%20in%20Alberta_FINAL.pdf.

97   Anthony Giddens, *The Politics of Climate Change,* 2nd ed. (Cambridge: Polity Press, 2011), 104.

98   These rankings are based on 2011 emissions. See Union of Concerned Scientists, "Each Country's Share of CO2 Emissions," http://www.ucsusa.org/global_warming/science_and_impacts/science/each-countrys-share-of-co2.html#.WDYqUqIrL5U.

99   Paul Webster, "Canada's Dirty Little Kyoto Strategy," *Globe and Mail*, June 3, 2006, F7.

100   Jaccard, Hein, and Vass, "Is Win-Win Possible?" 1; Marc Jaccard, "Want an Effective Carbon Policy?: Heed the Evidence," *Policy Options*, February 2, 2016, http://policyoptions.irpp.org/magazines/february-2016/want-an-effective-climatepolicy-heed-the-evidence/.

101   It should be noted, though, that 12 of the 18 coal-fired electricity generating units in Alberta that will be closed by 2030 were going to shut down due to regulations passed by the Harper Conservative government. The federal Conservatives, not the provincial New Democrats, should receive credit for closing down two-thirds of Alberta's coal-fired electricity generation in 2030. See Alberta Energy, "Phase-out of Coal-Fired Emissions in Alberta" (March 2016), http://www.energy.alberta.ca/Org/pdfs/FSCoalPhaseOut.pdf.

102   Fifty-five percent of Alberta's electricity in 2014 came from coal-fired generation. Although coal is also the primary source of electricity in Saskatchewan and Nova Scotia, the province of Alberta generates more coal pollution than the other two provinces combined. See Alberta Energy, "Phase-Out of Coal-Fired Emissions in Alberta"; Alberta, "Phasing Out Coal Pollution," http://www.alberta.ca/climate-coal-electricity.aspx.

103   Leach et al., *Climate Leadership: Report to Minister*, 11.

104   S. M. Lipset, *Agrarian Socialism: The Cooperative Commonwealth Federation in Saskatchewan* (Berkeley: University of California Press, 1950), 309.

105 Terry Boston, "Letter to The Honourable Rachel Notley," September 30, 2016,   http://www.alberta.ca/documents/Electricity-Terry-Boston-Letter-to-Premier.pdf. About the essential elements Alberta needed to implement, Boston wrote: "Based on the input from 25 investment institutions and two of the largest independent power producers in North America, two essential elements are required for the level of investments for reliable capacity and renewable energy. First, is the provision of voluntary payments for the six coal plants with remaining life beyond 2030. Second, is continued confidence that Alberta's power market design produces competitive results which are fair and efficient, while encouraging the future investments needed to maintain reliability during the transition to cleaner sources of generation."

106 My thanks to Jim Lightbody for this observation.

10

Conclusion: Market Fundamentalism in the Tar Sands

"Given a system entirely dependent upon market functions for the safeguarding of its existential needs, confidence will naturally turn to such forces outside the market system which are capable of ensuring common interests jeopardized by that system."
—*Karl Polanyi,* The Great Transformation, *1944*

Market Fundamentalism and the Character of Exploitation

Canada is no stranger to resource booms. Dawson City, Cobalt, Kirkland Lake, Val-d'Or, Hemlo, and most recently Fort McMurray testify to their prominence in Canadian history. This book has focused on the post-1995 tar sands rush, has tried to explain that boom, and has tried to show some of its impacts on society and nature.

The potential for the post-1995 tar sands boom arose from several quarters. The addiction to oil that followed the birth and maturation of the Hydrocarbon Age was an essential ingredient.[1] The evolving nature of the international petroleum economy was also important, especially the petroleum demand/production profile in the United States. In the early 1970s, it seemed certain that US oil production from the lower 48 states had peaked. In 1988, Alaska oil production did the same at just over two million barrels per day. The resulting declines in US domestic production combined with increased US consumption from 1985 through to the first years of this century created a yawning production/consumption gap. Increased American dependency on foreign oil to satisfy its craving resulted. Imports as a share of US consumption were on the rise after 1985. So too was the percentage of that fix supplied by dealers from that notoriously turbulent region, the Middle East, and other unstable regions. When the Gulf War erupted in 1990, OPEC production as a share of US consumption had spiked back to 25.2 percent from a low of 11.6 percent in 1985.[2] The continental orientation of Canadian oil production and infrastructure, reinforced by the free trade agreements of 1989 and 1994, positioned Alberta's tar sands well to play a greater role in the American search for secure sources of petroleum.

Technological change also increased the potential for the tar sands to supply a fix for American cravings. The switch to truck and shovel operations in the mining sector delivered impressive operating cost reductions. In 2003, Suncor was very close to maximizing this type of cost savings. A company executive could tell a conference on energy security in North America that the company's operating costs were approximately US $9.50 per barrel.[3] These cost reductions made an established tar sands miner such as Suncor profitable over the "normal" range of oil prices ... normal at the dawn of the twenty-first century was a range of between $20 and $30 per barrel.

The potential for a boom is one thing; it took government choice and action for it to materialize. Here the state took its cue from what Alberta's global competitors were doing. A liberal renaissance was afoot. Norway, Great Britain—even Russia and Venezuela—were reducing the state's share of petroleum rents in order to attract investors. This encouraged Canadian governments to follow suit. Of most relevance and concern to Alberta's energy minister in the early 1990s was Venezuela's *La Apertura Petrolera*. Burned by the nationalization of foreign oil assets in Venezuela in 1976, the multinationals required especially lucrative financial incentives before they would consider partnering with PDVSA to exploit the Orinoco's extra-heavy oil deposits. Venezuela slashed royalty rates, from nearly 17 percent to 1 percent, and cut corporate taxes in half. Billions in investment dollars followed these measures. Alberta chose to follow Venezuela's lead.

Mimicking the Venezuelan royalty concessions, and introducing the "generic royalty regime" more generally, was government's most important contribution to the frenzied pace that exploiting the tar sands took. What is striking about this choice is the fact it was based on fallacies. First, a generic regime was deemed the right choice because of the supposed uncertainty that Alberta's existing royalty system created for investors in the late twentieth century. In the early 1990s, two different royalty regimes applied to the bulk of tar sands production. Syncrude paid 50 percent of its net profit to the provincial government; Suncor and Imperial's Cold Lake project paid either 5 percent of gross revenues or 30 percent of net revenues—whatever amount was greater. Certainly these agreements were different, but there really wasn't anything uncertain or mysterious about the Alberta royalty system, not least because most of the industry in the late 1980s was following the so-called Cold Lake regime. Since Alberta wasn't in the habit of reneging on the terms of its royalty agreements, it's hard to see where any troubling amount of uncertainty rested. A second fallacy asserted that royalties needed to be reduced in order to make the tar sands business profitable. This simply wasn't true. To reach exactly the opposite conclusion, one only had to read company annual reports or the accolades of the business press, or listen to the words of tar sands executives like Eric Newell, Rick George, Gwynn Morgan, or J. P. Bryan. Fallacious as these views were, they created and sustained a myth of the tar sands as a struggling, unprofitable sector of the Canadian petroleum industry. They were important political resources for those who insisted the state must reduce its share of economic rents.

The choice to sweeten the fiscal regime was complemented by the decision to let the market decide how much tar sands crude should flow out of northern Alberta. Government gave no thought to placing a cap on tar sands production. Let the market decide how much oil should be scraped and steamed out of the land. For a time in the 1960s the provincial government had restricted tar sands production. At that time the Manning administration did so to protect other elements of the provincial economy and society—those associated with conventional oil production. Unlike in the 1960s, the multinationals in the 1990s didn't have to lobby government to lift restrictions on production. At the end of the twentieth century, the prevailing view was that Alberta should produce as much tar sands crude as the American market wanted and produce it as quickly as possible. The elites preached rapid, unfettered development. The governing party, the official opposition in the provincial legislature, business, and trade unions all applauded the fiscal changes Alberta made to promote the tar sands. None called for a limit on how much of the province's nearly 170 billion barrels of bitumen should be turned into petroleum products.

On the one hand these decisions followed a well-worn path in Alberta, one where the provincial government generally treated the oil and gas industry well. Provincial fiscal concessions such as holidays from paying royalties on production typically were offered during tough times in the oil patch. The federal government joined Alberta in extending preferential pricing to tar sands production as part of the NEP. But the 1970s and early 1980s were a time when very modest state interests also featured in government policies. In the tar sands these interests appeared as the federal and provincial ownership stakes in Syncrude and the fleeting federal interest in marrying tar sands production to Canadian oil self-sufficiency.

Market fundamentalism dismissed the importance of these state interests. Under its influence, governments believed it was counterintuitive to see the state as having interests in the petroleum sector that couldn't be met, and met more effectively and efficiently, by reregulating the sector to maximize corporate profit-making potential. This was the logic of the free trade agreements. Corporate interests and markets generally would determine the "how much" and the destination of Canadian and American petroleum production. But if markets couldn't ensure that reserves would be maintained, the state was then welcome to offer corporations incentives to find and develop more oil and gas. Even passive and profitable investment positions, such as Alberta's position in the Syncrude consortium, violated market fundamentalism's strictures.[4] In the extreme, Alberta was prepared to privatize its voice in petroleum lands management along with its equity position. When the province liquidated the last of its position in Alberta Energy Corporation in 1993, it also transferred to the company the provincial voice in allowing access to the public lands found within the Cold Lake Air Weapons Range. A private company, not a government department, would play the primary provincial gatekeeping role to those 5,400 square kilometres (2,085 square miles).[5]

It became second nature in this petroleum version of market fundamentalism to delegate the key decision-making responsibilities to the private sector. Patricia Nelson bragged about how "awesome" her kitchen cabinet was. This collection of informal advisors—all drawn from industry—had told Nelson of the regulatory burden her government had placed on them. They generously answered Nelson's call for their "best and brightest" to go through her department's regulations and "identify those that are redundant, those that are duplicated, those that are overlapped, and those that are just not appropriate for today." They did "a tremendous job" and slashed the department's regulations in half; all the minister said she had to do "was bring it together."[6] The National Task Force on Oil Sands Strategies, the brainchild of tar sands companies, was created to perform similar responsibilities. Its industry-dominated subcommittees decided what needed to be done to attract billions of dollars in tar sands investments to Alberta, and the provincial and federal governments happily embraced the Task Force's vision.

Measured against the investment and production objectives of the National Task Force on Oil Sands Strategies, it may be impossible to exaggerate the success of market fundamentalism in the tar sands. The Task Force's blueprint for development thought that, if the state followed that design, anywhere between $21 and $25 billion would be invested in the tar sands by 2020. Production would triple as a result. The 2020 investment goal was exceeded in less than 10 years. Between 1999 and 2013, approximately $201 billion had been invested in the tar sands—more than eight times what the Task Force hoped to see by 2020.[7] Preliminary data from Statistics Canada stated that nearly $33 billion in new capital expenditures was invested in 2013 alone.[8] Production had tripled by 2009. In 2015, another record year for tar sands production, synthetic crude oil and non-upgraded bitumen production stood at 3.5 million barrels per day, more than four times the production of 1995.

But the Task Force also said that growth would be measured. Government could look to it for a "coordinated plan" that would deliver "staged and logical developments over time." In fact, what has unfolded in the tar sands has been anything but coordinated, staged, or logical. Instead growth has been explosive, exponential, frenzied. Alan Greenspan's phrase "irrational exuberance" applies just as well to the tar sands boom as it did to the speculative fever that afflicted stock markets in the 1990s.

This irrational exuberance, an atmosphere encouraged by market fundamentalism's impact on government decision-making, spawned a litany of damage, problems, and challenges. Evans writes about the disillusionment with neoliberal globalization that flows from society's failure to subordinate the market, to make the market serve social goals. One dimension of that failure is the "inability to govern markets and discipline capital so that capitalists themselves are protected from the potential chaos of unregulated markets."[9] The tar sands boom testifies to this dimension of society's failure. The Fort McMurray First Nation's submission to the 2015 royalty review panel identified the oil sands sector as both the driver of Alberta's economic boom and "the epicentre of inflation." Drawing on data from the Canadian Energy Research Institute, the submission reinforced the observation from Chapter Three about dramatic increases in tar sands supply costs during the boom. The First Nation noted how the supply costs of an in situ project and a stand-alone mining project had nearly quadrupled and quintupled respectively between 2004 and 2015. In 2015, those respective costs stood at $58.65 and $70.18 per barrel. At those rates of increase, rates far higher than the general rate of inflation, tar sands supply costs have risen over this period "at a rate that jeopardizes project viabilities."[10] The saving grace for projects during this period was the fact oil prices were rising significantly. But when oil prices plunge as they did from July 2014 to February 2016, such dramatic increases in supply costs become serious threats to these new projects.[11] Whereas on the eve of the boom Syncrude, Suncor, and Imperial Cold Lake were profitable at prices between $20 and $30 per barrel, the tar sands boom generation of projects would be very far from breaking even at those prices. Since predicting the future of oil prices is a fool's game, I won't hazard guesses about whether a new normal range of oil prices is likely to be established, when that range may appear, or what that price range would be. What we do know is that the viability of new or proposed tar sands projects now depends on much higher prices than was the case a generation ago. The billions of dollars poured into the tar sands has damaged the industry's competitiveness.

To some extent this heightened risk to capital should be attributed to market fundamentalism. It should be laid at the feet of the fiscal regime governments established in the 1990s. Generally speaking, companies are cost minimizers unless they operate in a regulatory setting that encourages "gold-plating."[12] This term refers to situations where companies spend excessively or overinvest because they can pass those extra costs on to their customers or consumers. When used in the context of the US military-industrial-complex, American taxpayers were those customers. They bore the costs of excessively expensive weapons systems. Although the generic royalty system and the fiscal regime's generous treatment of capital costs[13] likely didn't encourage overinvestment, these aspects of tar sands reregulation tolerated cost overruns. They were part of a regulatory approach that didn't impose financial discipline on companies. It didn't encourage companies to reduce cost overruns. Since companies would pay the 1 percent gross production royalty until payout, cost overruns were tolerated because they extended the timeframe for applying the 1 percent royalty. Higher royalty rates and less generous capital cost provisions would have provided project managers with additional incentives to reduce their costs.[14]

Market Fundamentalism and Nature

Nature paid a very high price for the choices animated by market fundamentalism. Visit Google Earth and take a virtual trip to the skies above the Fort McMurray area. Compare the lands being "disturbed" by tar sands exploitation now with the adjoining swathes of green. Zoom in and compare the colour of today's tailings reservoirs with the colour of water bodies such as McClelland Lake that haven't tasted the waste from bitumen mining. Use the historical imagery feature and compare the landscape as it was in 1984 with the legacy of tar sands mining as it exists today. Remember that, in your lifetime, more pits and more waste will be added to today's imagery as miners exploit every profitable acre of their leases.

The sacrifice of nature now being written in the latest chapter in the environmental history of Alberta is suggested well by how one term—sterilization—was used by the state during the last generation of project approvals. Sterilization results when recoverable barrels of bitumen are left in the ground. Sterilization results if government decides to protect exceptional natural areas, such as the McClelland Lake wetlands, from the steel of shovels. In this Canadian chapter of industrialization's relationship with nature, little of Alberta's boreal forest has been sterilized. The boreal landscape has been sacrificed to help satisfy our society's craving for oil.

For humankind, the far greater sacrifice Canadians and Albertans have tolerated and facilitated since the 1992 Rio Earth Summit concerns the climate. In a dark moment it's tempting to see the amount of misinformation peddled in the climate change debate as equal to the enormity of the task we face to ensure this planet is livable for our kind at the end of this century. Extreme statements and exaggerated claims litter both sides of the debate. Environmental commentary about the climate consequences of exploiting the tar sands can be fanciful. This charge applies equally well to the claims of successive governments about the seriousness of their efforts to make a meaningful contribution to this issue. It's nonsense to suggest that not developing any more of Alberta's bitumen would give the world a significantly better chance of meeting the most recent ambitions outlined in the 2015 Paris Agreement. At the same time, it's ethically deplorable to suggest that since Canada emits only approximately 1.6 percent of the world's greenhouse gas emissions we don't have a responsibility as a developed nation to play a leadership role in trying to realize the Paris Agreement's ambitions.[15] Authentic leadership demands Canada do more and that the tar sands should contribute real reductions in GHG emissions from current levels.

To date this hasn't happened, and it appears unlikely to happen in the next 10 to 15 years. The tar sands have emerged essentially unscathed from more than 25 years of international and national climate change politics. While environmental criticisms have gathered speed, they haven't slowed down the production of Alberta's "dirty oil" with its trademark greater level of GHG emissions. Political and corporate leaders partnered to create sales teams to market Alberta as a land that took climate change seriously. Alberta was, they told the public, the first jurisdiction in North America to require large industrial emitters of greenhouse gases such as the tar sands to meet a GHG intensity reduction target. Those teams generally avoided telling the public that companies could avoid reducing their emissions at all if they paid a $15 per ton indulgence into the province's Climate Change and Emissions Management Fund. As with so much tar sands policy in Alberta, important responsibilities for managing this aspect of the tar sands were handed off to an industry-dominated organization that wasn't very accountable to elected politicians, governments, and the public. The Climate Change Emissions Management Corporation's performance was little different from those produced by the National Task Force on Oil Sands Strategies or the Cumulative Environmental Management Association. To a significant degree, the funds gathered through the province's carbon tax on large emitters that didn't meet their emissions intensity reductions was recycled to those interests.

For the most part, Alberta addressed climate change with rhetoric—hot air if you like—during the Progressive Conservative years. From 1990 to 2005, GHG emissions from the tar sands doubled; by 2014 they had doubled again. From 1990 to 2005, Alberta's emissions rose from 175 Mt to 233 Mt. The tar sands accounted for 29 percent of that increase. From 2005 to 2014, the province's emissions rose by another 41 million tonnes to 274 Mt; the tar sands accounted for a staggering 82 percent of that increase. Over 24 years, as the world's appreciation of the seriousness of climate change grew, Alberta's emissions rose by 57 percent; the tar sands accounted for just over half of that 99-million-tonne increase.[16] What other jurisdiction in the developed world that claimed to take climate change seriously sported such an abysmal GHG emissions record?

The high price nature paid during the tar sands boom resulted in part from institutional and ideational features that predated market fundamentalism. Following the example set by the Texas Railway Commission, Alberta's energy regulators defined conservation as the efficient development of petroleum. As a former ERCB chairman explained to me nearly 10 years before the boom began, conservation in the contemporary sense of environmental protection wasn't a criterion the ERCB was obliged to consider when it evaluated the merits of oil and gas development applications.[17] The ERCB's "directly and adversely affected" test also predated the reincarnation of market fundamentalism. This institutional feature is an excellent example of the second face of power—where barriers are raised and decision-making agendas are set to prevent decision-making from dealing with interests that challenge the status quo.[18]

The boom years strengthened this institutional legacy hostile to valuing nature. The environmental side of the ledger also saw the state delegate its decision-making authority to industry. The industry-led Cumulative Environmental Management Association ensured that talk about the cumulative environmental effects of exploiting the tar sands would triumph over actions to minimize those effects. Talk, not action, in defence of nature was all the state would allow during the first 10 to 15 years of the boom. But, as environmental criticisms became more regular and spread beyond Canada's borders, even talking about nature came to raise the hackles of provincial and federal politicians. Alberta's environment department censured the Oil Sands Environmental Coalition when a moderate member of the coalition like the Pembina Institute published negative media about the tar sands. Government refused to accept or consider the organization's statements of concern on vital environmental issues such as managing Alberta's growing tailings reservoirs. Even talk would also be more difficult to offer, since these matters were transferred to the Alberta Energy Regulator and were subject to the stricter "directly and adversely affected" test, not a "directly affected" test. Legal standing to voice concerns in the Alberta regulatory setting became more difficult to establish.

The federal government also endeavoured to make it more difficult to voice environmental criticisms of tar sands projects. Natural Resources Minister Joe Oliver's vitriolic attack against "environmental and other radical groups" in the winter of 2012 foreshadowed federal legislation to restrict opportunities to advance environmental objections to exploiting the tar sands. Changes to the *National Energy Board Act* made it more difficult for the "radicals" who ran rampant in Minister Oliver's imagination to satisfy the Act's participation criteria. Rewriting the *Canadian Environmental Assessment Act* not only made it more difficult for the public to qualify to participate in assessments, but also struck in situ tar sands projects, where most of the future of tar sands industrialization rests, from the list of industrial projects that would trigger a federal environmental assessment. As in Progressive Conservative Alberta, Conservative Ottawa's response to louder voices opposing tar sands exploitation was to try to silence them.

The environmental community had high hopes this record would change after Alberta elected the first centre-left government in its history in May 2015. They should be disappointed with what they saw in the first 18 months of the Notley administration. The Notley government's approach to managing the toxic legacy of tar sands tailings reservoirs is as meek as the Progressive Conservative approach. During this time the Notley government did little more than reaffirm the Progressive Conservative approach to addressing the climate change dimension of the tar sands. The Climate Leadership Plan essentially recommended that the future path of tar sands GHG emissions should be determined by a market-based mechanism—carbon pricing. Under this plan's measures, Alberta's GHG emissions in 2030 are projected to be 270 million tonnes, a trivial 4 million tonnes (1.45 percent) less than the province's 2014 emissions total. Since the plan, to its credit, calls for the elimination of all coal-fired electricity generation by 2030, the trivial nature of Alberta's proposed GHG emissions reduction should be attributed in large part to anticipated increases in emissions from the tar sands. Financially, there's no reason to expect the taxes associated with this version of "climate leadership" will be any more onerous on tar sands producers than previous carbon taxing proposals. In 2003, Suncor and Syncrude concluded that if Ottawa imposed a $15 per ton carbon tax on their operations it would have a very marginal impact on their production costs; Suncor put those costs at between 20 and 27 cents per barrel; Syncrude estimated a range of 22 to 30 cents per barrel.[19] A yet-to-be revealed Carbon Competitiveness Regulation will replace the Specified Gas Emitters Regulation in 2018. If this replacement follows the Leadership Plan's recommendation, Alberta will continue to offer large GHG emitters a variety of ways to satisfy the government's GHG emissions ambitions. Buying their way out of making real reductions in their plants will continue to be an option for large emitters to "reduce" emissions. And, as noted in the last chapter, some economists expect large emitters with low carbon-intensity levels, including some tar sands producers, to profit financially from the "output-based allocations of emissions rights" proposed in the Climate Leadership Plan. The subsidy they receive from the provincial government may exceed the carbon tax they pay.

This lax treatment of the tar sands was affirmed, if not compounded, by Premier Notley's decision to introduce a cap on tar sands emissions, a measure not recommended in the Climate Leadership Plan. The premier didn't cap tar sands emissions below or even at the level (65.6 million tonnes) reported in the national greenhouse gas emissions inventory Canada submitted to the United Nations Framework Convention on Climate Change in 2016. Instead, Alberta's cap on tar sands emissions was set at 110 million tonnes. This cap amounts to a 68 percent increase in tar sands emissions from 2014 levels. With such a generous emissions limit, this NDP measure complements, rather than rejects, the Progressive Conservative history of measures that have been toothless in reducing GHG emissions from the tar sands. Using the production/emissions history of the tar sands as a rough guide to the future, this 110 Mt cap may turn out to be academic. Between 2005 and 2014, tar sands production increased by 1.17 million barrels per day to 1.99 mbd; the sector's GHG emissions rose by 33.6 million tonnes over this period. Under the pessimistic or conservative assumption that the Climate Leadership Plan doesn't produce any of the improvements in GHG emissions intensity it strives for, this history suggests that at least another 1.17 mbd of tar sands production could come on stream (with an additional 33.6 Mt of GHG emissions) before emissions approached the 110 Mt cap. It's difficult to see this NDP measure—even assuming it isn't removed or modified by future governments—as representing a serious impediment to tar sands expansions in the forseeable future. The more likely constraint on expansion was noted earlier—the escalating supply costs associated with the current generation of tar sands projects.

Canadian public policy still clearly privileges the tar sands over nature. This privilege has also been promoted by political messaging, by political spin doctors. The Notley government indulges in the same doublespeak about its contribution to addressing climate change as did its Progressive Conservative predecessors. Exaggerated labels are attached to government reports and legislation. The bravado the Progressive Conservatives showed in labelling their 2008 climate change strategy *Alberta's 2008 Climate Change Strategy: Responsibility/Leadership/Action* is equalled in the NDP's choice of title for its flagship climate change strategy document: *Climate Leadership: Report to Minister*. The bar for climate change leadership in Alberta is a very low one indeed if it may be satisfied by a 1.45 percent or 4-million-tonne reduction in emissions in 2030 from 2014 levels. Alberta's leadership doesn't look any more admirable if it's seen instead as calling for Alberta's GHG emissions in 2030 to be 16 percent higher than the 233 Mt the province emitted in 2005. This reality didn't give pause to Alberta's Environment and Parks Minister Shannon Phillips before saying that Alberta's *Oil Sands Emissions Limits Act* showed "the world that energy-producing jurisdictions can establish limits and work and thrive in a carbon constrained future."[20] She looked forward to telling the 22nd Conference of the Parties meeting in Marrakech "what is possible from an energy-producing jurisdiction" and that Alberta was "a world leader on climate action."[21]

Should the world really want other oil-producing jurisdictions that are increasing their production to follow Alberta's version of climate leadership? In 2015, Texas had more than tripled its oil production from 2005 production levels, to 3.462 mbd.[22] The state's GHG emissions in 2005 were 785.68 Mt. If the Lone Star State replicated Alberta's proposed 2005 to 2030 greenhouse gas emissions trajectory, it could emit 911.4 Mt in 2030, 120 million tonnes more than the World Resources Institute calculated the state's GHG emissions to be in 2011.[23] Or, if the Russian Federation used Alberta's proposed 2005 to 2030 emissions trajectory as its guide, Russia's 2030 emissions could rise by 337.7 million tonnes from their 2005 level. This 16 percent increase would send 249.1 million tonnes more greenhouse gases into the atmosphere than Russia emitted in 2013.[24] If the United States followed Alberta's "16 percent" climate leadership prescription, it would abandon the progress made in reducing GHG emissions while nearly doubling American oil production from 2005 to 2015.[25] Given the context established by the Progressive Conservatives' neglect of serious climate change policy, perhaps what the Notley government has delivered qualifies as a type of leadership. I think, however, that the Notley path that should be portrayed in much more modest terms; it's hardly the case that Alberta is now "a world leader on climate action."

Market Fundamentalism and Countermovements

It is never a given that a strong protective countermovement will arise to challenge market fundamentalism. Such a countermovement has yet to appear in the politics of the tar sands. Block, Somers, and Evans all claim that a variety of conditions must be met in order for effective countermovements to emerge. Opportunities, location in the structure of power, resources (including organizational capacities), ideology—all may be relevant to explaining the emergence and effectiveness of the opposition to the post-1995 reregulation of the tar sands.

The privileged position of petroleum in Alberta's political economy, due to its centrality to material prosperity, has always raised obstacles to challenging its needs and desires. This position was a fundamental obstacle to building a movement that could challenge reregulation. Petroleum's privilege in the tar sands was augmented by the position labour took as the National

Task Force on Oil Sands Strategies crafted the vision for exploiting Alberta's bitumen. Labour stood with, not against, capital when it came to reregulation. The tension between labour and capital may be seen as one important characteristic of Polanyi's double movement, a movement that historically has allowed workers to win some concessions from the market, concessions Lindblom might call market reform or Block might have called the rationality of capitalism. This tension didn't exist in the early to mid-1990s. Trade unions joined business leaders in lobbying the state for a new fiscal regime for the tar sands. Schisms appeared once the juggernaut of industrialization was picking up speed and oil prices rose impressively. But nature never benefited from those ruptures, focused as they have been on issues such as royalties, labour shortages, and upgrading more of Alberta's bitumen in the province. On the eve of the boom, this elite unity also was found in the Alberta legislature. There the Liberal official opposition joined the Progressive Conservative government in endorsing the reregulation of the tar sands. If a nature-focused countermovement was to emerge, it would be led and populated by environmentalists and First Nations.

Political institutions played a vital role in denying opportunities for an effective provincial or national countermovement to emerge to oppose unfettered tar sands growth. Project proposals were channelled through and considered by provincial regulatory processes notoriously inhospitable to allowing a broad cross-section of environmentalists to participate and question the scale and pace of development. With the passage of time, these processes and rules were adjusted to make these opportunities even scarcer. Societal opposition to growth was simply regarded as less and less legitimate. The state, at both the provincial and federal levels, changed the rules of its hearing processes to make it more difficult for society's opponents to voice their concerns. Whatever alternative vision these opponents might have for accommodating the ambitions of tar sands developers on the boreal landscape wasn't welcome. The Cumulative Environmental Management Association should be seen in a similar light. Industry's dominance in CEMA ensured that environmentalists and First Nations would at best have significant difficulties in furthering their efforts to moderate the boom's ecological excesses.

The difficulties critics encountered were aggravated, in some cases, by a want of organizational capacity. This may have been particularly important with respect to First Nations. First Nations, unlike most provincial or national environmental groups, virtually were guaranteed standing in Alberta regulatory hearings. Living in the midst of tar sands industrialization opened the door to participation. But they don't appear to have had the financial or personnel resources needed to take advantage of that opportunity, especially in the first decade of the boom. Comparing the breadth and sophistication of the Mikisew Cree First Nation's intervention at CNRL's Horizon hearings with First Nation interventions prior to Horizon supports this view. CNRL's $155,000 contribution to the MCFN's environmental assessment work is primarily responsible for the qualitative chasm between that submission and what the MCFN had been able to submit previously. Earlier projects from Syncrude, Suncor, Shell, and True North Energy might have faced stronger First Nation opposition if First Nations had better organizational capacities. This point was also illustrated by the difficulties the Athabasca Chipewyan First Nation had in coping well and responding effectively to the avalanche of consultation referrals industry sent their way. The imagery of David and Goliath is compelling here.

It's also important to recognize that the emergence of a strong domestic countermovement to reregulation was hampered by the fact that strings were attached to the funds First Nations received from industry and government. Funding was contingent on a general willingness of First Nations to accommodate themselves to industrialization. Government and industry didn't give First Nations the opportunity to contribute to the blueprint for exploiting the tar sands. But they were quite happy to give First Nations opportunities to benefit materially from the boom.

These strings and other aspects of industry's behaviour are reminders that it's naive to believe that industry won't try to defend their visions of market fundamentalism from society's challengers. In some cases, that defence produced open, direct conflict, but conflict that never boiled over into the streets. Industry played the capital strike card very effectively in the wake of the 2007 Alberta Royalty Review Panel report. They used their prominence in the economy to good effect and extracted concessions from the government. On most occasions, government was a partner, not an antagonist. Here too the public relations campaigns that industry and government developed in the wake of episodes such as the Aurora tailings reservoir incident shine light on this explicitly conflictual face of the tar sands' defence. Industry also defended its development vision through efforts to coopt and compromise potential critics in the First Nations communities. They have encouraged First Nations to join hands with them and exploit nature for material gain. Given histories of impoverishment and decimation of traditional Aboriginal commercial vocations such as trapping (decimated by environmentalist opposition), it shouldn't be a surprise to see thoughtful leaders of First Nation communities want to join the tar sands boom. Those who have a one-dimensional view of First Nations, seeing them as only steadfast, unwavering opponents of environmentalism, have missed a crucial aspect of the place of Aboriginal peoples in the tar sands boom. This missing piece contributes importantly to the failure of a strong domestic counter-movement to emerge.

Industry's efforts to coopt and compromise have also sapped some of the potential for provincial environmentalists to play a stronger role in the development of a countermovement. The Pembina Institute has played an important role in shaping the tone of the environmental opposition to the tar sands. Their publications are very valuable in understanding the scale and ecological consequences of the tar sands. Through their interest in the lands at the heart of the tar sands boom, they were able to participate and raise questions others could not about the wisdom of market fundamental-ism's prescription for northeastern Alberta. But the impressive organizational capacity that allows Pembina to play these important roles is due in part to the Institute's strategy to derive significant portions of its revenues from tar sands operators. These are the very companies that have turned the boreal landscape into one of sacrifice and that are the major contributors to the growth of Canadian GHG emissions. Pembina's collaborative instincts made the Institute a good candidate to work with industry and, intentionally or not, help industry and government to weaken the environmental critique.

Some of the frustration experienced by those who see the need for a protective countermovement to challenge reregulation in the tar sands rests in what was noted above. Opportunities have suffered when interests between possible antagonists coincide rather than diverge. At times, the interests of labour, First Nations, and environmentalists have been more congruent with industry than Polanyi's double movement might suggest. Opportunities for a provincial or national countermovement to develop as well have suffered due to institutions, particularly by how precepts of market fundamentalism have been institutionalized into regulatory processes, environmental assessment processes, and ad hoc industry-led and dominated organizations. The latter have few, if any, accountability linkages to elected officials. These institutions matter so significantly here because of the ideas they embody.

When George Koch drew attention to the fact that, in only seven years, tar sands developers incurred $7.3 billion in cost overruns he asked: "So where's the outrage?"[26] There wasn't any. The version of market society that took root in Alberta's political landscape was one where these excesses were excused. While they weren't applauded, they certainly weren't condemned either. This tolerance for market excess should be seen as reflecting a faith in the market. There was widespread faith that these overruns could be excused due to the growth they were part of. Imagine the scorn and rebuke government would have earned if it reported those volumes of red ink to its electors as part of a successful effort to boost employment and gross domestic product. If such bumps on the tar sands road were natural, so too was the idea that the state should be little more than a hospitable concierge. "We're here to deliver the services required," Premier Stelmach said. "There is no such thing as touching the brake or anything like that."[27]

The ideological power of the market, its promises and excesses, also help to explain the support the tar sands have enjoyed among some First Nations leaders and their communities. Collapsing oil prices explain why Chief Boucher of the Fort McKay First Nation saw his salary sag to $375,000 in the 2015–16 fiscal year from $675,000 in 2014–15.[28] Such tremendous wealth among the leaders of this First Nation, even after the collapse in oil prices, is due overwhelmingly to the First Nation's oil and gas businesses. Why wouldn't the First Nation leadership view the market in a positive light?

The same could be said of the Pembina Institute. Its collaborative approach reflects an important accommodation with market ideology. In early 2017, the Institute held its annual unGALA in Toronto, an event where "cowgirls and cowboys ride herd on climate policy." There were plenty of opportunities then to sponsor those Pembina wranglers. For $15,000 you could join Cenovus, CIBC, ConocoPhillips, Enbridge, RBC, Scotiabank, and Suncor as "Clean Energy Champions." For $25,000 you could have joined TD as a silver sponsor; a cheque for $35,000 could have bought you a gold sponsorship like Shell Canada. The Institute's platinum and presenting sponsorships, requiring donations of $50,000 and $75,000 respectively, hadn't been snapped up when I last checked. Free cowboy hats were provided for all unGALA attendees.[29]

The compelling and enduring nature of the ideology of market fundamentalism in Alberta is underlined by the initial suite of measures the Notley government aimed at the tar sands. A banker and a chief economist for an investment firm were part of the four-member team the premier endorsed to review Alberta's royalty regime. Staying the course on royalties was a predictable result of their work. What did the NDP government do about the permissive, accommodative stance the Progressive Conservatives had signalled they would take toward the blight of tailings reservoirs on the boreal landscape? Embrace it. Implement it. The province's climate leadership plan is meek in its treatment of the tar sands. It's difficult to see the 110+ million tonne regulatory cap on emissions from the tar sands as a measure establishing a meaningful limit on the sector's GHG emissions in the near to medium term. That four tar sands CEOs stood with the premier as she detailed Alberta's leadership intentions might have suggested as much. So too does Alberta's decision to leave it to the market to determine what emissions reductions the tar sands sector will actually contribute toward meeting the province's less than ambitious 2030 emissions target.

There is no doubt that Premier Notley was dealt a terrible hand of economic cards to play when she assumed office in 2015. As oil prices sank and jobs vanished, Canadians, but especially Albertans, were reminded about petroleum's significance to general material wealth. The structural weight of petroleum, its privileged position in the Alberta and Canadian political economies, may well mean that a government of any ideological temperament cannot stray very far from catering to the market in its policies. But at the same time we should appreciate history and recognize that this structural weight and importance resulted from government decisions animated by ideology, not by necessity.

"Lacking a responsive nation state," Evans wrote, "it becomes difficult for social movements to gain traction around progressive agendas at the national level."[30] This describes well the situation we have detailed here. Ideology, interests, and institutions crippled the chances of responsiveness. This absence provided the impetus for opposition to go beyond Canada's borders to challenge the tar sands boom. Taking the case against the tar sands to international audiences, particularly politicians and consumers in the United States—the destination for virtually all tar sands production—was an opportunity that the overmatched Canadian environmentalists and First Nations ultimately took. President Obama's rejection of the Keystone XL pipeline was the clearest success of this transnational evolution of the environmental critique. This success, short-lived as it turned out to be, suggested still that the institutions and politics of nation states may remain essential to the prospects of success for transnational opposition. American political institutions, the presidential permission required for international pipelines, is fundamental to understanding the initial success of the opposition against Keystone XL. Presidential belief and aspirations, along with electoral politics, also contributed to success for the environmentalists during the Obama administration. Failure would have been more likely if Obama hadn't aspired to being seen as a climate change leader and if 350.org hadn't worked very hard to make Keystone XL an election issue.

The Future

The situation described by Polanyi, where forces emerge to successfully challenge the interests threatened by market fundamentalism in settings such as the tar sands, isn't upon us yet. Actors who regard Alberta's boreal ecosystem as little more than a petroleum reservoir have prevailed there for decades. Looking ahead, there are perhaps more reasons to suspect there is more gas in market fundamentalism's tank and that its run in the tar sands isn't over yet.

Internationally, President Donald Trump is one of those reasons. Trump declared his support for the Keystone XL pipeline project during the 2016 election campaign, and approving the pipeline was one of his first acts as president. In March 2017, the State Department issued the permit the Obama administration had denied TransCanada. Raised from the grave, Keystone XL can still expect a fight from organizations like 350.org and the Sierra Club. Legal challenges, demonstrations, and efforts to win the support of electors and candidates in the 2018 midterm elections are all avenues the pipeline's opponents may try to take. Michael Brune, executive director of the Sierra Club, vowed: "We will defeat this pipeline in the courts and the court of public opinion."[31] Trump's scorn for the scientific consensus on climate change could also bode well for the continued importance of market fundamentalism in petroleum politics and policy generally. Displaying a level of parochialism on par with his narcissism, President Trump announced his intention to withdraw the United States from the Paris Agreement on Climate Change.[32] The United States will join Nicaragua and Syria as the only members of the United Nations that do not subscribe to that nonbinding agreement.[33] The appointments of Scott Pruitt, Rex Tillerson, and Rick Perry to the positions of Environmental Protection Agency administrator, Secretary of State, and Secretary of Energy respectively also confirm the Trump administration's enthusiasm for the petroleum sector. Pruitt is a climate change skeptic. Tillerson, as ExxonMobil's CEO, oversaw the expansion of the ExxonMobil subsidiary Imperial Oil Ltd. in the tar sands. Perry's disdain for regulation was seen in his call to eliminate the Department of Energy altogether. It would be very surprising if they didn't run their organizations in ways promoting further increases in petroleum production.

Trump's naked enthusiasm for an America-first style of capitalism, however, is a double-edged sword. A Trump version of market fundamentalism in energy isn't necessarily one that would benefit the tar sands. Trump's desire to create jobs in America may lead to efforts to reregulate the American oil economy in ways to improve the cost competitiveness of the more expensive production flowing from shale oil plays such as Eagle Ford in Texas and the Bakken in North Dakota. If successful, those efforts could spell trouble for recent and future tar sands production and expansions. The inflated supply costs that the disciples of market fundamentalism delivered in Alberta could threaten the tar sands, especially if an improvement in US shale oil competitiveness and production dampens the prospects of oil prices returning to the US$100 level. Raising the oil price level needed for profitability in the tar sands—that's one of the risks of the reregulated tar sands that wasn't associated with developing bitumen in the early 1990s.

Domestically, the rules and institutions that facilitated the boom have remained largely untouched by new administrations in Edmonton and Ottawa. This institutional legacy is powerful and constitutes an important obstacle to challenging the state of the reregulated tar sands.

On the other hand, we may be on the cusp of change where impotent past challenges to the tar sands could be replaced by more powerful and effective critiques. Such environmental challenges to the future of the tar sands might arise from domestic politics. But in order to be more responsive, the state would have to change substantially. The many institutional biases identified previously that benefit market/business-led tar sands development would need to be tackled. Furthermore, leaders of political parties would need to be convinced that their electoral fortunes would suffer fatally if they didn't deliver more assertive policies on issues central to the health of nature such as climate change, protected areas, and reclamation. Such convincing may require a degree of mass political organization and mobilization Canadian environmentalism hasn't seen yet. Here is where Canadian opponents of the tar sands may be able to profit from the transnational network and strategies of an organization like 350.org. Such future campaigns should consider carefully the international institutional landscape and target those jurisdictions that offer access and resources to interests that, to this point in time, have been disadvantaged in the political struggle between petroleum and nature in Alberta's boreal forest.

Notes

1   Daniel Yergin coined the phrase "Hydrocarbon Age" in *The Prize.*
2   United States Department of Energy, Energy Information Administration, *Annual Energy Review* (September 2012), https://www.eia.gov/totalenergy/data/annual/showtext.php?t=ptb0507.
3   Ashar, "Canada's Oil Sands."
4   Alan J. MacFadyen and G. Campbell Watkins, *Petropolitics: Petroleum Development, Markets and Regulations, Alberta as an Illustrative History* (Calgary: University of Calgary Press, 2014), 160–61.
5   The completely privatized Alberta Energy Corporation, not a department of the Alberta government, shared responsibility with the federal government when it came to allowing access to the 5,400 square kilometres of the Cold Lake Air Weapons Range that fell within Alberta's boundaries.
6   Nelson, interview, 8, 12.
7   Alberta Energy, "About Oil Sands: Facts and Statistics," http://www.energy.alberta.ca/OilSands/791.asp.
8   Statistics Canada, *Public and Private Investment in Canada, Intentions, 2014* (Ottawa: Statistics Canada, 2014), 18.
9   Evans, "Is an Alternative Globalization Possible?," 277.

10   Fort McMurray First Nation, "Submission to 2015 Alberta Royalty Review Panel," 15.

11   The Energy Information Administration reported that the monthly spot price of WTI at Cushing, Oklahoma, fell from US$103.59 per barrel in July 2014 to $30.32 in February 2016. See United States Department of Energy, "Cushing, OK WTI Spot Price FOB."

12   Petter Osmundsen, "Risk Sharing and Incentives in Norwegian Petroleum Extraction," *Energy Policy* 27, no. 9 (September 1999).

13   One generous feature of the fiscal system was that it allowed the full expensing of fixed capital costs rather than requiring those costs to be amortized over the life of a project. See Macnab, Daniels, and Laxer, *Giving Away the Alberta Advantage*, 54.

14   The Fort McMurray First Nation submission to the 2015 royalty review panel supported increasing royalties in part on the grounds that such a move would reduce excessive investment in the oil sands. Fort McMurray First Nation, "Submission to 2015 Alberta Royalty Review Panel."

15   Environment and Climate Change Canada, "Global Greenhouse Gas Emissions," http://www.ec.gc.ca/indicateurs-indicators/default.asp?lang=en&n=54C061B5-1.

16   If the GHG emissions of the conventional oil and natural gas sectors are included, then Alberta's petroleum sector accounted for 63.1 Mt or 64 percent of Alberta's GHG emissions increase between 1990 and 2014. Environment and Climate Change Canada, *National Inventory Report 1990–2014, Part 3*, 81.

17   Canadian Society of Professional Biologists, Alberta Chapter and Alberta Society of Professional Biologists, *Seeking Consensus: The Public's Role in Environmental Decision Making* (Edmonton: Alberta Society of Professional Biologists, 1988), 104–05.

18   Lukes, *Power: A Radical View*; Peter Bachrach and Morton S. Baratz, "Decisions and Nondecisions: An Analytical Framework," *American Political Science Review* 57, no. 3 (September 1963).

19   "Kyoto Impact Minimal, Suncor Says," *Globe and Mail*, 10 January 2003; "Kyoto Oil Sands 'Scare' Eases," *Globe and Mail*, 10 January 2003; "Trust Puts Kyoto Costs at Up to 30 Cents a Barrel," *Globe and Mail*, 25 January 2003.

20   Claudia Cattaneo, "Alberta's NDP Puts Oilsands on a Leash by Moving Law to Place Cap on Emissions," *Financial Post*, November 1, 2016.

21   Alberta, "Alberta Updates World on Climate Leadership Plan," media release, November 8, 2016, https://www.alberta.ca/release.cfm?xID=43788B7D1B7F4-B61F-859C-F8294334EB975598.

22   In 2005, Texas produced 1.076 mbd of crude oil. See Energy Information Administration, "Texas Field Production of Crude Oil," https://www.eia.gov/dnav/pet/hist/LeafHandler.ashx?n=pet&s=mcrfptx1&f=a.

23   World Resources Institute, "CAIT U.S. State Greenhouse Gas Emissions" (Washington, DC: World Resources Institute), http://www.wri.org/resources/data-sets/cait-historical-emissions-data-countries-us-states-unfccc.

24   Russian GHG emissions data are calculated using the Historical Emissions tool from World Resources Institute, "CAIT Climate Data Explorer, 2015" (Washington, DC: World Resources Institute). The data for 2005 are from http://cait.wri.org/historical/Country%20GHG%20Emissions?indicator[]=

Total%20GHG%20Emissions%20Excluding%20Land-Use%20Change%20and %20Forestry&indicator[]=Total%20GHG%20Emissions%20Including%20 Land-Use%20Change%20and%20Forestry&year[]=2005&country[]=Russian% 20Federation&sortIdx=NaN&chartType=geo.The data for 2013 are from http:// cait.wri.org/historical/Country%20GHG%20Emissions?indicator[]=Total%20 GHG%20Emissions%20Excluding%20Land-Use%20Change%20and%20 Forestry&indicator[]=Total%20GHG%20Emissions%20Including%20Land- Use%20Change%20and%20Forestry&year[]=2013&country[]=Russian%20 Federation&sortIdx=NaN&chartType=geo.

25   American oil production rose from 5.184 mbd in 2005 to 9.415 mbd in 2015. See Energy Information Administration, "U.S. Field Production of Crude Oil," https://www.eia.gov/dnav/pet/hist/LeafHandler.ashx?n=pet&s=mcrf pus1&f=a. US GHG emissions declined from 7,378.8 Mt in 2005 to 6,870.5 Mt in 2011. See United States Environmental Protection Agency, "Fast Facts from the Inventory of US Greenhouse Gas Emissions and Sinks: 1990–2014," https://www.epa.gov/sites/production/files/2016-06/documents/us_ghg_ inv_fastfacts2016.pdf.

26   George Koch, "Money Pit: Think the Federal Government Is the Champion of Wasting Money?," *National Post Business Magazine*, July 1, 2004.

27   Canadian Broadcasting Corporation, "Stelmach Prepares to Take Charge as Premier" (December 4, 2006), http://www.cbc.ca/news/canada/edmonton/ stelmach-prepares-to-take-charge-as-premier-1.575588.

28   "Financial Statements, Fort McKay First Nation, Schedules of Salaries, Honoraria, Travel Expenses and Other Remuneration, Year Ended March 31, 2016," http://fnp-ppn.aadnc-aandc.gc.ca/fnp/Main/Search/DisplayBinaryData. aspx?BAND_NUMBER_FF=467&FY=2015-2016&DOC=Schedule%20 of%20Remuneration%20and%20Expenses&lang=eng; "Financial Statements, Fort McKay First Nation, Schedules of Salaries, Honoraria, Travel Expenses and Other Remuneration, Year Ended March 31, 2015," http://fnp-ppn.aadnc- aandc.gc.ca/fnp/Main/Search/DisplayBinaryData.aspx?BAND_NUMBER_ FF=467&FY=2014-2015&DOC=Schedule%20of%20Remuneration%20 and%20Expenses&lang=eng.

29   Pembina Institute, "unGALA 2017," http://www.pembina.org/event/ ungala-2017.

30   Evans, "Is an Alternative Globalization Possible?," 275.

31   Brady Dennis and Steven Mufson, "As Trump Administration Grants Approval for Keystone XL Pipeline, an Old Fight Is Reignited," *Washington Post*, March 24, 2017.

32   Donald Trump, "Statement by President Trump on the Paris Climate Accord," June 1, 2017, https://www.whitehouse.gov/the-press-office/2017/06/01/ statement-president-trump-paris-climate-accord; Oliver Milman, David Smith, and Damian Carrington, "Donald Trump Confirms US Will Quit Paris Climate Agreement," *Guardian*, June 1, 2017.

33   Haroon Siddique, "US Joins Syria and Nicaragua on Climate Accord 'No' List," *Guardian*, June 1, 2017.

Appendix 1: Oil Sands Production, 1995–2015, BPD (000s)

Year	Synthetic Crude Oil (SCO)	Non-Upgraded Bitumen	Total	SCO as percentage of Total Production
1995	281.783	200.015	481.798	58.5
1996	281.154	216.369	497.523	56.5
1997	289.331	298.765	588.096	49.2
1998	308.200	344.681	652.881	47.2
1999	323.296	347.197	667.977	48.4
2000	320.151	347.197	667.348	48.0
2001	349.084	375.501	724.585	48.2
2002	440.915	401.289	842.204	52.4
2003	508.845	446.721	955.566	53.3
2004	598.789	487.460	1,086.249	55.1
2005	546.584	518.279	1,064.863	51.3
2006	657.913	596.273	1,254.186	52.5
2007	687.475	632.754	1,320.229	52.1
2008	653.510	650.994	1,304.504	50.1
2009	765.469	723.327	1,488.796	51.4
2010	794.402	818.674	1,613.076	49.2
2011	862.332	881.201	1,743.533	49.5
2012	913.279	1,008.254	1,921.533	47.5
2013	935.922	1,148.518	2,084.440	44.9
2014	953.534	1,350.420	2,303.954	41.4
2015	976.177	1,549.807	2,525.984	38.6

Source: Alberta, Alberta Energy Regulator, "ST98 Executive Summary Report Data, Figure 10 and Figure 11," https://www.aer.ca/data-and-publications/statistical-reports/report-data. The thousands of cubic metres per day figures reported by the AER have been converted to thousands of barrels per day.

References

ABC News. "Hunting for Oil Canada." *Nightline*, July 28, 2008.

ACDEN. "ACDEN New Facility Walkthrough." YouTube video, 6:15. Uploaded May 23, 2013. https://www.youtube.com/watch?v=ut8H1Hq2hBw.

ACDEN. "ACDEN: The Strategic Service Provider." http://www.acfnbusinessgroup.com/.

Alaska Department of Revenue, Tax Division. *Alaska Oil Production, Production History FY* 1959–2012.* http://www.tax.alaska.gov/sourcesbook/Alaska Production.pdf.

Alberta. *Albertans & Climate Change: Taking Action.* October 2002.

Alberta. "Albertans to Benefit from a More Efficient, Effective Regulatory System." News release. October 24, 2012. https://alberta.ca/release.cfm?xID=3316894717280-EB7E-BBC2-D83D1C8E1B1F8C34.

Alberta. *Alberta's First Nations Consultation Guidelines on Land Management and Resource Development.* Edmonton: 2007. http://indigenous.alberta.ca/documents/First_Nations_and_Metis_Relations/First_Nations_Consultation_Guidelines_LM_RD.pdf

Alberta. "Alberta's New Royalty Framework Speech." Edmonton: January 29, 2016. https://www.alberta.ca/release.cfm?xID=401538F1E58AB-B873-40B1-E9C9A284B7AF4D22.

Alberta. "Alberta Updates World on Climate Leadership Plan." Media release. November 8, 2016. https://www.alberta.ca/release.cfm?xID=43788B7D1B7F4-B61F-859C-F8294334EB975598.

Alberta. "Chair Named to Manage Provincial Climate Change Fund." News release. May 6, 2009. https://www.alberta.ca/release.cfm?xID=2588916EB7350-94B1-016E-779CDCE024F9CDBE.

Alberta. "Climate Leadership Plan Speech." Media release. November 22, 2015. https://www.alberta.ca/release.cfm?xID=38886E9269850-A787-1C1E-A5C90ACF52A4DAE4.

Alberta. "Legislation Backs Alberta's Plan to Reduce Emissions." News release. April 7, 2003. https://alberta.ca/release.cfm?xID=14168.

Alberta. "Let's Talk Royalties." https://letstalkroyalties.ca/.

Alberta. *Lower Athabasca Region—Tailings Management Framework for the Mineable Athabasca Oil Sands.* Edmonton: March 2015.

Alberta. "The Panel: Peter Tertzakian." https://letstalkroyalties.ca/panel/peter-tertzakian/.

Alberta. "Phasing Out Coal Pollution." https://www.alberta.ca/climate-coal-electricity.aspx.

Alberta. "Premier Stelmach Delivers Historic, New Royalty Regime for Alberta." News release. October 25, 2007. https://alberta.ca/release.cfm?xID=22384D8D0CC20-9549-7D32-2CF5FDADC70214D2.

Alberta. "Province Takes Meaningful Steps Toward Climate Change Strategy." Media release. June 25, 2015. https://www.alberta.ca/release.cfm?xID= 38232B11A8C17-0B34-BB8E-6B03088D90D1C786.

Alberta. "Province to Capture Feedback on Royalty Recommendations." News release. September 25, 2007. http://alberta.ca/release.cfm?xID= 221663DDF2206-A43B-D590-E8244B31BFA13C82.

Alberta. "Washington Mission Aims to Build on Alberta-US Relations: Stevens to Stress Environmental Stewardship in Oil Sands Production." News release. April 23, 2008. https://alberta.ca/release.cfm?xID=233637BF323A2-EABD-EFD8-8048078D8B29257A.

Alberta Chamber of Resources. *Learning from Experience: Aboriginal Programs in the Resource Industries*. Edmonton: Alberta Chamber of Resources, January 2006.

Alberta Chamber of Resources. *Representative Costs for Mineable Oil Sands Projects*. Edmonton: Alberta Chamber of Resources, 1987.

Alberta Chamber of Resources, Oil Sands Task Force. *Athabasca Oil Sands Opportunities for Economic Growth*. Edmonton: Alberta Chamber of Resources, August 1987.

Alberta Economic Development. *Oil Sands Industry Update*. Edmonton: Alberta Economic Development, March 2004.

Alberta Economic Development. *Oil Sands Industry Update*. Edmonton: Alberta Economic Development, Spring 2005.

Alberta Employment, Immigration, and Industry. *Oil Sands Industry Update*. Edmonton: Alberta Economic Development, 2006.

Alberta Employment, Immigration, and Industry. *Oil Sands Industry Update*. Edmonton: Alberta Employment, Immigration, and Industry, 2007.

Alberta Energy. *1994–1995 Annual Report*.

Alberta Energy. *1995–1996 Annual Report*.

Alberta Energy. *1996–1997 Annual Report*.

Alberta Energy. *1997–1998 Annual Report*.

Alberta Energy. *Energy Security for Canada: The Oil Supply Option*. Edmonton: Alberta Energy, August 1987.

Alberta Energy. "Facts and Statistics." Edmonton: Alberta Energy, 2017. http://www.energy.alberta.ca/oilsands/791.asp.

Alberta Energy. "Phase-out of Coal-Fired Emissions in Alberta." Edmonton: Alberta Energy, March 2016. https://open.alberta.ca/dataset/9cc07f29-aee3-4c09-b13f-a7e22b59fef1/resource/3a1ec661-0375-4b7b-9e52-be043e6c269f/download/2016-03-FS-Coal-Phase-Out.pdf.

Alberta Energy and Utilities Board. *Application by Suncor Inc. Oil Sands Group for Amendment of Approval No. 7632 for Proposed Steepbank Mine Development, (Decision No. 97–1)*. Calgary: Alberta Energy and Utilities Board, 1997.

Alberta Energy and Utilities Board. *Application by Syncrude for the Aurora Mine, (Decision No. 97–13)*. Calgary: Alberta Energy and Utilities Board, October 1997.

Alberta Energy and Utilities Board. *Polaris Resources Ltd. Applications for a Well Licence, Special Gas Well Spacing, Compulsory Pooling, and Flaring Permit Livingstone Field*. Calgary: Alberta Energy and Utilities Board, December 16, 2003. http://www.aer.ca/documents/decisions/2003/2003-101.pdf.

Alberta Energy and Utilities Board. *Report of the Joint Review Panel Established by the Alberta Energy and Utilities Board and the Government of Canada EUB Decision*

2004–005: Canadian Natural Resources Limited, Application for an Oil Sands Mine, Bitumen Extraction Plant, and Bitumen Upgrading Plant in the Fort McMurray Area. Calgary: Alberta Energy and Utilities Board, January 27, 2004.

Alberta Energy and Utilities Board. *Report of the Joint Review Panel Established by the Alberta Energy and Utilities Board and the Government of Canada, Decision 2004–009: Shell Canada Limited, Applications for an Oil Sands Mine, Bitumen Extraction Plant, Cogeneration Plant, and Water Pipeline in the Fort McMurray Area.* Calgary: Alberta Energy and Utilities Board, February 5, 2004.

Alberta Energy and Utilities Board. *Report of the Joint Review Panel Established by the Alberta Energy and Utilities Board and the Government of Canada EUB Decision 2006–128: Albian Sands Energy Inc., Application to Expand the Oil Sands Mining and Processing Plant Facilities at the Muskeg River Mine.* Calgary: Alberta Energy and Utilities Board, December 17, 2006.

Alberta Energy and Utilities Board. *Shell Canada Limited: Muskeg River Mine Project, (Decision 99-2).* Calgary: Alberta Energy and Utilities Board, 2002.

Alberta Energy and Utilities Board. *TrueNorth Energy Corporation: Application to Construct and Operate an Oil Sands Mine and Cogeneration Plant in the Fort McMurray Area (Decision 2002-089).* Calgary: Alberta Energy and Utilities Board, 2002.

Alberta Energy and Utilities Board. *Report of the Joint Review Panel Established by the Alberta Energy and Utilities Board and the Government of Canada, EUB Decision 2006–128 (Albian Sands Energy Inc.).* Calgary: Alberta Energy and Utilities Board, 2006.

Alberta Energy Regulator. "AER Bulletin 2014-31: Changes to the Guidelines for Submission of a Predisturbance Assessment and Conservation and Reclamation Plan." Calgary: Alberta Energy Regulator, October 9, 2014. http://www.aer.ca/documents/bulletins/AER-Bulletin-2014-31.pdf.

Alberta Energy Regulator. "AER Suspends Directive 074: Tailings Performance Criteria and Requirements for Oil Sands Mining Schemes." News release. March 13, 2015. https://www.aer.ca/about-aer/media-centre/news-releases/news-release-2015-03-13.

Alberta Energy Regulator. "Directive 074: Tailings Performance Criteria and Requirements for Oil Sands Mining Schemes." Calgary: Energy Resources Conservation Board, February 2009.

Alberta Energy Regulator. "Directive 085: Fluid Tailings Management for Oil Sands Mining Projects." Calgary: Alberta Energy Regulator, July 14, 2016.

Alberta Energy Regulator. "ERCB Conditional Approval of Final Two Tailings Plans Ends Initial Phase of Directive 074." (News release). December 17, 2010. http://www.aer.ca/about-aer/media-centre/news-releases/news-release-2010-12-17-nr2010-20.

Alberta Energy Regulator. "ERCB Conditionally Approves Tailings Plan for Shell Muskeg River Project." News release. September 20, 2010. http://www.aer.ca/about-aer/media-centre/news-releases/news-release-2010-09-20-nr2010-13.

Alberta Energy Regulator. *Report of the Joint Review Panel Established by the Federal Minister of the Environment and the Energy Resources Conservation Board, Decision 2013 ABAER 011: Shell Canada Energy, Jackpine Mine Expansion Project.* Calgary: Alberta Energy Regulator, 2013.

Alberta Energy Regulator. *ST98–2013: Alberta's Energy Reserves 2012 and Supply/Demand Outlook 2013–2022,* Calgary: Alberta Energy Regulator, 2013.

Alberta Energy Regulator. *ST98–2014: Alberta's Energy Reserves 2013 and Supply/ Demand Outlook 2014–2023*. Calgary: Alberta Energy Regulator, 2014.

Alberta Energy Resources Conservation Board. *Energy Resources Conservation Board Rules of Practice* (Alberta Regulation 252/2007). Edmonton: Alberta Energy Resources Conservation Board, 2010.

Alberta Energy Resources Conservation Board. *2012 Tailings Management Assessment Report, Oil Sands Mining Industry*. Calgary: Alberta Energy Resources Conservation Board, June 2013.

Alberta Energy Resources Conservation Board. *Report of the Joint Review Panel Established by the Federal Minister of the Environment and the Energy Resources Conservation Board, Decision 2011–005: Total E&P Joslyn Ltd., Application for the Joslyn North Mine Project*. Calgary: Energy Resource Conservation Board, 2011.

Alberta Environment. *Alberta's 2008 Climate Change Strategy: Responsibility Leadership/ Action*. Edmonton: Alberta Environment, January 2008.

Alberta Environment. *Albertans and Climate Change: A Plan for Action*. Edmonton: Alberta Environment, 2002.

Alberta Environment. *Annual Report 2010–2011*.

Alberta Environment. *Regional Sustainable Development Strategy for the Athabasca Oil Sands Area*. July 1999.

Alberta Environment. *Sustainable Times*. Issue 1 (April 2000).

Alberta Environment. *Sustainable Times*. Issue 2 (November 2000).

Alberta Environment. *Sustainable Times*. Issue 4 (October 2001).

Alberta Environment and Alberta Sustainable Resource Development. *Annual Report 2014–2015*.

Alberta Environment and Alberta Sustainable Resource Development. *Regional Sustainable Development Strategy for the Alberta Oil Sands Area, Progress Report, July 2001*.

Alberta Environment and Parks. *Oil Sands Mine Reclamation and Disturbance Tracking by Year*. http://osip.alberta.ca/library/Dataset/Details/27.

Alberta Environment and Parks. "Total Area of the Oil Sands Tailings Ponds over Time." March 4, 2015. http://osip.alberta.ca/library/Dataset/ Details/542.

Alberta Environment and Parks. "Total Volume of the Oil Sands Tailings Ponds over Time." March 4, 2015. http://osip.alberta.ca/library/Dataset/Details/545.

Alberta Environmental Protection. *Fort McMurray-Athabasca Oil Sands Subregional Integrated Resource Plan*. Edmonton: Alberta Environmental Protection, 1996.

Alberta Federation of Labour. "The Bitumen Glut Has a Silver Lining." January 30, 2013. http://www.afl.org/bitumen_glut_has_silver_lining_6xph6dfam m9y4lliy8jvoz1ulo4.

Alberta Federation of Labour. "Royalty Policy Is the Biggest Decision Any Alberta Government Has to Make: Advice to Government on Energy and Royalty Policy." January 2016. https://d3n8a8pro7vhmx.cloudfront.net/afl/pages/ 2770/attachments/original/1454352012/AFL_Advice_on_AB_energy_and_ royalty_policy_26Jan201r2FINAL.pdf?1454352012.

Alberta Finance. "Expert Panel to Examine Alberta's Royalty Regime." News release. February 16, 2007. https://alberta.ca/release.cfm?xID= 21056CB7A4991-EBE3-078B-B875B4E7E86EBE6A.

Alberta Health Services. "Fort Chipewyan Cancer Study Findings Released." News release. February 6, 2009. http://www.albertahealthservices.ca/news/releases/2009/Page500.aspx.

Alberta Justice. "Royalty Review Industry Liaison Meetings." Mimeo, n.d.

Alberta Legislative Assembly. "MLA Remuneration—Effective April 1, 2014." http://www.assembly.ab.ca/lao/hr/MLA/MLA%20Remuneration%20April%202014.htm.

Alberta Oil. "CAPP Says Industry Working to Establish Mutually Respectful Relationships: An Interview with CAPP's Greg Stringham." April 9, 2014. https://www.albertaoilmagazine.com/2014/04/establishing-mutually-respectful-relationships-capp-greg-stringham/.

Alberta Oil and Gas Conservation Board. *Report on an Application of Atlantic Richfield Company, Cities Service Athabasca, Inc., Imperial Oil Limited and Royalite Oil Company, Limited under Part VI A of the Oil and Gas Conservation Act (OGCB Report 68-C).* Calgary: Alberta Oil and Gas Conservation Board, December 1968.

Alberta Oil Sands Consultations Multistakeholder Committee. *Peace River Hearings: Transcripts.* September 14, 2006.

Alberta Oil Sands Consultations Multistakeholder Committee. *Phase Two, meeting transcript.* Calgary, morning session. April 23, 2007.

Alberta Royalty Review Advisory Panel. *Alberta at a Crossroads: Royalty Review Advisory Panel Report,* 2016.

Alberta Royalty Review Panel. *Our Fair Share: Report of the Royalty Review Panel to the Hon. Lyle Oberg, Minister of Finance.* Edmonton: Department of Finance, 2007.

Alberta, Saskatchewan, and Quebec. *Security of Supply: An Opportunity for Canada.* Edmonton: Alberta Energy, January 30, 1987.

Alberta Treasury Board and Finance. *Fiscal Plan 2016–19.* 2016. http://finance.alberta.ca/publications/budget/budget2016/fiscal-plan-complete.pdf.

Alberta Wilderness Association. "Government Disregards Own Guidelines to Fast-track Policy Review. Changes Would Allow Oilsands Mining in Sensitive Wetland." News release. April 8, 2002. https://albertawilderness.ca/wordpress/wp-content/uploads/20020408_nr_awa_mcc_government_disregards_guidelines.pdf.

Alberts, Sheldon. "Obama Has Oilsands in His Sights; Pledge to Reduce Dependence on 'Dirty' Oil a Warning to Alberta Producers." *Vancouver Sun,* June 25, 2008, A12.

Albian Energy Inc. (Albian) and Oil Sands Environmental Coalition (OSEC). *Issue Resolution Document for the Proposed Muskeg River Mine Expansion Project.* August 21, 2006.

Albian Sands Energy Inc. *Application for Approval of the Muskeg River Mine Expansion Project.* Vol. 1, *Project Description.* April 2005.

Albian Sands Energy Inc. *Muskeg River Mine Expansion Project.* Vol. 2, *Air Quality, Noise and Environmental Health.* April 2005.

Alvarez, Pierre R. "Business Interest Associations and the Canadian State: A Case Study of the Independent Petroleum Association of Canada." Master's thesis, Department of Political Studies, Queen's University, 1986.

Anderson, Ronald. "Lalonde's Plans Felt Major Policy Blunder." *Globe and Mail*, November 20, 1980, B2.

Anderson, Ronald. "Longer-Term Costs Flow from Cheap Oil." *Globe and Mail*, April 9, 1986, B2.

ARC Financial Corp. "The Alberta Royalty Review Submission by ARC Financial Corp." Presented by Peter Tertzakian, Chief Energy Economist, Calgary, May 23, 2007, 4.

Arrowsmith, Lisa. "Oil Sands Giant Says 'Sorry' for Dead Ducks." *Globe and Mail*, May 3, 2008.

Ashar, Mike. "Canada's Oil Sands: A Globally Competitive Resource, Remarks by Mike Ashar, Executive Vice President, Suncor Energy Inc." Conference on Energy in the North American Market: Innovation, Investment and a More Secure Future, Washington, DC, June 12, 2003.

Asia Pulse. "Greenpeace Opposes Suncor Refinery Planned for Australia." March 7, 2000.

ATB Financial. *ATB 2015 Annual Report.* http://www.atb.com/SiteCollectionDocuments/About/annual_reports/atb_2015_annual_report.pdf.

Athabasca Tribal Council. "ATC, Industry and Federal Government Sign Ground-Breaking Agreement." January 24, 2000. http://atc97.org/finance-administration/federal-government.

Athabasca Tribal Council. "Industry Capacity Building Agreement." August 4, 1999. http://atc97.org/finance-administration/industry-capacity-building-agreement.

Auditor General of Alberta. *Annual Report of the Auditor General of Alberta 2006–2007.* Edmonton: Auditor General of Alberta, September 2007.

Auditor General of Alberta. *Report of the Auditor General of Alberta.* Edmonton: Auditor General of Alberta, October 2008.

Auditor General of Alberta. *Report of the Auditor General of Alberta.* Edmonton: Auditor General of Alberta, October 2012.

Austen, Ian. "Canadians Investigate Death of Ducks at Oil-Sands Project." *New York Times*, May 1, 2008.

Avery, Bryant. "Fort McKay Writes Off Gov't, Will Deal with Plants Directly; Surviving in the Land of Giants." *Edmonton Journal*, March 22, 1997, E1.

Avery, Bryant. "Way of Life Sees Drastic Changes." *Edmonton Journal*, March 22, 1997, E4.

Babiak, Todd. "No Answers Coming as to How Tainted Political Fixer Got Job." *Edmonton Journal*, April 9, 2011, A5.

Bachrach, Peter, and Morton S. Baratz. "Decisions and Nondecisions: An Analytical Framework." *American Political Science Review* 57, no. 3 (Sep. 1963): 632–42. https://doi.org/10.2307/1952568.

Bankes, Nigel. "Oil Sands Emission Limit Legislation: A Real Commitment or Kicking It Down the Road?" *Ablawg.ca* (blog), November 3, 2016. http://ablawg.ca/2016/11/03/oil-sands-emission-limit-legislation-a-real-commitment-or-kicking-it-down-the-road/.

Bankes, Nigel. "Separation of Powers and the Government's Response to the Judgment in *Pembina Institute v. Alberta (Environment and Sustainable Resources*

Development), 2013 ABQB 567." *Ablawg.ca* (blog),October 11, 2013. http://ablawg.ca/2013/10/11/separation-of-powers-and-the-governments-response-to-the-judgment-in-pembina-institute-v-alberta-environment-and-sustainable-resources-development-2013-abqb-567/.

Barker, Jim, Dave Rudolph, Trevor Tompkins, Alex Oiffer, Francoise Gervais, and Grace Ferguson."Attenuation of Contaminants in Groundwater Impacted by Surface Mining of Oil Sands, Alberta, Canada." Paper presented to the International Petroleum Environmental Conference, Houston, Texas, November 6–9, 2007. http://www.cec.org/sites/default/files/submissions/2006_2010/9182_10-2-rsub-appendix_v-_uwaterloo_suncor_leakage.pdf.

Bayulgen, Oksan. *Foreign Investment and Political Regimes: The Oil Sector in Azerbaijan, Russia, and Norway.* Cambridge: Cambridge University Press, 2010. https://doi.org/10.1017/CBO9780511676048.

Berry, David. "The Disobedient Albertans." *Alberta Views* 13, no. 5 (June 2010).

Berton, Pierre. *The Klondike Quest: A Photographic Essay 1897–1899.* Toronto: McClelland and Stewart, 1983.

Berton, Pierre. *Klondike: The Last Great Gold Rush 1896–1899.* 2nd ed. Toronto: McClelland and Stewart, 1972.

Betancourt, Rómulo. *Venezuela: Oil and Politics.* Boston: Houghton Mifflin Company, 1979.

Bielawski, Ellen. *Rogue Diamonds: Northern Riches on Dene Land.* Vancouver: Douglas & McIntyre, 2003.

Block, Fred. "Karl Polanyi and the Writing of *The Great Transformation.*" *Theory and Society* 32, no. 3 (2003): 275–306. https://doi.org/10.1023/A:1024420102334.

Block, Fred. "A New Era of Regulation?" *States, Power, and Societies* 15, no. 1 (2009): 1, 3, 5.

Block, Fred. "Polanyi's Double Movement and the Reconstruction of Critical Theory." *Revue Interventions économiques* 38 (2008): 1–14.

Block, Fred. "The Ruling Class Does Not Rule: Notes on the Marxist Theory of the State." *Socialist Revolution* 33 (1977): 6–28.

Block, Fred. "Swimming Against the Current: The Rise of a Hidden Developmental State in the United States." *Politics & Society* 36, no. 2 (2008): 169–206. https://doi.org/10.1177/0032329208318731.

Block, Fred. "Understanding the Diverging Trajectories of the United States and Western Europe: A Neo-Polanyian Analysis." *Politics & Society* 35, no. 1 (2007): 3–33. https://doi.org/10.1177/0032329206297162.

Block, Fred, and Margaret R. Somers. *The Power of Market Fundamentalism: Karl Polanyi's Critique.* Cambridge, MA: Harvard University Press, 2014. https://doi.org/10.4159/harvard.9780674416345.

Boothe, Paul. "Alberta's Greenhouse Gas Plan: A Glass Half Full or Half Empty?" *Maclean's,* November 24, 2015. http://www.macleans.ca/economy/economicanalysis/albertas-greenhouse-gas-plan-a-glass-half-full-or-half-empty.

Boothe, Paul, Félix-A. Boudreault, and Christopher Frankel. "Getting to 2030: Comparing and Coordinating Provincial Climate Policies." Toronto: Institute for Competitiveness & Prosperity, October 2016.

Boothe, Paul, Mel Cappe, and Christopher Ragan. "A Federal Carbon Price Demonstrates Policy Progress, Perils." *Globe and Mail*, October 16, 2016.

Boston, Terry. "Letter to The Honourable Rachel Notley." September 30, 2016. https://www.alberta.ca/documents/Electricity-Terry-Boston-Letter-to-Premier.pdf.

Boucher, Jim, and George Arcand, Jr. *2014 Management Discussion and Analysis, Fort McKay First Nation, Alberta*. September 15, 2014. http://fnp-ppn.aandc-aadnc. gc.ca/fnp/Main/Search/DisplayBinaryData.aspx?BAND_NUMBER_FF= 467&FY=2013-2014&DOC=Schedule%20of%20Remuneration%20and%20 Expenses&lang=eng.

Boué, Juan Carlos. "Enforcing *Pacta Sunt Servanda*? Conoco-Phillips and Exxon-Mobil versus the Bolivarian Republic of Venezuela and Petróleos de Venezuela." *Centre of Latin American Studies, University of Cambridge*. Working Papers Series 2, no. 1.

Boutilier, Guy. "Interview with Guy Boutilier." By Adriana A. Davies. *Petroleum History Society Oil Sands Oral History Project*, December 12, 2012, transcript, 8. http://www.glenbow.org/collections/search/findingAids/archhtm/extras/ oilsands/Boutilier_Guy.pdf.

BP. *BP Statistical Review of World Energy June 2014*. http://www.bp.com/content/ dam/bp-country/de_de/PDFs/brochures/BP-statistical-review-of-world-energy-2014-full-report.pdf.

BP. *BP Statistical Review of World Energy June 2015*. http://biomasspower.gov.in/ document/Reports/BP%20statistical%20review-2015.pdf.

Braid, Don. "Really, Just How Scary Is Notley?" *Calgary Herald*, April 30, 2015, A4.

Braid, Don. "Sorry, Mr. Stelmach, This Is One Big Compromise." *Calgary Herald*, October 26, 2007.

Bramley, Matthew. *An Assessment of Alberta's Climate Change Action Plan*. Drayton Valley, AB: Pembina Institute for Appropriate Development, September 2002.

Bramley, Matthew. *The Case for Deep Reductions: Canada's Role in Preventing Dangerous Climate Change*. Vancouver: David Suzuki Foundation and Pembina Institute, 2005. https://www.pembina.org/pub/536.

Braudel, Fernand. *Memory and the Mediterranean*. New York: Vintage Books, 2001.

Breen, David H. *Alberta's Petroleum Industry and the Conservation Board*. Edmonton: University of Alberta Press, 1993.

Bregha, François. *Bob Blair's Pipeline: The Business and Politics of Northern Energy Development Projects*. Toronto: James Lorimer and Company, 1979.

Broder, John M., and Dan Frosch. "Rejecting Pipeline Proposal, Obama Blames Congress." *New York Times*, January 18, 2012.

Broder, John M., and Dan Frosch. "US Delays Decision on Pipeline Until After Election." *New York Times*, November 10, 2011. http://www.nytimes. com/2011/11/11/us/politics/administration-to-delay-pipeline-decision-past-12-election.html?_r=0.

Brooke, James. "Canada Is Unlocking Petroleum from Sand: Digging for Oil." *New York Times*, January 23, 2001, C1.

Brookings Institution. *U.S.-Alberta Energy Relations: A Conversation with Premier Alison Redford*. Washington, DC: Brookings Institute, 2013. https://www. brookings.edu/wp-content/uploads/2013/03/20130409_alberta_energy_ redford_transcript.pdf.

Brooymans, Hanneke. "Cameron Gets First Look at Oilsands." *Edmonton Journal*, September 28, 2010, A1.

Brooymans, Hanneke. "Mikisew Cree Withdraw Constitutional Challenge of Mining Project." *edmontonjournal.com*, September 23, 2010.

Brooymans, Hanneke. "Syncrude Duck Deaths Kept Quiet; Province Aware 1,606 Ducks Killed on Tailings Pond, Not 500 Originally Reported to Public." *Edmonton Journal*, April 1, 2009, A1.

Brunnen, Ben. "Upstream Oil and Gas Industry Outlook." Calgary: Canadian Association of Petroleum Producers, 2015. www.capp.ca/~/media/capp/customer-portal/documents/272494.pdf.

Burke, Marie. "Metis Concerned about Expansion." *Windspeaker*, February 1999, 39.

Business Wire. "Suncor Earnings Increase 70% in the Quarter." April 21, 1994.

Buss, Karen E. "Letter to the Honourable Jim Prentice, Minister of the Environment, Energy Resources Conservation Board, and Canadian Environmental Assessment Agency." April 7, 2009. www.pembina.org/reports/letter-to-ceaa-ercb-april-07-2009.pdf.

Calgary Herald. "Where the Leadership Contenders Stand: The Herald Examines Candidates' Positions on Six Key Policy Issues." November 25, 2006, A17.

Campbell, Carolyn. "Birds and Tar Sands Tailings Ponds: Ever Safe to Land?" *Wild Lands Advocate* 22, no. 2 (April 2014).

Campbell, Colin J., and Jean H. Laherrère. "The End of Oil." *Scientific American* (March 1998).

Canada. *Northern Frontier, Northern Homeland: The Report of the Mackenzie Valley Pipeline Inquiry*. 2 volumes. Ottawa: Minister of Supply and Services Canada, 1977.

Canada Mortgage and Housing Corporation. *Housing Market Insight: Alberta*. December 2016. https://www.cmhc-schl.gc.ca/odpub/esub/68779/68779_2016_M12.pdf?fr=1501858642166

Canada Mortgage and Housing Corporation. *Rental Market Report: Canada Highlights*. 2016. https://www.cmhc-schl.gc.ca/odpub/esub/64667/64667_2016_A01.pdf?fr=1501859287406

Canada Newswire. "Canada and Alberta Announce Strengthened R&D Effort for Oil Sands and Heavy Oil." March 19, 1993.

Canada Newswire. "Syncrude Sets New Oil Production Mark." September 18, 1992.

Canada. Parliament. Senate. *Proceedings of the Standing Senate Committee on Aboriginal Peoples, 36th Parliament, 1st Session, Issue 23*, March 16, 1999.

Canada School of Energy and Environment. *Annual Report, 2009–10*.

Canadian Association of Petroleum Producers. "Capital Investment in Canada's Oil and Gas Industry Down 62% in Two Years." News release. April 7, 2016. http://www.capp.ca/media/news-releases/capital-investment-in-canada-oil-and-gas-industry-down-62-per-cent-in-2-years.

Canadian Association of Petroleum Producers. *Crude Oil: Forecast, Markets & Transportation*. Calgary: Canadian Association of Petroleum Producers, 2015.

Canadian Association of Petroleum Producers. "New Tailings Regulations: Directive 085." *Context: Energy Examined (CAPP's member magazine)* 4, no. 3 (August 2016).

Canadian Association of Petroleum Producers. *Oil Sands: Benefits to Alberta and Canada, Today and Tomorrow, Through a Fair, Stable and Competitive Fiscal Regime*. Calgary: Canadian Association of Petroleum Producers, 2007.

Canadian Association of Petroleum Producers. "Royalty Panel's Report Flawed; Industry Committed to Working Constructively with Government." News release. September 24, 2007.

Canadian Association of Petroleum Producers. "Royalty Report Sets Stage to Review Alberta's Competitiveness: CAPP." News release. January 29, 2016. http://www.capp.ca/media/news-releases/royalty-report-sets-stage-to-review-albertas-competitiveness-capp.

Canadian Association of Petroleum Producers. *Statistical Handbook for Canada's Upstream Petroleum Industry.* http://www.capp.ca/publications-and-statistics/statistics/statistical-handbook.

Canadian Association of Petroleum Producers. "Submission: Bitumen Pricing Methodology for SEC Reserves Disclosure." Calgary: Canadian Association of Petroleum Producers, September 2005.

Canadian Society of Professional Biologists, Alberta Chapter, and Alberta Society of Professional Biologists. *Seeking Consensus: The Public's Role in Environmental Decision Making.* Edmonton: Alberta Society of Professional Biologists, 1988.

Canadian Broadcasting Corporation. "Bruce Carson, Former Harper Aide, Not Guilty of Influence-Peddling." November 17, 2015. http://www.cbc.ca/news/politics/bruce-carson-not-guilty-influence-peddling-1.3322811.

Canadian Broadcasting Corporation. "Cancer Rate in Fort Chipewyan Cause for Alarm: Medical Examiner." March 10, 2006. http://www.cbc.ca/news/canada/edmonton/cancer-rate-in-fort-chipewyan-cause-for-alarm-medical-examiner-1.609695.

Canadian Broadcasting Corporation. "Cancer Rates Not Higher in Fort Chipewyan, Investigation Concludes." July 19, 2006. http://www.cbc.ca/news/canada/edmonton/cancer-rates-not-higher-in-fort-chipewyan-investigation-concludes-1.575738.

Canadian Broadcasting Corporation. "'Comprehensive' Review of Fort Chipewyan Cancer Rates Announced." May 22, 2008. http://www.cbc.ca/news/canada/edmonton/comprehensive-review-of-fort-chipewyan-cancer-rates-announced-1.720133.

Canadian Broadcasting Corporation. "Fort Chipewyan Rejects Alberta Cancer Board Study." November 10, 2008. http://www.cbc.ca/news/canada/edmonton/fort-chipewyan-rejects-alberta-cancer-board-study-1.752332.

Canadian Broadcasting Corporation."Local Doctor Doubts Report on Fort Chipewyan Cancer Rates." July 25, 2006. http://www.cbc.ca/news/canada/calgary/local-doctor-doubts-report-on-fort-chipewyan-cancer-rates-1.600942.

Canadian Broadcasting Corporation. "Oilsands-Area Hamlet Supports Whistleblower MD." March 5, 2007. http://www.cbc.ca/news/canada/oilsands-area-hamlet-supports-whistleblower-md-1.636759.

Canadian Broadcasting Corporation. "Stelmach Prepares to Take Charge as Premier." December 4, 2006. http://www.cbc.ca/news/canada/edmonton/stelmach-prepares-to-take-charge-as-premier-1.575588.

Canadian Natural Resources Limited."Canadian Natural Resources Limited Expresses Concerns over the Royalty Review Panel Report." News release. October 9, 2007. http://www.cnrl.com/upload/media_element/131/01/1009_royalty_review.pdf.

Canadian Natural Resources Limited. *Horizon Tailings Management Plan.* 2009. https://www.aer.ca/documents/oilsands/tailings-plans/CNRL_2009_Horizon_TailingsPlans.pdf.

Canadian Oil Sands Trust. *Annual Report.* 2001.

Canadian Oil Sands Trust. "Canadian Oil Sands Discusses Royalty Changes." (News release). October 26, 2007. http://www.newswire.ca/fr/news-releases/canadian-oil-sands-discusses-royalty-changes-534540301.html.

Canadian Press. "Alberta Rejects a Bailout for West Edmonton Mall." *Toronto Star*, March 18, 1994, B7.

Canadian Press. "Major Syncrude Project Depends on Rising Oil Price." *Globe and Mail*, July 29, 1987, B6.

Canadian Press. "Oilpatch Plans Offensive Against Alta Royalty Review Report." September 24, 2007.

Canadian Press. "Still Alberta's Prerogative to Say Who Speaks at Oilsands Reviews." October 4, 2013.

Canes, Michael E., and Rachael G. Jonassen. *EISA Section 526: Impacts on DESC Supply, Report DES86T1*. LMI Government Consulting, March 2009. www.dtic.mil/get-tr-doc/pdf?AD=ADA502264.

Carbery, Jim. "Fort McKay." Presentation to Global Energy Security Forum, Florida International University, February 21, 2012. http://energyforum.fiu.edu/events/2012/canadian-oil-sands/jim-carbery.pdf.

Cardinal, Harold. *The Unjust Society: The Tragedy of Canada's Indians*. Edmonton: M. G. Hurtig, 1969.

Carlisle, Tamsin. "Arden Haynes: Man in the Middle." *Financial Post*, January 28, 1991, 7.

Carson, Bruce. "Notes for a Speech on 'Banff Dialogue' and Canada's Plan to Reduce Carbon." June 19, 2009. https://drive.google.com/file/d/0B_0MqnZ4wmcMNTkxMU1jZkpoNDA/view?pli=1.

Carter, Jim. "Breaking New Ground: Syncrude's Partnerships with Aboriginal People." Speaking Notes for Jim Carter, Resource Expo 2002: Business Agreements for Profit. Calgary Alberta, December 3, 2002.

Cattaneo, Claudia. "$3B Boost for Oilsands." *Financial Post*, November 25, 1997, 1.

Cattaneo, Claudia. "20% Hike in Royalties Would Cost US $26B," *Financial Post*, September 26, 2007.

Cattaneo, Claudia. "Alberta's NDP Puts Oilsands on a Leash by Moving Law to Place Cap on Emissions." *Financial Post*, November 1, 2016.

Cattaneo, Claudia. "Oilpatch New International Whipping Boy; CAPP Aims to Debunk Impact of Inaccuracies." *Financial Post*, February 19, 2008, FP 3.

Cattaneo, Claudia. "Secret Deal on Alberta's Oilsands Emissions Limits Divides Patch." *Financial Post*, December 1, 2015.

Cattaneo, Claudia. "Secret Oilsands Deal Spurred by Alberta NDP's Concern over Project Cancellations, Green Group Says." *Financial Post*, December 3, 2015.

Cattaneo, Claudia. "A Slap in the Face for Alberta." *National Post*, October 26, 2007.

Cattaneo, Claudia, and Jon Harding. "Royalties Hike Would Kill 'Golden Goose.'" *National Post*, September 20, 2007.

Center for Biological Diversity. "Oil Shale and Tar Sands." n.d. http://www.biologicaldiversity.org/programs/public_lands/energy/dirty_energy_development/oil_shale_and_tar_sands/.

Chase, Steven. "Klein Giving Away Alberta Oil, Gas Riches: Study Think-Tank Finds Province Collects Less Royalties, Taxes than Two Other Peers." *Globe and Mail*, November 10, 1999, B1.

Chastko, Paul. *Developing Alberta's Oil Sands: From Karl Clark to Kyoto*. Calgary: University of Calgary Press, 2004.

Chen, Yiqun. *Cancer Incidence in Fort Chipewyan 1995–2000*. Alberta Cancer Board, 2009.

Chiasson, Cindy. "Pembina Ruling Shines Spotlight on Need for Reform." Environmental Law Centre. October 4, 2013. http://elc.ab.ca/pub-archives/pembina-ruling-shines-spotlight-on-need-for-reform/.

Chiasson, Cindy. "Single Energy Regulator Bill a Poor Deal for Alberta's Environment." Environmental Law Centre. November 1, 2014. http://elc.ab.ca/?s=Single+energy+regulator+a+poor.

Chipewyan Prairie Dene First Nation Group of Companies. "Companies." http://cpgroupofcompanies.com/companies/.

Church, Maria. "Fort Chipewyan Celebrates Opening of Elders' Care Centre." *Northern Journal*, May 19, 2014. https://norj.ca/2013/10/fort-chip-elders-care-centre-to-open-by-spring/.

CIBC World Markets. "Equity Research Industry Update—The New Alberta Oil Sands Royalty Regime." October 26, 2007.

Cilliers, Roland. "Aboriginal Association Marks $1B in Suncor Business." *Fort McMurray Today*, May 27, 2009.

Climate Change and Emissions Management Corporation. *2010 Call for Proposals Guide and Instructions*. September 2010.

Climate Change and Emissions Management Corporation (CCEMC). *2013/2014 Annual Report*.

Clinton, Hillary Rodham. "Remarks on Innovation and American Leadership to the Commonwealth Club." Excerpts. Global Washington. October 15, 2010. http://globalwa.org/2010/10/secretary-clintons-remarks-on-innovation-and-american-leadership-to-the-commonwealth-club/.

Crothers, Michael, and Ed Whittingham. "On the First Anniversary, Much to Celebrate, and Even More to Do." *Globe and Mail*, November 22, 2016, B4.

Cryderman, Kelly. "Not on an 'Anti-Tar-Sands Crusade', Neil Young Says." *Globe and Mail*, January 19, 2014. https://www.theglobeandmail.com/news/national/neil-young-concludes-anti-oilsands-concert-series-with-show-in-calgary/article16398977/#dashboard/follows/.

Cryderman, Kelly. "Obama and the Oilsands; 'Dirty Oil' Debate Back in Spotlight." *Calgary Herald*, February 22, 2009, A1.

Cummins, H. J. "New Oil Pipeline Across State Approved; It Would Be a Boon to the North Central US, Supporters Argued. Foes Cited Extracting Methods Used for the Oil." *Star Tribune*, November 26, 2008, 2D.

Dacruz, Michelle. "First Nations Partner with Suncor in Business." *Fort McMurray Today*, October 4, 2002, A8.

Daily Oil Bulletin. "Reshaping a Giant: Syncrude Ownership 1965–2015." October 4, 2015. http://www.dailyoilbulletin.com/supplement/daily-infographic/2015/10/5/reshaping-giant-syncrude-ownership-1965-2015/#sthash.LGp7oZv8.dpbs.

David Suzuki Foundation. *Seizing Alberta's Climate Leadership Opportunity*. Vancouver: David Suzuki Foundation, September 2015. http://www.davidsuzuki.org/publications/downloads/2015/Addressing%20Climate%20Change%20in%20Alberta_FINAL.pdf.

Day, Michael J. "A New Tenure Option for Alberta Oil Sands." In *Heavy Crude and Tar Sands: Hydrocarbons for the 21st Century, Fifth International Conference on Heavy Crude and Tar Sands,* Volume 4, edited by Richard F. Meyer, 427–72. Caracas: Petróleos de Venezuela, S.A., 1991.

"Declaration of US and Canadian Environmental and Conservation Leaders on US–Canada Cooperation on Climate, Energy, and Natural Areas Conservation." June 4, 2009. https://www.pembina.org/reports/us-can-ceo-declaration.pdf.

Democracy Now. "10,000 Surround White House to Protest Keystone XL Tar Sands Oil Pipeline." November 7, 2011. http://www.democracynow.org/2011/11/7/10_000_surround_white_house_to.

Dennis, Brady, and Steven Mufson. "As Trump Administration Grants Approval for Keystone XL Pipeline, an Old Fight Is Reignited." *Washington Post,* March 24, 2017.

De Souza, Mike. "Update 1—Canada's Alberta to Introduce Economy-Wide Carbon Tax in 2017." *Reuters News,* November 22, 2015.

Dewar, Elaine. *Cloak of Green: The Links Between Key Environmental Groups, Government and Big Business.* Toronto: Lorimer, 1995.

Doer, Gary. "Letter to the Honorable Chuck Hagel, Secretary, US Department of Defense." Public Comment on Department of Defense (DOD) Notice: Environmental Assessments; Availability, etc.: DLA Energy Mobility Fuel Purchasing Programs. April 18, 2013. https://regulations.gov/.

Doern, G. Bruce, and Brian W. Tomlin. *Faith and Fear: The Free Trade Story.* Toronto: Stoddart Publishing, 1991.

Doern, G. Bruce, and Glen Toner. *The Politics of Energy: The Development and Implementation of the NEP.* Toronto: Methuen, 1985.

Dow Jones News Service. "Sun Says Canadian Oil Pact Will Increase 1982 Earnings." September 2, 1981.

Dow Jones News Service. "Suncor Plans $355 Million Oil Sands Plant Expansion." July 27, 1982.

Dowie, Mark. *Losing Ground: American Environmentalism at the Close of the Twentieth Century.* Cambridge, MA: MIT Press, 1995.

Dykstra, Matt. "NDP Proposes to Rejig Alberta's Royalty Structure." *Edmonton Sun,* April 10, 2015.

Ebner, David. "Report Finds Alberta Still a Bargain, Even with Higher Royalties." *Globe and Mail,* September 26, 2007.

Ebner, David. "Suncor, Syncrude May Feel Less Pain from Royalties Increase." *Globe and Mail,* September 27, 2007.

Ebner, David, and Norval Scott. "Energy Stocks Plunge After Call to Raise Royalties." *Globe and Mail,* September 19, 2007.

Edelman, Peter. "The Worst Thing Bill Clinton Has Done." *Atlantic,* March 1997.

Edmonton Journal. "500 Fowl Symbols Tarnishing Alberta." May 1, 2008, A18.

Edmonton Journal. "We're Lucky to Have an AG with Chutzpah." October 4, 2008, A18.

Edwards, Rob. "RBS in Battle with the Cree First Nation over Dirty Oil Development Project on Tribal Lands." *Herald Scotland,* April 18, 2010.

Encana. "Encana Plans to Cut About $1 Billion from 2008 Alberta Investments Royalty Panel Report Adopted in Full." News release. September 28, 2007. https://www.encana.com/news-stories/news-releases/details.html?release=609981.

Energy Mines and Resources Canada. *The National Energy Program, 1980.* Ottawa: Supply and Services Canada, 1980.

Energy Policy Institute of Canada. *A Canadian Energy Strategy Framework: A Guide to Building Canada's Future as a Global Energy Leader.* August 2012.

Enhanced Energy Recovery and Refining News. "Development Strategy for North America." 18, no. 8 (March 1, 1995).

Environment Canada. *National Inventory Report 1990–2005: Greenhouse Gas Sources and Sinks.* Ottawa: Environment Canada, April 2007.

Environment and Climate Change Canada. "Global Greenhouse Gas Emissions." http://www.ec.gc.ca/indicateurs-indicators/default.asp?lang=en&n=54C061B5-1.

Environment and Climate Change Canada. *National Inventory Report 1990–2014: Greenhouse Gas Sources and Sinks in Canada (Canada's Submission to the United Nations Framework Convention on Climate Change).* Ottawa: Environment and Climate Change Canada, 2016.

Esping-Andersen, Gosta. *The Three Worlds of Welfare Capitalism.* Princeton, NJ: Princeton University Press, 1990.

Evans, Peter. "Is an Alternative Globalization Possible?" *Politics & Society* 36, no. 2 (2008): 271–305. https://doi.org/10.1177/0032329208316570.

Farnsworth, Clyde H. "Business Technology: Unlocking Oil in Canada's Tar Sands." *New York Times,* December 28, 1994.

Feeney, Lauren. "Why the Sierra Club Broke Tradition to Protest the Keystone Pipeline." *Moyers & Company.* February 13, 2013. http://billmoyers.com/2013/02/14/sierra-club-lifts-120-year-ban-on-civil-disobedience-to-protest-keystone-xl-pipeline/.

Fekete, Jason. "Oilsands Plan Needed Now, Lougheed Says." *Edmonton Journal,* September 3, 2006, A3.

Fekete, Jason. "Tory Candidates Skeptical of Alberta Royalties Review." *Calgary Herald,* July 13, 2006, A5.

Fekete, Jason, and Renata D'Aliesio. "Oilsands Royalties Put Under Review: Industry Welcomes Move." *Calgary Herald,* December 14, 2006, D1.

Fekete, Jason, and Tony Seskus. "Stelmach Under Fire." *Calgary Herald,* October 26, 2007.

Fekete, Jason, and Tony Seskus. "Tories Desert Klein: Premier 'Shocked' Party Has Turned Against Him." *Calgary Herald,* April 1, 2006, 1.

Ferguson, Derek. "Tories vs. Tories over Alberta Oil." *Toronto Star,* January 8, 1987, A14.

Financial Post. "Alberta Energy Branch Restructuring Praised." February 16, 1994.

Financial Post. "Fossil Fuels Targeted." April 28, 1993.

Financial Post. "FP500: 2013." http://www.financialpost.com/news/fp500/2013/index.html.

Financial Post. "Oil Strategy Is Outdated." January 14, 1993, 14.

First Energy Capital. "Integrated & Large Caps: Better to Boil Your Bitumen!" Calgary: October 26, 2007.

First Energy Capital. "Job Losses Quantified—A Look at the Alberta Royalty Impact." Calgary: October 10, 2007.

First Energy Capital. "Oil Sands – A Totally Bitumen Deal!" Calgary: October 26, 2007.

Fisher, Matthew. "Chretien and Getty Chat about Katimavik and Oil Prices." *Globe and Mail*, April 2, 1986, A9.

Fitzsimmons, R. C. *The Truth about Alberta Tar Sands: Why Were They Kept Out of Production?* Edmonton: 1953.

Flanagan, Erin, and Jennifer Grant. "Losing Ground: Why the Problem of Oilsands Tailing Waste Keeps Growing." Drayton Valley, AB: Pembina Institute, July 2013. https://www.pembina.org/reports/losing-ground-oilsands-tailings-fs.pdf.

Fluker, Shaun. "Amended Rules of Practice for the Alberta Energy Regulator: More Bad News for Landowners and Environmental Groups." *Ablawg.ca* (blog), December 11, 2013. http://ablawg.ca/2013/12/11/amended-rules-of-practice-for-the-alberta-energy-regulator-more-bad-news-for-landowners-and-environmental-groups/.

Fluker, Shaun. "Bill 2 *Responsible Energy Development Act*: Setting the Stage for the Next 50 Years of Effective and Efficient Energy Resource Regulation and Development in Alberta." *Ablawg.ca* (blog), November 8, 2012. http://ablawg.ca/2012/11/08/bill-2-responsible-energy-development-act-setting-the-stage-for-the-next-50-years-of-effective-and-efficient-energy-resource-regulation-and-development-in-alberta/.

Fluker, Shaun. "The Case of the 1600 Dead Ducks: The Verdict Is In—Syncrude Guilty under the Migratory Birds Convention Act." *ABlawg.ca* (blog), June 30, 2010. http://ablawg.ca/2010/06/30/the-case-of-the-1600-dead-ducks-the-verdict-is-in-syncrude-guilty-under-the-migratory-birds-convention-act/.

Fluker, Shaun. "The Jurisdiction of Alberta's Energy and Utilities Board to Consider Broad Socio-Ecological Concerns Associated with Energy Projects." *Alberta Law Review* 42, no. 4 (2005): 1–14.

Fluker, Shaun. "The Smoking Gun Revealed: Alberta Environment Denies Environmental Groups Who Oppose Oil Sands Projects the Right to Participate in the Decision-Making Process." *Ablawg.ca* (blog), October 3, 2013. http://ablawg.ca/2013/10/03/the-smoking-gun-revealed-alberta-environment-denies-environmental-groups-who-oppose-oil-sands-projects-the-right-to-participate-in-the-decision-making-process/.

Folio. "Long-Time Politico Brings Expertise to Alberta-Led Centre of Excellence." 45, no. 23, August 15, 2008.

Fong, Jennifer. "Greenpeace Wants Inquiry into Duck Deaths; Province's Investigation Too Close to Industry, Environmental Body Says." *Vancouver Sun*, May 6, 2008, A4.

Foote, Lee. "Threshold Considerations and Wetland Reclamation in Alberta's Mineable Oil Sands." *Ecology and Society* 17, no. 1 (2012): 35–45. https://doi.org/10.5751/ES-04673-170135.

Fort McKay First Nation. "Financial Statements Fort McKay First Nation, Schedules of Salaries, Honoraria, Travel Expenses and Other Remuneration, Year Ended March 31, 2014." http://fnp-ppn.aandc-aadnc.gc.ca/fnp/Main/Search/DisplayBinaryData.aspx?BAND_NUMBER_FF=467&FY=2013-2014&DOC=Schedule%20of%20Remuneration%20and%20Expenses&lang=eng.

Fort McKay First Nation. "Financial Statements Fort McKay First Nation, Schedules of Salaries, Honoraria, Travel Expenses and Other Remuneration, Year Ended March 31, 2015." http://fnp-ppn.aandc-aadnc.gc.ca/fnp/Main/Search/DisplayBinaryData.aspx?BAND_NUMBER_FF=467&FY=2014-2015&DOC=Schedule%20of%20Remuneration%20and%20Expenses&lang=eng.

Fort McKay First Nation. "Financial Statements Fort McKay First Nation, Schedules of Salaries, Honoraria, Travel Expenses and Other Remuneration, Year Ended March 31, 2016." http://fnp-ppn.aadnc-aandc.gc.ca/fnp/Main/Search/DisplayBinaryData.aspx?BAND_NUMBER_FF=467&FY=2015-2016&DOC=Schedule%20of%20Remuneration%20and%20Expenses&lang=eng.

Fort McMurray First Nation. *Submission to 2015 Alberta Royalty Review Panel* (Assisted by Paul Precht Energy Economics Ltd.). September 2015.

Foster, Peter. "The Gang of Four's Oil Cap Blunder." *Financial Post*, December 4, 2015.

Francis, Diane. "Canada's Ailing Oil Sands Plants Desperately Need Government Aid." *Toronto Star*, May 1, 1986, E3.

Freeman, Alan. "Alberta's Gift to Culture." *Globe and Mail,* June 7, 2006, R1.

Freeman, Alan. "Mr. Klein Goes to Washington with Oil Message; Festival Aimed at Raising Awareness." *Globe and Mail*, June 28, 2006, B9.

Fund, John H. "Learning from Canada's Reagan." *Wall Street Journal*, February 23, 1995.

Gazette (Montreal). "Syncrude Signs Two Agreements Providing Jobs, Grants for Indians." July 5, 1976.

Geddes, Ashley. "Oilsands Task Force Eyes Future Expansion." *Financial Post*, May 25, 1995.

Geman, Ben. "Canada Warns US Against Using Energy Law to Bar Fuel from Oil Sands." *Greenwire*, February 28, 2008.

Giddens, Anthony. *The Politics of Climate Change.* 2nd ed. Cambridge: Polity Press, 2011.

Giddens, Anthony. "The Rise and Fall of New Labour." *New Statesman*, May 17, 2010.

Gillies, Rob. "Will Canada's Oil Boom Be an Environmental Bust?" *Associated Press*, August 24, 2008.

Gilmour, Brad, and Bruce Mellett. "The Role of Impact and Benefits Agreements in the Resolution of Project Issues with First Nations." *Alberta Law Review* 51, no. 2 (2013): 385–400.

Giovannetti, Justin, and Jeffrey Jones. "Alberta Carbon Plan a Major Pivot in Environmental Policy." *Globe and Mail*, November 22, 2015.

Globe and Mail. "Athabasca Tribal Council Inks Historic Oil Sands Deal." March 16, 2001.

Globe and Mail. "Greenpeace Protests Oil-Sands Expansion." March 7, 2000.

Globe and Mail. "Kyoto Impact Minimal, Suncor Says." January 10, 2003.

Globe and Mail. "Kyoto Oil Sands 'Scare' Eases." January 10, 2003.

Globe and Mail. "Trust Puts Kyoto Costs at Up to 30 Cents a Barrel." January 25, 2003.

Goldstein, Lorrie. "Trudeau Adopts Harper's Climate Targets." *Toronto Sun*, September 19, 2016.

Goodman, Lee-Anne. "US Set to Approve Keystone XL Pipeline." *Globe and Mail*, October 20, 2010.

Gordon, Andrea. "Suncor Plans Step Up in Spending." *Toronto Star*, May 1, 1987, E5.

Gordon, Deborah, and Yevgen Sautin. "Opportunities and Challenges Confronting Russian Oil." Washington, DC: Carnegie Endowment for International

Peace, May 28, 2013. http://carnegieendowment.org/2013/05/28/opportunities-and-challenges-confronting-russian-oil/g6x5.

Greenpeace. "Alberta Climate Plan an Historic First Step But More Needs to Be Done." News release. November 22, 2015. http://www.greenpeace.org/canada/Global/canada/pr/2015/11/AB-climate-statement.pdf.

Greenpeace Canada. "Statement: NDP Win Opens Door to Greener Economy in Alberta." May 6, 2015. http://www.greenpeace.org/canada/Global/canada/pr/2015/05/AlbertaElection.pdf.

Greenspan, Alan. "The Challenge of Central Banking in a Democratic Society." Remarks at the Annual Dinner and Francis Boyer Lecture of the American Enterprise Institute for Public Policy Research, Washington, DC. December 5, 1996. http://www.federalreserve.gov/boarddocs/speeches/1996/19961205.htm.

Haavardsrud, Paul. "Environmental Tug-of-War Clouds Oilsands Future." *Calgary Herald*, October 25, 2005, A8.

Haggett, Scott. "Oil Sands Duck Deaths Tragic, Imperial CEO Says." *Reuters News*, May 1, 2008.

Hall, Peter, and David Soskice, eds. *Varieties of Capitalism: The Institutional Foundations of Comparative Advantage.* Oxford: Oxford University Press, 2001. https://doi.org/10.1093/0199247757.001.0001.

Hall, Peter A., and Rosemary C. R. Taylor. "Political Science and the Three New Institutionalisms." *Political Studies* 44, no. 5 (1996): 936–57. https://doi.org/10.1111/j.1467-9248.1996.tb00343.x.

Hansen, James. "Silence Is Deadly." June 3, 2011. http://www.columbia.edu/~jeh1/mailings/2011/20110603_SilenceIsDeadly.pdf.

Harding, Jon. "Oilsands Hit Back at 'Dirty' Tag: Industry Launches Website as US Mayors Threaten to Stop Buying 'Tarsands' Fuel." *Calgary Herald*, June 24, 2008, A1.

Harding, Jon. "US Mayors Target 'Dirty Oil;' Oilpatch Website Takes On Critics." *Calgary Herald*, June 24, 2008, A1.

Harper, Tim. "US Capital Faces Alberta Invasion; Province Kicks Off Massive Two-Week Lobbying Blitz." *Toronto Star*, June 26, 2006, A2.

Hawkes, David C., and Bruce G. Pollard. "The Evolution of Canada's New Energy Policy." In *Canada: The State of the Federation 1986*, edited by Peter M. Leslie. Kingston, ON: Institute of Intergovernmental Relations, 1987.

Healing, Dan. "Reactions Cool to New Tailings Pond Rules; Implementation Is 'Going to Be a Challenge'." *Calgary Herald*, February 4, 2009, D4.

Henton, Darcy, and Dan Healing. "Tailings Rules Given 'Teeth'; New Oilsands Regulations Designed to Clean Up Province's Image After 500 ducks Killed in Syncrude Pond." *Edmonton Journal*, February 4, 2009, A1.

Hoberg, George, and Jeffrey Phillips. "Playing Defence: Early Responses to Conflict Expansion in the Oil Sands Policy Subsystem." Canadian Journal of Political Science 44, no. 3 (September 2011): 507–27. https://doi.org/10.1017/S0008423911000473.

House of Commons. Standing Committee on Environment and Sustainable Development. *Keeping a Promise: Towards a Sustainable Budget: Report of the Standing Committee on Environment and Sustainable Development.* Ottawa: Canada Communication Group, 1995.

House of Commons. Standing Committee on Finance and Economic Affairs. *Minutes of Proceedings Standing Committee on Finance and Economic Affairs, 33rd Parliament, 2nd Session*, Issue no. 112, September 23, 1987.

Huismann, Wilfried. *Pandaleaks: The Dark Side of the WWF*. Bremen: Nordbook UG, 2014.

Ibrahim, Mariam. "Alberta NDP 'Got It Wrong on Royalties,' Labour Leader Gil McGowan Says." *Edmonton Journal*, February 1, 2016.

Imperial Oil. *Kearl Oil Sands Project: 2009 Annual Tailings Plan Submission, September 30, 2009*. https://www.aer.ca/documents/oilsands/tailings-plans/Imperial_2009_Kearl_TailingsPlans.pdf.

Imperial Oil Resources Ventures Limited. *Kearl Oil Sands Project—Mine Development (Regulatory Application)*. Vol. 5, *Air and Noise*. July 2005. http://www.acee.gc.ca/050/documents_staticpost/cearref_16237/KR-0007-5.pdf.

Indian Association of Alberta. *Citizens Plus: Alberta Red Paper*. Edmonton: 1970.

Indian and Northern Affairs Canada. "Minister Nault Signs Capacity Building Agreement with Athabasca Tribal Council to Promote Natural Resource Industry Partnerships." *Canada NewsWire*, January 9, 2003.

Ingram, Matthew. "Royalty Critique Doesn't Add Up." *Globe and Mail*, November 16, 1999.

International Energy Agency. *World Energy Outlook 2013 (Executive Summary)*. Paris: International Energy Agency, 2013.

Ipsos-Reid. *Canadians and Americans Give Their Views on North American Energy Issues*. March 1, 2004. https://www.ipsos.com/en-ca/canadians-and-americans-give-their-views-north-american-energy-issues?language_content_entity=en-ca.

Irving, Jacob. *Oil Sands: An Industry Overview*. Oil Sands Developers Group, January 28, 2009.

Jaccard, Marc. "Want an Effective Carbon Policy?: Heed the Evidence." *Policy Options*, February 2, 2016, 2. http://policyoptions.irpp.org/magazines/february-2016/want-an-effective-climatepolicy-heed-the-evidence/.

Jaccard, Marc, Mikela Hein, and Tiffany Vass. "Is Win-Win Possible?: Can Canada's Government Achieve Its Paris Commitment ... and Get Re-Elected?" Burnaby, BC: Simon Fraser University School of Resource and Environmental Management, September 20, 2016.

Jacobs, John. "CCPA-NS Presentation to the Public Review Commission on Oil and Gas Exploration off the Coast of Cape Breton." Canadian Centre for Policy Alternatives, January 2002. https://www.policyalternatives.ca/publications/reports/ccpa-ns-presentation-public-review-commission-oil-and-gas-exploration-coast-cap.

Jaremko, Gordon. "Fort McKay Becoming Power Hub: Aboriginal Vision Guides $9.7–Billion Project Horizon with New Town, Jobs." *Edmonton Journal*, December 29, 2004, G1.

Jaremko, Gordon. "Is Alberta's Treasury Extracting a Fair Share?: Oil Price Has Tripled Since Compact Made to Jumpstart Oilsands Investment." *Edmonton Journal*, September 16, 2006.

Jaremko, Gordon. *Steward: 75 Years of Alberta Energy Regulation*. Calgary: Energy Resources Conservation Board, 2013.

Johnston, Daniel. *International Petroleum Fiscal Systems and Production Sharing Contracts*. Tulsa, OK: Penwell Publishing, 1994.

Jones, Jeffrey. "Analysis—Talk Is Cheap, Skeptics Say of Oil Sands Message." *Reuters News*, June 24, 2008.

Jones, Jeffrey. "Royalty Panel Member Fires Back at Critics." Reuters, September 28, 2007.

Jones, Jeffrey. "Update 1—Syncrude Duck Deaths Now Triple Initial Tally." Reuters, March 31, 2008.

Jorgensen, Miriam, and Rachel Starks. *Forwarding First Nation Goals Through Enterprise Ownership: The Mikisew Group of Companies*. Paper prepared for Aboriginal Leadership and Management, The Banff Centre, April 2014. http://nni.arizona.edu/application/files/2314/6179/0332/2014-4_mikisew_case_study.pdf.

Kalgoorlie Miner. "Ducks Doomed in Canadian Sludge Lake." May 1, 2008.

Karl, Terry Lynn. *The Paradox of Plenty: Oil Booms and Petro-States*. Berkeley: University of California Press, 1997.

Katzenstein, Peter J. *Small States in World Markets: Industrial Policy in Europe*. Ithaca, NY: Cornell University Press, 1985.

Kaur Communications. "Reactions from Around the World to Government of Alberta's New Climate Change Strategy." *Canada News Wire*, November 22, 2015.

Keith, David. "The Real Bruce Carson Scandal." *Toronto Star*, September 22, 2015. https://www.thestar.com/opinion/commentary/2015/09/22/the-real-bruce-carson-scandal.html.

Kennett, Steven. *Integrated Resource Management in Alberta: Past, Present and Benchmarks for the Future* (Occasional Paper #11). Calgary: Canadian Institute of Resources Law, 2002.

Khanna, Paul. "Summaries of the Deputy Minister Meetings with Industry and the Alberta Government on Oil Sands Outreach and Communications, March 16, 2010." March 25, 2010. https://drive.google.com/a/ualberta.ca/file/d/0B46zsDD7Xqu3NzIxNmVhYmEtMTQoNCooNzVkLTkoZDgtMGJiYThmNzA1ZWQz/view?pli=1.

Kidd, Kenneth. "Pumping Profits." *Globe and Mail*, November 15, 1991, P21.

Klein, Naomi. *This Changes Everything: Capitalism vs. the Climate*. Toronto: Alfred A. Knopf Canada, 2014.

Kleiss, Karen. "Alberta Not Meeting Government's Own Emissions Targets." *Edmonton Journal*, February 28, 2013.

Knight-Ridder Tribune Business News. "Foreign Companies Racing to Get Piece of Venezuela's Oil Action." November 9, 1997.

Koch, George. "Money Pit." *National Post Business*, July 2004.

Korchinski, Donna. "Drillers Turning to Alberta's Tar Sands." *Financial Post*, June 14, 1994.

Kuletz, Valerie. *The Tainted Desert: Environmental and Social Ruin in the American West*. New York: Routledge, 1998.

Kunzig, Robert. "Tar Sands Yield Millions of Barrels – But at What Cost?" *National Geographic* 215, no. 3 (March 2009): 34–59.

Laxer, Gordon. "Alberta's Plan Guts Efforts to Cut Greenhouse Gases." *Winnipeg Free Press*, December 10, 2015, A11.

Law, Jonathan, and John Smullen, eds. *A Dictionary of Finance and Banking*. 4th ed. Oxford: Oxford University Press, 2008.

Leach, Andrew, Angela Adams, Stephanie Cairns, Linda Coady, and Gordon Lambert. *Climate Leadership: Report to Minister*. Edmonton: Government of Alberta, 2015.

LeBlond, Nancy, and Sasha Brown. "Training Options That Would Increase Employment Opportunities for Local People in Resource Extraction Projects in Northern Communities: Final Report." Prepared for Manitoba Research Alliance on Community Economic Development in the New Economy, November 2004. https://mbresearchalliance.files.wordpress.com/2012/11/32land_reclamation_rev.pdf.

Lewis, Jeff. "Oil Sands Growth Plans at Risk under Alberta's New Climate Rules." *Globe and Mail*, November 23, 2015.

Lewis, Jeff. "Suncor Reaches $4.2-Billion Deal with Canadian Oil Sands." *Globe and Mail*, January 18, 2016.

Lindblom, Charles. "The Market as Prison." *Journal of Politics* 44, no. 2 (1982): 324–36. https://doi.org/10.2307/2130588.

Lipset, S. M. *Agrarian Socialism: The Cooperative Commonwealth Federation in Saskatchewan*. Berkeley: University of California Press, 1950.

Lisac, Mark. *Alberta Politics Uncovered: Taking Back Our Province*. Edmonton: NeWest Press, 2004.

Lisac, Mark. *The Klein Revolution*. Edmonton: NeWest Press, 1995.

Luff, Glenn. "Corporate Alberta and First Nations Meet to Promote Economic Partnership." *Grassroots: Aboriginal Business in Alberta*. Ottawa: Minister of Indian Affairs and Northern Development, Spring 2001. http://publications.gc.ca/collections/Collection/R12-14-2001-1E.pdf.

Lukes, Steven. *Power: A Radical View*. 2nd ed. Padstow, UK: Palgrave Macmillan, 2005. https://doi.org/10.1007/978-0-230-80257-5.

Macdonald, Jim. "Alberta's Energy Regulator Issues Tough New Directive for Oilsands Tailings Ponds." *Canadian Press*, February 3, 2009.

Macdonald, Jim. "Alta Minister Rejects Public Inquiry into 500 Dead Ducks in Oilsands Tailings Pond." *Canadian Press*, May 5, 2008.

Macdonald, Jim. "Only Five Ducks Saved from Syncrude Tailings Pond, 500 Perish in Oilsands Wastes." *Canadian Press*, April 30, 2008.

MacFadyen, Alan J., and G. Campbell Watkins. *Petropolitics: Petroleum Development, Markets and Regulations, Alberta as an Illustrative History*. Calgary: University of Calgary Press, 2014.

MacLean, Mairi. "This Job Requires Heavy Lifting: Mikisew Cree Put Heart in Slings." *Edmonton Journal*, September 27, 2002, F1.

Macnab, Bruce, James Daniels, and Gordon Laxer. *Giving Away the Alberta Advantage: Are Albertans Receiving Maximum Revenues from Their Oil and Gas?* Edmonton: Parkland Institute, 1999.

Mahony, James. "Alberta Government Makes Oilsands Policy Shift." *Daily Oil Bulletin*, October 27, 2005.

Malcolm, Andrew H. "Canadian Tar Sands: Hope and Challenge." *New York Times*, February 15, 1982.

Mansell, Robert L., and Michael B. Percy. *Strength in Adversity: A Study of the Alberta Economy*. Edmonton: University of Alberta Press, 1990.

Mansfield, Becky. "Rules of Privatization: Contradictions in Neoliberal Regulation of North Pacific Fisheries." *Annals of the Association of American Geographers* 94, no. 3 (2004): 565–84. https://doi.org/10.1111/j.1467-8306.2004.00414.x.

Manzano, Osmel, and Francisco Monaldi. "The Political Economy of Oil Contract Renegotiation in Venezuela." In *The Natural Resources Trap: Private Investment*

Without Public Commitment, edited by Federico Sturzenegger and William W. Hogan, 409–66. Boston: MIT Press, 2010. https://doi.org/10.7551/mitpress/9780262013796.003.0020.

March, James G., and Johan P. Olsen. "The New Institutionalism: Organizational Factors in Political Life." *American Political Science Review* 78, no. 3 (1984): 734–49.

Markusoff, Jason. "Alberta's Image Getting Makeover to Battle Its Environmental Rep." *Edmonton Journal*, April 24, 2008, B8.

Marr-Laing, Thomas. (with Gail MacCrimmon). *Downsizing, Deregulation, and Regionalization: The Weakening of the Alberta Government's Role in Environmental Protection*. Drayton Valley, AB: Pembina Institute, 1997.

Marr-Laing, Thomas, and Chris Severson-Baker. *Beyond Eco-terrorism: The Deeper Issues Affecting Alberta's Oilpatch*. Drayton Valley, AB: Pembina Institute for Appropriate Development, February 1999.

Marsden, William. *Stupid to the Last Drop: How Alberta Is Bringing Environmental Armageddon to Canada (and Doesn't Seem to Care)*. Toronto: Alfred A. Knopf Canada, 2007.

Marsh, Brandon. "Preventing the Inevitable: The Benefits of Contractual Risk Engineering in Light of Venezuela's Recent Oil Field Nationalization." *Stanford Journal of Law, Business and Finance* 13, no. 2 (2008): 453–87.

Martin, Patrick. "Getty's Call Unsolicited, Yamani Says." *Globe and Mail*, April 9, 1986, A4.

Masson, Richard, and Bryan Remillard. *Alberta's New Oil Sands Royalty System*. Edmonton: Alberta Energy, 1996.

Maugeri, Leonardo. *The Age of Oil: The Mythology, History, and Future of the World's Most Controversial Resource*. Westport, CT: Praeger, 2006.

Mayer, Jane. "Taking It to the Streets." *New Yorker* 87, no. 38, November 28, 2011.

McCarthy, Shawn. "Canada's Carbon Challenge: Turning Promises into Reality." *Globe and Mail*, January 22, 2016.

McClenaghan, Theresa. "Bill C-38: Federal Budget Bill 2012 Implications for Federal Environmental Law." *Canadian Environmental Law Association*, June 2012. http://www.cela.ca/sites/cela.ca/files/Bill-C-38-Federal-Budget-Bill-Review-and-Implications.pdf.

McConnell, Grant. *Private Power and American Democracy*. New York: Alfred A. Knopf, 1966.

McConnell, R. G. *Report on a Portion of the District of Athabasca Comprising the Country Between Peace River and Athabasca River North of Lesser Slave Lake*. Ottawa: Queen's Printer, 1893. https://doi.org/10.4095/286121.

McGowan, Elizabeth. "NASA's Hansen Explains Decision to Join Keystone Pipeline Protests." Reuters, August 29, 2011. http://www.reuters.com/article/idUS257590805720110829.

McGowan, Gil. "AFL Presentation to Alberta Royalty Review Panel." Calgary, Alberta. May 23, 2007.

McIntosh, William K. "Building Sustainable Relationships: A Compendium of Leadership Practices in Aboriginal Engagement and Sustainability." Toronto: Canadian Business for Social Responsibility, 2005. http://www.eldis.org/vfile/upload/1/document/0708/DOC21483.pdf.

McKenzie, Kenneth J. "Make the Alberta Carbon Levy Revenue Neutral." *SPP Briefing Paper* (University of Calgary School of Public Policy) 9, no. 15 (April

2016). https://www.policyschool.ca/wp-content/uploads/2016/05/carbon-levy-revenue-neutral-mckenzie.pdf.

McKibben, Bill. *Oil and Honey: The Education of an Unlikely Activist.* New York: Henry Holt and Company, 2013.

McLellan, Anne. "Interview with Anne McLellan." By Adriana A. Davies. *Petroleum History Society Oil Sands Oral History Project,* July 11, 2011, transcript. http://www.glenbow.org/collections/search/findingAids/archhtm/extras/oilsands/McLellan_Anne.pdf.

Meili, Dianne. "Oilsands Boom Creates Uneasy Wealth in the North." *Alberta Sweetgrass: The Aboriginal Newspaper of Alberta* 14, no. 6 (May 2007).

Meyer, Richard F., and Emil D. Attanosi. "Heavy Oil and Natural Bitumen—Strategic Petroleum Resources." US Department of the Interior, US Geological Survey Fact Sheet 70–03 (August 2003). https://pubs.usgs.gov/fs/fs070-03/fs070-03.html.

Mikisew Cree First Nation. "Response to the Multi-Stakeholder Committee Phase II Proposed Options for Strategies and Actions and Submission to the Government of Alberta for the Oil Sands Strategy." June 2007.

Miley, Frances, and Andrew Read. "Jokes in Popular Culture: The Characterization of the Accountant." *Accounting, Auditing & Accountability Journal* 25, no. 4 (2012).

Millington, Dinara, and Carlos A. Murillo. *Canadian Oil Sands Supply Costs and Development Projects (2012–2046).* Calgary: Canadian Energy Research Institute, 2013.

Milman, Oliver, David Smith, and Damian Carrington. "Donald Trump Confirms US Will Quit Paris Climate Agreement." *Guardian,* June 1, 2017.

MM Limited Partnership. "The Mikisew Energy Services Group." http://www.mesg.ca/pages/company.htm.

Moen, Andrea B. *Demystifying Forestry Law: An Alberta Analysis.* Edmonton: Environmental Law Centre, 1990.

Mommer, Bernard. *The New Governance of Venezuelan Oil.* Oxford: Oxford Institute for Energy Studies, 1998.

Morgan, Geoffrey. "Anyone Who Emits Carbon Will Pay, Alberta Says as It Releases Tough Climate Change Policies." *Financial Post,* November 22, 2015.

Morgan, Geoffrey. "Cenovus Energy Inc. Warns of 'Negative' Fallout If NDP Changes Royalty Structure." *Financial Post,* April 29, 2015.

Morgan, Gwynn. "Populism Tramples Principle in Alberta." *Globe and Mail,* October 29, 2007.

Motherwell, Cathryn. "Suncor to Pump $250-Million in Oil Sands: Report Says $21-Billion Needed over 20 Years." *Globe and Mail,* November 16, 1994, B1.

National Energy Board. *2015 Oil Exports and Imports Summary.* 2015. https://www.neb-one.gc.ca/nrg/sttstc/crdlndptrlmprdct/stt/crdlsmmr/2015/smmry2015-eng.html.

National Energy Board. *Canada's Oil Sands: Opportunities and Challenges to 2015: An Update.* Calgary: National Energy Board, 2006.

National Energy Board. *Canada's Oil Sands: A Supply and Market Outlook to 2015.* Calgary: National Energy Board, 2000.

National Energy Board. *Canadian Energy Supply and Demand 1985–2005.* Ottawa: Minister of Supply and Services Canada, 1986.

National Energy Board. *Estimated Production of Canadian Crude Oil and Equivalent, Annual (1998–2015).* https://www.neb-one.gc.ca/nrg/sttstc/ crdlndptrlmprdct/ stt/stmtdprdctn-eng.html.

National Task Force on Oil Sands Strategies. *Final Report: A New Era of Opportunity for Canada's Oil Sands.* Edmonton: Alberta Chamber of Resources, 1995.

National Task Force on Oil Sands Strategies. *The Oil Sands: A New Energy Vision for Canada.* Edmonton: Alberta Chamber of Resources, 1995.

National Task Force on Oil Sands Strategies. *A Recommended Fiscal Regime for Canada's Oil Sands Industry, Appendix C: Fiscal Report.* Edmonton: Alberta Chamber of Resources, 1995.

Natural Resources Canada. "CSR Case Study: Syncrude Canada Ltd. Earning Its Social License to Operate." Ottawa: Natural Resources Canada, 2004. https:// www.commdev.org/userfiles/files/1077_file_syncrude_e.pdf.

Natural Resources Canada. "An Open Letter from the Honourable Joe Oliver, Minister of Natural Resources, on Canada's Commitment to Diversify Our Energy Markets and the Need to Further Streamline the Regulatory Process in Order to Advance Canada's National Economic Interest." January 9, 2012. http://www.nrcan.gc.ca/media-room/news-release/2012/1/1909.

Natural Resources Canada. "Selected Crude Oil Prices Monthly—2000." http:// www.collectionscanada.gc.ca/webarchives/20071116044435/http://www2. nrcan.gc.ca/es/erb/prb/english/view.asp?x=476&oid=523.

Natural Resources Canada. "Selected Crude Oil Prices Monthly—2005." http:// www.collectionscanada.gc.ca/webarchives/20071120173540/http://www2. nrcan.gc.ca/es/erb/prb/english/view.asp?x=476&oid=1008.

Natural Resources Defense Council. "Alberta Tar Sands Feed US Addiction to Oil." Press release. June 30, 2006. https://www.nrdc.org/media/2006/060630.

Natural Resources Defense Council. "Don't Buy It; Tar Sands Oil Is Still Dirty." Press release. April 29, 2008. https://www.nrdc.org/media/2008/080429-1.

Natural Resources Defense Council. "Environmental Groups Fight Attempt to Repeal Crucial Climate Provision from 2007 US Energy Bill." Press release. May 8, 2008. https://www.nrdc.org/media/2008/080507a.asp.

Natural Resources Defense Council. "Letter to the Governors of the Western Governors' Association on Tar Sands." June, 26, 2008. https://www.nrdc.org/ resources/letter-governors-western-governors-association-tar-sands.

Natural Resources Defense Council. "Strip Mining for Oil in Endangered Forests." June 1, 2006. https://www.nrdc.org/resources/strip-mining-oil-endangered-forests.

Natural Resources Defense Council and Sierra Club of Canada. *America's Gas Tank: The High Cost of Canada's Oil and Gas Export Strategy.* 2002.

Natural Resources Defense Council, Western Resource Advocates, and Pembina Institute. *Driving It Home: Choosing the Right Path for Fueling North America's Transportation Future.* June 2007. https://www.nrdc.org/sites/default/files/ drivingithome.pdf.

Nelson, Patricia. "Interview with Patricia Nelson." By Brian Brennan. *Petroleum History Society Oil Sands Oral History Project.* June 28, 2012, transcript, 9. http:// www.glenbow.org/collections/search/findingAids/archhtm/extras/oilsands/ Nelson_Patricia.pdf.

Nelson, Paul, Naomi Krogman, Lindsay Johnston, and Colleen Cassady St. Clair. "Dead Ducks and Dirty Oil: Media Representations and Environmental

Solutions." *Society & Natural Resources* 28 (2015): 345–59. https://doi.org/
10.1080/08941920.2014.948241.

New York Times. "A Good Call on the Pipeline." January 18, 2012.

New York Times. "Canada Oil Accord Is Praised." September 3, 1981.

Newell, Eric. "Aboriginal Employment at the Athabasca Tar Sands." *Canadian Business and Current Affairs: Canadian Speeches* 7, no. 5 (September 1993).

Newell, Eric. "Interview with Eric Newell." By Robert Bott. *Petroleum History Society Oil Sands Oral History Project*. May 25, 2011, transcript. http://www.glenbow.
org/collections/search/findingAids/archhtm/extras/oilsands/Newell_Eric.pdf.

Newell, Eric P. "The Oil Sands: A New Energy Vision for Canada." Remarks by Eric P. Newell, President, Alberta Chamber of Resources at the Launch of the Report of the National Task Force on Oil Sands Strategies. Edmonton, Alberta. May 18, 1995.

Ng, Harry M. "Letter to Donald Martin, Project Manager for NEPA, DLA Installation Support for Energy." American Petroleum Institute Comment on DOD-2013-OS-0055-0001. April 22, 2013. https://regulations.gov/.

Nikiforuk, Andrew. *Dirty Oil: How the Tar Sands Are Fueling the Global Climate Crisis*. Greenpeace Canada, September 13, 2009. http://www.greenpeace.org/canada/
en/campaigns/Energy/tarsands/Resources/Reports/tar_sands_report/.

Nikiforuk, Andrew. *Tar Sands: Dirty Oil and the Future of a Continent*. Vancouver: Greystone Books, 2008.

Nissan, Salman, and Ed Osterwald. *In-Province Upgrading: Economics of a Green-field Oil Sands Refinery (Prepared for Alberta Federation of Labour)*. Competition Economists Group, April 7, 2014. http://www.unifor.org/sites/default/files/documents/
document/ceg_economics_of_in-province_upgrading_in_alberta_final_07_
april_2014.pdf.

Norway Petroleum Directorate. *Annual Report 1980*.

Obama, Barack. "Remarks in Las Vegas, Nevada." June 24, 2008. Online by Gerhard Peters and John T. Woolley, *The American Presidency Project*. http://www.
presidency.ucsb.edu/ws/?pid=77554.

Oil and Gas Journal. "Canadian Oilsands, Heavy Oil Adjusting to Tough Economics." July 11, 1994.

Oil Sands Community Alliance. "About OSCA." http://www.oscaalberta.ca/
about-osca/.

Oil Sands Community Alliance. "The Oil Sands Developers Group Changes Name as It Aligns Focus on Socio-Economic Issues." Press release. October 29, 2013. http://www.oscaalberta.ca/wp-content/uploads/2015/08/FINAL-Press-Release-for-transition.pdf.

Oil Sands Environmental Coalition. *OSEC Hearing Submission Regarding Albian Muskeg River Mine Expansion Project, EUB Application No. 1398411, EPEA Application No. 004–20809 and Water Act File No. 60330*. August 25, 2006.

Oil Sands Environmental Coalition. *Submission in the Matter of a Joint Panel Review by the Alberta Energy and Utilities Board and the Government of Canada, (Imperial Oil Resources Ventures Limited for the Kearl Oil Sands Project)*. October 12, 2006. http://
www.ceaa-acee.gc.ca/050/documents_staticpost/cearref_16237/kr-0062.pdf.

Olsen, Sue. "The 'Delegated Administrative Organization' in Alberta." *Canadian Parliamentary Review* 20, no. 3 (Autumn 1997): 5–7.

O'Neill, Katherine. "Report Casts Doubt on MD's Claims about Alberta Reserve's Cancer Rates." *Globe and Mail*, November 8, 2009.

Organisation for Economic Cooperation and Development. *Government at a Glance 2009.* Paris: OECD, 2009.

Organisation for Economic Cooperation and Development. *OECD Database on Trade Unions.* https://stats.oecd.org/Index.aspx?DataSetCode=UN_DEN#.

Osmundsen, Petter. "Risk Sharing and Incentives in Norwegian Petroleum Extraction." *Energy Policy* 27, no. 9 (September 1999): 549–55. https://doi.org/10.1016/S0301-4215(99)00045-2.

Park, Gary. "Alberta Wants Oil Sands Included in Global Crude Oil Reserves." *Petroleum News* 7, no. 32 (August 11, 2002).

Park, Gary. "New Royalty Expected to Boost Oil Sands Production." *Platt's Oilgram News* 73, no. 232 (December 4, 1995).

Partridge, John. "US Market Pundit Flees 'Socialist' North." *Globe and Mail,* September 19, 2007.

Pate, Thomas J. "Evaluating Stabilization Clauses in Venezuela's Strategic Association Agreements for Heavy-Crude Extraction in the Orinoco Belt: The Return of a Forgotten Contractual Risk Reduction Mechanism for the Petroleum Industry." *University of Miami Inter-American Law Review* 40, no. 2 (2009): 347–81.

Pay Dirt: Alberta's Oil Sands—Centuries in the Making, directed by Matt Palmer. 2005. Calgary: Pay Dirt Pictures, 2005. DVD.

Pay Dirt: Alberta's Oil Sands—Making the Unconventional Conventional, directed by Matt Palmer. 2005. Calgary: Pay Dirt Pictures, 2005. DVD.

Pembina Institute. "Alberta Oilsands Development Takes Centre Stage at Smithsonian: Canadian and US Environmental Groups Bring Environmental Costs into the Spotlight." Media release. June 27, 2006. http://www.pembina.org/media-release/1250.

Pembina Institute. *Annual Report 2004.* http://www.pembina.org/reports/pembina-ar-2004.pdf.

Pembina Institute. "Canadian Environmental Groups Issue Declaration on Oilsands Development." Media release. December 1, 2005. http://www.pembina.org/media-release/1166.

Pembina Institute. "Foreign Affairs Access to Information on Section 526." November 29, 2010. http://www.pembina.org/reports/foi-foreign-affairs.pdf.

Pembina Institute. "Government Must Rein in Disorderly Development, Balance with Environmental Protection." Media release. September 19, 2006. http://www.pembina.org/media-release/1286.

Pembina Institute. "Imperial Oil Reckless Regarding Global Warming Implications of Kearl Oilsands Mine." Media release. November 15, 2006. http://www.pembina.org/media-release/1336.

Pembina Institute. "Implementation and Enforcement Critical to Success of First Attempt at Tailings Regulation." Media release. February 3, 2009. www.pembina.org/media-release/1776.

Pembina Institute. "Managing Oil Sands Development for the Long Term: A Declaration by Canada's Environmental Community." December 1, 2005. http://www.pembina.org/reports/OS_declar_Full.pdf.

Pembina Institute. "Oilsands Responsible for Up to Half of Canada's Emissions Growth." Media release. November 29, 2005. http://www.pembina.org/media-release/1164.

Pembina Institute. "Pembina Reacts to the Results of the Alberta Election." Media release. May 5, 2015. https://www.pembina.org/media-release/pembina-reacts-to-the-results-of-the-alberta-election.

Pembina Institute. "Shell Breaks Global Warming Promise for Oilsands Projects." Media release. April 8, 2009. http://www.pembina.org/media-release/1808.

Pembina Institute. "Suncor Project Should Not Go Ahead As-Is: Energy Utilities Board Must Set Tough Limits on Greenhouse Gas Emissions." Media release. July 13, 2006. http://www.pembina.org/media-release/1256.

Pembina Institute. "unGALA 2017." http://www.pembina.org/event/ungala-2017.

Pembina Institute. "US Decisions on Tar Sands Imports Will Impact First Nations Communities, Leaders Say." Media release. September 22, 2010. http://www.pembina.org/media-release/2087.

PennEnergy. "Online Research Center: Worldwide Fiscal Systems Improve for Investors, Favor Oil over Gas." January 1, 1998.

Petro-Canada. "Petro-Canada's Letter to Alberta Premier Regarding Royalty Review Recommendations." News release. October 3, 2007.

Phillips, Shannon. "Head in the Sands." *Alberta Views* 11, no. 10 (December 2008).

Pigeon, Marc-André. "Tax Incentives and Expenditures Offered to the Oil Sands Industry." Ottawa: Library of Parliament, January 27, 2003.

Plourde, André. "On Properties of Royalty and Tax Regimes in Alberta's Oil Sands." *Energy Policy* 38, no. 8 (2010): 4652–62. https://doi.org/10.1016/j.enpol.2010.04.025.

Poelzer, Greg. "Aboriginal Peoples and Environmental Policy in Canada: No Longer at the Margins." In *Canadian Environmental Policy: Context and Cases*, 2nd ed., edited by Debora L. VanNijnatten and Robert Boardman. Don Mills, ON: Oxford University Press, 2002.

Poitras, George. "Canada's Bloody Oil." *Guardian*, August 24, 2009. https://www.theguardian.com/commentisfree/2009/aug/24/climate-camp-canada-oil-tar-sands.

Polanyi, Karl. *The Great Transformation: The Political and Economic Origins of Our Time.* Boston: Beacon Press, 2001.

Polczer, Shaun. "First Nation's Chief Has Gone from Fighting Oil Industry to Embracing It." *Calgary Herald*, November 9, 2006, A20.

Porter, Michael E. "America's Green Strategy." *Scientific American* 264, no. 4 (1991): 264.

Porter, Michael E., and Claas van der Linde. "Toward a New Conception of the Environment-Competitiveness Relationship." *Journal of Economic Perspectives* 9, no. 4 (1995): 97–118. https://doi.org/10.1257/jep.9.4.97.

Powell, Brenda Heelan. *Demystifying Forestry Law: An Alberta Analysis.* 2nd ed. Edmonton: Environmental Law Centre, 2003.

Pratt, Larry. *Energy: Free Trade and the Price We Paid.* Edmonton: Parkland Institute, 2001.

Pratt, Larry. "Energy, Regionalism and Canadian Nationalism." *Newfoundland Studies* 1, no. 2 (1985): 175–99.

Pratt, Larry. "Energy: The Roots of National Policy." *Studies in Political Economy* 7, no. 1 (1982): 27–59. https://doi.org/10.1080/19187033.1982.11675694.

Pratt, Larry. *The Tar Sands: Syncrude and the Politics of Oil.* Edmonton: Hurtig Publishers, 1976.

Pratt, Larry, and Ian Urquhart. *The Last Great Forest: Japanese Multinationals and Alberta's Northern Forests*. Edmonton: NeWest Press, 1994.

Pratt, Sheila. "An Audit Too Far: The Stelmach Government Pledged Accountability—Until Fred Dunn Discovered Their Billion-Dollar Giveaway." *Alberta Views* 13, no. 8 (October 2010).

Precht, Paul. "Interview with Paul Precht." By Adriana A. Davies. *Petroleum History Society Oil Sands Oral History Project*. January 29, 2013, transcript, 10, 12. http://www.glenbow.org/collections/search/findingAids/archhtm/extras/oilsands/Precht_Paul.pdf.

Precht, Paul, and Greg Stringham. "Fiscal Treatment of Oil Sands Development in Alberta." In *The Fourth UNITAR/UNDP International Conference on Heavy Crude and Tar Sands, Proceedings,* Volume 1: *Government, Environment (August 1988)*, edited by Richard F. Meyer and Ernest J. Wiggins. Edmonton: Alberta Oil Sands Technology and Research Authority, 1989.

Pritchard, Timothy. "Syncrude Plant Expansion Halted; Energy Policy Cited." *Globe and Mail*, January 14, 1981, B1.

Radler, Marilyn. "Worldwide Reserves Increase as Production Holds Steady." *Oil & Gas Journal* 100, no. 52 (December 23, 2002): 113–45.

Reddekopp, Neil. "Theory and Practice in the Government of Alberta's Consultation Policy." *Constitutional Forum constitutionnel* 22, no. 1 (2013): 47–62.

Redford, Alison. "Keystone Is Responsible Oil Sands Development." *USA Today*, February 25, 2013.

Richards, John, and Larry Pratt. *Prairie Capitalism: Power and Influence in the New West*. Toronto: McClelland and Stewart, 1979.

Rogers, Dan. "Canadians Seek Tax Relief to Develop Sands." *Journal Record*, June 7, 1995.

Rosenberg, Howard, and Charles S. Feldman. *No Time to Think: The Menace of Media Speed and the 24-hour News Cycle*. New York: Bloomsbury, 2008.

Ross, Elsie. "Regulator Demonstrate[s] Its Independence Through Its Actions, Says ERCB Head." *Daily Oil Bulletin*, December 22, 2008.

Royal Canadian Mounted Police, Commercial Crime Section. *Information to Obtain a Production Order* (Police File # 2012–1046508). https://drive.google.com/a/ualberta.ca/file/d/0B6wfH8hIAchFbEF4c2NsazlXVUE/view.

Rutledge, Ian. "UK Energy Policy and Market Fundamentalism: A Historical Overview." In *UK Energy Policy and the End of Market Fundamentalism*, edited by Ian Rutledge and Philip Wright. Oxford: Oxford University Press, 2010.

Samuels, Alana. "America's Once-Robust Safety Net Is No More." *Atlantic*, April 1, 2016.

Sankey, Paul, and Ryan Todd. "Oil Sands Royalty Review: The Bolivarian Republic of Alberta." Global Markets Research, Deutsche Bank, September 28, 2007.

Schlosser, Kolson L. "US National Security Discourse and the Political Construction of the Arctic National Wildlife Refuge." *Society & Natural Resources* 19, no. 1 (2006): 3–18. https://doi.org/10.1080/08941920500323096.

Scott, Norval. "Alberta Set to Unveil New Rules for Oil Sands Waste." *Globe and Mail*, November 26, 2008, B3.

Scott, Norval. "Environmentalists Target Oil Sands Investors." *Globe and Mail*, September 16, 2008.

Seskus, Tony. "A Bigger Piece of the Pie." *Calgary Herald*, October 3, 2007, 3.

Seskus, Tony, Jason Fekete, and Lisa Schmidt. "Royalty Report Rattles Stocks; Oilpatch Issues Warning; I Won't Be Bullied: Premier; Klein 'Fears' for Oilsands." *Calgary Herald*, September 20, 2007.

Seskus, Tony, and Lisa Schmidt. "Tories to Hear Review Gripes." *Calgary Herald*, September 21, 2007.

Sharpe, Sydney. "'Generic' Oilsands Royalty Seen as Boost to Industry." *Financial Post*, December 1, 1995, 3.

Shell Canada Ltd. *Oil Sands Performance Report 2015*. April 22, 2016. http://www.shell.ca/en_ca/promos/energy-and-innovation/oil-sands-performance-report-2015/_jcr_content.stream/1463441702776/00cfc57a8625b41538e c24a2fc9d2e7160147b85367300b8dd8b9cb735aa1736/she-2055-oil-sands-performance-report-2015-final1.pdf.

Sheppard, Mary Clark. *Oil Sands Scientist: The Letters of Karl A. Clark 1920–1949*. Edmonton: University of Alberta Press, 1989.

Siddique, Haroon. "US Joins Syria and Nicaragua on Climate Accord 'No' List." *Guardian*, June 1, 2017.

Simmons, Matthew R. *Twilight in the Desert: The Coming Saudi Oil Shock and the World Economy*. Hoboken, NJ: John Wiley and Sons, 2005.

Simon, Bernard. "Old Habits Die Hardest: Canada's Energy Policy." *Financial Times*, March 12, 1987.

Simons, Paula. "Alberta Blindsided by US Fuel Law; Ottawa, Province Must Work Together to Protect Our Interests on Capitol Hill." *Edmonton Journal*, September 16, 2008, A12.

Slocum, Dennis. "Profit Falls 87 Per Cent at Suncor." *Globe and Mail*, April 25, 1986, B1.

Slocum, Dennis. "Suncor Raises Commitment to Alberta Oil Sands Plant." *Globe and Mail*, July 21, 1987.

Slowey, Gabrielle. *Navigating Neoliberalism: Self-Determination and the Mikisew Cree First Nation*. Vancouver: UBC Press, 2008.

Slowey, Gabrielle A. "The Political Economy of Aboriginal Self-Determination: The Case of the Mikisew Cree First Nation." PhD dissertation, University of Alberta, 2003. http://www.collectionscanada.gc.ca/obj/thesescanada/vol2/001/nq88048.pdf.

Snyder, Jesse. "A Fine Mess: The AER's Directive 074." *Alberta Oil: The Business of Energy*, July 28, 2015. https://www.albertaoilmagazine.com/2015/07/alberta-energy-regulator-directive-074/.

Solo, Robert, Daniel R. Fusfeld, and James M. Buchanan. "Three Reviews of Charles E. Lindblom's *Politics and Markets: The World's Political Economic Systems*." *Journal of Economic Issues* 13, no. 1 (1979): 207–17. https://doi.org/10.1080/00213624.1979.11503617.

Southerst, John. "Through the Wringer." *Canadian Business* (August 1993).

Spaling, Harry, Jannelle Zwier, William Ross, and Roger Creasey. "Managing Regional Cumulative Effects of Oil Sands Development in Alberta, Canada." *Journal of Environmental Assessment Policy and Management* 2, no. 4 (December 2000): 501–28. https://doi.org/10.1142/S1464333200000461.

Starko, Jim. "Alberta Economic Development Projects Receive Ministerial Kick-Off." *Grassroots: Aboriginal Business in Alberta*. Ottawa: Minister of Indian Affairs and Northern Development, Spring 2001.

Statistics Canada. "Chipewyan Prairie First Nation, Indian Band Area, Alberta (Code 630470) (table)." *National Household Survey (NHS) Aboriginal Population Profile. 2011 National Household Survey.* Statistics Canada Catalogue no. 99–011-X2011007. Ottawa: November 13, 2013. http://www12.statcan. gc.ca/nhs-enm/2011/dp-pd/aprof/details/page.cfm?Lang=E&Geo1=BA ND&Code1=630470&Data=Count&SearchText=Chipewyan%20Prairie% 20First%20Nation&SearchType=Begins&SearchPR=01&A1=All&Custom=& TABID=1.

Statistics Canada. "Division No. 16, CDR, Alberta (Code 4816) (table)." *National Household Survey (NHS) Aboriginal Population Profile. 2011 National Household Survey.* Statistics Canada Catalogue no. 99–011-X2011007. Ottawa: November 13, 2013. http://www12.statcan.gc.ca/nhs-enm/2011/dp-pd/aprof/details/page.cfm?Lang=E&Geo1=CD&Code1=4816&Data=Count&Se archText=Division%20No.%2016&SearchType=Begins&SearchPR=01& A1=All&B1=All&GeoLevel=PR&GeoCode=4816&TABID=1.

Statistics Canada. "Fort McMurray #468 First Nation, Indian Band Area, Alberta (Code 630468) (table)." *National Household Survey (NHS) Aboriginal Population Profile. 2011 National Household Survey.* Statistics Canada Catalogue no. 99–011-X2011007. Ottawa: November 13, 2013. http://www12.statcan. gc.ca/nhs-enm/2011/dp-pd/aprof/details/page.cfm?Lang=E&Geo1= BAND&Code1=630468&Data=Count&SearchText=Fort%20McMurray%20 #468&SearchType=Begins&SearchPR=01&A1=All&Custom=&TABID=1.

Statistics Canada. *Public and Private Investment in Canada, Intentions, 2014.* Ottawa: Statistics Canada, 2014.

Statistics Canada, and Sharanjit Uppal. "Unionization 2011." http://www.statcan. gc.ca/pub/75-001-x/2011004/article/11579-eng.pdf.

Steele, Amy. "Boomtown Challenges." *See Magazine*, December 15–December 21, 2005.

Steele, Colonel S.B. *Forty Years in Canada: Reminiscences of the Great North-West with Some Account of His Service in South Africa.* New York: Dodd, Mead and Company, 1915.

Stephenson, Amanda. "ERCB Waives Tailings Penalties: Technology More Difficult than Expected." *Calgary Herald*, June 12, 2013.

Sterritt, Angela. "Athabasca Chipewyan First Nation Makes the Best of Oil Money." CBC, April 2, 2014. http://www.cbc.ca/news/indigenous/ athabasca-chipewyan-first-nation-makes-the-best-of-oil-money-1.2579126.

Stewart, David K., and Anthony M. Sayers. "Leadership Change in a Dominant Party: The Alberta Progressive Conservatives, 2006." *Canadian Political Science Review* 3, no. 4 (December 2009): 85–107.

Stiglitz, D. Joseph. "Moving Beyond Market Fundamentalism to a More Balanced Economy." *Annals of Public and Cooperative Economics* 80, no. 3 (2009): 345–60. https://doi.org/10.1111/j.1467-8292.2009.00389.x.

Suncor Energy Inc. *Big Plans—Annual Report 1997.* https://inis.iaea.org/search/ searchsinglerecord.aspx?recordsFor=SingleRecord&RN=29066158.

Suncor Energy Inc. *2002 Annual Report.*

Suncor Energy Inc. *Annual Report 2015.* http://www.suncor.com/en-CA/ investor-centre/financial-reports/annual-disclosure.

Suncor Energy Inc. "Report on Sustainability 2013: CEO Message." http:// sustainability.suncor.com/2013/en/about/ceo-message.aspx.

Suncor Energy Inc. "Suncor Energy Releases 2013 Report on Sustainability." News release. July 17, 2013. http://www.suncor.com/newsroom/news-releases/1741591.

Suncor Energy Inc. "Suncor Sees Possibilities, Outlines Environmental Goals in Sustainability Report." June 18, 2009. http://www.suncor.com/newsroom/news-releases/1088547.

Symonds, William C. "Congratulations—You Struck Sand." *Business Week*, December 18, 1995.

Syncrude. "Industry Signs Agreement with Athabasca Tribal Council." News release. January 9, 2003.

Syncrude. *Pathways: Aboriginal Review 2012.* http://www.syncrude.ca/assets/pdf/Syncrude-Pathways-2012.pdf.

Syncrude. "Submission to the Oil Sands Multi-Stakeholder Consultation Panel—Fort Chipewyan, AB." October 4, 2006.

Tait, Carrie. "Total Shelves $11-Billion Oil Sands Mine." *Globe and Mail*, May 30, 2014, B1.

Taylor, Graham D. "Sun Oil Company and Great Canadian Oil Sands Ltd.: The Financing and Management of a 'Pioneer' Enterprise, 1962–1974." *Journal of Canadian Studies/Revue d'Etudes Canadiennes* 20, no. 3 (1985): 102–21. https://doi.org/10.3138/jcs.20.3.102.

Tertzakian, Peter, and Kara Jakeman. "The Fiscal Pulse of Canada's Oil and Gas Industry, First Quarter 2015." Calgary: ARC Financial Corp., April 2015.

Tetley, Deborah. "'The Richest Poor Place in the World': Garages and Sheds Provide Shelter in Black Gold City." *Calgary Herald*, October 21, 2005.

Thomas, Richard. *Boreal Forest Natural Region of Alberta.* Edmonton: Environmental Protection, 1998.

Thomas, Richard. *The Final Frontier: Protecting Landscape and Biological Diversity within Alberta's Boreal Forest Natural Region.* Edmonton: Alberta Environmental Protection, 1998.

Thompson, Isha. "Mikisew Cree Activist Garners International Attention." *Alberta Sweetgrass* 17, issue 9 (2010). http://www.ammsa.com/publications/alberta-sweetgrass/mikisew-cree-activist-garners-international-attention.

Thomson, Graham. "Game of Numbers, and Semantics." *Edmonton Journal*, October 26, 2007.

Thomson, Graham. "'It's Way Bigger Than We Thought,' Says CAPP." *Edmonton Journal*, September 19, 2007.

350.org. "Over 800,000 Americans Tell the Senate: Stop Keystone XL." February 14, 2012. https://350.org/over-800000-americans-tell-senate-stop-keystone-xl/.

Timoney, Kevin P. "A Study of Water and Sediment Quality as Related to Public Health Issues, Fort Chipewyan, Alberta" (on behalf of the Nunee Health Board Society, Fort Chipewyan). December 2007. https://sites.ualberta.ca/~swfc/images/fc-final-report-revised-dec2007.pdf.

Timoney, K., and P. Lee. "Environmental Management in Resource-Rich Alberta, Canada: First World Jurisdiction, Third World Analogue." *Journal of Environmental Management* 63, no. 4 (2001): 387–405. https://doi.org/10.1006/jema.2001.0487.

Tombe, Trevor. "Here's How Much Carbon Pricing Will Likely Cost Households." *Maclean's* October 11, 2016, http://www.macleans.ca/economy/economicanalysis/heres-how-much-carbon-pricing-will-likely-cost-households/.

Tombe, Trevor. "Here's What We Know—and Don't Know—about Alberta's Carbon Tax." *Maclean's* November 23, 2015, http://www.macleans.ca/economy/economicanalysis/heres-what-we-know-and-dont-know-about-albertas-carbon-tax/.

Tordo, Silvana, with Brandon S. Tracy and Noora Arfaa. *National Oil Companies and Value Creation* (World Bank Working Paper No. 218). Washington, DC: World Bank, 2011.

Toronto Star. "Oil Sands Industry Seeks $2.8 Billion Tax Break." May 20, 1995, SA2.

Toronto Star. "Syncrude Canada Raises Profile with First-Ever Annual Report." May 25, 1992, C5.

Treaty Alliance Against Tar Sands Expansion. "First Nations and Tribes Sign New Treaty Joining Forces to Stop All Tar Sands Pipelines." News release. September 22, 2016. http://www.treatyalliance.org/wp-content/uploads/2016/09/TAATSE-PR-Treaty-Signing-EN-FINAL.pdf.

Trescott, Jacqueline. "The Truck Stops Here: Energy Exhibit Rankles Environmentalists." *Washington Post,* June 8, 2006, C01.

Tristone Capital Inc. "Energy Investment Research – Conventional Oil Hammered, Oil Sands Hit, and Where's the Clarity on Conventional Gas?" October 26, 2007.

Trump, Donald. "Statement by President Trump on the Paris Climate Accord." June 1, 2017. https://www.whitehouse.gov/the-press-office/2017/06/01/statement-president-trump-paris-climate-accord.

Tupper, Allan, Larry Pratt, and Ian Urquhart. "The Role of Government." In *Government and Politics in Alberta,* edited by Allan Tupper and Roger Gibbins, 31–66. Edmonton: University of Alberta Press, 1992.

Union of Concerned Scientists. "Each Country's Share of CO2 Emissions." http://www.ucsusa.org/global_warming/science_and_impacts/science/each-countrys-share-of-co2.html#.WDYqUqIrL5U.

United Kingdom Department for Business, Energy & Industrial Strategy. *Crude Oil and Petroleum: Production, Imports and Exports 1890 to 2015.* https://www.gov.uk/government/statistical-data-sets/crude-oil-and-petroleum-production-imports-and-exports-1890-to-2011.

United States Conference of Mayors. "2008 Adopted Resolutions—High-Carbon Fuels." 76th Annual Meeting, Miami, 20–24 June 2008. https://www.nrdc.org/sites/default/files/air_08062301a.pdf.

United States Department of Energy, Energy Information Administration. *Annual Energy Review.* September 2012. https://www.eia.gov/totalenergy/data/annual/showtext.php?t=ptb0507.

United States Department of Energy, Energy Information Administration. *International Energy Outlook 2003.* https://www.eia.gov/outlooks/archive/ieo03/index.html.

United States Department of Energy, Energy Information Administration. *Petroleum & Other Liquids: Cushing, OK WTI Spot Price FOB.* https://www.eia.gov/dnav/pet/hist/LeafHandler.ashx?n=pet&s=rwtc&f=m.

United States Department of Energy, Energy Information Administration. "US Crude Oil Imported Acquisition Cost by Refiners." https://www.eia.gov/dnav/pet/hist/LeafHandler.ashx?n=PET&s=R1300____3&f=M.

United States Department of Energy, Energy Information Administration. *US Imports by Country of Origin.* https://www.eia.gov/dnav/pet/pet_move_impcus_a2_nus_epoo_imo_mbblpd_a.htm.

United States Department of the Interior, Bureau of Land Management. "Oil Shale and Tar Sands Leasing Programmatic EIS Information Center." http://ostseis. anl.gov/index.cfm.

United States Department of State. "Keystone Pipeline Presidential Permit." March 14, 2008. https://2001-2009.state.gov/r/pa/prs/ps/2008/mar/102254.htm.

United States Department of State. "Keystone XL Pipeline Project Review Process: Decision to Seek Additional Information." Press release. November 10, 2011. http://alternativeenergy.procon.org/sourcefiles/state_department_KeystoneXL_press_release_nov_10_2011.pdf.

United States Department of State. "President Meets with President Fox and Prime Minister Martin." March 23, 2005. https://2001-2009.state.gov/p/wha/rls/rm/2005/q1/43847.htm.

United States, White House. "Statement by the President on the Keystone XL Pipeline." November 6, 2015. https://obamawhitehouse.archives.gov/the-press-office/2015/11/06/statement-president-keystone-xl-pipeline.

Upstream. "Alberta Tries to Break into US Psyche." March 24, 2006, 24.

Urquhart, Ian. "Alberta's Land, Water, and Air: Any Reasons Not to Despair?" In *The Return of the Trojan Horse: Alberta and the New World (Dis)Order*, edited by Trevor W. Harrison. Montreal: Black Rose Books, 2005.

Urquhart, Ian. "Blacklisted: Pembina Institute v. Alberta." *Wild Lands Advocate* 21, no. 4/5 (October 2013).

Urquhart, Ian. "Borders, Boundaries, and the Politics of Petroleum Pipelines." *Journal of Borderland Studies* (forthcoming).

Urquhart, Ian. "The Devil Is in the Details: Implementing the Kyoto Protocol." In *Braving the New World: Readings in Contemporary Politics*, 3rd ed., edited by Roger Epp and Thomas Bateman. Scarborough, ON: Nelson Thomson Learning, 2004.

Urquhart, Ian. "Institutions and Environmental Politics: The Keystone XL Pipeline Controversy." Paper presented at the Annual Meeting of the Midwest Political Science Association, Chicago, IL, April 2015.

Urquhart, Ian. "A Modest Proposal?: Diversity and the Challenge of Governance in Northern Alberta." *Northern Review* Issue 25/26 (Summer 2005): 92–105.

Urquhart, Ian. "Sleeping with the Enemy?—Is Safe Sex Possible?" *Wild Lands Advocate* 15, no. 6 (2007): 28–9.

Varcoe, Chris. "Tailings Ponds, Pipeline Leaks Keep Heat on AER." *Calgary Herald*, July 16, 2016, B1.

Verlicky, Elaine. "Investors Stick with Their Oil-Sands Projects—One of the World's Richest Mineral Deposits." *Petroleum Economist*, January 13, 1993.

Vernon, Raymond. *Sovereignty at Bay: The Multinational Spread of US Enterprises.* London: Longman, 1971.

Waddell, Christopher. "Federal Aid to Be Given to the West." *Globe and Mail*, May 1, 1986, B1.

Wall Street Journal. "Alberta Cuts Royalties, Plans Expansion Loan for Oil Sands Plants." April 29, 1986.

Wallace, Jim. *Forty Mile to Bonanza: The North-West Mounted Police in the Klondike Gold Rush.* Calgary: Bunker to Bunker Publishing, 2000.

Washbrook, Kevin. "Why Are People Cheering Alberta's Climate Plan?" *The Tyee*, December 16, 2015. https://thetyee.ca/Opinion/2015/12/16/Cheering-Alberta-Climate-Plan/.

Weber, Bob. "Alberta to Implement Carbon Tax in Climate Change Policy." *Canadian Press*, November 22, 2015.

Weber, Bob. "Alberta's Premier Designate Fleshes Out Plan for Oilsands Royalty Review." *Canadian Press*, December 13, 2006.

Webster, Paul. "Canada's Dirty Little Kyoto Strategy." *Globe and Mail*, June 3, 2006, F7.

Welsh, Larry. "Canada Pushing Forward Heavy Oil and Tar Sands." *Reuter News*, August 3, 1987.

Western Report. "Newell's $21B Ambition: Syncrude Declares Tar Sands a 'National Priority.'" December 5, 1994.

Wheaton, Sarah. "Obama's Fragile Climate Legacy." *Politico*, December 13, 2015. http://www.politico.com/story/2015/12/climate-change-obama-paris-216716.

Williams, Peggy. "The Orinoco." *Oil and Gas Investor* 17, no. 11 (1997).

Wood, James. "NDP's Call for Royalty Review Heats Up as Alberta Election Issues." *Calgary Herald*, April 29, 2015.

Wood, James. "Notley's Carbon Plan Wins Praise from Ontario, Federal Leaders." *Calgary Herald*, November 23, 2015.

Woodward and Company Lawyers LLP. "Athabasca Chipewyan First Nations—Written Submission to Participate in the Hearings and Notice of Question of Constitutional Law" (Document #465). Canadian Environmental Assessment Agency, October 1, 2012. http://www.ceaa-acee.gc.ca/050/documents-eng.cfm?evaluation=59540&page=3&type=0&sequence=0.

World Energy Council. *Survey of Energy Resources 2007.* London: World Energy Council, 2007.

World Meteorological Organization. "Globally Averaged CO2 Levels Reach 400 Parts per Million in 2015." Press release. October 24, 2016, http://public.wmo.int/en/media/press-release/globally-averaged-co2-levels-reach-400-parts-million-2015.

Worth, Jess. "'Bloody Oil': Canadian First Nations Internationalize Their Struggle Against the Most Destructive Project on Earth." *New Internationalist*, Issue 427 (November 1, 2009).

Woynillowicz, Dan. "Letter to Director, Northern Region, Alberta Environment, and Shauna Cartwright, Alberta Energy and Utilities Board, re Albian Sands Energy Inc.—EPEA Application No. 004-20809 (Muskeg River Mine Expansion), EUB Application No. 1398411 (Muskeg River Mine Expansion), and Water Act File No. 60330 (Muskeg River Mine Expansion)." Pembina Institute for Appropriate Development for the Oil Sands Environmental Coalition, August 2005.

Woynillowicz, Dan, Chris Severson-Baker, and Marlo Raynolds. *Oil Sands Fever: The Environmental Implications of Canada's Oil Sands Rush.* Drayton Valley, AB: Pembina Institute, 2005.

Yedlin, Deborah. "Anxiety Hangs over Oilpatch; It's Hard to Conclude Stelmach Got It Right." *Calgary Herald*, October 26, 2007.

Yergin, Daniel. *The Prize: The Epic Quest for Oil, Money, and Power.* New York: Free Press, 1991.

Younie, Angela. "Prehistoric Microblade Technology in the Oilsands Region of Northeastern Alberta: A Technological Analysis of Microblade Production at Archaeological Site HiOv-89." Master's thesis, Department of Anthropology, University of Alberta, 2008.

Yurko, W. J. "Development of the Alberta Oil Sands." Address to the Engineering of Canada Conference, Edmonton, Alberta. April 17, 1974.

Index